Israel at 50

Israel at
50

A Journalist's Perspective

John Hohenberg

 Syracuse University Press

Library of Congress Cataloging-in-Publication Data
Hohenberg, John.
    Israel at 50: a journalist's perspective / John Hohenberg.
      p. cm.
    Includes bibliographical references and index.
    ISBN 0-8156-0518-8 (alk. paper)
    1. Israel—History. I. Title. II. Title: Israel at fifty.
DS126.5.H58   1998
956.9405—dc21   97-51946

For Jo Ann, Pam, and Eric

John Hohenberg, a distinguished journalist and political and diplomatic correspondent in New York, Washington, D.C., and overseas, witnessed many of the critical events described in this book during Israel's infancy as an independent state fifty years ago. A professor of journalism at Columbia Graduate School of Journalism from 1950 to 1976, Professor Hohenberg also served as the administrator of the Pulitzer Prizes and secretary of the Pulitzer board from 1954 to 1976. His recent works include *The Bill Clinton Story, Foreign Correspondence: The Great Reporters and Their Times,* 2d ed., *The Pulitzer Diaries: Inside America's Greatest Prize,* and *Reelecting Bill Clinton: Why America Chose a "New" Democrat,* all published by Syracuse University Press. *Israel at 50* is his eighteenth book.

Contents

PART THREE | Between War and Peace

PART FOUR | Israel and the Middle East

PART FIVE | Israel vs. Palestinians

Introduction: *On Reality and Miracles*

When Israel was born in 1948 during a war waged by its enemies, the nation's first prime minister, David Ben-Gurion, remarked, "In Israel, to be a realist, you must believe in miracles."[1]

Ben-Gurion was first of all a realist. That, regardless of whatever miracles he believed in, is why his influence on both its philosophy of government as well as its growth still is greater than that of any of his successors. Without his stern and often irascible guidance, the shape of Palestine itself would be quite different today.

As Israel has developed, its first fifty years have been marked by rapid growth, an expanding economy, a first-rate fighting force, and a population of more than 5 million people. There also have been setbacks, the worst being the uproar over breaches in the Oslo peace accords with the Arabs that harmed both sides.

Even so, with Israel's continued strong links to the United States, together with the downfall of the Soviet Union, its great enemy, there is reason to expect a substantial increase in its population, its industries, and its trade balance, provided a durable peace can at last be attained in a part of the world that sorely needs it. That above all else is the basis of hope for the future.

Given such reasonable security, which Ben-Gurion in his time would have considered the greatest miracle of all, Israel's rise can also become a greater benefit to its neighbors as Egypt and Jordan already have demonstrated. Nor is the American-Israeli relationship a one-way street. As Iraq's 1990 attack on oil-rich Kuwait emphasized, together with the Iraqi missile assault on Israel at the time, Israel still guards the approach to Middle East oil fields—a compelling reason for the continuing American-Israeli alliance that extends to Egypt, Jordan, and Turkey as well.

From the outset, Ben-Gurion's Israel was President Truman's concern, for he permitted only eleven minutes to elapse before he announced American recognition of the new nation once it had been declared simultaneously in Tel Aviv and at the United Nations in New York.

In a letter to the first president of Israel, Ben-Gurion's associate, Chaim Weizmann, Truman wrote: "I trust that the present uncertainty, with its terribly burdensome consequences, will soon be eliminated. We will do all we can to help by encouraging direct negotiations between the parties looking toward a prompt peace settlement."[2]

To that, the first UN secretary-general, Trygve Lie of Norway, added his conviction that Israel's survival was an obligation of the world organization, for he wrote at the time: "The invasion of Palestine by the Arab states was the first armed aggression which the world has seen since the end of World War II. The United Nations could not permit that aggression to succeed and at the same time survive as an influential force."[3]

So there it was—the future of Israel as seen by the leaders of the United States and the United Nations. After fifty years, it follows that the progress, as well as the continued support of Israel, still must be linked largely to its alliance with the United States and its dependence on the goodwill of the world's leading nations in the UN.

However important Prime Minister Ben-Gurion's miracles may have been that helped bring Israel into being, the reality remains that it will continue indefinitely to need the strongest support of the United States and other world leaders in the UN for the next century. No small state, regardless of its location, can be considered entirely secure of itself in a brutal world—and that goes for Israel as well as all the rest.

In the commentary on Israel's past, present, and future that follows, I intend to stress the realities that an independent, self-governing State of Israel has had to overcome in the Middle East, the issues it still faces now and in the century yet to come, and the role it continues to occupy as an American ally and a member of the United Nations. However important the memory of the Holocaust may have been in rallying world opinion behind the formation of a Jewish state after World War II, the hard truth will have to be recognized from now into the next century that Israel, like its neighbors, will be expected to progress toward improving relations in a highly competitive world.

During a lifetime's concern with national and international affairs, I witnessed many of the events described herein at the onset of this commentary on Israel and the Middle East. In some of them, I participated as a reporter, researcher, or American government servant employed at various times by the State or Defense Departments and their adjuncts. I was at the White House, too, although not as frequently.

My United Nations record is stronger, for I was a New York newspaper correspondent for the UN's formative years and, thereafter, a Columbia University professor with a full schedule plus a weekly one-day assignment for selected graduate students at the UN for almost twenty-six years.

Along with more recent sources, therefore, I have used my notes, diaries, and letters with the enormous available literature on Israel and the Arabs, including the memoirs of major figures on both the Israeli and Arab sides. I have the liveliest recollection, too, of the first UN representatives of the Jewish Agency for Palestine, including Moshe Sharett, Abba Eban, Golda Meir, and others who helped Ben-Gurion in many different ways during Israel's formative years.

For the UN, there are lively memories, too, of such secretaries-general as Trygve Lie and Dag Hammarskjold, as well as such outstanding American public servants as Ralph Bunche, the first of the UN's winners of the Nobel Peace Prize. I also have my own contribution to Israel's earliest years—a large supplement published by Dorothy Schiff's *New York Post* detailing a month-long visit to the new State of Israel that took me north of Dan and south of Beersheba.

On the basis of this beginning I maintained my study of Israel through the years, trying to keep up with the memories and histories of leading figures as well as the daily events I discussed so often in my university classes and weekly visits to the UN.

This, in sum, has now become the background for my commentary on Israel in Asia, the continent that fascinated me through six long lecture tours during the latter part of my services at Columbia and other universities here and abroad. Whatever history there may be in these pages appears as necessary background to the opinions I have formed of Israel's past, present, and future.

As for my purpose, I can do no better than quote President Truman again, this time in his reply during his 1948 presidential campaign to his unsuccessful Republican rival, Gov. Thomas E. Dewey of New York:

The subject of Israel . . . must not be resolved as a matter of politics in a political campaign. I have refused consistently to play politics with the question. I have refused, first, because it is my responsibility to see that our policy in Israel fits with our foreign policy throughout the world; second, it is my desire to help build in Palestine a strong, prosperous, free and independent democratic state. It must be large enough, free enough and strong enough to make its people self-supporting and secure.[4]

The goals President Truman set for the development of Israel, in all truth, have been fulfilled. For the future, the peace accords between Egypt, Jordan, and the Palestine Liberation organization—all entered into with the support of the United States—have set the course for a new era in which the long-held goal remains the settlement of the remaining issues between Israel and its neighbors and the beginning of genuine peaceful coexistence.

In the founding of the state fifty years ago, Prime Minister Ben-Gurion and his colleagues in government had to count on miracles as realities. And that, accordingly, is how I have begun this work as one of the surviving journalists who recorded the delirious events of May 14, 1948, at the United Nations and in the Middle East.

PART ONE | **Founding the State**

1. The Rebirth of a Nation

Britain was weary after World War II. The magnificent leadership of Winston Churchill now was history and striped-pants diplomacy had become the order of the era beginning in 1947. So it happened early that year, after being set upon in Palestine by rival Jewish and Arab forces and severely damaged, that the British decided to give up their quarter-century of control over Palestine on the western fringe of Asia.

The first to receive word of the surrender of power was the big, good-natured Norwegian, Trygve Lie, secretary-general of the United Nations, known affectionately to his colleagues and the press as "Trigger" Lie after a pompous Chinese was heard to so mispronounce his first name. But Trygve or Trigger, take your pick, was not quite sure what to do about the British pull-out so he called on his resident expert in the handling of difficult causes, an American, Ralph Bunche.

Bunche, the head of the UN's Trusteeship Department in the world organization's temporary headquarters at Lake Success, Long Island, was strong and tough. Moreover, being black, he had a sure inner sense about conflicts among minority groups that had been under the rule of a greater power. So the first decision he and Lie reached was to deny the British an immediate meeting of the full membership of fifty-seven nations in the UN General Assembly to receive the surrender of what was called the Mandate over Palestine. The British had accepted that from the old, half-forgotten League of Nations in 1922. The reason for the decision was not basically anti-British; it simply was a question that neither Lie nor Bunche could answer: Who takes control when the British move out?

It was self-evident that the Jews and Arabs were locked in a furious power struggle; to have accepted the British default without a decision on who was to win control would have put the UN in a completely un-

3

tenable position, or so Lie had concluded. The League of Nations, after all, had died as the repository of lost causes and neither Lie nor Bunche wanted to approve the UN's descent into the same graveyard of failed diplomacy.

So there was a stall at the UN in the refurbished aircraft factory at Lake Success, Long Island, that served as the home of the secretariat of the UN and its Security Council, the eleven-member reigning body in which each of the so-called Big Five—the United States, the Soviet Union, Britain, France, and Nationalist China—had insisted on the authority to veto any proposition at issue. The Soviets already had demonstrated the usefulness of that device, having vetoed the American-sponsored Baruch Plan under which any nation unlocking the secret of the atomic bomb would be forced to swear off the use of the big bang (except, that is, the United States, which had ended World War II with two such fatal blasts on Japanese soil).

The Security Council, therefore, was no alternative to the decision Lie and Bunche had reached on delaying a meeting of the General Assembly, and so the UN was put in the untenable position of merely waiting for developments.

Perhaps, some suggested hopefully, the British might change their minds and start all over again in Palestine by reconciling Jewish aspirations for statehood with Arab needs for homes and jobs. But there was not a chance of that. The British representative to the UN, Sir Alexander Cadogan, an old hand at the diplomatic game of verbal thrust and parry, already had said, "Having failed so far, we now bring the Palestine question to the UN in the hope that it can succeed where we have not."

Lie then looked back hopefully at the jigsaw puzzle of the Balfour resolution's wording on which the League had based its approval of the Mandate. That still offered nothing of consequence as might have been expected of a British foreign secretary, of vintage circa 1917, Arthur James Balfour, who had satisfied everybody and nobody with his declaration:

> His Majesty's Government view with favor the establishment in Palestine of a National Home for the Jewish people, and will use their best endeavors to facilitate the achievement of this object, it being clearly understood that nothing shall be done which may prejudice the civil and religious rights of the existing non-Jewish communities in Palestine or the rights and political status enjoyed by Jews in any other county.

Lie and Bunche finally decided that maybe they could force a decision of sorts from the Big Five acting as a separate, unofficial grievance committee, with three other delegations added for action as a preparatory group to decide the fate of Palestine and its warring peoples. Right off, cables went from Lake Success to the Big Five delegations and three others to recommend UN action on the future of Palestine. But once again, Lie had no luck and Bunche had run out of ideas. The Big Five would not accept the responsibility and the British, more than any others, were adamantly opposed. They wanted to be relieved of Palestine and that was that.

Longingly, Lie recorded his feelings then: "Now in 1947, a permanent Jewish homeland seemed at least a partial solution to the problem of hundreds of thousands of refugees languishing in European camps and driven by natural instinct to seek haven outside a continent stained in Jewish blood."[1]

But how was that to be achieved at the UN? The problem seemed to defy rational solution, if indeed the fifty-seven-member nations could agree on anything that required a diplomatic formula.

A shocked world at the same time was trying as best it could to save the gaunt and half-starved survivors of the Holocaust. Although Adolf Hitler's persecution of the Jews had been on record from the day he seized power in Germany, the extent of the wartime tragedy, as it spread to central and eastern Europe, seemed beyond belief. And yet, the 6 million dead of the Holocaust, too, were a record that had been kept with fiendish efficiency.

Out of an estimated 7.5 million Jews in Europe at the onset of World War II, only about 1.5 million survived now in hastily formed Red Cross holding camps. In the immediate postwar era, these pitiful beings had become the objects of a struggle between the Jewish Agency for Palestine, the Arab Higher Committee, and the British mandatory power.[2]

During the war, there had been a Jewish Brigade from Palestine that fought side by side with the British and hailed Winston Churchill as a hero, but all that was forgotten now. And the British successors to Churchill did not have his ability to instill loyalty among the masses to a cause in which he believed. It is difficult to imagine, accordingly, that a Churchill-led government would have approved of limiting Jewish immigration to Palestine as his successors did and failed to enforce their decision. As a result, European ships chartered by the Zionist cause were depositing surviving Jewish refugees at Palestine ports at the rate of about a thousand a week early in 1947. And the veterans of the wartime Jewish Brigade now were fighting both the Arabs and the British to try to save their coreligionists.[3]

However, some refugees never made it because the British navy, under orders, was intercepting ships bearing illegal immigrants wherever possible and returning them to displaced-persons camps on the island of Cyprus in southern Europe. Even so, week by week, the cause of a Jewish homeland continued to gain in strength as weapons purchased mainly through Czechoslovakia arrived for use by the Haganah, the Jewish Agency's army, and its affiliates, the Stern gang and the Irgun Zvai Leumi.

Under these circumstances the British decided to leave Palestine, and the Arab Higher Committee had to face up to the prospect, once the British forces departed, of fighting with other Arab support against the determination of David Ben-Gurion and his fellow Zionists to restore a Jewish nation in Palestine. It was clear enough by then that the Jews would settle for nothing less, which is what basically caused the British to decide to pull out while it still was possible.

That decision, primarily, so alarmed the Arab peoples whose homes were in Palestine that hundreds of thousands of them fled mainly to neighboring Jordan, the remainder taking refuge in Egypt, Syria, Lebanon, and Iraq. Statistics in so fluid a situation are notoriously unreliable but among my notes, taken from Arab sources in 1950, the estimates of Arab flight from Palestine between 1946 and 1950 range from six hundred thousand to eight hundred thousand; at the very least, it would seem that the hasty departure of the British reduced the Arab majority in Palestine from more than a million to perhaps 250,000 on the fringes of what was to become Israel.[4]

Under such circumstances, the British on April 2, 1947, announced that they were giving up their mandatory power over Palestine and asking the UN to make recommendations for the future government of the area. Now there was no way Lie could avoid an early special session of the General Assembly, which drew delegates from all member-nations.

However, as Lie and Bunche had expected, the special assembly session that met on April 28, 1947, merely complicated the proceedings.

Unable to halt the fighting between Arab and Jewish forces and faced with the reality of a British troop withdrawal, the delegates contented themselves with a decision to turn the problem of Palestine's future into an issue for a new eleven-nation committee called UNSCOP—the UN Special Committee for Palestine—before adjourning without future action.

So, instead of an eight-nation committee including the Big Five, the original proposal developed by Lie and Bunche, what the UN now produced was a bigger and more diverse group that still could not agree on how Palestine was to be governed after the British left. UNSCOP thereafter could agree only that the British mandate should end and the UN should grant "independence" to the entire area after a transitional period under UN supervision. Also, there was a self-serving declaration of respect for places holy to the three great religions involved in the area but at that point the eleven-nation advisory group split.

Seven of the eleven called for the partition of Palestine, which would have created a Jewish state, an Arab state, and a UN trusteeship over Jerusalem as a separate entity. A minority of three, each of whom had a large Muslim population, called instead for an Arab-dominated federal state in which the Jews would be a minority. The Australian delegate abstained.

Secretary-General Lie's conclusion, once UNSCOP had adjourned, was as follows: "What had emerged was a clear victory for the principle of partition. The international community . . . had decided that two states should be created. As Secretary General, I took the cue and, when approved by delegates for advice, frankly recommended that they follow the majority plan."

Next, the General Assembly was called into a regular session that failed to ratify the partition plan or discard it for some other proposal that as yet had not been formulated. Once spokespersons for the Jewish Agency in Palestine agreed to the partition proposal, it was apparent that a majority would be inclined to support the UNSCOP recommendation. Only countries with large Muslim populations opposed the recommendation.

But the British attitude remained fluid. As the vote on partition approached, it was apparent that the majority still expected somehow that the British armed forces would remain in Palestine even after partition was approved in the assembly to see that an orderly transfer of authority occurred in an area where Jewish and Arab armed forces already were preparing for war. That, however, was just another diplomatic delusion. It should have been apparent to all concerned that the British were leaving as quickly as possible precisely because their armed forces had no intention of taking still another beating in the middle of a renewed Arab-Jewish conflict.

It already was evident to neutral observers in Palestine that the Jewish and Arab forces were preparing for battle if the UN partition plan won the assembly's approval. Neither was satisfied with the proposal as it was being drafted in the UN preparatory to the assembly's decisive vote on partition.

The Arabs were to receive western Galilee, the West Bank of the Jordan River, an Egyptian-Sinai strategic area, and a narrow ledge of land along the Mediterranean even then known as the Gaza Strip. The Zionists, deeply disappointed, did not want to settle for their allocated part of the Mediterranean coastline north of Haifa that ran southward to the Gaza Strip through eastern Galilee and the Negev desert. Jerusalem, as always under UN planning, had been reserved for a separate trusteeship held by the world organization.

Ben-Gurion, who had taken charge of armed preparations on the Jewish side, expected a major Arab attack once partition was finally approved and tried to weld the competing Jewish military units into a single fighting force under a former officer of the Jewish Legion, Chaim Laskov. But it was not easy to bring Haganah, the Irgun, and the Stern gang into unity to face the emergency, for all needed arms now and someone had to raise the money to buy more military weaponry. While Laskov did the best he could at reorganization, Golda Meir was dispatched to the United States to raise the necessary money.

The decisive vote in the UN Assembly, for which a two-thirds majority was required, came on November 29, 1947, with the United States, the Soviet Union, most of Europe, Latin America, and the Commonwealth outside Britain piling up the necessary majority, 33 to 13. The Arab response was announced: the six major Arab delegations walked out—Egypt, Saudi Arabia, Iraq, Yemen, Syria, and Lebanon. As for the British, having abstained in the voting, that delegation announced it could not enforce partition and set a deadline of May 14, 1948, for the departure of its armed forces from Palestine.

That had been the date for a new UN commission of five—the Philippines, Denmark, Panama, Czechoslovakia, and Bolivia—to make suitable arrangements for the implementation of partition. The trouble with that proposal, however, was that the rival forces in Palestine were skirmishing—the Jews for a fight for independence, the Arabs in defense of their people and their homes. And the British forces gave fair warning to all concerned that they would be out of Palestine by May 15, the day after their self-imposed deadline.

Although the UNSCOP partition vote had been hailed in Tel Aviv, Haifa, and the Jewish farm collectives with singing and dancing as the results were broadcast across the land, there was no rejoicing now. Ben-Gurion memorialized the occasion by writing: "The Jewish people will not fall short at this great hour of the opportunity and the historic responsibility that have been given to it. The restored Judea will take an honorable place in the Holy Land, the Near East and the world at large."

With full-scale war in prospect and preliminary fighting under way, Ben-Gurion moved for a showdown within his ranks just three days before the scheduled British departure on May 15. He summoned an emergency meeting of the provisional government he had set up for the new Jewish state, warned its members that he expected at least sixty thousand Jewish deaths in an all-out Arab attack, and asked for a vote on whether a UN demand for an immediate truce would be acceptable. The possibility of a truce was voted down at that meeting by a 3 to 2 margin. And then, apparently, Ben-Gurion's biographer declared, he decided he would announce the rebirth of a Jewish state in Palestine if the UN either deadlocked or sought a truce in the first stages of war.

The tensions increased during the seventy-two hours before the British forces were to leave. The Security Council had met repeatedly at Lake Success over the possibility of ordering a truce, but both sides now were holding back pending the expected British departure, so no council action was taken. However, another special session of the assembly was in session at Flushing Meadow as the deadline approached and the U.S. delegation suddenly appeared to be wavering on partition. Former Senator Warren Austin, the chairman of the American UN delegation, began talking trusteeship instead of partition.

However, as Secretary-General Lie observed, there was not much support at the assembly for a last-minute switch to trusteeship despite an American suggestion that U.S. troops might possibly be assigned to a proposed UN force to police such a temporary UN rule in Palestine. The wavering American position by that time had so irritated the secretary-general that he had privately suggested to Senator Austin that they both should resign their UN posts in protest against a switch from partition.

Austin's retort, as Lie quoted him: "Why, Trygve, I didn't know you were so sensitive."⁵

So the decisive moment of the special assembly approached on May 14, 1948, with the approval of three resolutions—one that supported a Security Council truce initiative, another to name a mediator to work with the five-member UN Truce Commission to preserve peace, and a third to protect the various holy places in Jerusalem in the event of war. But in its climactic hour, the special assembly left standing the majority vote of the previous year for partition.

When that word was flashed to Tel Aviv, Ben-Gurion, standing under a portrait of the founder of Zionism, Theodor Herzl, announced the rebirth of the Jewish state with the name of Israel saying, "We, members of the People's Council, representatives of the Jewish Community of Eretz Israel and the Zionist movement . . . by virtue of our natural and historic right, and on the strength of the resolution of the United Nations General Assembly, hereby declare the establishment of a Jewish state in Eretz Israel, to be known as the State of Israel."*

In the Museum of Art in Tel Aviv, where Ben-Gurion had spoken, the new flag of Israel was unfurled to the delight of the people—the Star of David in the middle of two broad stripes of white and blue. Those who had heard him and cheered arose and sang the anthem, "Hatikvah" (hope), for surely this was at last a day of hope for the survivors of the Holocaust wherever they were.⁶

Even at the onset of the information age, all this did not become immediately known in the cavernous UN auditorium at Flushing Meadow as it headed toward adjournment. I recall I was at the typewriter at the small *New York Post* office at Flushing Meadow, preparing my account of the proceedings, when one of the reporters who worked with me came running in to announce that the Jewish delegation had just declared its own state in Palestine. I had barely finished substituting an opening paragraph about this for one that reported a UN deadlock when a third member of our staff entered announcing that the Jewish state's new name would be Israel.

After that, I decided I had better move into the assembly hall for a better view of the proceedings when the U.S. delegation announced

*Eretz means land in Hebrew; "Land of Israel."

President Truman had just recognized the State of Israel. From then on, the developments out of Flushing Meadow, Washington, and Tel Aviv so preoccupied everybody in the news business that we could not take the time, for the moment, to try to find out how all this had happened and why it had happened.

This was to be left for another day. But that night of May 14, 1948, was one to remember fifty years later after all the Arab-Israeli conflicts in the Middle East beginning with the War of Independence.

2. A Leader for Israel

It is tempting to speculate, at least for the romantically inclined, that this David Ben-Gurion, a chunky, hard-bitten, sixty-two-year-old politician, through some inner miracle of personality had transformed himself into another Moses leading his people into the Promised Land. Or perhaps, alternatively, into an elderly David suddenly come into superhuman strength to defeat the Arab Goliath.

But no, considering the earthy reality of Ben-Gurion and his weakness for oratorical flourishes, it simply will not do to try to re-create him in terms of the People of the Book, his own people, no matter how fervently he may have believed in them. That is not at all the way he exerted his influence then or later over the future of these newly created Israelis and the other millions who were to join them in the rebirth of an ancient nation.

This, after all, was no heroic George Washington, or even a magnetic Mahatma Gandhi, each able in such vastly different ways to arouse their people to struggle for their freedom against seemingly impossible odds. For that is what it took in the early years of the atomic era, seemingly, to bring an ancient Israel back into being Palestine.

But was there not something else, too, that this sometimes bumbling politician in his sixties could contribute, a factor that was crucial in transforming a fearful, scattered, and often downtrodden people into a million passionate crusaders fighting for their freedom in the deserts of the Middle East against overwhelming odds? A future prime minister, Shimon Peres, then in his twenties but already wise beyond his years, had this to say about Ben-Gurion:

> I do not believe the state would have been created without him.
> . . . Ben-Gurion ran the war down to the smallest detail. His chief of
> staff, Yaacov Dori, was still on his sickbed and effectively *hors de com-*

bat. Moreover, Ben-Gurion was forced to contend with relentless, seething opposition both from the former high command of the Haganah [the Zionist army]—and especially from its main fighting force, the Palmach—and from the ranks of the younger officers whom he had brought into the top echelons of the new army.

But how was this possible for so elderly a politician without military experience gained on the field of battle? In his early history, it is true, he had enlisted in the British-supported Jewish Legion* organized by the combat-minded Vladimir Jabotinsky to fight under the Union Jack in World War I. But unfortunately, Ben-Gurion had been dumped into an Egyptian field depot, not Palestine, and had never heard a shot fired in anger, although he carried a gun and wore a British-supplied uniform.

In the ensuing years, back in Palestine and working among his people as a dedicated Zionist, he had somehow developed the enormous and all-consuming will that would accept nothing less than a Jewish state in Palestine, an Israel with an army of zealots who stood up to the British-trained Arab Legion under difficult conditions. It seems like a contributed explanation for Ben-Gurion's leadership and the unchallenged results he obtained from his tireless massing of supplies from abroad, his changes in command, his daring in ordering sudden shifts of the slender forces he was able to mobilize. But it is the only explanation that fits the results that history has recorded—the rebirth of the Jewish state in Palestine.

To quote once more from his successor, Peres: "The War of Independence lasted a year and a half. The actual fighting was conducted in spasms, with truce periods declared between rounds [by the UN]. We took advantage of those truces to build up both the state and the army. This was truly a war of the few against the many; the few, moreover, had few arms, while the many had many."

The military-minded might also suggest that the Arab armies from Egypt, Jordan, Syria, Lebanon, and Iraq—plus two locally organized Palestinian forces—were neither as highly motivated nor as well trained and organized as the smaller Israeli force that withstood their attacks. Surely, that is a fair assumption but it would be difficult, on the evidence of history, to dispute Peres's assumption that Ben-Gurion did make the difference.

*The Legion fought for Britian in World War I, the Brigade in World War II.

In any event, not everything that happened in Palestine directly after May 14, 1948, can be attributed to vacillations of British and American policy, the general tendency among the diplomatic community nowadays in accounting for the continued presence of a Jewish state among the nations of the earth. It would seem, therefore, that this latest leader of Israel, this imperious, steel-willed Ben-Gurion, is worth more examination together with his heritage, his education, training, and experience as a leader of Zionism.

Now in the depths of the atomic era, so many things have changed, including the heightened presence of the United States military in the Saudi Arabian oil field. Moreover, Nazi Germany, Fascist Italy, the Soviet Union, and militarist Japan no longer exist. Still, the Middle East remains dangerously unsettled, for Israel, the Palestinian Arabs, and the surrounding Arab states—except Egypt and Jordan—have been unable to resolve their differences. A complete settlement of outstanding issues continues to be elusive despite America's heightened pressure based in part on its ever-growing need for foreign oil.

Ben-Gurion's handling of Arab problems in Israel and his negotiations with his neighbors, therefore, remain pertinent for today and tomorrow.

There was nothing particularly significant about Ben-Gurion's birth in a Russian empire marked by ferocious repression of all its peoples, including the helpless Jewish minorities who were repeatedly assaulted with death-dealing pogroms at the pleasure of some official who catered to the anti-Semitism of the mob.

The future leader of Israel was born David Gruen, or Green, to a large Jewish family in 1886 in the Polish town of Płońsk, then a part of czarist Russia.

His father, Avigdor Gruen, was able to maintain a legal practice to support his wife and ten children while working tirelessly for the creation elsewhere of a Jewish national home. On most nights, young David remembered there was a discussion at home between his father and their Jewish neighbors over when and where such a Jewish state could be created that would be free of the dread Russian pogroms and all the other poisonous aspects of anti-Semitism that flowed from them.[1]

All this was years before the Austrian journalist Theodor Herzl published his path-breaking work, *The Jewish State*, in 1896 in his native

Vienna and thereby selected Palestine as the proposed site of an Israel re-created in a quite different and far more competitive modern world. Once the book came into print and was smuggled into Russia, the nightly discussions that David listened to, wide-eyed, took form around that far-off land designated in the Old Testament as the repository of milk, honey, and Jewish settlements.

These hopeful Jewish hostages to misfortune in a czarist empire could not contemplate, as David well understood even in his early years, how such a state could be formed by newcomers against the opposition of its mostly Arab peoples—and particularly against the wishes of its current rulers, the Ottoman Turks, who had held Palestine for well-nigh four centuries. But then, to a schoolboy, Turks and Arabs were only vague figures compared to the dream so vividly stated by his father—a Jewish homeland.

In this manner David began the training of a middle-class (to dignify his economic status) Russian Jew in his native Płońsk. Besides the Polish and Russian languages he had to know for his eventual registration in a public school, he began learning Hebrew at home at the age of three from his paternal grandfather, a member of the family. For an American child today, having trouble enough with English grammar, the notion of being fluent in three languages before attending public school may seem far-fetched, but this was the way an educated person's life began among the Jews of Russia toward the end of the nineteenth century and well into the twentieth.

That, in any event, was how David was introduced to *cheder,* the Hebrew school, and three years later the public school in Płońsk. This, too, was how an educated Jewish person began training for life in Czarist Russia at the end of the nineteenth century, without expensive athletic programs, movies, or even school parties and dances to relieve the monotony of long hours of instruction. The teacher was an autocrat, to be obeyed without question; the pupil was expected to follow orders.

In so strained an environment, young David did well in Hebrew learning at home and in the mingled Polish and Russian instruction at the public school of Płońsk. He read widely, wrote well, and learned to play chess with the skill of an adult but seldom was permitted to join other children at play when he was not at home studying or sharing in the tasks of so large a household. In this manner he reached maturity for a Jewish lad of 13, when he achieved the status of bar mitzvah, training under the supervision of a rabbi in the reading of the Torah.

What excited him even more, about the same time, was his father's announcement that the fabled Theodor Herzl of Vienna would soon be visiting Płońsk, apparently the equivalent of today's routine book tour by an author, this one to sell his well-received book *The Jewish State*. To meet the great man in Płońsk, for David and his father, was a sufficient honor; to welcome him into their home, however briefly, was an event that became a lifelong influence upon the growing youth who remembered the grave, black-bearded Viennese journalist with both reverence and enthusiasm.

In this manner, apparently, the ideal of a Jewish state in Palestine became fixed in David's mind as a lifelong objective and even an ideal for a career that was, with relatively few interruptions of significance, devoted to the realization of a Jewish state in Palestine.[2]

When David was seventeen and in high school in Płońsk, the violence of a 1903 pogrom at Kishinev, in the Russian district of Bessarabia, sent a tremor of horror through every other Jewish community in the Russian empire. People in Płońsk knew perfectly well that, but for the accident of the Russian choice of Kishinev, they themselves might have been the victims of senseless state murders by the score.

The shock to a sympathetic outside world was so great that the British suggested publicly the possibility of establishing a Jewish national refuge in their African colony of Kenya, but the Turks in Palestine remained stubbornly silent. The pressures for Jewish emigration to Palestine already were rising, and seven World Zionist Congresses had urged still more Jews to apply after Kishinev. But for a Jewish state in Kenya, World Zionism was not impressed.

The impetus for settlement of Jewish émigrés in Palestine became intense. In Płońsk, David, an impatient teenager, began arguing for greater emphasis on a Jewish return to Palestine, something the Turks even now were not encouraging even if they did accept a few thousand additional Jewish settlers annually despite the protests of the Arab residents and their chieftains.

When word of Herzl's death in 1904 at forty-four reached Płońsk by way of his obituary in the *Vienna Neue Freie Presse*, David's feelings must have intensified, for there is a record of a rabbi's rebuke to him for suggesting the creation of a Jewish self-defense force in Płońsk of all places. Such ideas, older Jews in the community worried, might well bring down the wrath of the Russians on themselves. So the only result of David's daring was an apologetic attitude among the elders of the Jewish community for the youth's conduct.

The incident increased David's impatience with life in Płońsk. However, when he sought with his father's permission to complete high school in the nearby great city of Warsaw, he was told with brutal frankness by the residence authorities that they had long since filled the Jewish quota for education in that city. And so, at nineteen in the early summer of 1906, without his father's permission, he set out on a Russian tramp steamer for the port of Jaffa in Palestine with a few of his Płońsk schoolmates.

It was his first break with his past, his first encounter with his future life, but the immediate result was frustration and disappointment. His first experience in Jaffa was a heartache; far from a promising port of entry to a future home for Israel, this was a run-down Arab city that more closely resembled the remains of an abandoned junkyard, some of its citizens in rags, its future a miserable blank.

Still, David fumbled his way through several poorly paid beginners' jobs in the relatively small Jewish community until, shortly, he received a letter from home that he had been drafted into the Russian army. Now, this was a serious matter, particularly for a Jewish youth, because he realized that his father would be heavily fined if there were the slightest delay in his scheduled appearance for induction.

There was no help for him. He had to return as quickly as possible to Płońsk, where he was inducted as a Russian soldier and briefly served at a distant post before deserting. Evidently, his desertion did not reflect on his family, for there is no record of a fine or other punishment in the last years of the tottering czarist regime.

It was the young Zionist's good fortune, on his second venture in Palestine, that he made his way back to Jaffa safely and this time joined the Jewish community as a writer for a weekly newspaper called *Ahdut* (unity). Conforming to general Zionist practice, he now changed his name to that of a Jewish activist, Josef Ben-Gurion, who had been executed by the Romans in A.D. 70 for opposing their rule in Palestine.

As Ben-Gurion, David made rapid progress and even talked for a time of applying to law school at a Turkish university in Constantinople. But that soon became impossible, for a revolt of young Turks deposed the reigning sultan in Constantinople, which complicated the lives of the Jewish colonials in Palestine. At one point, to appease the jittery Turk officials in Palestine, the inexperienced young journalist even suggested that the paper might ask all Jews in Palestine to become Turkish citizens.

However, when a Jewish meeting for that purpose was announced in the paper, only a few showed up, the idea was dropped, and Ben-Gurion concluded that appeasement would not work—something he never forgot.

By that time, he had become an official of the Zionists' World Organization and an editorial writer for *Ahdut*. He seemed likely to achieve his aim of attending law school in Constantinople before the Greek-Turkish war in the Balkans began in 1912, when he was twenty-six. The Greek invasion of Turkey, however, made that impossible. Even when the dismayed Turks sued for peace after having lost some territory to the invaders while retaining control of Palestine, it did appear that the prospect of a Jewish homeland in Palestine under Turkish auspices was a lost cause.

Ben-Gurion finally did attend law school, but the coming of World War I in 1914 forced an abrupt about-face. This time, when Turkey entered the war on the side of the German kaiser, who was attacking Britain, France, and Russia, the Turks in Palestine started a "holy crusade" against the Russian czar and his subjects. The immediate result in Palestine was a headlong flight of Russian Jews for safety elsewhere, during which Ben-Gurion and some of his colleagues wound up in New York City in 1915. He was then in his thirtieth year, penniless and looking for work when his Zionist training saved him. On the basis of a fast study of English and sympathetic American audiences, he became a Zionist fund-raiser in the United States.

For the first time in his life, Ben-Gurion was living in a land where there was constitutional protection of freedom of speech and religion, a free press, and the right of people to assemble peacefully for a redress of their grievances.[3] Since early in the twentieth century, refugees by the tens of thousands from central, eastern, and southern Europe had been arriving in the United States each month—an exodus that was remarkable in its intensity. Merely to walk the streets of New York City, and particularly on the Lower East Side of Manhattan, as Ben-Gurion so often did, was to realize the difference that America was making in the world.

The Statue of Liberty, her torch held high on Liberty Island, was no illusion; her savior, Joseph Pulitzer of the *New York World*, who had brought her from France and financed her placement on her pedestal in New York harbor, himself had been an immigrant from Hungary and knew firsthand the pressures that had forced so many to seek refuge in this new land of promise. Whatever social and economic pressures there were against minorities then elsewhere in the United States, such prejudice was seldom visible in New York City. And as American Zionists sent Ben-Gurion across the land as a lecturer and fund-raiser once his English had sufficiently improved, what he saw and experienced convinced him more than ever that a home for displaced Jewry in Palestine was both practical and feasible.

The realization that the North and South in America, even a half-century after the Civil War, had not made a suitable economic and social adjustment did not dismay him. Moreover, although he could neither understand the seriousness of America's racial problem nor condone the prejudice against millions of black Americans, the response of the American Jewish communities to the Zionist appeal heartened him and strengthened his resolution to help create a Jewish homeland once the war ended.

He noted, too, in his travels across the broad land, that a price also had to be paid for religious freedom; here in America, the Jewish community already was being divided into Orthodox and Conservative synagogues and Reform temples, with varying practices that drew criticism from opponents. And there still were hate groups in America that, small though they were and scant as their influence might be, still had to be faced and dealt with as menaces to religious freedom.

Yet, overall, there was strength and hope in the sheer variety and size of the United States and its resources, something that Ben-Gurion would never forget all the rest of his years. His first visit to America would not be his last, nor would he leave without visible evidence of a permanent change in his life.

Not long after his arrival in New York City he had met another Jewish refugee from Russia, Paula Munweiss, of Minsk, who was working at a clinic and as lonely in a great city in this new land as he was. It was a fortunate encounter for both of them; soon, they were dating regularly and making certain to see each other whenever Ben-Gurion returned from one of his nationwide Zionist tours. Together, they shared the excitement of discovery on November 2, 1917, when the

New York newspapers carried the British announcement of the Balfour declaration's pledge of a Jewish national home in Palestine, together with all its qualifications.[4]

By that time, the United States had entered World War I on the side of the Allies, and the British were recruiting in New York City for volunteers for their Jewish Legion, something that almost immediately attracted Ben-Gurion. He and Paula were married in December 1917, moved to a small apartment in Brooklyn, and were expecting their first child when he was summoned for service in the Jewish Legion. However, by the time the war ended a little less than a year later, he was still waiting in Egypt with other uniformed British Legionnaires to see action in battle, and Palestine had fallen into British control, marking the end of the Turkish rule.

It was late in 1919 before Ben-Gurion was back home in a quite different Palestine, living with Paula and their infant daughter, Geula, in the recently founded town of Tel Aviv. Now, having survived one Arab massacre of the Jews who were flocking to a British-controlled Palestine, he realized that the British promise of a Jewish national home in the disputed area had been a wartime British maneuver to arouse world sentiment against the Turks. And so, his main interest now as a Zionist leader was to help mobilize recruits for what was then a new Jewish army, the Haganah, under the leadership of his former commander in the Jewish Legion, Vladimir Jabotinsky.

The struggle for Jewish freedom in Palestine had entered a new and even more critical stage; as Ben-Gurion belatedly realized, the Zionist cause now was under attack from all the surrounding Arab states as well as the armed Arabs within Palestine. The League of Nations was too weak to be of any use to the beleaguered Jewish population. They would have to be organized, trained, and armed to defend themselves because nobody else would do it for them.

3.   The War of Independence

The way wars begin and are fought will constantly surprise the novice, as Dwight David Eisenhower once observed. And that was as true of Israel's War of Independence as it has been for other conflicts closer to Ike's experience.

Even so, the successful Allied commander in World War II may have had something to do with David Ben-Gurion's leadership of a Jewish citizen army in its first engagements in 1948. For under Ike's sponsorship the champion of Israel's rebirth visited Europe's displaced-persons camps after Nazi Germany's collapse and also saw the tragic evidence of the horrors of Auschwitz and Bergen-Belsen.

The future leader of Israel said at the time, "From the tragic few miraculously saved, I bring two prayers. One, for the unity of Israel. The second, for a Jewish state, a call that goes out from the dead millions to surviving Jewry and the conscience of the world."

On returning to Palestine, Ben-Gurion assumed the post of commander in chief of the citizen forces that would resist the Arabs after the British pull-out. But as the British departed at midnight on May 14, 1948, as planned, the Jewish commander was beset with conflicting advice from his sharply divided staff. Most wanted him to stick to standard military doctrine and attack the advancing enemy force of Egyptians in the Negev desert to try to deflect them from the heart of newly formed Israel. What Ben-Gurion insisted upon, instead, was a desperate gamble to cut off Arab forces centered in Jerusalem by severing the Tel Aviv–Jerusalem road near the town of Latrun.

Some of his senior officers warned that success at or near Latrun was by no means assured, for the troops there were largely inexperienced; some were poorly armed and undependable in a crisis. Still, Ben-Gurion persisted and finally had his way as the commander in chief.

21

By that time, the situation at Latrun had deteriorated without the knowledge of the commander on that front. Unable to anticipate the unexpected, a part of the Eisenhower doctrine of warfare, the corps commander there had been cut off from his forward unit near the Latrun road. There, a dismayed twenty-year-old platoon commander was alone with his group of equally inexperienced soldiers, unable to communicate with the main force because a stray Arab bullet had silenced his radio.

The platoon leader, Ariel Sharon, a future defense minister of Israel, did not know whether to advance or to move his unit back to safety. And so, at dawn, the Arab forces discovered the exposed Israelis and annihilated them. The rest of the Jewish troops at Latrun apparently had abandoned them during the night without notice or at least that was Sharon's conclusion.

In a furious fire fight with the enemy, Sharon saw fifteen of his thirty-five men killed in action, another eleven wounded, including himself, and some others missing. A sixteen-year-old trooper, his jaw shattered by a bullet, had half-dragged, half-carried his platoon commander to safety. And at the Hadassah Hospital in Tel Aviv, where Sharon was taken, the doctor who operated on him called him lucky because a bullet had hit him in the groin, not his heart, and he would survive.

So it turned out that the fortunes of war, which seemed to have favored Ben-Gurion everywhere else as commander in chief over the advancing Arabs, turned against him at Latrun and permitted the enemy to retain control of Jerusalem—the great prize of the War of Independence. Shimon Peres, then the most junior of Ben-Gurion's officers at headquarters, concluded that their dispute with their chief that night had cost them control of both Jerusalem and Latrun.

As for Lieutenant Sharon, he wrote afterward in bitterness of spirit, "I hardly knew who had been left alive," then added after talking to parents of some of his troops, "In their silence, I imagined I could hear them saying that they had given the most precious things they had into my hands. And now, where were they, you who are still alive? Tell me, they were saying, where are our sons?"[1]

Inevitably, within the rickety Israeli order of battle, there were other internal clashes, some of them misunderstandings, others deliberate provocations aimed at the commander in chief by ambitious subordinates. Under the circumstances, such things were bound to happen when arms purchased from Czechoslovakia, Italy, and France were arriving in Israel despite effective arms embargoes that had been levied against the struggling Jewish nation by Britain and even the United States. No one questioned how or why the Communist Czechs were selling precious rifles and larger armaments to the beleaguered Israelis despite the Soviet Union's pro-Arab policy; however, as long as the greedy Czechs were willing to accept hard cash in the form of American dollars, the needs of warfare were promptly supplied. And the dollars, thanks to fund-raisers like Golda Meir, continued to flow from America.

Less than a month after the war began, there was a threat of civil strife over the ownership of weapons that had arrived in Israel from France aboard the SS *Altalena* despite a purported French arms embargo. After Ben-Gurion claimed the cargo for the Haganah, there was—so he accused Menachem Begin—a counterclaim from the Irgun Zvai Leumi, which, like the Stern Gang, tried to maintain a separate organization despite the war.

For the rest of his life, Begin, himself a future prime minister of Israel, denied he had tried to deflect the *Altalena*'s arms to the Irgun after Ben-Gurion seized the shipment for the national army, which was in dire need of them. At one point, the ship was even shelled in the struggle over the arms.[2]

And that, too, illustrated the Eisenhower thesis of the surprises inherent in warfare that can not be anticipated.

The UN mediator who had been appointed a few hours before the onset of the war, Count Folke Bernadotte, the president of the Swedish Red Cross, meanwhile had been trying to end the continual struggle of the new Jewish state against its enemies. After the fighting had continued for two weeks, Bernadotte was encouraged by the passage of a UN Security Council resolution calling for all sides to accept a truce. What the Swedish champion of peace had to do was to shuttle from the Jewish side to each of the participating Arab opposition forces to obtain a multilateral cease-fire. That in itself proved to be a major accomplishment no matter how shaky the truce itself seemed to be.

Bernadotte persevered. Once having negotiated a cease-fire on

May 28, he persuaded all sides to try for a more permanent truce, and somehow kept the guns silent through part of June. During this period the Israelis were furiously stockpiling arms, food, and other supplies for a resumption of the fighting. But more important, they also were working to build a new road to the Old City of Jerusalem by hewing and clearing rocks from a mountainside. Using a similiar Allied performance in World War II as their model, the Israelis called it their Burma Road.

When the fighting resumed, Count Bernadotte pleaded with the UN for stronger action, and on July 15 the Security Council, in a tough-sounding resolution, ordered a cease-fire as "a threat to the peace." It was the first time the UN Charter's forceful chapter 7 had been invoked to call upon all sides "to desist from further military action," while the mediator set up the necessary truce machinery for a second time.

What this amounted to was a threat of sanctions, meaning punishment against violators. And though the Arabs seemed confident that the UN ultimately would favor them, because the new Israel at that stage was not even a UN member, they were cautious enough to halt their attacks. Now the key to the war seemed to both sides to be Jerusalem, where the British officered Arab Legion of Jordan (then known as Transjordan under King Abdullah) was being besieged by the Israeli forces that had used their new road effectively.

In the second phase of the fighting, the Syrians, Lebanese, and the smaller Iraqi forces had been hurled back from northern Galilee, and the Palestinian Arabs no longer were a factor in the fighting. But the Jordanian forces holed up in Jerusalem and the even larger Egyptians in the south still were major elements in the conflict. In all truth, Israel would not be secure while these armies were in Palestine.[3]

The first truce negotiated by Count Bernadotte with only a few UN observers to help him had lasted from June 11 to July 9, 1948. The second truce, as ordered by the Security Council, went into effect on July 18 with more than five hundred UN observers scattered through the various areas of the fighting in Palestine. Count Bernadotte, Ralph Bunche of the UN, and other truce officials operated from the island of Rhodes in the Mediterranean.

There had been no time period or closing date for the second truce, so Count Bernadotte began to work on concrete proposals to both sides to try to obtain a peace settlement. In this effort, he was continually encouraged by his friend, Secretary-General Lie, from Lake Success. On September 16, the count wrote to Lie from Rhodes: "I think that with appropriate General Assembly action now the back of this problem can be broken. It will be a terrible tragedy if the opportunity is not seized. I hope to see you in Paris within a few days."

Three Jewish terrorists assassinated Count Bernadotte in Jerusalem the next day. For the UN, Bunche cabled that the murder was "a planned, cold-blooded attack in the new city of Jerusalem." Colonel André Pierre Serot, one of the UN's observers, was slain with him.

For the Israeli government, Moshe Shertok (later Sharett) cabled the UN his government's "outrage" and blamed "desperadoes and outlaws who are execrated by the entire people of Israel." He added, the "government of Israel has adopted most vigorous and energetic measures to bring assassins to justice and eradicate evil."

But all that could not bring Count Bernadotte back to life. And even though Bunche at once took over as temporary mediator, the shock of the assassination was worldwide. As Lie wrote later, "The enormity, the barbarism, the primeval stupidity of the act were engulfing. And our grief was still more bitter."

After a state funeral for the count and Colonel Serot, the second truce was repeatedly broken by fighting in Galilee in the north of Israel and also in the south beginning at Beersheba where Israeli forces took on the Egyptians and routed them in a pitched battle. The UN General Assembly already was meeting in Paris but its pleas for peace were ignored.

By mid-October 1948, there was spreading conflict by a now well-armed and confident Israeli fighting force. The siege of Jerusalem was broken at last by the Haganah, but the Old City was still held by the Arab Legion. In the north, the Syrians and Lebanese were set back within their borders and the Iraqis also were routed. In the Negev, which the Egyptians had virtually encircled, their front was permanently shattered except for the Sinai Peninsula and the Gaza Strip.

"On February 27, 1949, a final cease fire was signed with the Egyptians and by early March there was no more fighting anywhere," the youthful Ariel Sharon wrote. "With the end of the war and recognition by many of the world's states, Israel had emerged from its traumatic birth as a nation."[4]

It was not easy to make peace between the warring states; however, Bunche's position as mediator, replacing Bernadotte, was officially confirmed by the UN and he took vigorous action at once to bring the parties together on the island of Rhodes. For forty-two days, the imperturbable American suggested, urged, even pleaded with the Israeli and Arab delegations to negotiate a workable peace agreement while Secretary-General Lie in New York supported his efforts by separate talks with the Egyptian and Israeli delegations to the UN.

In Lie's words, it was Bunche's "skill and dedication" that brought about an armistice agreement on February 24, 1949, between Egypt and Israel. Next came the Lebanese-Israeli pact on March 23, followed by a similar treaty with Jordan on April 3, and Syria on July 20. On the initiative of the UN, the International Court of Justice at the Hague ordered Israel to pay reparations to Count Bernadotte's family, upon which the Israel government, in one of its first actions after the war, acceded in promptly providing a negotiated amount.

And at last, on May 11, 1949, the reborn State of Israel was formally admitted to membership in the UN. It was, Secretary-General Lie wrote in his fourth annual report, "one of the epic events of history, coming at the end not merely of 30 years, but of 2,000 years of accumulated sorrows, bitterness and conflict."

Even so, peace has still to be attained in Palestine with the creation of the Arab state envisaged in the UN's original partition resolution. And toward century's end, even though Egypt and Jordan had signed permanent peace agreements with Israel, the companion Arab state remained a commitment that fell short of attainment.[5]

Once Israel held its first democratic elections on January 25, 1949, installing Chaim Weizmann as president and Ben-Gurion as prime minister, with a single-house parliament, the Knesset, President Truman announced the United States had given the new nation *de jure* recognition.

As for the *de facto* recognition of Israel that Truman announced almost immediately after the proclamation of the new nation on May 14, 1948 (May 15 in Israel), it became a part of the Democratic Party's platform on which he ran for election that year. He never did offer any defense of the embargo on American arms that was almost immediately slapped on a state that was fighting for its life. In the long run, it did not matter.

What counted much more was the amount of financial support that came from the American government and private donors over the years without which Israel's development would have been almost fatally flawed. That the Soviet Union did not do more for the Arab states, some of whom became its faithful clients almost until the collapse of the Communist regime in 1991, was one of the accidents of history that benefited Israel.

President Truman did have to put up with much opposition within his government when he persisted in his support of Israel. The Arabs had backing in the State Department—the president called such state officials people "in the second and third echelons" but their point of view was important enough for him to make a last-minute switch before the British retreat to a trusteeship for Palestine.

However, once the president learned Ben-Gurion would proclaim the State of Israel on the night the British left Palestine, his decision to recognize the new nation immediately became a priority. In his memoirs, he reflected that a trusteeship for Palestine under the UN "was not a bad idea at the time," but the transfer back to formal recognition of the new state took precedence once it came into being.

"I was told," Truman wrote in his memoirs, "that to some of the career men of the State Department, this announcement [recognizing Israel] came as a surprise. It shouldn't have been if they had supported my policy."

Truman reflected that every president has been faced with the problem of how to prevent career officials from imposing their view on policy instead of carrying out a chief executive's orders. President Franklin Roosevelt, he recalled, had carried on direct negotiations during World War II with Churchill, Stalin, and others, thereby short-circuiting the State Department. The reason Truman did not follow FDR's practice of running his own State Department in the White House was that Truman intended to see to it that the State Department followed his lead.

And in the end, he and the nation at large appeared to be satisfied. To President Weizmann of Israel, Truman wrote after Weizmann's re-election on November 29, 1948:

> My feeling of elation on November 3d [the day after election day] must have approximated your feelings of one year ago today and on May 14th and on several occasions since then.
> However, it does not take long for bitter and resourceful oppo-

nents to regroup their forces after they have been shattered. You in Israel have already been confronted with that situation and I expect to be all too soon. So I understand very well your concern to prevent the undermining of your well-earned victory."[6]

In Israel meanwhile, Prime Minister Ben-Gurion was taking on the task of fashioning a new nation with serene self-confidence and a fighting spirit—an attitude that seemed to him to have worked out fairly well in the largest and richest democracy on earth.

4.   A Tour of Israel

For a little more than a month in the spring of 1950, I traveled in Israel from north of Dan to south of Beersheba, including a visit to partly occupied Jerusalem. On every side, the wreckage of the War of Independence remained in evidence.

In view of the manifest strength of the Jewish state today, a half-century after its successful struggle against five invading Arab armies, it is worth recalling what enormous problems faced the embattled Prime Minister Ben-Gurion, his first cabinet, and his exhausted people with the coming of the UN-arranged armistice.

What follows is less a sentimental account of travel than a comparison of the devastated land I remember with the thriving nation that exists today. Whatever notes I have of that journey support my memory of the people and places I visited.[1]

Israel and its five million people now occupy an area in Palestine the size of the state of New Jersey, which has a population 40 percent larger. But in 1950, the country as I saw it was terribly crippled by war and barely able to feed its million or so people, let alone the thousands of immigrants who clamored for admission and citizenship.

Few would have believed it possible then for so harassed and burdened a people to survive, let alone prosper. Old Jerusalem, the eastern part of the Holy City that is so much smaller than the modern establishment, still was occupied by Jordan's Arab Legion, and I could see signs of fairly recent fighting there as well as at Lydda Airport after my arrival.

I saw the slit trenches from which the soldiers of the Haganah had fought their foes, the earth still muddy from recent rains. There were coils of barbed wire nearby, bent and rusted, and other evidence in abandoned helmets and torn parts of uniforms mainly of Israeli sol-

29

diers who had tried so hard to fight their way from their Burma Road into the heart of the Holy City.

Parts of the forty-mile highway from Tel Aviv to Jerusalem, mostly built under fire by Jewish soldiers, forced my Israeli driver and escort to swing twenty miles off the direct route to the ancient city to reach the King David Hotel, my destination. And there, in the heart of Jerusalem and its three hundred thousand people, I realized for the first time the viciousness of the combat between the Haganah and the Arab Legion.

From my hotel room, I saw the Arab Legionnaires on patrol in the Old City and the shabby remains of houses bitterly fought over, their doors and windows smashed, their roofs pierced by shell fire. It was shattering evidence of the status of Jerusalem at the time, a city that had known more of war than peace for thousands of years and very likely would face more of it before long.

For Americans who may think of so distant and half-forgotten a war as a mere blip of history, such sights as these might have been sobering. Yet, even for the people of Jerusalem as I saw them that day of my arrival, they appeared to be going about their business and other routines without fear of the passing files of the enemy among them.

Nor was there any concern among the leaders of the Israeli government whom I had known at the UN in New York and to whom I talked at length that week.[2] They accepted the enemy among them as a fact of life, taking proper precautions but not letting the presence of the invaders dismay them. This is how it was for the Jews of the Middle East who had escaped the Holocaust. And this is how it would continue to be for years on end.

What had changed was the reality of the Jewish state for which these people had battled and on which they now depended for their lives against the hostile Arabs. It was a sobering recognition, for me at least, of how Jewish life in Palestine would have to be preserved in the hostile environmental of the Middle East, which was so strikingly different from the peaceful assurances of life in America.

However, nobody I interviewed in the Israeli government of 1950, mostly people I had known and worked with as a journalist at the UN while reporting on the trials of the formative Jewish state, acted any differently from the people they represented. Ben-Gurion himself still was firmly in control as the prime minister, with Moshe Sharett as foreign minister together with the Cambridge don from South Africa, Abba Eban, and the Milwaukee schoolteacher, Golda Meir, among others in his regime. It was government under extreme pressure, to be sure, but a government nevertheless that tried its best to represent its newest constituents as well as the relatively small percentage of Arabs who had not taken flight from a war-torn land.

Outside Jerusalem, as I headed north with my car, driver, and escort, there were calmer sights in the hundreds of kibbutzim, the socialist-type farm settlements that were such a prominent feature of rural Israel.[3] I saw numerous places where workmen were putting up new buildings on communal farms and in the myriad small towns through which I was driven. Usually, it seemed to me that mainly older men were doing much of the work of reconstruction and development while younger people, including many women, tended the cows, sheep, and poultry in fenced enclosures.

One of the striking features of the land, even though a settled peace was far distant, seemed to me to be the presence of schools everywhere for children, youth, and adults. All Israel appeared to be on a learning binge, or so my escort, a member of the government, assured me. I could not doubt the description. The schools, many of them nearly finished, could not be dismissed as a mere fantasy; this was a shining part of the reality of the new Israel state.

And it meant even more for the future than it did for the remnants of warfare that were in evidence on every side during my travels that early spring of 1950.

Despite this show of progress in Israel toward a peacetime economy, there also appeared to be an alertness among the farm settlements to the possibility of a return to wartime danger—a sudden Arab raid, a burst of shell fire from a concealed position, a continued threat in the very midst of such peaceful rural scenes.

I particularly remember one kibbutz at which we stopped: Ma'aleh Hamishmar, a seemingly prosperous farm settlement surrounded by large fir and cypress trees plus well-tended flower gardens. Still, on the outskirts of the apparently peaceful area, I saw a sandbagged machine gun emplacement, a bomb shelter—mainly for women and children, so I was told—and walls of farm buildings that had been scarred by rifle fire.

This rural fortified point had held out against Arab attackers, who vastly outnumbered the defenders who now returned to work on their communal farm. The working families it supported continued to go about their business with an air of calm, but I noticed that some still carried rifles or side arms. Peace here was a sometime thing.

It was, however, typical of such communal life in Israel in 1950, for I saw other farm settlements on the way north past Dan that were even better armed plus had guards to give the alarm in the event of sudden danger. This, surely, was a new country that desperately had to cling to the lifeline of independence for which its people had fought. No one could possibly mistake the signs of those who wanted peace but were also prepared for instant reversion to another difficult fight for life.

Anyway, my escort, driver, and I were given a fine communal lunch in the dining hall with a score or so of others from Ma'aleh Hamishmar, not so much because I was a visiting American journalist but a stranger within their gates. The spirit of the place attracted me more than the remaining signs of its part in the War of Independence.

Much the same thing happened when we drove to what was once an Arab village from which the residents had fled and now was called Ein Kerem on a Judean hill some distance from Jerusalem. The place was now totally Jewish, but I still saw graphic evidence of its former inhabitants, something that troubled me without turning me against the current owners.

It simply was difficult for me to understand such emergency transfers of property in wartime—but it was something I had to get used to in the Middle East. For the Arabs, when victorious, did much worse in the form of torture and other personal indignities against Jewish residents in the countryside when they were trapped.

These were among the starker facts of the kind of life Jews had to put up with in their newly created state in the Middle East.

Now, part of Ein Kerem was devoted to farmland where new arrivals strange to Israeli ways spoke many languages but also were trained in Hebrew if they needed it. Another part of the settlement was set up as a school for these newcomers with Jewish farmers doing double duty in the evening as teachers for continually new arrivals. Somebody had to break them in to perform a fair share of the communal duties in these Israeli agricultural communities.

In due course, so I was told, some of the newcomers eventually would become individual farmers, called *moshavniks* in the Israeli lexicon, and work their share of land in the less frequent *moshavim* communities I also was shown. But whether I was driven to either the kibbutzim or *moshavim* settlements, the effect on me was identical. By working the soil and sharing the hardships it entailed, the Israelis who took to the land were making the most strenuous and necessary contributions to the future nation.

I do not want to give the impression that all Israel, as it then existed, was a gigantic communal farm where all shared in the labor or worked a separate farm for themselves. I would only suggest that at that time, individual or communal farm profits must have been hard to come by.

It was, in any event, not only agricultural produce that was gathered and sold; as the trip lengthened, I also saw many of the products of communal and individual factories in this mixed socialist/capitalist economy. Among them were furniture, toys, kitchenware, wooden and iron framework for beds and sofas, and places where mattresses and the like were being turned out.

This, too, was a period when Israel's thriving export trade was developing with European countries, Britain and Belgium in particular, and markets almost as large in North Africa and South Asia, especially India, plus transport by air and sea. To that end, I was often told by factory managers and others of their plans and hopes for the future together with the price of the products they were selling.

When I asked about the Arabs who had fled from the places some of the Israelis now occupied, I was told that many were held in displaced-persons camps under UN supervision pending their transfer either to Arab-occupied areas or to the few Arab settlements that remained in Israel—perhaps 15 percent of Palestine's population at the time.

If the pressures on Israel for the developing Arab need for resettlement continued to rise in those early days of statehood, there also was anxiety in neighboring Arab lands where many of the refugees wanted to make new homes.

It is no figment of the imagination that such pressures threatened some of the weaker Arab governments, especially Lebanon and Jordan. Syrian and individual Arab organizations like Hezbollah, the so-called Party of God, had virtually occupied south Lebanon until the Israelis, in self-defense, moved into the Golan Heights north of their border. And as for Jordan, early in the reign of King Hussein, Palestine refugees more than once were termed a likely threat to his sovereignty.

It also became evident as early as 1950 that Israel needed most of all an immediate outlay of finances and labor for housing construction.

Too many Jewish families along my route were living in cramped and uncomfortable circumstances; here and there I even saw tents being used to accommodate the overflow of immigrants for whom even the smallest apartment might have seemed heaven-sent.

In the year of my visit, the government's plans, with American and other financing, included the construction of at least fifty thousand new houses. But even that seemed barely sufficient to meet the needs of a population that already had exceeded one million, was heading toward the six million it expected at century's end, and, according to a Tel Aviv University study, might rise to a state of nine million early in the next century.

The one city in Israel that I had wanted to visit for more than a day was Tel Aviv, "the Hill of Spring," which was destined even then to become the nation's largest although it had been in existence for less than four decades. With 375,000 people in 1950, it already was more populous than Jerusalem. Indeed, some of its inhabitants were calling it a "little Paris," mainly because it had become the cultural as well as the commercial center of the land.

Except for the babel of languages I heard in the dozens of cafés where people passed a spare hour or two, I might have been more inclined to think of it as a miniature New York City. But the description did not fit, as far as I was concerned, being a born New Yorker; what Tel Aviv reminded me of to a greater extent was pre-Hitler Vienna with its formerly large Jewish population and its fervent interest in music and the arts as well as commercial affairs.

Whatever the new Jewish city's antecedents, Tel Aviv was impressive. I took to wandering about by myself of an evening during my time there, sampling the entertainment and the cafés, and during the daytime tried to absorb some of the broadening commercial activity so vital to Israel's place in the world between Europe, North Africa, the Middle East, and Asia. It already was apparent that Tel Aviv had become a major center for transactions between these parts of the world and would continue to expand by reason of its central location for global trade.

From Damascus to Baghdad, Cairo to Beirut, and Amman to Riyadh, there were larger and far older world centers in the area, but Tel Aviv already was a worthy rival for all of them. It was not merely due to the city's location at the head of the Mediterranean; it was a mix of Israeli know-how as well as its commercial and geographic outlook.

In Israel, there still is a saying that I remember: "Jerusalem represents the past, Haifa the future but Tel Aviv is the present." That's the way it is in Israel.

What I recall principally about the latter part of my journey in Israel were the stark contrasts in both the main centers of population and the countryside. North of Dan, I could see the mountains of Lebanon and the fortifications of the enemy in the distance. And later, when our car swung south, my escort and the driver had to caution me continually against expecting too much either of the land or people as we followed the River Jordan along which Arab forces were generally in possession of the West Bank.

But in the Mount Hermon area, I saw indications of renewed development for the lake country—Huleh, the Sea of Galilee, and the Dead Sea, lowest spot on earth. There, a small-scale model of the American Tennessee Valley Authority was taking shape for the irrigation of at least a part of the Negev desert.

I recall how disappointed I was at Beersheba at the head of the sun-baked Negev desert in the south of Israel, looking out over vast stretches of sand without even a sign of human habitation. My escort reminded me, in a matter-of-fact way, that the Jewish scientific community hoped to extract potash and equally valuable chemicals from the area, all in good time. But I saw no sign of such activity and concluded, there in the south of a beleaguered Jewish state, that I had seen the end of its resources.

More than a decade later, I learned how wrong I had been in reaching so hasty a conclusion. For at the head of the desert, in a suburb of Beersheba, Israel later created its first nuclear reactor with French assistance at a center called Dimona.[4] From that project, nuclear-generated electricity one day would help bring light and power to the nation's factories and homes. And perhaps, with the mastery of plutonium technology and the provision of heavy water, the ultimate atomic defense of Israel, too, would be achieved.[5]

And so, as my 1950 tour of Israel ended, I had seen something more than the Jewish state as it then existed; what I was introduced to also was a glimpse of the future.

5. Democracy under Fire

Israel's experiment with democracy, the first in the Middle East, was remarkable in a part of the world that had profoundly mistrusted self-government for much of its history.

In an oil-rich region that still was mainly subject to arbitrary rule by military dictators or monarchs, it was a novel experience in the latter part of the twentieth century to deal with a leadership that remained subject to the people it represented as well as to parliamentary approval of its decisions.

That in itself was bound to increase the hostility to Israel of neighboring Arab governments, particularly when most of them had to cope with the resettlement of Arab refugees from Middle East wars.

It was with good reason that UN Secretary-General Trygve Lie, after a 1951 visit to Israel and four of the Arab states it had defeated in the 1948–49 War of Independence, said of the losing Arab rulers, "In Egypt, Syria and Lebanon, the burning question remained that of the existence of Israel. There was hatred, bitter hatred."

He apparently excepted only Jordan, among the embattled states he visited, from his general observation.

The secretary-general said the UN already had spent $50 million caring for the Palestinian refugees in huge camps for displaced peoples totaling 850,000, including 450,000 who had sought refuge in Jordan, 130,000 in Lebanon, another 130,000 in Egypt, 85,000 in Syria, and the rest scattered elsewhere.

Lie specified that repatriation was impossible. He argued that the refugees, therefore, would have to be settled where they currently were located, something the Arab governments would not accept. What these leaders wanted, Lie said, was Israeli payments for "fantastic claims," his description. As for Israel, the Jewish leaders told him they

36

felt unable to pay more than a fraction of fair compensation for lost Arab homes but they continued to freeze the bank accounts of absent Arabs.

By contrast, the UN leader said, Israel then was caring for masses of Jewish refugees who were arriving daily from Arab and European areas. However, his assessment of the Arabs was sharper because he blamed them for trying to upset the UN decision to partition Palestine and concluded, "I earned the appreciation of the Jews and the condemnation of the less objective of the Arabs."

Even so, he predicted it would take a long time to bring about a lasting peace in the Middle East.[1]

In the government of Israel, Prime Minister Ben-Gurion and his cabinet already had to cope with major problems in the defense of their infant state, the support of their growing Jewish population, and the development of the Palestinian areas that had been seized from the Arabs in the War of Independence.

It was no simple matter that Ben-Gurion now was undertaking in his sixties—to unite and rebuild the spirit and shattered outlook of people who had been hounded, persecuted, and scattered to the ends of the earth. This basically was the purpose of his government with its one-house parliament and assortment of political parties in a land taken mainly from his enemies. Even among his own cabinet, he had skeptics, critics, and naysayers who might not always follow where he wanted to lead them.

The Mapai, a historic part of the Zionist movement almost from the beginning, could be described with the founding of Israel as a centrist organization with strong left-of-center labor elements that would eventually make it a labor party. In its early days, however, it had a broad middle-class appeal with support from intellectuals, school and university people, and professional and women's organizations. Although mildly socialist in its economic outlook, it was violently anti-Communist mainly because of Soviet support for the Arabs.

With Ben-Gurion as its leader, the Mapai dominated the proceedings of the Knesset in its earliest years. The usual majority of parliament at the time was firmly behind the prime minister so that he was not easily challenged in his first term in high office.

The opposition, such as it was, consisted of the more conservative politicians, people like Menachem Begin, the hard-headed leader of the Irgun Zvai Leumi, and some of the religious parties that allied themselves with him. It would one day become the larger right wing Likud Party but now it was known as the Gachal and had relatively little effect on the governance of the land. It may have approximated the influence of the National Religious Party at times, but Begin himself did have a following and would be heard from one day as Israel grew stronger and more diverse.

Among the dozen or so smaller parties that tended to follow the leaders, shifting alliances mainly out of benefit to their leadership, there was one worth mentioning for as long as the Soviet Union and world communism remained an aggressive force. It was called the Mapam and it was boldly Communist, always following the Communist line. Just how the Mapam could exist under the circumstances remained a puzzle to outlanders who came to Israel and observed the Knesset in action for the first time.

It was not that Mapam had a great deal of influence. But that a Jewish nation in Palestine dependent on the United States could tolerate such hostile membership in its parliament demonstrated only that Israel was in truth a free country under the circumstances. Fortunately for all concerned, Mapam's brand of communism didn't even outlast the Soviet Union.

Ezer Weizman, the president of Israel at this writing, is the authority for the statement that no single party in the Knesset can gain a majority of the Israeli parliament's 120 seats, because the government is made up of one of the two major parties plus alliances with many other smaller parties. This kind of rule through coalition partners makes for much political pretzel bending, as the past has repeatedly shown.

In the Knesset itself, Israel's more than 2 million voters toward century's end do not choose individual candidates, as in the United States, but cast ballots for the party of their choice. The current rule is that the number of seats a party wins is determined by the number of votes it receives, with fifteen thousand to twenty thousand votes per election being worth one seat. The party slate that gets the most seats then contracts with the splinter parties for the seats necessary for a majority of sixty-one (although in the case of Golda Meir, at the end of her rule, she headed a minority party in the Knesset while awaiting the outcome of an election to replace her government and the bargaining that went with it). A party primary system—a late addition—selects individuals.

But even as dominant a figure as Ben-Gurion in his latter years could not take possession of a Knesset dominated by younger candidates for leadership, particularly after he turned his back on his Mapai Party and founded another smaller splinter party. That move caused Labor, a coalition partner of Mapai, to dominate governments in Israel for thirty years before finally being overthrown to the amazement and concern of the outvoted leading figures of Labor/Mapai. It followed that the left-leaning Labor/Mapai then had to watch helplessly while a new and inexperienced Likud Party, composed of Menachem Begin's Herut Party and its smaller allies, put the nation on a center-to-right course it had never before experienced with results that few anticipated.[2]

Other individuals fairly worshiped Ben-Gurion, and others tolerated him for his ability as a leader; all of them were important to Israel from the beginning. Among them were Levi Eshkol and Shimon Peres, both future Labor prime ministers; others, such as Moshe Dayan, played a leading role in cabinets of both the Left and the Right; and the most remarkable among the women who had given their lives to the cause of a Jewish nation in Palestine, Golda Meir.

Born Golda Mabovich in 1898 in Kiev, Russia, she had been brought to the United States when she was eight by her immigrant parents, educated and trained as a teacher in Milwaukee, then at twenty-three resettled in Palestine with her husband, Morris Meyerson, as pioneering Zionists. Within a few years, she was among the leaders of the Jewish labor federation, Histadrut, and joined such stalwarts as Ben-Gurion, Sharett, and others in the effort to strengthen the Jewish state.

Repeatedly after World War II, Mrs. Meir was in evidence at the UN as a member of the Jewish Agency delegation. In New York City and elsewhere in America, she also became identified as a fund-raiser for the Jewish state with help from such American Jewish leaders as Rabbi Abba Hillel Silver and Bernard M. Baruch. And soon she became recognized as a fixture in the governance of Israel and a future prime minister.

If Mrs. Meir was not as popular in Israel as she should have been, it was principally because she refused to stay hidden in the women's sections of Orthodox synagogues; in a sense, therefore, she helped emancipate women in the Middle East as well as the Jewish state. Hers became a unique contribution to both Zionism and feminism in Israel.[3]

The role of the UN, too, continued to be of major importance in the efforts of the Jewish leadership to solidify the existence of Israel in world opinion. The task was difficult, and particularly so after the unruly Stern gang conspirators carried out their assassination of Count Bernadotte.[4] It was all very well to argue, as some tried to do, that such tragedies by extremists in new nations had also marred the beginnings of other countries, notably the United States. This was a reference to the 1804 duel in which former vice president Aaron Burr killed Alexander Hamilton.

The parallel, however, was far from apt; in any event, nothing really softened the harsh response of world opinion against Israel for Bernadotte's murder until his successor, the American political scientist Ralph Bunche, by sheer persistence was able to arrange for an end to the War of Independence in 1949. The Nobel Peace Prize that came to him afterward not only reflected credit on the UN but it also recognized the mediator's ability to silence the guns of war—a settlement that came in good time for a well-nigh exhausted Israel.

What Bunche was able to achieve, especially after what had happened to his predecessor, deserves emphasis in any estimate of the basic rationale behind the rise of Israel as a nation. He was forty-four years old, and the first black division head in the American State Department, when he transferred to the UN as chief of its Trusteeship Department in 1946 after World War II. Until 1941, when he had joined the American Office of Strategic Services during World War II, he had been a Howard University professor; at the UN, he quickly came to the attention of Secretary-General Lie who had implicit faith in his judgment.

As Lie said after the news came of the Nobel award: "The award filled me with pride; it not only expressed the admiration the entire world felt for an outstanding American, but also . . . it represented a tribute to the United Nations and its Secretariat for their role in the settlement of international disputes."[5]

What Bunche was unable to rectify was the status of Jerusalem and the tremendous problem presented by the Arab refugees. For although Israel, with the help of the United States government and citizenry, was able to resettle the growing influx of refugees from Europe and elsewhere, the Arab countries either deliberately or through lack of resources could not do much about their own refugee problem. And that, as matters developed, could not help arousing more difficulties and greater hatred for the new nation that had imposed itself amid the Arab world.

The UN tried to maintain its proper role to assist in the settlement of Arab refugees. Harold Evans, an American Quaker, was appointed a Special Municipal Commissioner for Jerusalem on the recommendation of the General Assembly, but the Arab countries refused to cooperate with him even though it would have been in their interest to do so. And after the War of Independence, when the General Assembly sought to internationalize the Holy City, both the Arabs and the Israelis opposed that move and killed it. They split the city instead, with the Arabs holding the smallest part, the almost ruined part, or Old Jerusalem as it was known.

As a result, the assembly and the Conciliation Commission remained in the UN framework, but neither side was willing to trust its fate entirely to the UN. For in 1947, the West's cold war with the Soviet Union already was under way, as Winston Churchill signaled in his celebrated "Iron Curtain" speech at Westminister College in Fulton, Missouri, on March 5. In President Truman's presence, the old Lion of Britain warned of an "indefinite expansion" of Soviet power and doctrine because, as he put it, "From Stettin in the Baltic to Trieste in the Adriatic, an Iron Curtain has descended across the continent."

Soviet influence in the Arab world, as matched against the Anglo-American and French assistance for Israel, had been just one of the results in the Middle East. Another, which apparently began a few months after the end of the War of Independence, was the onset of organized raids into Israeli territory by Arab terrorists known as the Fedayeen. Within the next three years, the Gaza Strip and Sinai Peninsula as well as the West Bank and Lebanese and Jordanian borders were affected.

The assaults took many forms. Some were ambushes staged in Jewish farmlands. Others booby-trapped fields, mined roads, and touched off small raids by Arab groups at almost any time. The result eventually led to Israeli reprisals in kind but it took a long time for Ben-Gurion to authorize them as the cold war deepened. If the hardships thereafter delayed Israel's effort at reconstruction, the Arabs also had to suffer the consequences of their campaign.

Middle East terrorism and the Israeli responses became in effect a part of the global cold war between the Soviet Union and the West even though Churchill, in his Fulton speech, had tried to emphasize his warning that the West's direct response to Soviet tactics could constitute the first line of attack in the cold war. However, the Arabs who accepted Soviet support might well have taken Churchill's caution against the consequences of their alliance when he defined neutral status in the cold war as follows: "Special associations between the members of the UN which have no aggressive point against any other country, which harbor no design incompatible with the Charter of the UN, far from being harmful, are beneficial and, I believe, indispensable."[6]

So it came about; whether Israel and the Arabs may have hoped to be disassociated with the cold war, their respective loyalties sooner rather than later drew them into this long and wearing contest. To be sure, the Soviets may not have actively participated in the rising tide of terrorist raids on Israel but there was no doubt of Moscow's support for the Fedayeen in their long campaign against the Jewish state. It followed that American and Anglo-French interests in the cold war were bound to range them on the side of Israel when the Jewish state, in the years immediately after the War of Independence, was seriously threatened by Arab terrorist attacks.

The main theater of cold war operations consisted of the West's response to the Soviet challenge—the Truman Doctrine, the Marshall Plan, and the North Atlantic Treaty Organization under which the member-nations mobilized their armed resources. In the Middle East, the response was less awesome once Israel decided to strike back against Arab terrorism but it did have an effect and that is what counted.

Just why Ben-Gurion delayed his response to the Fedayeen raids had become a concern to those about him, particularly his top general, Moshe Dayan, when the prime minister decided to move in 1953. But the manner of the response was curiously limited, considering the effect it was having on the exposed farm population of the Jewish state.

What finally happened was the beginnings of a combined parachute and commando strike force consisting of one battalion of limited size at the outset. It was called Unit 101 and it was under the command of the still youthful Ariel Sharon, who had been asked to interrupt his studies for a university degree to return to the tougher life of an Israeli soldier. What he was told to do was to plan and train his people for commando tactics in the hope of discouraging further terrorist attacks.

His first target was set for a village called Kibbiya in 1953 near the Jordanian border from which Arab terrorists were believed to have originated a recent strike against a nearby Israeli village in which they killed a mother and her two infant children. Before the raid took place, however, this Israeli pilot effort against terrorism was sufficiently important for General Dayan to interview the commander, Sharon.

That first commando strike force, consisting of fewer than two hundred troops, had trained hard, was heavily armed, and each member of a special assault group went into action carrying a ten-kilo pack of explosives on their backs. Dayan approved and Sharon gave the order for combat action.

It was clear, as Unit 101 went into combat for the first time, that this was no ordinary assault on an Arab village. In the depths of the much larger cold war, the world would judge whether the Israelis at last were ready to respond to Soviet-supported Arab terrorism.

A firefight on the outskirts of the Arab village, Kibbiya, preceded the Israeli assault on the Arabs' homes late that night. In the encounter a small group of Arab village guards was killed by the Jewish invaders. After that, as Sharon reported, all forty-two stone houses in the village were destroyed but there was no count of casualties other than the dozen or so guards who had been killed. Unit 101 then retreated, its mission completed with the use of the TNT blasts that leveled the stone houses.

However, when the Jordanian radio later that night reported the first Israeli commando attack, Sharon was surprised by the announcement that sixty-nine villagers had been killed in the raid including a number of women and children. He concluded that, instead of fleeing when they heard the first Jewish attack in the firefight, the villagers had not believed there would be a serious Israeli response.

Regardless of the criticism of Israeli tactics that followed, Prime Minister Ben-Gurion was satisfied with Israel's commando response to Arab terrorism. When he summoned the commando leader, Sharon, this was the verdict: "It doesn't make any difference about what will be said about Kibbiya around the world. The important thing is how it will be looked at here in this region. This is going to give us the possibility of living here."

That, too, became a part of Ben-Gurion's democracy under fire in the renewed struggle between Israel and its enemies. Now it would be terror against terror along the borders between the Jewish state and its Arab enemies. And sooner or later, the Western powers as well as the Soviet Union would also become involved in this widened war in the Middle East.[7]

6. Crisis over Suez

An international crisis erupted over the Suez Canal in 1956. It was caused mainly by the attempt of the Egyptian dictator Gamal Abdel Nasser to make his country a great power in the Middle East. Instead, it led to war.

Nasser's problem was complicated not only by his ambition but also by his hatred of Britain and France, the controlling powers behind the Canal, as well as his efforts to punish Israel.

The dictator's rise to power had been spectacular. As a career officer in the Egyptian army, he had led a revolt in 1952 that unseated King Farouk, wrecked the leadership of Gen. Muhammad Naguib two years later, and in 1956 succeeded him as the unopposed elected president of Egypt.

Nasser's next moves were even more drastic. He nationalized the Suez Canal by seizing it from its private operation by a British-French company, then forced a British army to leave the area in Egypt it had occupied by treaty for many years. Everything happened so fast that the British seemed unsure what to do about it. However, the French and the Israelis soon were conferring on a retaliatory strike against Nasser and inviting the British to side with them.

All this time, nobody was paying much attention to President Eisenhower in the United States, who also had dealings with Nasser, mainly because Ike was preoccupied with his campaign for reelection in 1956. And that turned out to be a mistake for all concerned.

Egypt's fundamental problem for a long time had been its lack of sufficient arable land to cultivate in order to feed its rapidly growing population. Except for a comparatively narrow strip in the valley of the

Nile, little could then be produced elsewhere in Egypt to sustain its people.

For years, therefore, various Egyptian rulers had considered building what was called a High Dam at Aswan on the Nile to increase the river's breadth across a much wider area at the proper time of the year for greater food production. Foreign experts had called the project feasible, but also had concluded that it would require the creation of an artificial lake near Aswan, the removal of at least a hundred thousand people, and the expenditure of upward of $1 billion.

Still, when Nasser took power in Egypt, this was what he wanted to construct for his people. First he tried to promote the Aswan High Dam with the British, but they did not have the money to lend him. The United States was a much better possibility, but Nasser's clumsy tactics ruined his chances when the Americans discovered he also was trying to negotiate with the Soviet Union. In the end, he lost out with both Washington and Moscow.

Then, mainly out of sheer desperation, he took control of the Suez Canal, ousting the private Anglo-French owners, forcing the British troop withdrawal, and then proceeding to collect all fees from the Canal's traffic in ships, which proved to be a bountiful source of revenue for the eventual construction of the Aswan High Dam. All this may have seemed to the dictator to be well within his rights because the Suez Canal was basically Egyptian; however, he did not take account of the sensibilities of the British and the French after they were summarily ejected from the Canal.[1]

About the Israelis, Nasser cared even less. He had been severely wounded while fighting with the army against the Israelis in their War of Independence and he had never forgotten it. So regardless of what Prime Minister Ben-Gurion may have thought, Nasser's first move as the new owner of the Canal was to prohibit all Israeli shipping from using the Strait of Tiran leading to the Gulf of Aqaba at the southern end of the hundred-mile waterway. That decree seemed to make permanent the ban on Israeli shipping through the Canal that had been invoked now and then ever since 1950.

For Israel, the Nasser decree constituted a serious setback to its developing trade with its potential markets in West Africa and South Asia. Protests would have done no good; if the Egyptian dictator had already taken on the British and the French, he obviously would have paid no attention to the Israelis.

Even so, it happened that the Israelis were conferring with the French at the time of the Suez crisis for the purchase of heavy armaments—a negotiation that very quickly developed into a suggested conference with Britain about a punitive expedition against Nasser's Egypt and possibly even the return of the Suez Canal to international ownership.

All three opposing nations had common interests, but the ties between Frence and Israel were particulary close. France, as it turned out, had been the only one of the great Western powers that had refused to clamp an arms boycott on Israel during the War of Independence, thereby supplying the hard-pressed Jewish state with some of the urgently needed war supplies it could not buy from the Communist Czechs.

Although Israel had since made rapid progress in promoting its business and industry as well as its defensive strategy, the British and the Americans still refused to lift their arms embargo. But by chance, as the Suez crisis was developing, the Israelis were beginning to receive a $100 million supply of heavy armaments they had purchased from the French during a secret conference held in late June 1956 outside Paris.

This was how it came about that the Israeli Defense Forces (IDF) in mid-July of 1956 gratefully accepted the French delivery of seventy-two Mystère aircraft and two hundred tanks together with ammunition and other needed items. It was understood by both sides that another deal for big guns was to follow. Even in the inflated economies of Europe toward century's end, that kind of arms delivery would have seemed impressive; in midcentury, as may be imagined, the Israelis were delighted.[2]

Just to prove they meant business and would fill more orders, the French made General Dayan, still the leading Israeli commander, an officer of the Legion of Honor. It followed that the British-French talks about Nasser now became a three-sided negotiation when an Israeli official was asked how much time the Israelis would require to fight their way across the Sinai Peninsula and grab the Canal. The first Israeli estimate was two weeks, including a massive parachute drop at the outset, which seemed to the French worth considering. But the British were not too sure they wanted to participate, and Prime Minister Ben-Gurion, at that point, also was not prepared to give his approval, let alone ask for the support of his cabinet and that of the always uncertain Knesset.

Although these preliminary British-French-Israeli conferences were secret in the wake of Nasser's seizure of the Suez Canal, there was a surprising response in the United States, where almost anything—even such distant matters as the Suez Canal and the Aswan High Dam— soon become fodder for a presidential campaign. To the annoyance of Secretary of State John Foster Dulles, he became the target of congressional charges that he had "triggered" the Egyptian seizure of the Suez Canal by denying the Egyptian ambassador's request for an American loan for the Aswan High Dam.

What the record of State Department briefings for news people showed was that before Nasser's possession of the Canal, Dulles has been ready to turn down Egyptian ambassador Ahmed Hussein's request for congressional approval of a loan when the envoy exclaimed that he already had a counteroffer from Moscow. To that, Dulles retored, "Well, then, if you already have the money, there is no need of our support. The offer is withdrawn."

Subsequently, Dulles also was quoted as saying he acted out of resistance to "moral blackmail," and President Eisenhower, at his farm at Gettysburg, Pennsylvania was annoyed. In Cairo, Nasser was quoted by his foreign minister, Fawzi Bey, as saying, "This is not a withdrawal. It is an attack on the regime and an invitation to the people of Egypt to bring it down."

Later, during a congressional hearing on the subject, Dulles told Senator Clifford Case, "There is one thing I want to make clear, Senator. I do not believe in the U.S. being blackmailed, and any time I sense a purpose on the part of any country to try to get money out of us by threatening that if we don't pay the money it will do something, at that point I say, 'Nothing doing!'"

All this was preliminary to President Eisenhower's even more forceful entry into the controversy just before the American election day in November 1956, when he sought reelection.[3]

Israel's motives for joining an Anglo-French coalition military action against Egypt were threefold. The Fedayeen terrorist attacks against border farms and towns still had not been stopped. Egypt was in a threatening position, massing its troops on the Sinai Peninsula. Most important of all, the Israelis believed it necessary to reopen their blocked route to the Canal in the Strait of Tiran to pursue their trade in West Africa and South Asia.

While General Dayan now was talking with French operatives and even Foreign Minister Golda Meir was involved, although as always she was suspicious, Prime Minister Ben-Gurion still was withholding his consent as the cabinet seemed divided. That summer, too, the British also were not inclined to rush ahead, preferring for their own reasons to wait until fall.

Prime Minister Anthony Eden was uncomfortable when Nasser continually attacked the Western powers in speeches before howling mobs in Cairo and Alexandria. At one of these appearances, the Egyptian dictator charged that the West was "punishing Egypt because she refused to side with military blocks." But at the same time, Nasser was careful to specify he was also rejecting Soviet assistance (by that time, Moscow also had refused him).

In defense of his seizure of the Canal, Nasser had said, "This money is ours and this Canal belongs to Egypt because it is an Egyptian liability company. . . . We dug this Canal with our lives, our skulls, our bones, our blood."[4]

Eden, in response, cabled Eisenhower to urge a "firm stand" by the United States with Britain to make certain that the influence of both parties in the Middle East was not "irretrievably undermined." But Ike was not buying the British line. When he sent a special envoy to Britain, it was merely to try to cool everybody off and let the future determine whether Nasser would be up to running the Suez Canal, a primitive operation by comparison with the highly mechanized locks of the Panama Canal in the Americas.

That did not satisfy Eden, who would have felt safer with the United States at his side in any military action against Nasser. The British leader went so far in late summer as to compare Nasser to Mussolini and urge joint action to set up an international commission for control of the Suez Canal.

Now Ike's reply was icy: "There must be no grounds for our several peoples to believe that anyone is using the Canal difficulty as an excuse to proceed forcibly against Nasser."[5]

Ben-Gurion in Israel still had his doubts about Britain's willingness to fight with France and Israel for the right to control the Suez Canal, but he was well aware that Israel could do nothing by itself to maintain the right to use the Canal. He also relished the chance to take a crack at his terrorist tormentors based on the Gaza Strip and, perhaps, in the Sinai Peninsula as well.

However, near summer's end, the Israeli prime minister saw that

Nasser was still very much in control of the Canal, Israel was still shut out, and the Arab terrorists still were operating with little restraint on the nation's southern and Mediterranean borders to the north of the Gaza Strip.

At that time, moreover, a twenty-two-nation conference met in London to try to bridge the gap between Nasser's control of the Suez Canal and what some called the rights of individual users of the Canal. Because the Soviet Union was among the nations represented at the meeting, together with neutrals such as India, Indonesia, and Ceylon (now Sri Lanka), it followed that the American secretary of state was in an uncomfortable position. If he deviated from the Anglo-French position for international control of the Canal, he would be offending America's historic allies; if not, the chances of a real diplomatic solution of the Suez crisis were nil.

Under such grievous circumstances, Dulles made a brave attempt at proposing international control of the Canal with a strong advisory role for a committee of users backed by the United Nations. To that, India's V. K. Krishna Menon, a leader of the UN's neutrals, pointed out with convincing logic that Nasser was in charge of the Canal and would continue to be unless he were overthrown, which was unlikely. Therefore, Krishna Menon argued, the best that could be expected was a nominal role for a committee representing the users of the Canal together with the undiminished authority of the Egyptian government.

President Eisenhower, who was preparing at the time in the United States for his fall campaign for reelection, seemed more drawn to the neutralist point of view advocated by Krishna Menon than to Dulles's proposal, but he also understood the position of his secretary of state, who could not very well offend America's two closest allies. So, in effect, Ike told Dulles to do the best he could, which was very little.

On the showdown at the conference late in August, eighteen nations accepted Dulles's proposed substitute for Nasser's control, knowing perfectly well that it would change nothing. The Soviet Union, Indonesia, and Ceylon backed Krishna Menon's neutral position. And Nasser quickly rejected the eighteen-nation proposal when it was presented to him. As Krishna Menon had said, Nasser was in charge and he meant to keep control of the Canal unless he was forcibly removed.

So France was ready to act in September and Britain was still committed, but seeking further delay. It now was left to Ben-Gurion to decide whether Israel should lead the attack on Egypt with Britain and

France later joining in the assault. What the Israeli prime minister asked for was a signed guarantee that all three would carry out in good faith any program that won their final agreement. He simply refused to accept a British proposal that Israel should lead the attack with the British and French following after forty-eight hours. That would not do, Ben-Gurion said; nor did he support a French suggestion for a pretense of an Egyptian attack as the cause of the three-nation offensive. When the strategy meeting ended, there was an understanding that all three nations would strike at the Canal at the same time, but Ben-Gurion still reserved his acceptance.

It was clear enough that none of the three wanted to leave Nasser in control of the Canal but all were embarrassed about so aggressive an attack to remove him.

As late as mid-October, when there was a brief but bloody battle between the Arab Legion of Jordan and Israeli paratroops who attacked a Jordanian village in retaliation for a terrorist raid, there was a stern British warning to Israel that such moves might bring about retaliation under a British-Jordanian treaty. If Israel did not trust the British, the feeling was mutual.[6]

Time was running out now for all the nations concerned with the use of the Suez Canal, and that included Egypt. Instead of his defiant attitude of the summer, Nasser now was instructing Fawzi Bey, his foreign minister, to accept the concept of an international advisory board in his control of the Suez Canal. Next, a new UN secretary-general, Dag Hammarskjold of Sweden, received a private British proposal listing six principles that should govern any UN settlement of the Suez Canal crisis. Hammarskjold promptly made them public.

The British and French delegations to the UN became active on orders from their governments because negotiations seemed to be close at hand that could lead to a settlement of the crisis over the Canal—one that might very well leave Nasser in charge of the operation under UN and user surveillance. As for the British principles for a settlement, the doves at the UN suggested they also might be a part of the negotiations to ease the crisis.

However, at the same time, the CIA's U-2 spy planes in late October were reporting evidence of military action in the Middle East. French fighter aircraft were landing at Israeli airfields. In Israel itself, some type of mobilization appeared to be under way. At Malta, the RAF was active and the British navy's troop ships were coming in for loading.

On the diplomatic front, too, at least one American ambassador, Douglas Dillon, in Paris, noted that his British and French colleagues either were missing or uncommunicative toward the end of October. In general, he reported to Washington, the French as a group were "clamming up."

All this was sufficiently disturbing to Secretary of State Dulles in the closing days of the 1956 presidential campaign to notify President Eisenhower of all the strange developments, diplomatic and military. Ike concluded hastily that Israel, on general principles, needed a warning—just why, he apparently was not sure, but he guessed that an attack on Jordan was likely. That, at least, is how the president's warning to Tel Aviv was phrased by Dulles just before Britain, France, and Israel were scheduled to begin their invasion of Egypt by seizing the Suez Canal.

7.   War with Egypt

The war against Egypt began on the afternoon of October 29, 1956, with a parachute drop of about four hundred Israeli troops near the southern end of the Suez Canal.

From 150 miles to the west about the same time, a mechanized battalion of about a thousand Israelis raced across the Sinai Peninsula to link up with their paratroops, who were fighting that night against a small force of Egyptians that had been trapped in the Mitla Pass in the southern Canal zone.

At the critical juncture, as scheduled, the British and French issued their contrived demand to both the Israelis and Egyptians to accept a cease-fire. The Israelis promptly accepted, although they did not stop shooting right away. President Gamal Abdel Nasser—not suspecting the ruse—at once rejected it as he had been expected to do.

By that time, the British and French, under their agreement with the Israelis, should have been landing their forces from ships off Port Said at the northern terminus of the Canal zone, but they were late and did not get into the fight for days after the Israelis had been fully committed. Prime Minister Ben-Gurion by nightfall also had sent another Israeli column into the Gaza Strip, the source of so much Egyptian terrorist activity, to do as much damage as possible to his foes.

Except for the Anglo-French delay in joining the war once the Israelis had made the opening moves as agreed upon, everything now was supposed to be on schedule. Overnight, other Israeli columns were heading south along the borders of the Sinai Peninsula. One on the west was going south along the Gulf of Suez below the Canal zone toward Sharm el-Sheik on the shores of the Red Sea; another on the east of the Sinai was following the shoreline of the Gulf to Elat and the Strait of Tiran off the Sharm central point where the strait leads to the Red Sea.

All this had been planned by General Dayan with the approval of Prime Minister Ben-Gurion. Ariel Sharon, now a twenty-eight-year-old brigade commander in the Israeli army, was at the head of the mechanized column speeding across the Sinai desert to link up with the paratroops already engaged in fighting at the Mitla Pass. By next morning, October 30, the Israelis were successful everywhere; in the bloody battle outside the Mitla Pass, a convoy of the enemy had been surprised with a toll of 260 dead and more than a hundred wounded.[1]

By that time, however, the British and French still had not landed troops at Port Said and Port Fuad at the head of the Suez Canal as scheduled, although there had been scattered allied bombing here and there. However, it appeared that the Israelis alone were on the attack by land, and an international storm was rising against them. The Soviet Union was threatening to intervene, and in the United States, even though President Eisenhower was in the last week of his reelection campaign (election day was November 6 that year), he already was responding in disbelief over the actions of three of America's closest allies.

Before the shooting began, Secretary of State Dulles had sent word to London to inquire into British intentions, having been warned by some puzzling military moves, particularly a mobilization by the Israelis. Accordingly, the American ambassador, Winthrop Aldrich, dined on October 28 with Foreign Minister Selwyn Lloyd of Britain, who professed ignorance of Israeli intentions but said he had warned the Israelis not to attack Jordan. As for another question by Aldrich over whether Israel intended to attack Egypt, the British diplomat pleaded a lack of information.

The next night, six hours after the invasion began in the Sinai Peninsula, President Eisenhower arrived back in Washington from a campaign speech in Virginia. Dulles was ready for him with a White House conference that included military leaders from the Pentagon and the American intelligence people who had been caught flat-footed. Ike immediately blamed Ben-Gurion for the Israeli initiative in starting the fighting and told Dulles to take the case to the UN with a demand for sanctions. By that time, the Americans were aware that the Soviets were just as annoyed.

To make certain that the world knew the United States was not taking part in this latest Middle East war, the president also issued a public reaffirmation of the Tripartite Declaration of 1950 in which the United States, Britain, and France had pledged cooperation to maintain peace in the Middle East. The British did not make matters any better when Sir Pierson Dixon, the British envoy to the UN, told his American opposite, Henry Cabot Lodge, that the Tripartite Declaration was now "ancient history."

While the UN Security Council convened next morning, October 30, Ike was demanding an explanation from Prime Minister Anthony Eden, who promptly blamed everything on Nasser by saying his hostility had relieved the tripartite powers of their obligations, if any. To that, Ike violently disagreed, then became outraged when he was told of the Anglo-French ultimatum to Egypt to quit fighting after the Israeli attack.

What happened then was old-style UN of the cold war period except that the Soviets' Andrei Gromyko was not wielding the veto; instead, the British and French calmly vetoed an American proposal before the Security Council calling for a cease-fire, an Israeli withdrawal, and a directive to all other UN members to refrain from the use of force. Still, Ike's inherently sunny disposition caused him to predict that all would be well if he could persuade the Israelis to stop fighting.

But that fragile hope died with news later on October 30 that the British were bombing strong points on the Egyptian side. Nasser then realized he had been trapped into a war with Britain and France, and not just with the Israelis. At once he pulled his armed forces from the Sinai front and prepared for a defensive war by blocking them from other early engagements. By that time, not only the United States but also the Soviet Union was demanding an armistice, and the UN's resolutions took force from the strange union of the cold war's foremost antagonists.

By early November, besides defending Egypt's interest, Nasser had sunk several vessels, including a blockade ship sideways across the Suez Canal, preventing anybody from using it for many months.[2]

Prime Minister Ben-Gurion, General Dayan, and the rest of the Israeli high command realized as soon as the Americans appealed to the UN that the jig was up. Then, knowing the British and French action at the head of the Suez Canal was limited, they staged a cleanup campaign on the Sinai Peninsula as quickly as possible. It was not enough for them to have purged the Gaza Strip outside the Sinai of terrorists—those Arabs soon would be back and the Israelis once again would have to contend with them. But while the Jewish forces had the chance and the Security Council was still deliberating in New York, they wound up Operation Kadesh, as they called it, by piercing the Egyptian strongholds in the southern Sinai from which Nasser had withdrawn his army.

As Sharon observed at the time, the Israelis did not know when they would be back in the areas and they took advantage of the opportunity to crisscross it, level the strongholds, and take as many prisoners and arms caches as they could. It had by that time become apparent even to the most enthusiastic military mind that there was bound to be a UN cease-fire, particularly when it became known that President Eisenhower had demanded it.

Within only about a hundred hours of intense activity on the Sinai Peninsula, therefore, Israeli forces swarmed south from the first battle at the Mitla Pass and linked up with another arm of the Israeli offensive at the southernmost point of the peninsula, Sharm el-Sheik. They kept the defenses the Egyptians had erected to close the Strait of Tiran, hoping to maintain a clear water route to the Red Sea in the south and, in the opposite direction, through the Gulf of Suez and the Suez Canal itself to the north.

However, at the height of the Israeli offensive, when all strong points in the Sinai had been seized, the British and the French at the head of the Suez Canal already were slackening their efforts in the knowledge that a UN-ordered cease-fire was imminent. The Soviet prime minister, Nikolai Bulganin, had acted independently of the UN by demanding an immediate cease-fire of Israel under the threat of immediate Red Army intervention. At almost the same time, Ben-Gurion received a letter from President Eisenhower, which was equally firm in calling for an end to the fighting. Clearly, the Anglo-French-Israeli effort, ill-starred from the outset, would have to be abandoned, and all the territory the Israelis had seized on the Sinai would have to be given up.

About the best that could now be hoped for on the Israeli side was that Egypt would be obliged to permit Israeli shipping to use the Suez Canal once peace was restored to the area. But even that was far from certain, for Nasser had sunk so many ships to blockade the waterway that it would take an inordinate amount of time and effort to make it available to traffic by sea once again. It was, in sum, a case of snatching defeat from the jaws of victory.

As for Nasser's ultimate objective to raise enough money through the collection of Suez Canal fees to build the Aswan High Dam, that also had become a far-distant dream now shattered by the war that had been imposed on him. Considering the power and strength of the forces arrayed against him, it was a miracle of sorts that he had even been able to survive thus far.

By November 3, having achieved all its objectives in a lightning offensive, Israel was ready to obey a UN demand for a cease-fire, and Nasser already had done so. The Israelis gave in the following day mainly because the British and French landings at the head of the Suez Canal still had not occurred. That happened belatedly on November 5, but Prime Minister Eden at the same time sought Anglo-French membership in a proposed UN force to safeguard the Canal "to be stationed between the combatants."

The UN General Assembly, which had served the cease-fire demand on the combatants after the British-French veto had blocked Security Council action, did not dignify Eden's perfidy with recognition, and the opposition in the House of Commons booed him. That he bothered to try to foist his cover story on an unbelieving world was an outrage in itself, for with Israeli's agreement to a cease-fire, the Suez War, in effect, was over.

The final act in this strange offensive came on November 5 with the Anglo-French parachute drops, after which the European allies occupied Port Said and Port Fuad at the head of the blocked Suez Canal. It did them no good, even if they briefly persuaded Ben-Gurion to reconsider his compliance with the cease-fire. The French premier, Guy Mollet, and Eden made a final attempt to persuade the UN to let them join the UN force that was temporarily taking over the Suez Canal, but Secretary-General Hammarskjold would have none of it. No great power, including the Americans and Russians, would be part of the UN occupation.

A great neutral, Jawaharlal Nehru, the prime minister of India, had the last word on this long-distance debate. He called the attack on Egypt "naked aggression."[3]

President and Mrs. Eisenhower voted early on that election day, at their polling place near their farm at Gettysburg, Pennsylvania, then flew to Washington in *Air Force One*. Upon their arrival at the White House, Ike learned that his efforts to restore peace to the Middle East had succeeded with the refusal of the last-gasp efforts of the British and French to retain a role in the operation of the Suez Canal. A disappointed Ben-Gurion, also shut out of the Canal's UN management, at last had the satisfaction of having halted Arab terrorist activity from the Gaza Strip at least for the time being. But for all the brilliance of General Dayan's strategic assault on Nasser's Canal stronghold across the Sinai Peninsula, the Israeli hold on conquered Egyptian territory was temporary. By the following March, it would have to be given up.

If there were any doubt about the correctness of President Eisenhower's campaign to undo the Anglo-French-Israeli offensive against Egypt, the success of his reelection campaign speedily dispelled it. Far from being hurt by standing out alone in the West against three of America's allies, the American electorate gave him the greatest political victory of his career that night when the results were tallied. New York state alone gave him a 1,600,000-victory.

In the popular vote, Ike defeated his respected Democratic opponent, Adlai E. Stevenson, by more than 98.5 million votes—35,585,316 to 26,031,322. And in the electoral college, having carried forty-one states to Stevenson's seven, the vote was 442 to 39. In both the popular and state votes, therefore, Ike's victory over Stevenson exceeded the totals he achieved over the same opponent in 1952—more than enough evidence that the so-called Jewish vote in the United States remained heavily in his favor regardless of his cease-fire demand that Ben-Gurion had to accept against the resistance of his British and French allies.

Prime Minister Eden bore the blame for the failure of the Egyptian war and had to resign in favor of his associate, Harold MacMillan. The French premier, Guy Mollet, participated with MacMillan in discussions with Eisenhower and Dulles over the strengthening of the NATO (North Atlantic Treaty Organization) alliance. And soon, in 1957, all were concerned once again with Nasser's repeated efforts to play off the Soviets' interests against the Western powers. In this extremity, Ben-Gurion now kept Israel aloof from further entanglements, having been obliged to yield its conquered territories in the Sinai and the Gaza Strip with the completion of arrangements for peace with Nasser. What the temporary UN force did make possible for Israel, once the Canal was cleared and reopened, was the assurance that it now could safely be used by Israeli shipping. But for as long as Nasser continued in authority, that did not seem to be a very effective guarantee, and it was interrupted, as expected, during a latter-day war that suited Nasser's convenience.

As for the French part in the Suez fiasco, Prime Minister Mollet did not last in office either. He was replaced in June 1957 by Maurice Bourges-Maunoury, but only for a relatively brief time. And after him came Gen. Charles de Gaulle, who was much more difficult to deal with.

For Ben-Gurion at seventy-one, it was a time for reflection. He had retired before to a home in the Israeli desert and he would do so again. But as always, when the nation called him, he invariably returned to service. Now, however, the position was increasingly difficult, because Nasser, always an Arabist and an Egyptian first, had regained almost everything he had lost in the Suez War and even now was experimenting with a renewed relationship with the Soviet Union.

King Hussein of Jordan, for one, felt threatened. And the Lebanese and even the Syrians were nervous about Soviet inroads in the Middle East. As far as Ben-Gurion's role and Israel's were concerned, however, the foe to be watched more carefully than ever was an Egypt that was inclined toward Communist influence under Nasser.

The Egyptian dictator had once threatened to seek Moscow's financial help to construct the Aswan High Dam. And the interruption of his scheme for profiting from the seizure of the Suez Canal, in all likelihood, seemed to the Israelis to foreshadow a resumption of his courtship of Moscow. Under those circumstances, regardless of Ben-Gurion's feelings about President Eisenhower's defense of Egypt in the truncated war over the Suez Canal, there was no alternative to Israel's continued dependence on the United States in the ever shifting alliances of the Middle East.

That, however, was never guaranteed. With the encouragement of Secretary Dulles, an effort was made in the United States Congress directly after the Suez War settlement to punish Israel not only by suspending government assistance to the Jewish state but also by eliminating tax credits for gifts to Israel from private American sources.

But that was too much for the congressional opposition. At a briefing for the leaders of Congress in mid-February 1957, the Senate Republican leader, William Knowland, warned that the proposed American sanctions against Israel would cause him to resign from

the United States delegation to the UN. And the opposition Democratic leader, Lyndon Baines Johnson, himself a future president, also
objected.

Still, President Eisenhower persisted, going to the length of making public his threat to invoke sanctions against Israel. And this time,
Ben-Gurion decided it was time to seek peace with Ike and, to effect it,
he withdrew the last Israeli forces from the heights overlooking the
Strait of Tiran. It was difficult for the aging leader of Israel but he had
no choice.[4]

8.   Treasure in the Desert

Few would have suggested an atomic future for Israel after its rebirth in the Middle East, least of all the United States.

The Americans at the time alone exerted nuclear power in a war-weary world and had attempted, in the failed Baruch plan before the United Nations, to halt any other country from doing so. True, the Baruch plan had been aimed principally at blocking the Soviet Union from achieving atomic parity; however, it also would have choked off all others, from close allies, such as Britain and France, even to little ones, such as Israel.

The Soviets, nevertheless, touched off their first nuclear blast in 1949, the British and French did so soon afterward, and within a decade there were estimates that at least twoscore nations were able to generate atomic power for peaceful purposes. Because the nuclear process for two-thirds of its development is the same for war as for peace, it was evident that the atomic club eventually would be considerably enlarged.

But what of Israel's chances, seemingly so alone in the Middle East among the 350 million people spread for almost three thousand miles from Egypt to Pakistan? Even within the reborn nation itself, at the outset the skeptics could not give much for its chances at atomic parity.

The Jewish state did have resources, mainly the nuclear scientists who had fled from the Nazi threat in Europe. But when Prime Minister Ben-Gurion and his top advisers began probing for those who were willing to risk their reputations and their future prospects to found an atomic industry within Israel's borders, most of them backed off while making polite noises of mingled regret and eternal friendship.

It was in effect almost as intimidating a response as the elderly Bernard M. Baruch, in his twilight years, had encountered in the UN

61

when he had presented his proposal to stop the development of the atom for warlike purposes.

True, years have passed since 1946 when the American atomic initiative came before the UN and Baruch presented the first—and last—effort before the Security Council to halt the development of the atom for weaponry.

It has been even longer since the American atomic initiative was presented before the UN Atomic Commission, where the veto did not apply, but it is still worth considering how futile the American effort really was to inhibit the growth of the nuclear threat in wartime. To begin with, Baruch himself was no atomic expert; he would not have been able to say more than a greeting to Albert Einstein. In presenting his atomic plan, he called on all nations, including his own, to surrender their war-bent nuclear explosives to an international authority, yet to be created, and to yield forever the use of the veto to preserve their atomic status.

As might have been expected, the Soviet's Andrei Gromyko was the first to object, and eventually he killed the Baruch proposal with a veto before the Security Council. But even years later, during a Columbia faculty discussion, one of our most distinguished nuclear physicists, Prof. Isaac Isidor Rabi, bitterly attacked the Baruch plan as a fraud the United States had perpetrated on the international community. I would say in reviewing the history of the failed project that such emotional high voltage was not required to make certain an American delegation at the UN would not attempt to put over a new Baruch initiative.

This one never had a chance to begin with.

To assemble the materials needed for an attempt to create an atomic industry for peaceful uses was surely necessary for the world of the twenty-first century. Uranium ore could not readily be found everywhere on earth—America's came from Africa in a secret project initiated by a Columbia University geologist in war-time. And heavy water, not just ordinary H_2O, was not available by turning on a tap marked "cold" in the kitchen. Nor were other necessary elements and the skills needed to combine them available in any factory with a steam boiler or whatever devices could be used to obtain a useful result.

Moreover, what could be done about an element such as plutonium that did not exist in nature but would have to be manufactured if it were to be used in creating a nuclear device for destructive wartime uses? Even considered on an entirely theoretical basis, such problems as these could not be waved aside impatiently by a patriotic leader such as Ben-Gurion in Israel, who believed quite sincerely—and accurately—that his country would not long exist without a nuclear industry of its own.

Now and then, as Ben-Gurion persisted in trying to realize part of his vision of a future for Israel's nuclear industry, some of his scientists would argue with him that the notion in itself was absurd. One of the most respected of the veterans who had helped found the Jewish state, Abba Eban, called the concept a "worthless alligator" when he returned to the Ben-Gurion cabinet after a decade as the Israeli ambassador to the United States.

That response, in itself, was mild compared with what the prime minister had to endure from his other close associates in the founding of the Jewish state. And yet, he did have a point when he thought of the millions of people who would one day try to eke out a living in the narrow space squeezed between the Jordan River and the Mediterranean Sea directly north of the uninhabited Negev desert, which even the nomads tended to avoid when possible.

The question that the prime minister could not resolve for himself was where the money would come from to make Israel self-supporting in the next century if not in this one. For despite all the goodwill of the supportive American-Jewish community, which still contributed so much to the upkeep of Israel, such financial support could not be expected to continue forever. Nor would the Arab hostility to the presence of the Jewish state in Palestine be expected to wane in the foreseeable future.

No, as Ben-Gurion saw the future, in no way could Israel continue to exist unless some way were found to make the country self-supporting. No matter how talented the Israelis could be as traders and regardless of how shrewdly they could bargain with the outside world, their government could not forever count on handouts from abroad to sustain a Jewish presence in the Middle East.

That in substance, was why the prime minister persisted in reading as much current literature on the nuclear subject as he could find.

Sometimes, in his search for answers to the questions he himself raised about Israel's future, he even offended some of his closest collaborators. Once, the always-sensitive Golda Meir hastened to meet him in response to his summons only to be reminded by him that she soon would be making another trip to the United States—she remained the nation's champion fund-raiser—but, he asked, would she mind very much buying some new books that he needed but could not find in Israel?

Of course, Golda was put out, and she was by no means alone. However much the country depended on Ben-Gurion, he was no diplomat—and it was just as well. The striped-pants set by itself would never have conceived and created a new country.

How often Ben-Gurion talked wistfully of the treasures buried in the scorched earth of the Negev desert—the phosphate, potash, and other minerals that could one day be extracted and made to yield at least a part of the money needed to balance the country's income with its outgo. When he could, the prime minister and his wife lived in a small home they maintained in a desert *kibbutz* rather than the relative luxury of Tel Aviv or the spiritual comfort of Israeli-occupied Jerusalem (the Arabs still maintained a foothold on old Jerusalem to the east).

When Ben-Gurion dared to do so, he also would expound on the necessity for developing a process to desalinate sea water in order to add to the always-slender water resources of the Jordan River and its tributaries, the Dead Sea, and the few other areas used for the irrigation of the country's precious farmland. But always, among the few closest to him, he would return to the dire need to manufacture nuclear power in sufficient volume to make Israel solvent.

It was something more than a preachment. Instead, it became a tenet of his faith that he and the people who trusted in his leadership would somehow find the treasure that his senses told him would be uncovered in the Negev desert.

That, in essence, was why he concentrated on the site of the country's first nuclear community, Dimona, which was founded as an adjunct to Beersheba and the first nuclear reactor that began unromantically as a mere hole in the ground—and a big one at that. What he never lost was his faith. And that became all-important to the future of Israel.[2]

The world did not stand still during the years of doubt and trial for the Jewish state in Palestine. For although the United States continued to exert leadership in atomic development even after the Russians showed off their own nuclear capacity in 1949, the Americans lagged surprisingly in the development of the almost equally important long-range missiles.

Here, the Soviet Union was clearly the leader in the years immediately after World War II. With mistaken complacency, American scientists refused to acknowledge the Soviet ability to launch intercontinental ballistic missiles to take the lead temporarily in what was called "the balance of terror." This was the development that Moscow tried to exploit during the 1962 Cuban missile crisis that caught the Americans almost completely by surprise.

The contrast between Soviet enterprise and leisurely American procedure in the long-distance missile field was striking. In the late summer of 1957, for example, the Americans still were reported to be working on intermediate-range missiles when the Soviets proclaimed, quite accurately, as it turned out, that they had flown the first intercontinental ballistic missile. To show how greatly they had progressed in the missile field, the Soviets emphasized their leadership with the launching of the first satellite around the earth, accomplished with a new and powerful rocket engine.

Premier Khrushchev took pride in Moscow in the new Soviet *Sputnik*, something the Americans could not immediately duplicate. When they did produce a satellite of their own, it was a flop when a test run failed after the usual ballyhoo. The ultimate result was a congressional investigation, the reorganization of the Defense Department, and the American attempt to recover lost ground with a series of small satellite trial runs. It was the first time in years that the American leadership in national defense had been cracked.

In his 1958 State of the Union message to Congress, President Eisenhower demanded more money at once to catch up with the Soviets in the development of long-range missiles and for the creation of submarines capable of carrying and shooting missiles toward the enemy whenever necessary. To balance the presentation, he pleaded for more assistance for developing countries—something the Soviets now were making an effort to do in the Middle East to outflank the United States and nullify any advantage that might result from bases among allies, such as Saudi Arabia or Israel. "Safety through strength!" was the burden of Ike's message.[3]

As a small state virtually isolated between the two nuclear giants,

Israel's position had never before seemed so helpless. To its government and to its people, its dependence escalated dramatically in the two decades since it had been proclaimed a nation reborn. A single long-range missile that reached its mark in the Jewish state would take a terrible toll in lives; a nuclear bomb, accurately aimed, would be even more catastrophic.

The back-and-forth between President Eisenhower and Premier Khrushchev held a morbid fascination for the People of the Book as potential victims of this tense international rivalry. With a certain amount of relief, therefore, the Israelis, together with the Palestinians among them and the Arab enemies surrounding them, learned of an effort by the Americans and the Soviets to arrange for a moratorium in atomic testing.

Premier Khrushchev made the first offer in the spring of 1958, under which he decided unilaterally to end atomic testing. After consultation with Britain and France, President Eisenhower agreed to a year's suspension of nuclear testing, with a suggestion that, dependent on the installation of international inspection and control, there would be an annual extension of his voluntary test ban. Despite Russian protests of American trickery, what happened was that the arrangement eventually was extended to include all future members of the revolutionary atomic society.

To have permitted continued testing of atomic weapons, without the strictest limits, would have been an encouragement to violators to continue to pollute the atmosphere with possibly fatal consequences for all forms of life on this planet, including the world's peoples.

The situation surely was dangerous enough when only the United States and the Soviet Union were testing atomic weapons. A joint congressional committee reported at the time that a nuclear attack on the United States could, if it spread destruction nationwide, kill at least 50 million people and injure as many as 20 million others, make half the nation's homes unusable, and contaminate food supplies and farmlands.

What so devastating a nuclear attack would do to defenseless small countries such as Israel and its Arab neighbors could be imagined only with horror. It followed that the inauguration of test-ban treaties then and later for each new member of the atomic club became a major public concern wherever the public was permitted to know the truth about the threats to the earth and its peoples. For anybody who had seen Hiroshima, as I did on two flights over Japan, this race for nuclear parity was the greatest of reasons for arms-limitation treaties that carried realistic provisions for enforcement.

The ultimate result of the exchange between the United States and the Soviet Union included Khrushchev's antics on his American and United Nations visits as well as Vice President Richard Nixon's Moscow debates. All this did not prove very much on either side, but it did give the Americans time to catch up with the Soviets' leadership in ballistic missiles. Otherwise, the benefits to the world's peoples were dubious, and that was especially true for small countries such as Israel and the surrounding Arab states.

It was typical of Eisenhower's sensible nature that he concluded his two terms in the White House with an American commitment to world peace in his last global tour. "Our basic aspiration," he said, "is to search out methods by which peace in the world can be assured with justice for everybody." He concluded, "I want to prove that we are not aggressive, that we seek nobody else's territories or possessions; we do not seek to violate anybody else's rights."[4]

It was a simple pledge of faith. And yet, how it would be received by Israel's enemies in the Middle East was, as always, of concern to its people. And they had the most to lose—their country, reborn after two thousand years.

Israel's efforts to attain nuclear strength were rewarded after five years with a certain amount of progress. Under Ben-Gurion's leadership, the Israelis raised money, found a group of young and enthusiastic nuclear physicists to resolve some of their problems of national defense, imported necessary material for the construction of atomic plants, and involved French assistance to complete their first nuclear reactor at Dimona.

Understandably, the crises were numerous and increasingly grave when viewed against the threatening background of American-Soviet rivalries. But, as Ben-Gurion so often warned, the greatest disaster for Israel would have been to watch the struggle of the giants and do nothing.

The prime minister began his first nuclear campaign with a close-knit, trustworthy group of Israeli nuclear experts, directed by Shimon Peres from the Defense Ministry, who worked with the French staff at

Dimona. Gradually, other Israelis were shifted to the rim of the desert to create the treasure of nuclear operation, without which there could be no Jewish nation of the future.

What counted most now was the closeness of the cooperative association with the French in a unique binational effort to resolve Israel's power problem. Much depended on the friendship of François Mitterrand, the French minister of justice, when he became interested in the survival of the Jewish state as an ally of France as well as the United States.

During this period the Israelis directly involved with the nuclear power project would have been virtually helpless without superior French knowledge and experience in the uses of atomic energy.

A moment of decision came for both the French and the Israelis, who had created so close a working relationship just after Sen. John F. Kennedy's victory in the presidential election of 1960. Andrei Gromyko, the Soviet foreign minister at the time, protested the French involvement in Israel's atomic development with a hasty trip to Paris. Apparently, a Soviet spy plane had obtained pictures of the large development at Dimona on the fringes of the Negev desert; that, together with knowledge of France's cooperation with the Israelis, led to the Soviet diplomat's conclusion about the objective of the project there.

It was a critical time for the Israelis. But after some hesitation, the French stood by their pledge to maintain secrecy over the work being done at Dimona, and Gromyko had to leave Paris without having gained anything for his trouble.[5]

This is not to say that Israel had everything its own way in its colossal gamble for atomic power after that, for General de Gaulle meanwhile had been elected president of France in 1959 and, as always, he never was easy to satisfy. Even so, in due course, Ben-Gurion's desperate gamble paid off with the creation of a nuclear power reactor at Dimona and, some years afterward, another and larger reactor near Tel Aviv. But this by no means took account of the willingness of Israel's Arab neighbors to try to match the Jewish state's feat.

Such efforts in years to come would lead to Israel's first attack on an Arab atomic installation. But someone other than Ben-Gurion would have to assume the grave risk. It was mainly due to the farsighted policy of Israel's first prime minister that his successors were able to respond in kind to the nuclear threat of an Arab neighbor.

9.   Israel Fights for Life

Israel's struggle against Soviet power in the Middle East began immediately after the abortive Suez War, when Premier Khrushchev began to exert pressure in favor of the Arab states in the Middle East. He was convinced that he could capture the Arab world for his country and communism by supporting Nasser's Egypt in the aftermath of the Suez conflict.

There was a peasantlike simplicity about Khrushchev's bid for Arab favor. While recognizing Nasser as the aggrieved party in the combined British-French-Israeli attack, the Soviet leader now offered the Egyptian dictator strong financial support for his pet project, the Aswan High Dam.

That did it. Nasser not only accepted the financial assistance of the Soviet Union after being turned down by the West but he also started actively planning to clear land for his cherished Aswan project beginning in 1960—a shrewd challenge from the Egyptian to the West, particularly the United States and Great Britain, to reverse themselves and give him the money he had demanded.

For embattled Arab leaders in the Middle East, the tribute paid to Nasser was impressive. And for Israel, it was indicative of a shift in Soviet policy to stress Communist interest in the Arab cause. However, the United States was slow to respond in patching up relations with Britain, France, and Israel. And Israel, as a symptom of the strained relationship between the United States and its embarrassed allies, now objected to overflights of its territory by American and British aircraft—activities that suddenly had become necessary to shore up Western oil interests that were under Arab control, and a likely Soviet objective.

At first, the Americans and the British did not take Israeli objec-

69

tions seriously and continued their overflights where necessary; but, because the irritant was one of the few ways in which the Jewish state could show its displeasure to its allies, the protests continued and the overflights dwindled. What the Israelis evidently were trying to impress on Washington was that their continued military assistance in the area could not be taken for granted.

As Nasser's Soviet deal for the Aswan High Dam indicated, it was time for America and the West to realign their forces in the face of a determined advance for Soviet influence in the oil-rich Middle East. Charles E. Bohlen, the American ambassador to Moscow, already had warned Washington not to expect that the Soviets would be dropping Nasser as soon as it suited their convenience, a popular notion at the time. It had been Bohlen's view that what the Soviets hoped to accomplish in the Middle East was to separate America from its allies—a process that Eisenhower and Dulles had begun in their effort to halt the Suez War.

Now, with Moscow's interest in the Arab world developing momentum, it was Bohlen's opinion that it was time for America's policy makers to reconsider their position.[1]

Nikita Sergeivich Khrushchev, a coarse-mouthed, ill-mannered former miner in the Ukraine, had joined the Communist Party at twenty-four a year after Lenin and Trotsky seized control of Russia, and pushed his way to the top as premier of the USSR directly after the Suez War in 1958. He had been among Stalin's closest associates in World War II, and in 1953, after Stalin's death, he became part of the Soviets' "collective leadership." That, however, did not last long, for within three years he had replaced his colleagues, Georgii Malenkov and Nikolai Bulganin. And by 1956, in a celebrated "secret speech" before the Communist Party leadership in Moscow, he denounced Stalin's rule of terror.

That marked his approach at the outset to a policy of "peaceful coexistence" with the West, which the United States and the Western allies did not take seriously after he squelched rebellions in Poland and Hungary with Stalinist efficiency. But in his bid for influence among the Arab states, he was more successful, because the deepest mistrust among them centered on Israel, especially after it joined Britain and France in the Suez War. Whatever President Eisenhower did to halt the war and save Nasser, it was not enough to persuade many of the Arab leaders to look to the United States for leadership.

Instead, without dropping a bomb, the Soviet Union became the real beneficiary of the Suez War by impressing the Arab states in the Middle East with its support of Nasser's cause. To make sure that even the veriest dullard got the message, the Soviet propaganda apparatus sent crowds equipped with signs and slogans to stage protest rallies before the British, French, and Israeli embassies in Moscow. On November 17 and 18, after a truce had taken effect in the Western attack on Egypt, Khrushchev himself delivered a bitterly phrased speech each day against the "lackey," meaning Israel, and the "Great Lords," meaning Britain and France, who had tried to overthrow Nasser and seize the Canal.

What Khrushchev wanted, aside from making an impression on Nasser and the rest of the Arab world, was independence of transit for all parties in the Suez Canal (something the Soviets also insisted on in the Turkish-controlled Dardanelles). To insure his suddenly elevated standing in the Arab world, he helped Nasser settle a long argument with the Sudan over the effect of the proposed construction of the Aswan High Dam. After that, with the help of Soviet engineers and specialists in dam construction, the plans for the Aswan High Dam were drawn and Soviet financing was assured for a beginning of work in 1960.

This was no mere propaganda ploy. It was a huge undertaking that projected a program for a better life for many of Egypt's 60 million people. The first Aswan Dam, a modest project, had been completed by the British in 1902 and enlarged in 1934 to insure the irrigation of a million acres of land outside the valley of the Nile. In the new plans for the Aswan High Dam, which would be huge in length and 375 feet high, four miles south of the first dam, it would provide irrigation for 2 million additional acres of Egyptian land, most of it desert, through the construction of an enormous artificial lake to be named, suitably, after Nasser himself.

Once the enormity of this undertaking became widely known, together with Khrushchev's generous financing, there was a lot of rethinking in the higher echelons of both the American and British governments. And the estimates of Gamal Abdel Nasser as a mere braggart ultimately changed, along with the necessity in the West of maintaining a strong Israel to confront so resourceful a neighbor.

Even so loyal and accomplished a diplomat as Ambassador Bohlen agreed years later that the cancelation of American aid for Nasser's Aswan High Dam was a mistake. It was bound to be rectified in years to come, no matter what happened in American-Israeli relations.[2]

For Israel, the decade after the futile Suez conflict was a time for reorganization and reconstruction in which Ben-Gurion, as always, played a dominant role. Whether he was prime minister, defense minister, or a leader of the opposition in government, his view of Israel's role in the Middle East—and, indeed, the world—helped shape its future as well as the position of its enemies.

However, in the wake of the disappointment over the outcome of the Suez conflict, the Israelis had a difficult time while their internal political future was reorganized—always a source of confusion to the outside world. There were so many political parties, and such frequent changes in the composition of some of the major parties, that the net effect could scarcely be judged from the outside. And even among the domestic-party leaders, the political reorganization in Israel after the Suez conflict became a troublesome factor for the future.

A part of this undoubtedly was caused by the frequent revival of charges having to do with the Lavon affair—the controversial role of Pinhas Lavon as defense minister before and after his forced resignation. Without presuming to judge the rights and the wrongs of the matter, it lasted for so long that it could not help having a negative effect on the way the Israelis ran their internal affairs, even though, in an emergency, they seemed nearly always to turn to Ben-Gurion for leadership when others failed.

To illustrate the extent of the problem within Israel, Lavon became defense minister in the regime of Moshe Sharett as prime minister in 1955. It took Ben-Gurion's agreement to return to the defense ministry, replacing Lavon, to satisfy the unruly opposition that charged wrongdoing without further investigation. And eventually, Ben-Gurion served another term as prime minister and quit once again in 1960 in a protest when charges against Lavon were dropped.

During the succeeding regime of Levi Eshkol, Ben-Gurion again turned up in a dominant political role. The once-powerful Mapai had been split as a centrist party with a majority moving to the left as a wing supporting Labor. That, however, did not suit Ben-Gurion. In 1965, without any previous notice to his supporters, he announced to a small group of the faithful that he was forming an entirely new political party called Rafi, an acronym in Hebrew meaning Israeli Workers List.

Some of the idealistic younger group in government followed him, but Rafi did not do well in the elections that year when Eshkol easily commanded a majority and proceeded to form a government without any of Ben-Gurion's stalwarts. However, with another war looming on the Middle East horizon, the faction pledged to Ben-Gurion once again joined the government with Moshe Dayan as defense minister just before the opening movement of the next war with the Arabs took place.[3]

It was a testimonial to the economic strength of the new Jewish nation in the Middle East that the uproar of domestic politics—always a grievous fault in any representative government—could be set aside when the fate of the country itself was at stake. Whatever Israel's shortcomings, there never was a time in its first fifty years when its people failed to come together as war with the surrounding Arab nations threatened its existence. And that, above all else, is what strengthened the Israelis in their next unavoidable war with the still-combative Arabs.

There was one other factor of importance to Israel, its Arab neighbors, and the West that had markedly changed in the 1960s—the organization of the United Nations and its leadership. In the mid-1960s, from its modest early membership, the number of nations subscribing to UN principles and its Charter had reached 135—many more than the founders had contemplated. And that was not all, for at least 50 more countries would be admitted to the UN before the century's end. For sheer numbers, therefore, the UN membership had far exceeded the expectations and even the aspirations of its founders.

However, the very size of the world organization now was bound to become its fundamental weakness in its most important function under the Charter, the negotiation and preservation of peace among nations. Even in the Israeli wars that already had been fought in 1948–49 and the Suez War in 1956, the peacemaking function of the UN had left much to be desired. And in the new crisis that already was gathering headway in the 1960s, involving Israel and nearly all its Arab neighbors, it was far from certain that another conflict could be halted merely because there was a UN Emergency Force that supposedly was in control of the Suez Canal.

To be sure, Trygve Lie, the first secretary-general, had performed miracles with a relatively small and inexperienced UN peacekeeping staff and his successor, Dag Hammarskjold, had advanced the Norwegian's record. Upon taking over from Lie in 1957, the Swedish diplomat had to deal with an immediate crisis—the four hundred thousand Palestinians who had fled from their homes during the Israeli War of Independence and were still penned up in refugee camps scattered along the borders of Israel's neighboring Arab states. But in addition, the UN leaders had to try to hold down a rising number of raids by Arab forces against Israel together with Israeli reprisals that had begun even after the peace accords for the first conflict had been signed in 1949.

Such activity also continued against Israel from the Gaza Strip and the Golan Heights in Syria across the Lebanese frontier as well as the West Bank of the Jordan River. If the Israelis replied in kind, there was not very much the UN could do about that other than to remind the contending forces that their signed peace accords were supposed to mean what the parties had agreed to and were not to be ignored.

Despite all the handicaps, Hammarskjold refused to be discouraged in his various missions of peace. He led a UN mission to the capital of Communist China, Beijing, stationed UN peace observers in Lebanon and Syria as well as the Gaza Strip on Israel's borders, and tackled what seemed like an impossible prospect of civil war in the Congo.

On September 18, 1961, climaxing four years of intensive activity, Secretary-General Hammarskjold perished during a Congo flight when his plane crashed in a jungle. If anybody had ever persevered in what seemed like an almost hopeless struggle for world peace, this slender, patient Swedish diplomat had done so.[4]

As his successor, the member nations of the UN approved a fifty-four-year-old Burmese diplomat, U Thant, who had been the chief of his country's delegation to the world organization since 1947. Within a few months, this first Asian secretary-general was plunged into the heart of the Cuban missile crisis in which President Kennedy served a virtual ultimatum on Premier Khrushchev in 1962 to remove his missiles from Cuba or face the consequences of an American missile attack. It was the closest the world had come to witnessing atomic destruction since the first American A-bombs had been dropped on Hiroshima and Nagasaki to end the last phase of World War II against Japan.

The UN then had two major peacekeeping functions under way, the UNEF operation that kept the Suez Canal open after the end of that war in 1957 and the removal of the Cuban missile threat by Soviet forces against the Unites States. But the end was not yet for U Thant.

Two years later, in 1964, he had to intervene with another peace-keeping force on the island of Cyrprus. And after the end of that vigorous and eternally risky five-year term, he was besought by the UN to accept a second term as secretary-general. He undertook it reluctantly in 1966 just as the Vietnam War was escalating through President Lyndon Johnson's determination to send major United States forces into the Far East to put down the North Vietnamese and their Vietcong allies, both having Soviet aid.

Inevitably, being forced to work with limited manpower and funds for so many major peacekeeping operations, U Thant could not be blamed for becoming ever more cautious in committing his people and himself to separating warring peoples, large and small, and trying to persuade them with pleas rather than force to stop killing one another. Such was the handicap under which the UN faced the possibility of still more war in the Middle East.

Now, however, there was scant possibility of either American support for still another UN peacekeeping operation or a direct intervention between Israel and its hostile Arab neighbors to prevent still more conflicts involving the Jewish state.

For when President Johnson entered the White House after the assassination of President Kennedy in Dallas on November 22, 1963, he found himself in the middle of what seemed to have begun as a semisecret American war in Vietnam against the Communist North Vietnamese and their Vietcong allies in South Vietnam. It is difficult, so many years later, to re-create the almost fanatical anti-Communist atmosphere that shrouded American public life in the 1960s, but the urge to combat Moscow and Beijing was so great that the new president felt compelled to enlarge the scope of the conflict he inherited.[5]

In the mid-1960s, therefore, a major element of the armed strength of the United States was being committed to a guerrilla war on the mainland of Asia, a project against which General Eisenhower had repeatedly warned. Worse still, the more American forces were committed to fight an elusive and powerful enemy, the less chance there was for the United States to maintain its far more important commitments in Europe and the Middle East.

Saudi Arabia, at that time, was better able to defend its vast oil fields and those of its neighboring Arab states with minimal American assistance and, in fact, suffered not even a threat of war. But Israel's position, as a smaller and more endangered American ally, was not as favorable against a fully mobile Egypt, a strengthened Syria, and a Jordan that was defended by the veteran Arab Legion.

The first sign of a still larger conflict in the Middle East came in a peculiar—even a totally unexpected—manner. The Syrians, although smaller and not as well armed as Egypt, were wholeheartedly in the Communist camp by that time and anxious to attack Israel in any way that seemed possible to yield results. Accordingly, in 1963, Israeli scouts learned that the Syrians had inaugurated a policy of diverting water from a number of small tributaries of the Jordan River—streams that Israel desperately needed for its own often inadequate water supply.

What the Israeli military command did first was to send a fleet of armed aircraft over the Syrian capital of Damascus as a sign that war would follow the diversion of more Israeli river water. But the Syrians ignored the warning. And in the spring of 1967, President Nasser, too, was ready to take on Israel in warfare once again, for he ordered the UN Emergency Force out of the Suez Canal. And at the same time, he shut Israel out of the Canal for the first time since the War of Independence by closing the Strait of Tiran to Israeli shipping at the southern terminus of the Gulf of Aqaba.[6]

All too soon, Israel once again would be fighting for its life, while Khrushchev redoubled his support of Egypt and sought to make still further gains in the Middle East.

PART TWO | **Survival**

10. Dayan's War

Levi Eshkol, the sixty-eight-year-old veteran Israeli finance minister, had taken over as prime minister from the revered Ben-Gurion in 1963 and now faced the warlike challenge of Egypt and Syria with Jordan's Arab Legion as a likely ally.

Eshkol, a gentle soul and considerate to a fault, was very far from an adaptable war leader. By reputation, he had always been regarded as a skilled politician, resourceful at the give-and-take of debate in the Knesset and compromise with those who opposed him. But when every citizen knew that the nation's armed forces were prepared for an Arab onslaught, and fear of Egypt's newfound alliance with the Soviet Union was spreading in the spring of 1967, demands were rising on every side for Ben-Gurion to return to power.

At times, in the streets of Tel Aviv and Jerusalem, crowds would chant his name. And in the Knesset and elsewhere at political meetings, there were grave discussions of how Prime Minister Eshkol could be persuaded to yield his leadership to the eighty-one-year-old Ben-Gurion, the founding prime minister of Israel who had held high office for almost fourteen of the nineteen years of the Jewish state's existence. To the street people, it often seemed unthinkable that Israel could go to war once again without Ben-Gurion to lead the nation.

Consider the feelings of the street people.

Ben-Gurion, still strong and tough at sixty-two, had been prime minister for five years during and after leading the country in the War of Independence. For two years, he had given way to his close friend and collaborator, Moshe Sharett, who had led the fight for the Jewish nation before the UN, but even so the founder had remained in government as defense minister.

Then, in 1955, Ben-Gurion once again had resumed the leadership of government as prime minister except for a brief time in February 1961, when he resigned but was immediately persuaded to return to office. He stayed there, in charge of the nation's affairs, until 1963. But even when he gave up his cherished post to Eshkol, he still jealously guarded his role in the formation of government policy.

Two years later, in 1965, there was an irreparable difference between the two comrades-in-arms over policy toward the Arabs. Ben-Gurion, in retiring to private life, split the dominant Mapai Party by withdrawing to form his new political organization, called Rafi. He took with him Moshe Dayan and many other major figures in the long struggle to make Israel a viable independent state in the Middle East.

Then, still hearing the crowds in the streets chanting Ben-Gurion's name, Prime Minister Eshkol knew it was time to find a meeting of minds with his great predecessor at the head of Israel's government. He did so, openly and with good spirit, by forming a government of national coalition with Dayan, the author of the successful Suez War strategy, as defense minister and Gen. Yitzhak Rabin as chief of staff of the army.

That, however, did not take account of the distribution of the Arab population in Israel and the way they earned their living. At the peak of Israel's economic drive, there would be at least five hundred thousand Arabs living on the Gaza Strip and the West Bank who crossed daily into Israel where they were gainfully employed. That was something that leaders such as Nasser and Hafez al-Assad of Syria never seemed to take into account when they nurtured their plans for war on Israel—and still more war even after they had once failed. Quite naturally, the Arab workers whose jobs in Israel were forfeit in wartime thereby suffered the most immediate and direct loss—though not on the field of battle.

However, if the Arab leadership took account of such difficulties as these, they never made it known but pursued their vendetta with the Israelis for as long as they were given the Soviet guns and other military supplies for war—and still more. This is the way politics in the Middle East was ordered from the time of the birth of Israel until there was no more fight left in the hostile neighbors of the Jewish state.[1]

General Dayan, with his black eye patch, speedily became the leading military figure on the Israeli side as soon as he accepted the Ministry of Defense from Prime Minister Eshkol. Dayan had been outstanding from the time he was made the Israeli army's chief of staff when he was thirty-eight. Ben-Gurion, the prime minister at the time, learned quickly to rely on Dayan and trust his military judgment implicitly. He was either the author or the principal supporter of some of the key decisions that Israel adopted in line with his defense policy, among them the creation of a national electronics industry, a far-spreading weapons research and development operation, and, to top off everything else, the great nuclear reactor that had been built and installed on the rim of the Negev desert at Dimona.

Dayan's approach to his comrades in arms was not that of an isolated superior who handed down his commands from on high, then watched the common herd struggle to do his wishes. He was always careful to consult his division commanders and sometimes their chief officers as well, even during the 1967 war when it still was a young army, a new army, and one in which the officers and the enlisted men were not estranged from each other.

Dayan himself, in the memoranda left by his associates, did not adopt a pose of command in addressing a conference of his division leaders, let alone make the fatal mistake of talking down to a meeting of the Israeli cabinet. Its members came to him, deeply concerned, on the eve of battle in 1967, and worried that this youthful army would not be up to the task it was obliged to undertake.

That last conference before the fighting began, looking back after the war, had been crucial for Dayan and even more so for his commanders. For these military leaders seemed to be superbly confident that the troops they had trained and worked with in such close order would be more than a match for the more numerous and better-armed Egyptians. The civilian leaders of government, however, had been far from certain of the outcome; it was the army, therefore, that boosted civilian morale on the eve of battle, not the reverse.

Had the civilian state of mind been dominant just before the war began, there is no doubt whatever that the army would have begun its difficult assignment under an enormous handicap—a downcast morale that could have spelled disaster. It was, however, the Egyptians—despite their superior numbers and equipment, who were not at all sure of carrying the fight to the enemy. The conclusion had been reached logically and on the basis of a certain amount of hard evidence, and was not mere happenstance.

Through intelligence briefings, including interviews with captured Egyptians before the fighting began, the Israelis learned quickly enough that they were unlikely to have to confront an entirely battle-hardened army. On the contrary, the Egyptian prisoners taken before the fighting began seemed not to have the faintest idea of how to conduct themselves in the desert, a background for war that called for the utmost mobility, economy of movement whenever possible during the heat of the day, and Spartan habits in the use of precious water.

Still, on the basis of experience with wandering Egyptian soldiers, lost in the desert and picked up by roving Israeli troops, their training for desert warfare seemed to have been nil. Not that the Israelis expected to sweep aside their foes without much hard work. On the contrary, the division under Dayan's command had been combat trained to expect fierce resistance and hardship. But those who remembered the 1956 war, the older people in uniform, saw to it that the youngest recruits did not go into desert warfare without knowing how to deal with the special conditions they were bound to face at one time or another before the fighting ended.

In this desert war, the Israelis would encounter Egyptian mine fields in which a wrong move might mean the loss of an arm or a leg. There would be fighting in darkness, much of it as surprise attacks, and there would be shelling from the Egyptian long-range artillery. The Israelis would be using more parachute drops this time than they did in the 1956 war to create confusion, surprise, and even flight among the enemy if the attack was mounted in force. Under such circumstances, it was remarkable that the final conferences before the war began demonstrated that it was the civilians, very largely, who still doubted the outcome while the troops and their commanders seemed superbly sure of themselves.[2]

By this time, the Israelis had been well armed with aircraft, big guns, tanks, and an immense number of mobile troop carriers so that General Dayan, in making his plans with General Rabin, knew his forces could overwhelm the much larger Arab forces combined against them. However, from the outset, it was clear before a shot was fired that this could be no stop-go war, dependent on UN truces to renew supplies and shift forces to key strong points.

What Dayan had determined to do was to strike rapidly and in force at each of his enemies in turn, then come back from a different direction as soon as possible to clean up what he expected to be the remnants of the enemy forces that still were capable of resistance. His objective, however, never shifted—total command of the battlefield from the moment the war began.

No Israeli army had ever attempted so massive an offensive—and in so many directions—but the money that had been raised for Israel, and the American, French, Czech, and other arms that had been purchased, now were to be used forcefully and dramatically to turn back still another challenge to the Jewish state from its collective Arab enemies.

The Egyptian, Syrian, and Jordanian forces, by contrast, had been newly armed with Soviet weapons from tanks and mobile artillery personnel carriers, but it was anybody's guess how well they had been trained in the use of the new armaments and how thoroughly they had been drilled in battlefield conditions. Here Dayan truly expected his Israeli forces would prove themselves to be superior.

Whatever Israel's problems may have been in the final days before the onset of the war, in sum, they did not affect the military. But Eshkol still was having trouble forming his cabinet of national unity despite the adherence of Dayan, as a contribution from Ben-Gurion's Rafi Party. Ben-Gurion himself, even in his eighties, was inflexible in refusing to take any part in the Eshkol cabinet. Others among Eshkol's opponents, notably Menachem Begin of the conservative Likud Party, were in favor of a cabinet reflecting national unity, as were some others.[3]

Despite the immense political confusion within Israel's civilian regime, there was no doubt whatever about Soviet intentions just before the onset of the war. In Premier Khrushchev's efforts to gain dominance in the Middle East, which meant control of its oil resources, his objective was to undermine the leadership of the United States in the area, following Britain's decline, and reduce as much as possible American access to the area's massive oil potential.

The Soviet leader, now as a burlesque politician who had upset the diplomatic routine at the United Nations, clowned his way through a tour of leading American cities and then failed miserably to break the will of an American president, John F. Kennedy, in the missile crisis of 1962. What Khrushchev wanted to do in his union with the Arabs was to attack American power close to his own field of operations by striking at American oil imports from Saudi Arabia and against smaller oil states.

In the Soviet premier's calculations, therefore, it must have seemed imperative to him to encourage the Arab forces facing Israel, which, together with the Saudis, constituted America's allies in the region.[4] In any event, as Israeli intelligence operatives were well aware, Soviet rubles and heavy weapons had been lavished on Egypt seemingly regardless of cost. And on May 14, 1967, a well-armed force of at least 75,000 Egyptians was moving across the Sinai Peninsula from the Suez Canal and taking up advanced positions on the Israeli border.

Regardless of the calmness of the Israeli armed forces and their commanders, some of the members of Prime Minister Eshkol's cabinet panicked. In meetings with the military command only a few days before the beginning of hostilities, the civilian leadership appeared to be frightened of the coming clash, suggesting strategies that seemed to the military people to be absurd and expressing so much doubt that it could have been disheartening to those who had to do the fighting.

But one day early in June, Dayan had made his decision. The war would start without further delay on June 5, because the enemy was beginning to fortify key points in the desert that the Israelis intended to capture as quickly as possible. The point could not be ignored. To waste more time on idle speculation would be to grant the Egyptians a greater opportunity to strengthen their positions.

Moreover, it was not Egypt alone that was to be attacked, although Egyptian terrorist raids had been stepped up against Israel in recent weeks from the Gaza Strip. To the north, near Israel's border with Lebanon, Syrian troops once again had occupied the Golan Heights and were continuing their terrorist activities against Israeli towns and farms across the border.

Even if the Lebanese had objected, which they failed to do, it would not have mattered. The Syrians also were operating out of southern Lebanon as if it had been added to their own territory. Israel may have halted Syrian diversion of water from the tributaries of the Jordan River, but that did not interfere with the pre-invasion Syrian terrorist raids.

There was little that Lebanon could to do about Syrian dominance even if Lebanese warring factions of Muslims and Maronite Christians could have agreed on a functioning government. There was no army of consequence to defend the country from either the Syrians or the Israelis. It had been just another battlefield and its people were the victims of the contending nations.

In Jordan, to the southwest, there was a more serious threat—the British-officered Arab Legion on which King Hussein depended for his security. At that stage in the festering wars with Israel, Jordan's military did constitute a danger because it was a veteran, well-trained organization. To support the Arab forces in this looming war, all three national combatants made use of the disorganized Palestinian guerrillas who operated within Israel's borders with whatever help they could promote from such neighbors.[5]

Nasser was then forty-nine and firmly in power as Egypt's dictator, a career army officer and graduate of the Royal Military Academy whose ambition caused him to reach for ever more power in the Middle East. With his troops advancing across the Sinai Peninsula in mid-May and the UN Emergency Force relieved of its duties at the Suez Canal, he was in complete charge and could have done whatever he pleased. But for reasons he kept to himself, he was not prepared to start the war against the Israelis, so the large Egyptian force loitered in the desert while awaiting the order to advance.

There was more prewar activity on the Syrian frontier. Another professional soldier, President Hafez al-Assad, who had been graduated from the Syrian Military Academy at twenty-seven and risen through the army's ranks to general, commander in chief, and dictator, now was also waiting to attack the Israelis. As in Egypt, the Soviet influence was dominant in Syria but little was happening except for the usual hit-and-run commando tactics that drew continual Israeli fire.

The third important figure in this Arab mobilization against Israel was Hussein, king of Jordan, who has succeeded his father, King Abdullah, in 1953 at eighteen and held power ever since mainly through the strength of his Arab Legion.

Hussein was by no means as militant as either Hafez al Assad or Nasser for a very good reason—he would have been hard put to say whether he ruled more Jordanians than Palestinians. As the position in the Middle East was developing, the displaced Arab people, now totaling almost nine hundred thousand, were scattered in UN holding camps along Israel's borders and at least half of them had been absorbed within Jordan. So even though Hussein could see little advantage for himself in waging war against Israel, he did so more because of the Palestinians his country had been obliged to absorb than because of any benefit he would have gained through any victory over Israel.

With his forces seemingly waiting one on the other to begin the fighting, Generals Dayan and Rabin struck hard at the very center of the enemy's massed position in the desert with a major air attack on the Egyptians at dawn on June 5, then an armored thrust that came at them from the side and rear. With so unexpected and violent an onslaught that caught the enemy completely off guard, the Israelis launched what they would call their Six-Day War with all the weapons at their command.[6]

11. Two Days in June

Since a foggy dawn on June 5, more than three hundred Israeli fighter aircraft had been attacking every Egyptian airfield in the Sinai and others as far off as the Suez Canal zone.

There has been no quibbling about who started the war. The Israelis did, and with good reason: their existence depended on a quick and overwhelming victory against a foe of superior numbers and equipment. As an issue, they used the blockage of the Tiran Strait.

The Israeli assault developed in waves, a few aircraft strikes at a time. Because the offensive was such a surprise, the enemy aircraft in the Sinai were caught mostly on the ground while neatly parked in rows—and as easily destroyed with well-placed bombs and gunfire. The few enemy pilots caught in or near their aircraft for the most part were killed. The rest were struck at breakfast or in bed.

The scene in the Egyptian Sinai airfields was sheer chaos. Every few minutes, another flight of Israeli aircraft roared in for the kill, obstructed only by scattered gunfire that was almost completely ineffective at first. That morning, all told, most of Egypt's approximately four hundred aircraft were either destroyed or so severely hit that they were put out of action indefinitely.

Flustered by the suddenness of the onslaught, Cairo radio babbled on about mythical Egyptian strikes against Tel Aviv and even the Israeli part of Jerusalem, but continued to be silent about the catastrophic Egyptian aircraft losses. In fact, the distracted Egyptian commanders were in no position to give a running account of their own defeat—and probably would have been court-martialed if they had attempted to do so.

As for Gamal Abdel Nasser, there is no reliable testimony so long after the fact as to his feelings about the disaster that was wiping out his airpower. But by the following day, he had recovered his senses sufficiently to accuse the United States of having sent disguised American aircraft to the Israelis that then were used against Egypt. Of course, it was a lie.

By the time President Lyndon Johnson arose for breakfast that June 5 at the White House, given the difference in time with the Middle East, he could listen to almost any network TV news broadcast with a summary of the details of Israel's quick disposition of the Egyptian air force while having his Wheaties and coffee. For good or bad measure by that time, what he also must have heard was a phony bulletin attributed to Foreign Minister Abba Eban that the Egyptians had made the first move for war.

It was not so, as the Israelis freely admitted afterward. But that first day, they were not talking much either for publication or for broadcast, sensibly trying to keep their enemies from accurate knowledge of what already had been accomplished and what remained to be done.

Manifestly, much of Israel's airpower, about 50,000 to 55,000 troops and a mechanized ground force that included several hundred tanks, had been arrayed that morning against the Egyptians in the Sinai, but perhaps 20,000 soldiers were sent off to take care of assignments against Jerusalem where Jordanian troops occupied the Old City. For an operation of this magnitude, with the nation's existence at stake in the event of failure, neither General Dayan as the defense minister nor General Rabin as the field commander were taking anything for granted.[1]

It was just as well. As soon as the Syrians learned they were at war, having belated knowledge of the Israeli attack on Egypt, Syrian bombers were in the air punishing Haifa, the nearest Israeli port, and whatever Israeli air bases they could reach. In response, Israeli aircraft were bombing Syrian airfields and installations in the Golan Heights, taking a toll of at least fifty Syrian aircraft in their counterattack. As for Jordan, after Israel finished with the Syrian aircraft, at least two dozen of King Hussein's fighters were put out of action, most of Jordan's air force.

Hussein, however, was not through. Although the Israelis had not expected much retaliatory action from him, the many Palestinian refugees for whom he was responsible caused him to make a much more forcible response than had been anticipated. Worse still, as far as

Israel was concerned, Jordanian big guns were fired into both new Jerusalem and Tel Aviv to the consternation of the Jewish citizenry.

That front remained among the most active that first day. As response to the Arab Legion's fire, an Israeli bomber damaged King Hussein's palace in Amman and savaged the city with rockets before returning to its base. Subsequently, there was much Jordanian shelling in the Israeli-held portion of Jerusalem that took its toll of lives and damaged areas near the Knesset.

In the heat of the day, when Jordanian troops occupied the building in Jerusalem that housed the UN Truce Supervision force, the world organization was drawn into the fray briefly while the UN's people hastily transferred their headquarters to the nearest available hotel. The UN's people, including their families with small children, had felt themselves besieged in their regular quarters and were lucky to escape injury with both sides exchanging fire in a room-to-room gun battle.

As might have been expected once the combatants settled down to the desperate business of war, the center of action shifted from the shattered Egyptian front in the Sinai to the Jordanian sector mainly because it was here, in Jerusalem, that the greatest struggle of this short but vicious war would take place. The Israelis had expected that two hundred thousand of their own people in the modern city would be shelled and some might be killed or wounded as the fighting continued. What they did not expect was that the fighting continued and the most precious part of Palestine, the Old City of Jerusalem, became a center of the armed struggle, because it was, as it had always been, a symbol for deeply religious Arab peoples.

Now it was being defended courageously and bravely by Jordan's Arab Legion against the inroads of Israeli infantry from the new city. The problem was that the Jordanians were firing artillery rounds and rockets into the new city, mainly from hills outside the Old City, and the Israeli population was taking punishment.

The Knesset, in an emergency night meeting in the well-protected basement of the Parliament building, quite naturally was debating the urgent, if still delicate, question of what to do about safeguarding the Old City while the siege was continuing. All participants were well aware that any outbreak of fighting in the Old City that heightened tensions and resulted in mass killings would result in immediate and forthright international condemnation of those responsible.[2] The Christian world, too, was deeply concerned.

In addressing this question Prime Minister Eshkol took it on himself to make the most important decision of the day next to authorizing the surprise attack. He proposed, briefly and unemotionally in that basement meeting of his parliamentary associates, that Old Jerusalem would have to be seized from the Jordanians to end the menace of continual bombardment of the new city. Not a voice was raised in protest. And so, the responsibility for perhaps the greatest risk to the Old City settled on the prime minister without comment and without a vote.

How and when it would happen was left to the fortunes and misfortunes of war while the advantage still rested with the Israeli forces and their government. Whatever the Israelis planned, it would have to be carried out quickly, because past experience had shown that the UN would demand a cease-fire as soon as the delegates could be brought together for an emergency meeting in New York.

President Johnson, Secretary of State Rusk, and the Soviet premier, Aleksei Kosygin, had been exchanging messages for most of that first day of fighting, leading to an agreement by both sides to press for the UN cease-fire. At the time, mainly because of the erroneous Israeli claim that the Egyptians had fired first, there was some doubt as to who had begun the fighting but later in the day it did not seem to matter as the United States and the Soviet Union informally concluded that this war would have to stop.

As any old UN hand might have predicted, even after the Security Council convened at 9:30 A.M. on June 5, only a few hours after the Israelis had struck the first blow, the delegates could not agree on the terms of a cease-fire. The Soviets wanted the fighting to stop with all sides returning to their positions before the first Israeli attack. That, however, was no go, because it would have permitted the Egyptians to continue to blockade the Strait of Tiran against Israel, the move that started the fighting.

The United States called for a simple cease-fire, which was the Israeli position because it permitted the Jewish state to retain its territorial gains. Then the Soviets further complicated matters by demanding a resolution condemning Israel for starting the war, and that really upset most of the delegates.

So far, the UN negotiations were par for the course in international confusion and, as the hours wore on, it was apparent that nobody would put forward a resolution to which the majority could agree. And there was no guarantee, even so, that one of the Big Five would withhold a veto for one obscure reason or another.

At that point the French chipped in with a compromise that nobody understood and, as a last gasp for the day, the Indians produced their usual neutral resolution, which duplicated the original Soviet proposal for a return to previous positions after a cease-fire. And so, after a long day of tit for tat that gave not even the reporters a story, the Security Council adjourned, much to the relief of the Israeli delegation, because all its members really wanted now was time to permit their military to solidify their victory over the Arabs.

All that the Arab delegates could do in this version of UN procedures was to protest with vehemence the inability of the Security Council to stop a small war in the Middle East. That was, however, a very substantial motive within the Egyptian delegation that helped cause the delay; to obtain a UN cease-fire without an accompanying order to the combatants to return to their positions before the war started would have given Israel the fruits of victory. That, the Egyptians had insisted on day one of the war, would have to be a part of the cease-fire resolution, but it failed to pass.

Nasser's suspicions of American collusion with Israel in this latest war in the Middle East were based upon the Egyptian experience of 1956 in the Suez War when Britain and France had joined Israel in a three-sided attack against the Arab front. Moreover, the Egyptian dictator could not bring himself to believe that the Israelis, without great power assistance, could have wrought so much destruction to Egyptian air-power in so short a time on the opening day of this new and unexpected conflict.

Accordingly, it was to be expected that Nasser would strike back at the United States as soon as he found it convenient to do so. That happened on June 6, a Tuesday, the second day of the war, when Cairo Radio announced that Egypt had severed diplomatic relations with Washington, in the same broadcast in which the United States was accused of collusion in the Israeli air attack on June 5. At the time Israeli Foreign Minister Eban was flying to New York to try to stall a cease fire resolution in the Security Council.

When Eban entered the Security Council debate late that day, there still had been no agreed cease-fire resolution and the Israeli armed forces had virtually destroyed Egypt's mechanized armor as well as its air-power. Nasser's tanks and troop carriers, like his aircraft, had been caught unawares by Israeli bombers in the first two days of the war and damaged so thoroughly as to be ineffective in further combat in the Sinai Peninsula. The situation was so serious that the Soviet's Kosygin repeatedly telephoned President Johnson urging him to expedite a quick UN cease-fire resolution without conditions.

Whether the Egyptians liked it or not, Moscow now realized a continued argument about ordering a return to prewar positions would serve only to give the triumphant Israelis still more time to grab even more Arab territory in the Sinai and, as far as Syria and Jordan were concerned, additional areas on the West Bank, in Lebanon and Syria, too. That was why, by the time Eban arrived in the council chamber on Tuesday evening, the United States and the Soviet Union already had agreed on the wording of a simple cease-fire resolution without any limiting conditions.

The Israeli foreign minister, therefore, had the grace to strike a noble pose in a laudatory speech that was broadcast to a global audience. In it, he detailed Israel's reasons for striking at the Arabs and justified the assaults—and the gains—the Israelis had made against Egypt, Syria, Jordan, and Iraq. But, in token of the UN's desire for peace, he agreed to the unconditional resolution for a cease-fire.

While Eban still was being applauded, the Egyptian delegation, on instructions from Cairo, flatly rejected the demand for a cease-fire, because, so Cairo argued, the UN in effect was giving Israel a territorial victory by refusing to order a withdrawal to prewar boundaries. To support the angry retort from Nasser, Egypt's Arab allies joined him in breaking diplomatic relations with the United States. Thus, the pro-Egyptian lineup then included Syria, Lebanon, Jordan, Iraq, Algeria, Yemen, the Sudan, and Mauritius.

Still, after two days and nights of combat, the Israelis had been victorious wherever they struck at Egypt and Jordan, apparently having determined to do substantial damage to the first two before turning on the toughest, if not the strongest, among its Arab enemies, Syria.

As far as Egypt was concerned, Nasser's airpower had been so hard hit that it could function only spasmodically and then with little effect. Territorially, Egyptian armor had been so damaged that much of the Sinai Peninsula now was under Israeli control and even the Suez Canal itself seemed vulnerable more than 125 miles from the Israeli border. It would be weeks, regardless of Nasser's plans, before he could threaten Israel again as he had done with impunity in the past.[3]

Jordan's King Hussein, too, had been damaged by Israel's opening two-day assault, including the bombardment of the capital, Amman. A continuation of the war, now inevitable with Egypt's rejection of the UN cease-fire resolution, would mean an almost immediate Israeli assault on the greatest prize of the war, the conquest of the Old City of Jerusalem for which General Dayan now was prepared. The difficulty here was not so much the part of Jordan's Arab Legion that still was holed up behind the Old City's fortifications; the Arab force was vulnerable and could be forced to retreat.

No, the problem was the possibility of major damage to the ancient monuments within the Old City that were so respected by Christians and Muslims as well as Jews. And so, it was with the greatest reluctance that General Rabin, as field commander, prepared for a third and crucial day of combat against Arab forces in Jerusalem. It was a chance the Israeli government decided to undertake because of the benefit it would derive from making a united Jerusalem its capital. So great a prize, combined with the destruction of Soviet arms used by Egypt, Jordan and Syria, would solidify Israel's position against its Arab enemies in the Middle East.

As far as the United States was concerned, a greatly strengthened Israel would serve as a bridge between Turkey, to the northwest, and Saudi Arabia, to the south, safeguarding American oil interests against the rising pressures of the pro-Soviet Arab states from Iran and Iraq in the east to Algeria on the west African coastline.[4]

Later that June, on the twenty-third, President Johnson and Premier Kosygin had a summit meeting at Glassboro State College in New Jersey, but there still was no way of settling the tensions in the Middle East aroused by the shattering Israeli attacks on the Arab states that had been collaborating with the Soviets. Indeed, just about all that happened at Glassboro was an urgent plea by Robert McNamara, as secretary of defense, for a treaty on arms control between the two great adversaries, the United States and the Soviet Union.

The Arabs' refusal to change their aggressive stance toward Israel, even after the damage that had been inflicted on them, served to delay for some time any arrangement between the Soviets and the Americans to reduce tensions. And that, perhaps, could have been forecast on the basis of what happened to the Soviets' Arab client states early in June when Israel's attacks stripped them of much of the extensive armaments Moscow had provided. The resounding defeats of the first two days only foreshadowed the even greater problems of the Arab states in surviving the rest of the war.[5]

12.   Old Jerusalem Captured

The capture of Old Jerusalem, with its fifty thousand Muslim citizens and ten thousand Jordanian troops, was unexpectedly easy. On June 7, the third day of Israel's Six-Day War, that part of the ancient Jewish capital fell with most Israeli guns being fired in the air in token of victory. The Jordanians had withdrawn under cover of darkness.

To the surprise of the first Israeli troopers who burst into the Old City about 10:00 A.M., that was the position as it was reported to General Dayan as field commander. And within a few hours, all of Jerusalem had been returned to Jewish control for the first time in more than two thousand years.

At least two other generals heard the news early that morning and also rejoiced while fighting parts of the war elsewhere. In the Sinai desert, General Sharon envied General Dayan's triumph, and at the Sharm el-Sheik, far to the south, General Weizman was so excited that he regretted the Israelis had failed to plan on conquering Cairo, Amman, and Damascus as well.

In Old Jerusalem itself, a celebration already was under way at breakfast time on the ancient Temple Mount, but how long the attackers could enjoy their conquest was a good question.

This, however, was how the youthful paratroop heirs to Kings David and Solomon, together with civilians from Israeli modern Jerusalem, chose to enjoy their victory. And to the Western world, where there still was astonishment over Israel's successes of the first two days of the latest conflict, much of the public feeling in the United States and Europe was swinging sharply in Israel's favor. The decisive point of public interest, especially in New York and Washington, seemed to be rising popular enthusiasm that so new and small a reborn nation could be knocking down the giants of the Arab world, particularly Egypt and its allies, with such skill and speed of maneuver.

What did not seem to bother the West so much, and Israel itself not at all, was the latest wandering horde of Arab refugees that had been created in the earliest days of this grinding war when Israeli forces overran Arab population centers, wrecking many a town, home, and farm in the wake of their stunning attacks.

What the total of refugees now would be in the miserable UN centers, which lined the borders of Arab lands in the Middle East, no one could say while the cease-fire still was not being observed. But it was, as always, trapped civilians on both sides who would suffer the most.

The difference with the past was that the survivors of the Holocaust had undertaken to fight for their lives and the lives of their children. And now the Israeli banner, the blue and white six-pointed Star of David, was hoisted by the conquerors over the Dome of the Rock on the Old City's Temple Mount.[1]

While a scattering of Israeli troops paused to pray at the Western Wall of the Holy City—often called the Wailing Wall—the Muslim authorities waited patiently nearby for an Israeli commander to surrender their share of the historic city and arrange, so far as possible, for a continuation of the community's affairs.

Once the first-division commander appeared with brusque assurances that military occupation would be brief if order prevailed without resistance, there was temporary relief among the Muslims that few civilians would be routed from their homes and businesses in the Old City. How long that would last, as in any wartime situation, no one could say.

The fundamentals of life in Old Jerusalem, for the time being, were bound to be shaky under Israeli occupation.

More formal pronouncements were issued later that day by Prime Minister Eshkol, who swore an oath softly against the grim background of the Wailing Wall, that this time Israel would never surrender again its control of the ancient city as its capital. It was a ceremonial assurance that would depend eventually on the impression the protesting Arab states would make on the world community as represented at the UN.

The Israelis, both the political and military leaders, understood the temporary nature of their conquest all too well, which was what made their continual pledges of no retreat seem hollow and poorly timed. Still, that third day of this latest war with everything going Israel's way, those in charge of the Jewish state's destinies could not be blamed for assuring their own publics that what they had conquered by arms would not be given up across the tables of the UN.

And yet, even to the uninformed observer, it was plain enough in the attitude of the civilians, who represented the Arabs of the conquered Old City, that they were cooperating with the victors because they were forced to do so, not out of respect for the new order that had just come into being. And given such grudging obedience at the top of the civilian order, it must have been evident to the victors that the will of the conquered peoples to resist had not been broken. Nor would it be for many a year to come, particularly after their leaders already had reaffirmed that there would be no peace, no negotiations, and no contacts with the Israelis.

On the most important matter confronting all the combatants, the UN Security Council's cease-fire resolution, the situation of the Arabs that third day was so deplorable that they simply resisted accepting the UN proposal to quit fighting. As for Israel, Foreign Minister Eban's late Tuesday speech of acceptance still remained to be fulfilled by his military organization.

It was a case of "I'm willing to stop fighting but make the other guy do it first."

This was still the position in Old Jerusalem even though King Hussein's Jordan troops had long since retreated from combat in darkness, but his artillery continued lobbing shells into Israeli-occupied modern Jerusalem as a token that the war was still being fought. And so, in Washington, President Johnson was awaiting word from his Defense Department on when the Egyptians, Jordanians, and Syrians could be expected to accept the UN's cease-fire.

The trouble with Egypt and Jordan seemed to be that the command structure in each had been so shattered by Israeli attacks that it was difficult for both Nasser and King Hussein to get the word to their troops, or so their available military people contended.

And as for Syria, except for a forced cessation of its air attacks, its army had not yet been committed to battle while the Israeli forces were otherwise occupied. As for Iraq, after an opening demonstration of support for its fellow Arabs, its commanders seemed quietly to have separated themselves from further combat with the Israelis on the Syrian front—the last reported Iraqi activity.

By nightfall Wednesday in the Middle East, Egypt's airpower was a mere shadow of itself, its ground forces had been routed from the Sinai Peninsula, the Suez Canal was in danger of Israeli air strikes, and the Strait of Tiran had been reopened to Israeli shipping. It now seemed to be just a question of a few more hours before word of the cease-fire could be forwarded to the relatively few places where Egyptian forces continued to resist.

Jordan's plight was even worse. King Hussein had been ousted from control of Old Jerusalem, as the world already had learned, but he also had witnessed his forces being routed by Israeli troops under cover of their airpower. They now held the occupied West Bank of the Jordan River, the site of ancient Judea and Samaria, together with the cities of Hebron, Bethlehem, Jericho, and others. The Dead Sea area, too, had been lost to the Arab Legion and thousands of Jordanian prisoners already were in Israeli custody.

Unlike dictator Nasser, who gloomily continued to blame fictional United States forces and aircraft for his troubles despite common knowledge that the Israeli airpower by itself had been the dominant factor in the attack on Egypt, King Hussein was continually announcing to Israel that he already had agreed to the UN cease-fire, and why were the Israelis continuing to shoot? The answer was obvious. The Israelis did not trust the Jordanian king any more than he placed his faith in them.[2]

For this reason more than anything else, the Moscow-Washington hot line continued in use daily between Premier Kosygin and President Johnson. On June 4, the president was at breakfast when Kosygin again called from Moscow to charge that the Israelis were still shooting and the United States would have to stop its partner at once. To complicate the situation after breakfast that day, there were separate American-Israeli and American-Arab rallies outside the White House, each attended by several hundred people.

It so happened that morning also was General Dayan's zero hour for an all-out attack on Israel's particular devil, Syria, probably because he realized both Egypt and Jordan were almost out of the troops, the equipment, and even the will to keep fighting. To justify the latest assault, a formal Israeli complaint was lodged before the Security Council that same morning, accusing Syrian artillery of having shelled al-most a score of Israeli villages from the Golan Heights.

On Friday morning, June 9, the council ordered Secretary-General U Thant to warn Syria and Israel at once with a demand for immediate compliance to still another cease-fire—this one the first directed at the Syrians. Both at once agreed but, just as predictably, the Syrians soon were charging continual violations by Israel together with automatic Israeli denials. In all truth, as it was later determined, the Israelis were intent on chasing the Syrians out of their Golan Heights for good and the Jewish forces managed to do so.

The council meanwhile finally was satisfied that the Egyptians had heeded its repeated demands to stop the shooting, after which Cairo radio announced to a disturbed population that Nasser himself would have an important statement that evening on TV. When it came on the eve of the Muslim Sabbath, it was a stunner: the dictator was quitting. As he put it, hoarsely and dejectedly, the war against Israel had halted mainly because the United States and Britain, which he called the im-perialist powers, had powerfully armed the Jewish state. For the out-come, he formally accepted full responsibility, then suddenly aroused all Egypt as follows: "I have decided to give up completely and finally every official post and every political role and to return to the ranks of the public like every other citizen."

The abdication of the president was such a thundering surprise that protesting mobs jammed the main streets of Cairo within an hour and, later, his secluded home, to protest his resignation and demand his resumption of the nation's leadership. Call it a propaganda speech to arouse his supporters, as some Americans quickly did, or even a trick to demonstrate his strength with his own people, as still others suggested, but the net effect was very much in his favor. And mean-while, in Tel Aviv and the modern part of Jerusalem, the Israeli public was expressing its satisfaction over the end of Nasser's rule only to learn he had at once returned to power.

Still, with Egypt out of the war and Jordan making a last desperate stand against the advancing Israelis under cover of their airpower, Pre-mier Kosygin finally ran out of patience with his weak allies in the Middle East, the Security Council, and even the hot line between Moscow and the White House on which he had threatened President Johnson. Early on Saturday, June 10, the Soviet Union broke diplomatic relations with Israel.

Whether that was intended to activate the United States into putting Israel on a leash or simply saving the last of the Soviet's major allies in the area, Syria, Secretary of State Rusk could not be sure, but both he and President Johnson knew that Moscow now meant business. The phraseology of the warning to Israel, while clinging to diplomatese, was menacing in itself. An immediate halt in Israeli military action was demanded or the Soviets would act "with all the consequences flowing therefrom."

The Israelis, having just won the Golan Heights after routing its Syrian garrison, now had a clear shot at the main fortifications on the way to Damascus and already had bombed the Syrian capital. Like Egypt and Jordan, Syria also was on the run but it simply would not do for the United States to give up on an ally under direct Soviet threat. No president would have done it, certainly not Lyndon Johnson.

What he did do was to order the Sixth Fleet, with its two big aircraft carriers, to proceed directly into the eastern Mediterranean within easy bomber range of major Soviet bases. And the Soviets, though masters of rocketry and ICBMs, their threat in the Cuba crisis in 1962, still had not a single aircraft carrier.

Now the American message to Moscow was just as clear and bold as it had been in Cuba: the United States would not stand idly by in any major Soviet threat in the Middle East. As for the reply to Kosygin on the hot line (he had kept LBJ awake four times during the night with other calls), the president—in moderate tones—assured the Soviet leader that Israel had been asked to cease fire and would comply.

The president had no reason to mention the movements of the Sixth Fleet. The Soviets knew perfectly well that the fleet was on maneuvers near Italy and would realize at once the meaning of a change in its direction eastward. So the president's reply was accepted at the UN without comment, Israel complied with the cease-fire as soon as it secured the Golan Heights, and the Syrians took a final pounding from the air.

In this manner, still another major confrontation between the United States and the Soviet Union was averted over that weekend. The Security Council finally upheld a cease-fire resolution that did not condemn anybody or order anybody to return to previously held positions, although there was a statement to that general effect. What Israel did do that weekend was to cancel its armistice agreements that for almost two decades had marked its frontier with its Arab neighbors.

The only ones who were hurt in these complicated maneuvers

were the many thousands of Palestinians who lost their homes in the latest Israeli advance.[3]

However, the damage after what was called the Six-Day War became far greater than the crisis over the rising number of helpless Arab refugees, a problem that all sides passed to the UN without providing necessary money and personnel to handle it. The radical Arab states and their self-declared protector, the Soviet Union, refused first of all to accept defeat and soon were rearming for another savage phase of the struggle for control of the Middle East against the United States and its allies, including Israel, Saudi Arabia, the various small oil emirates, and Turkey.

In that extremity, there might have been hope for averting still more war in the area if there had been a real effort by all parties to resolve their difficulties. But the most that happened in the years that followed were a series of peace resolutions, tagged Nos. 242 and 338 within the UN, that were well intentioned even though the contending nations, as usual, differed vastly in the interpretation of their meaning. The net effort internationally, therefore, was to weaken still more the already overburdened authority of the UN as a peacekeeping organization.

How often it was over the years that those who followed the world organization's efforts heard their harassed leaders plead that the UN by itself could not make peace! It had, they said, been designed mainly to try to keep the peace once it rested on firm agreements between the parties.

Necessarily, it followed that Israel's great victories of 1967, climaxed by the seizure of all Jerusalem, settled nothing but led eventually to the rise of Arab terrorism. That created an increase in casualties for all the forces involved, and preparation for still another war before the victory celebrations in Old Jerusalem and elsewhere had concluded with a salute to the Star of David and the Star-Spangled Banner. That is how it was in the Middle East after the Six-Day War.[4]

13. Golda

The ranks of the founders of Israel were thinning. Most of their supporters and potential replacements were far from sure of one another. Directly after the 1967 war, every change at the top had become increasingly painful—and with good reason. The line of the old Zionists, the champions of Jewish statehood, was running out in the Palestinian land of their forefathers.

The first and greatest of the Israeli prime ministers, David Ben-Gurion, was in his eighties and in retirement at his desert retreat. The second prime minister, Moshe Sharett, who had been closest to Ben-Gurion and celebrated the rebirth of Israel before the UN on May 14, 1948, had died in 1955. Levi Eshkol, the victorious third prime minister, was in his late seventies directly after the Six-Day War and feeling the uncertainties of advancing age.

The next of the old Zionists in the probable line of succession, Golda Meir, was in her seventieth year during that conflict—the last of her predecessors to be born in the nineteenth century. She had been Eshkol's foreign minister until 1966, then served briefly as secretary-general of the Mapai Party, and, upon Eshkol's death in 1969, became his interim successor with an electoral triumph shortly afterward that confirmed her as the next prime minister. To silence the doubters, she made Gen. Moshe Dayan, the hero of the Six-Day War, her defense minister and thereby began leading her government in his reflected glory.

There was no real reason for the younger aspirants to leadership to be mumbling about Golda's alleged shortcomings—her sensitivity, her forcefulness, her pride, and her changes in position. Much, for example, had been made, mainly behind her back, of her opposition to Eshkol's appointment of Dayan as defense minister at the time of the hostilities that led to the 1967 war. Of course, such whispers ceased as soon as Dayan swiftly agreed with the new prime minister to be her chief of defense. As for the Israeli public, they applauded the new team and seemed satisfied, at least for the opening phase of the new administration, that the new prime minister would serve them well.[1]

Nevertheless, the rivalry among the younger aspirants for power all too soon became a feature of her administration. Of the lot, Yitzhak Rabin, forty-seven when Golda took over, hoped to become the first native prime minister, having been born in Jerusalem in 1922. There were others of importance who could not claim such distinction even if they were otherwise well qualified to lead the nation—among them Yitzhak Shamir, at fifty-three a hard-line intelligence operative; Shimon Peres, at forty-six a well-qualified veteran of earlier governments; and Menachem Begin, at fifty-six a hardworking nationalist who would one day share a Nobel Peace Prize for bringing about a long-awaited peace that included Egyptian recognition of Israel.

I stress the point about the difference in ages between the first group to hold power in Israel and their younger, well-qualified rivals because reliance on age and experience, although not necessarily a guarantee of superior wisdom, seems to have been an important factor in the decisions of Israeli leadership in the declining years of this century. Certainly, it did not hurt Prime Minister Meir at the outset of her administration.

Not every Israeli leader at the beginning of its rebirth after two thousand years has forecast its continued existence for the ages. On the night that Israel was declared a state in 1948, Sharett was asked at the UN by a *Chicago Tribune* reporter, Chesly Manley, "The Maccabeean Jewish state lasted two hundred years, so how long do you think this one will last?"

To which Sharett replied while hurrying from the UN, "I'll settle for two hundred years." So far as I know, Sharett never bothered to correct his estimate, nor was he ever subject to particular criticism for it when he became Israel's second prime minister.

The point should not be overlooked. High-flown American oratory about the permanence of a land dedicated to democratic ideals and personal freedom has seldom been involved in the Middle East either before or after the rebirth of Israel. And that may at least be a partial explanation for Prime Minister Meir's problems in maintaining Israel as a free country devoted to democratic ideals in a part of the world that has known very little of both.[2]

Unexpectedly, what bothered Meir more than anything else in her beginning as prime minister was the difficulty she experienced in putting together a cabinet that would represent national unity. To be sure, she had already assembled what was known as a "caretaker" government upon being chosen prime minister but more than a month passed after that before she could form the kind of coalition the strained situation demanded.

This was by no means because enthusiasm had abated for Israel's surprise six-day victory over the combined Arab states with their Soviet-supplied aircraft plus mechanized military vehicles from tanks to artillery and rocketry. On the contrary, after the conclusion of hostilities when the American public fully realized the extent of Israel's triumph, almost a half-billion dollars was raised in the United States for everything from Israeli bonds and the contributions to the United Jewish Appeal to large gifts from American individuals and families to other Jewish causes.

Within Israel itself, the euphoria, too, lingered on.[3] The victory celebrations continued, ever enlarged in scope, and Prime Minister Meir found that her efforts to form a cabinet of national unity were making a fine public impression even though opposition politicians were hanging back rather than quickly accepting offers of cabinet posts.

Curiously, it was not through Meir's maneuvers that the desired coalition cabinet came into being. Rather, it was the somewhat desperate plight of President Richard Nixon's administration in the United States that led directly to a solution of that problem of Israel's governance. What happened was quite plainly a response to an adverse judgment arrived at by the Nixon administration in trying to maneuver itself out of the troublesome position in Vietnam it had inherited from the previous Lyndon Johnson administration.

Nixon's secretary of state, William P. Rogers, together with his defense colleague in the new Republican cabinet, Mel Laird, both were doves on Vietnam and made no secret of their urgent desire to play down and if possible even liquidate the Vietnam War. But they were up against the new president's top foreign-policy adviser, Henry Kissinger, who already had announced to the Washington press corps that the Nixon people would not repeat the mistakes of the previous Johnson administration, adding, "We will make our own mistakes."

This may have been a political joke in the American capital; however, it was anything but when Rogers next weighed in with his proposal for the settlement of Israel's difficulties with Egypt, Jordan, and Syria. The American secretary of state publicly announced that he was negotiating directly with the Soviet Union in an effort to overcome Israel's difficulties in the Middle East. To observe that Prime Minister Meir and her colleagues were shocked is putting it mildly.

For, suddenly, an American secretary of state was pulling the rug from under an Israeli government by dealing with Moscow—and not even consulting the government of his Middle East ally. To meet the emergency, which occurred after more than forty days of Meir's efforts to form a government of national unity, the prime minister summoned an emergency session of her "caretaker" regime and included therein some of those who had been invited but delayed acceptance, among them the hawkish Menachem Begin, the one-time head of Irgun Zvai Leumi.

An angry and determined Prime Minister Meir faced her colleagues that December 10, 1969, for an American secretary of state had publicly disgraced her by sweeping aside the unspoken condition among allies, large or small, that there is *always* consultation before dealing with a common enemy, clearly the Soviet position at the time. To make the situation critical, what Secretary Rogers said he would do was to consult Moscow on what Israel's borders should be for the future.

That was the knife in the back to any Israeli who had any feeling for the country's tremendous victory in the Six-Day War. For an American secretary of state to seek Moscow's opinion on so tender a subject without even asking for Israel's recommendations placed Prime Minister Meir in an impossible position. The hawks, led by Begin, were jubilant. And the cabinet meeting, although lengthy and stormy, finally did decide on one unanimous response to Rogers: The rejection by Israel's government of the American diplomat's proposal to consult the Soviet government on what Israel's future borders should be.

Now the hawks could not wait to get into the Meir government. The leader, Begin, representing the far Right, accepted a post as minister without portfolio and his Herut-Gahal Party backed him. Next came a general who had resigned from the army, Ezer Weizman, who became minister of transport. And all at once, Prime Minister Meir was leading a coalition cabinet of national unity that was opposing an American secretary of state.[4]

That was the last heard of the Rogers plan to consult Moscow.

Minister Begin's role in the cabinet of national unity, unfortunately, was short-lived. He could not get along with the leading dove in the cabinet, the foreign minister, Abba Eban, conditioned to American policy by his long Washington experience as Israel's ambassador there. In this extremity, Prime Minister Meir based herself on the principle of trading conquered territory for peace, a familiar proposition among the doves in the cabinet, and the acceptance of Security Council resolution 242, which called for a lasting peace in the Middle East but also specified Israel's withdrawal from conquered areas.

By the middle of 1970, after a rough six-month existence, the Meir coalition broke up. What did it was the stationing of Russian missiles along the Suez Canal within easy range of major targets in Israel and a massive new supply of Soviet weapons to the Egyptian army that pumped new life into the Nasser government. The clashes between Israelis and Egyptians, which never had really ended, increased in number and violence—a state of war without any formal declaration.

Now Secretary Rogers came up with another proposal, this one a cease-fire and a declared end to belligerency provided all parties agreed to withdraw from occupied territories. What hurt even more was his hint that Israel might not receive any more U.S. weapons if prompt acceptance of these dictated terms was not forthcoming. Early in August 1970, the Meir government caved in and accepted the new Rogers plan without leaving the conquered area, which ended Begin's relatively brief experience as an Israeli government minister.[5]

By coincidence, a little more than a month later, on September 28, 1970, Gamal Abdel Nasser died and was succeeded, as luck would have it, by an Egyptian who saw a certain amount of merit in negotiating for peace with Israel, Anwar el-Sadat, a champion of the Palestine Liberation Organization (PLO) and its bedraggled-looking leader, Yasir Arafat.

But even Sadat, at the beginning of his regime, could not change Egyptian policy overnight. While the Meir government wavered and debated, with the right wing factions headed by Begin still rejecting the government of national unity, factionalism inevitably split the Knesset and the Israeli public at large. Within five years of the nation's greatest victory over the Arabs in the 1967 war, the Jewish state became increasingly vulnerable. And sadly, even at the head of government, there seemed to be neither a feeling, nor much less, knowledge of imminent danger.[6]

The reasons were complex, as was usual for almost any development in the Middle East at the time. For much of the summer of 1970, armed guerrillas centered in the refugee camps around Jordan had been openly defying King Hussein's authority in his Jordanian kingdom. Knowing that the monarch was threatened on one side by Israel and dependent to a large extent on his alliance with his Arab neighbors, Egypt and Syria, the loosely organized terrorists constituted themselves as a third force within the kingdom to such an extent that they were reputed to have defied the government and even collected taxes for their own use.

What it all came down to was a war within a war—King Hussein was fighting for his life against the Fatah, the guerrillas who were loosely linked with the Palestine Liberation Organization, and the Israelis who had routed the Jordanian army from Old Jerusalem in the 1967 war. The king was represented as being afraid for weeks of turning loose his relatively small army against the guerrillas and thereby being accused of breaking Arab unity. But as the Fatah mobsters grew bolder, he realized he would have to strike at the rebels or forfeit his crown to them.

Finally, on the night of September 17, 1970—Black September as it became known—Hussein ordered his army into action against the Fatah, resulting in a virtual slaughter of the mobsters in the refugee camps. Under the circumstances, because the king's Arab Legion could not easily tell the difference between a guerrilla and a peaceful refugee, the onslaught turned into a massacre before the guerrillas and their Fatah movement were smashed.

To Hussein's consternation at the height of his anti-Fatah offensive, the hard-line Syrians constituted themselves as the protectors of the guerrillas and dispatched a mechanized invasion force southward to take on the smaller Jordanian army. In despair, the king appealed to the United States for aid in this extremity; instead, luckily for the king, the Israelis intervened with a decisive show of force to block all roads south against the Syrian expeditionary army. That appeared to be what saved Hussein's regime in Jordan.

Rather than duel the Israelis for mechanized superiority, the Syrians turned back, the Jordanian cleanup of the Fatah guerrillas concluded without further incident, and toward the end of September, an uncertain peace was restored in the Middle East. Hussein, always the moderate who had dealt favorably with the Israelis on other occasions, now became a much more important factor in the search of American policy makers for a durable peace in the Middle East. And Israel, in consequence, began a quite different relationship with Hussein.

Whatever uncertainty there had been about Prime Minister Meir's administration in Israel was laid to rest for the time being. Without Begin, her cabinet of national unity surmounted the nation's latest test of strength in the Arab world and looked forward to an improved relationship later that fall with Anwar el-Sadat as Nasser's successor. As for Hussein, his regime in Jordan became the narrow bridge for dealings between Israel and the hostile powers of the Arab world—an arrangement that seemed to suit all sides even if it did not immediately produce the peace that they professed to seek.

As for the survivors of the Fatah guerrilla movement after losing several thousand of its boldest operatives, they transferred the center of their resistance from Jordan to the desperately weak southern regions of Lebanon where Syria maintained what was in effect an occupation force. From that point of vantage, both the Syrians and their surviving guerrilla allies resumed their continued terrorist attacks along their frontier with normal Israel. In that extension of the Middle East struggle, the principal victims were the approximately 1.2 million Maronite Christians, about 30 percent of Lebanon's 3.7 million people, who had to contend with the dominant Muslim population of the land.

The only international force for peace in the area remained the pathetically small UN force of border inspectors, who still had only two necessarily vague Security Council resolutions, 242 and 338, on which to rely for the creation of a durable peace in a part of the world that badly needed it. Somehow, rightly or wrongly, the more than 200 million Muslims in the Middle East were being led far afield in a long and anxious search for a better understanding with the Christian and Jewish minorities among them.[7]

It was a decisive moment for Israel, too, later that year of 1970, for negotiations had resumed with King Hussein. Prime Minister Meir seemed confident that an agreement could be reached with Jordan that would in turn influence the new government of Egypt, obviously more moderate than Nasser's. The presumption among Meir's advisers was that Hussein, having been bailed out by Israel in his emergency, was likely to grasp the opportunity for a peaceful settlement if granted decent terms.

What the Meir government offered him, however, was not much. It amounted to a plan devised by Gen. Yigal Allon, a close associate of General Dayan, in which Jordan would be given a narrow corridor of land leading from Amman to the other Arab areas on the West Bank of the Jordan, plus a few other minor considerations. It was not good enough; Hussein demanded Israel's removal from his occupied territories including the Old City of Jerusalem and wouldn't settle for anything less, including the much-discussed Allon plan. So, the opportunity passed and Hussein returned, however blemished by the Syrian attack, to the all-or-nothing Arab fold.

Had Mrs. Meir offered more generous terms, perhaps the outcome might have been different. No one will ever know. On the American side, there has often been quietly expressed regret that Kissinger, still President Nixon's foreign-policy adviser at the time, could not have taken a more active part in the proceedings as he did later while secretary of state after still more Middle East warfare.

What Hussein asked for in these initial talks with Mrs. Meir and her colleagues was his first position—return of all Israeli-conquered territories including Old Jerusalem, and he would agree to sign a peace treaty as the first major Arab leader to do so and thereby accept Israel as a regional partner. Mrs. Meir would not buy it, principally because General Dayan, as her defense minister, would not agree. And so, the brief moment for peace passed, but the Israelis, seemingly feeling more secure than the occasion warranted, returned to their own demand for the retention of all conquered territories.

The mere sight of all the seething refugee camps on the Jewish state's borders, with more than a million Arab victims of a quarter century of Israeli-Arab wars, should have been sufficient evidence that Israel could not peacefully exist in the Middle East until its presence could adjust to the realities of dealing with the Arab world.

Hard bargaining in itself was not a sufficient response.[8]

14.   Disaster!

Egyptian paratroops were dropping behind enemy lines with scant opposition well beyond the east bank of the Suez Canal. Others were crowding into boats that ferried them across the turgid waters while Israeli spotters were sounding the first warnings of a surprise attack. An Israeli trooper was heard dashing into battle, gun in hand, while shouting "Sh'ma Yisroel" [Hear, O Israel].

The date: Saturday, October 6, 1973, the Day of Atonement known in Hebrew as Yom Kippur, which marked the start of the fourth Arab-Israeli conflict, the Yom Kippur War. Through meticulous planning and secret mobilization, Egypt and Syria had sprung a thunderous surprise on an overly confident Prime Minister Meir and her defense minister, General Dayan, the hero of the Six-Day War.

The only commanding Israeli presence to show up along the front lines in the first hours after Egypt struck across the Canal and Syria slammed down from the north was Gen. Ariel Sharon, who came charging in at the head of an Israeli reserve division to try to halt the Egyptian drive across the Sinai Peninsula. It took hours for Israeli Phantom fighter planes to swoop over the Egyptian lines, which by that time had advanced so far into the Sinai that Israeli troops on the east bank of the Canal were trapped.

What had happened was that the new Egyptian president, Anwar el-Sadat, upon succeeding Nasser after his death, decided still another war was the only answer to Israel's refusal to yield any of the Arab territories it had conquered in the Six-Day War. Sadat had little trouble persuading Syria's Hafez al Assad to join him in a combined attack. But Jordan's King Hussein, still with a bitter memory of the Black September guerrilla attack against him, hung back until Egypt could win control of the Sinai and Syria and had reconquered the Golan Heights. Neither, of course, ever came to pass.

The only other participant, Iraq, sent in a swarm of MiG aircraft two days after the war began; it lost some of them to mistaken Syrian fire, and Israel's belated response did the rest. But the Sadat-Assad combine, with its superior planning and espionage, took a heavy toll from the surprised Israelis while a large part of their forces was caught at prayer on the holiest day of the Jewish year.[1]

Despite the fury of the Orthodox about being interrupted at prayer, Israel did not have much excuse for being surprised by the enemy on the Day of Atonement. Although President Nixon then was in deep political trouble at home, his Defense Department had long since provided Israel with the sinews of war—more than a half billion dollars' worth had been bought, paid for, and delivered well ahead of the new Arab offensive. Both the aircraft and the new mechanized armaments had been made a significant part of Israel's defenses.

As for the Soviet Union, a new dictator, Leonid Brezhnev, despite his skepticism of the combined Egyptian-Syrian potential for victory over Israel in a fourth war, granted the pleas of President Sadat on a visit to Moscow to seek a much larger shipment of Soviet aircraft and armaments than ever before. Backing the Arabs was just about the only chance the Communist giant still had to maintain influence in the Middle East against the rising pressures of the United States and its European partners.

If Brezhnev wanted at all costs to avoid a confrontation with the United States, as seemed likely at the time, the alternative he had was to encourage Sadat and the Egyptians in this latest gambit against Israel as one of America's allies in the Middle East along with Saudi Arabia and Turkey. That was what the Soviets finally decided to do, but the effective strategy of deception against both Israel and the United States remained Sadat's responsibility.[2]

On at least a score of occasions in the months preceding the onset of the Yom Kippur War, what Sadat and his people did was to call up their army reserves, then cancel the order, evidently hoping the real summons a few days before the Jewish holy day would pass unnoticed. That, evidently, is what happened.

This is not to say that at least a few among both the Americans and Israelis could not be fooled. Indeed, there were people in the American and Israeli defense and intelligence services who saw danger in the unwarranted muster of hundreds of thousands of Egyptians and other Arabs to combat in the fall of 1973. But their warnings of a forthcoming new Arab war with Israel went unheeded because they came from junior sources. Some such cautions were even suppressed.

A big show for peace meanwhile was staged by the latest champion to win worldwide recognition, Secretary of State Henry Kissinger, who shared a Nobel Peace Prize for ending the war in Vietnam. As late as a week before the Egyptian-Syrian attack on Israel, at Kissinger's urging, the Israeli and Arab foreign ministers decided on a meeting with him in November, following the scheduled Israeli elections, to start new peace negotiations. It also happened that this September 30 was also the day that the Egyptians secretly tipped the Syrians that October 6 would be the day for the joint assault on Israel.

But as the Arabs' tanks, heavy artillery, and infantry moved up, with the Egyptians massing for the assault across the Suez Canal and the Sinai Peninsula and the Syrians against the Golan Heights, the Israelis most certainly could see what was happening. And long afterward, the question was often asked, "Why were the Israelis fooled?"

Still, on October 4, three days before battle, the Israeli army chief of staff, Lt. Gen. David Elazar, told a group of Israeli newspaper editors that the masses of Egyptian and Syrian troops at the Israeli border were indeed fully equipped for battle but he doubted they wanted to stage another war with Israel. That same day at a meeting of the senior members of Prime Minister Meir's cabinet, including both Mrs. Meir and Dayan as well as Deputy Premier Yigal Allon, all were assured by their military intelligence that an Arab attack was unlikely. General Elazar did suggest a partial mobilization, but was turned down. And when the full cabinet met that night, the Arabs' massing of troops was ignored.

The military, however, was not quite as confident as the Israeli cabinet that the Arabs would remain at peace. At a CIA session on Thursday, October 4, in headquarters then at Langley, Virginia, the Israelis sent reassurances that the Arabs would not fight but they also provided accurate statistics on the impressive size and spread of both the Egyptian and Syrian mobilizations. That bothered the Pentagon.

And twenty-four hours before hostilities began, Dayan was sufficiently concerned to see Prime Minister Meir again with his chief of staff and intelligence director. This time, Mrs. Meir would have summoned the full cabinet once again, but most of them already had left for the Yom Kippur observance so it was no go.

Instead, she agreed to a low state of alert and a briefing of senior reservists. But nobody wanted to call up the reserves—before Yom Kippur—except for one retired soldier, Gen. Ariel Sharon. When he was summoned for his own briefing as a senior reservist and realized the extent of the twin Arab buildups, he asked for permission to mobilize his reserve division but was refused.[3]

The Egyptians now were so confident that their ruse had worked that they permitted the Cairo daily *El Ahram* to banner the Egyptian mobilization as a defense against an expected Israeli attack. If anything should have brought the Israelis to their senses, that was it. The unpleasant truth was that the highest echelons of the Israeli government and its army felt so smugly secure in one of the world's worse danger spots that they would not believe the formidable truth of the latest Arab plan for aggression when it was drawn to their attention by a leading Arab newspaper.

There was reason to be disturbed as well about the failure of American intelligence to report an imminent war close to the nation's interests in the Middle East until it happened. Among those most surprised was Secretary of State Kissinger, who was waiting for a report on the Middle East at his New York hotel before completing a draft of a forthcoming speech. He never did get it by bedtime for the best of reasons. By that time, it was early Saturday morning on the Sinai Peninsula and the Israelis finally had learned, to their distress, that the Egyptians already were about to launch their longboats in the Suez Canal for the mass crossing that would touch off the Yom Kippur War.

As a board of inquiry determined long afterward, both Prime Minister Meir and General Dayan were alerted shortly after dawn on October 6 by the chief of staff, General Elazar, with indisputable evidence that the Arabs would attack within hours. He pleaded for full mobilization, the summoning of all the reserves, and a preemptive first strike by the Israeli Air Force if possible before the Egyptians in particular swung into action. His superiors refused, still confident apparently that the troops they had in the Canal and Sinai area could handle anything the Arabs threw at them. And this after a substantial number already were on leave over Yom Kippur.

Mrs. Meir notified Kenneth Keating, the American ambassador, early that morning of Israel's decision to avoid a preemptive first strike and he in turn cabled the news to President Nixon in Washington and Secretary of State Kissinger in New York. But in no way did either the Israelis or the United States interfere with the plans approved by Sadat in Egypt and Assad in Syria for a coordinated strike at Israeli forces later that day—the hour finally was set at 2:00 P.M. From then on, the issue passed to the gods of battle.[4]

A larger number of the strong points along the east bank of the Suez Canal, a line created by Lt. Gen. Chaim Bar Lev, were held by only a few hundred middle-aged Israeli reserves with scant military training, and that afternoon all the hell of an unexpected war burst about them. Many of the regulars had been given the day off to pray with their families, so the unlucky substitutes suddenly had to face a deafening barrage from artillery dug into the sand dunes on the west side of the Canal; then came the terrible fire of thousands of Egyptian tanks in preparation for an all-out assault by the enemy infantry.

In the line of undermanned bunkers, the trapped Israelis on the east bank saw Egyptian troops in hundreds of rubber boats propelling themselves across the Canal—the main body that was to join the paratroops that had been dropped fifteen to twenty miles into the Sinai. Thousands of tanks, too, were ferried across the Canal but there was relatively little the few hundred Israelis in the bunkers and other strong points could do to stop the advance. Some were obliged to hold out for as much as a week while the fate of the invasion was being decided inland.

For this well-planned invasion to take back the 125-mile Sinai, much of it desert, the Egyptians also had brought with them an enormous store of new Russian-made weapons, including rockets and anti-tank missiles. The first wave of the invaders, too, had special machinery that made it impossible for the Israelis to set aflame the maze of pipes in the Canal that contained a gas that was to be used to repel an enemy. Toward evening, the Israeli reserves in the bunkers for the most part were isolated and out of action—those that had survived the shelling and the rockets—while the main body of the attackers now was fighting Israeli forces inland.

At the outset on the Egyptian front, therefore, the truth was that the overly confident Israelis, more intent on Yom Kippur prayers than fighting, were badly outmaneuvered. Only a few more than two hundred tanks were immediately available to try to repel the several thousand Egyptian tanks and armored troop carriers. As for the vaunted Israeli Air Force with its new American aircraft, it took hours even to get into action against Egyptian paratroop drops behind Israeli lines in the Sinai and the Soviet-made MiGs that applied such efficient air cover at the outset of the invasion.

It was impractical, too, to try to recall the many thousands of regular troopers who had been given the day off to pray with their families on Yom Kippur, so the Israeli high command had to depend on the mostly middle-aged reserves who were filling in for so many of the regulars. In sum, there never was another time in the early history of the revived Jewish state when it was so badly outmaneuvered by its Arab enemies—a disgrace in itself, no matter now valiantly the Israeli war machine finally began fighting hours after the Egyptian invaders had broken loose in the Sinai.[5]

On the Syrian front, which was restricted at first to the northern end of the Golan Heights, the Israeli response was more forceful because the area of combat was far more restricted. On the Golan's entrance that the Israelis held directly north of the Syrian border, the limited number of Israeli reserves in the bunker strong points had a better chance of cracking the oncoming Syrian regulars, their tanks, and their air cover even though the enemy had a backup of at least fifteen miles of the Israeli-occupied Golan along which to attack.

Unlike the far longer Sinai front of the Egyptians to the south, the Israelis facing the Syrians on the Golan could not have retreated even if the command had been given because there was no place to hide. It was therefore a case of standing up to the surprise of the enemy assault that day or being shot in their tracks. Under such drastic circumstances, the surprised Israeli forces, limited though they were, gave a magnificent account of themselves even though they had no air cover at the onset and the Syrian tanks outnumbered their own by almost nine to one. But the Israeli casualties, too, were great—a terrible price that had to be paid for their lack of preparedness against a savage and unrelenting enemy.

Although the Egyptian area of combat was much larger in the Sinai against the outmanned and surprised Israelis, the Syrians had a greater advantage along their much more concentrated front on the Golan. For once the Syrian armor was safely past the Israeli defenders; there were four routes open to the invaders directly into the heart of Israeli. These were the historic routes linking Damascus and Cairo that narrowed into a much broader highway as it swung along the Palestinian shore toward Gaza.

Once the Syrian armor could penetrate the Israeli lines on and around the Golan, the only remaining defenses that blocked the enemy advance into the Israeli heartland were a series of barbed-wire strong points marked either by watchtowers or elevated fortifications. It became obvious, therefore, in the opening phases of combat, that Dayan as defense minister could be held responsible for blocking what seemed to be an enemy plan for a union of forces somewhere to the north of Gaza.

But even with the knowledge of the extent of the invasion, Dayan did not seem prepared to commit all possible resources to the emergency defense of the nation that Yom Kippur. The two overwhelmed defense systems, in the Sinai to the south and the Golan on the north, struggled valiantly but with little hope of immediate relief in the early hours of the attack. It took many hours, in fact, for the Israeli forces to evacuate their own citizens, the settlers in the defense villages south of the Golan, in order to set up roadblocks against an expected Syrian surge to the south that could have threatened Tel Aviv had it developed. Only the valor of the emergency tank crews, their skill, and their luck against the oncoming Syrian armor averted what could have been a fateful Syrian penetration of the main Israeli defense system.

For more than twenty-four hours, the Israeli gunners, virtually without air cover until the pilots could be rounded up to serve in the emergency, held off the Syrian tanks and absorbed terrible punishment while holding their ground. What the Syrians accomplished that first day of their assault was to conquer the Mount Hermon sector at the cost of a severe loss of scores of tanks and their crews to Israeli resistance. Only after nightfall that first tragic day did the overwhelmed Israelis dare to relax their vigilance against the enemy armor.

That night, the first elements of the Israeli Air Force that had been able to function received massive reinforcements so that, from dawn on October 7, the defense at last could slow down the Syrian armor and at least halt its progress. Had the Syrian command not committed the error of seeking only to gain more territory instead of reducing the remaining Israeli strong points blocking a full-scale advance, the Syrians might have been more successful than they ultimately proved to be. But, fortunately for Israel, grave errors also were committed in the enemy's strategy that at last enabled the defense to halt the Syrian advance and turn back its leading elements.[6]

Under these conditions the Israeli Air Force, at virtual full strength, soared into action on both fronts the next day with shattering results against both the Arab fronts. Of the two, the Syrians, being the more concentrated, absorbed the largest losses and were stopped far short of their anticipated goals. But in the south, the Egyptians still slugged it out with the reinforced Israelis in the Sinai desert while retaining complete control of both banks of the Suez Canal despite the bypassed Israeli defenses there. In this manner the Yom Kippur War slowly ground to a halt within a week after two desperate Israeli counterattacks failed, and the agonized General Sharon pleaded at one point to be permitted to lead still a third such strike, only to be repulsed. What Sharon had proposed to do was to recross the Suez Canal at the head of his reserve division and any others that could be mustered to shock the Egyptians into a defensive posture. But the high command did not want to take a chance on him. It was, so Dayan reasoned, too early for Israel to attempt to seize the offensive.

There were differences, too, on the Arab side as the Israelis slowly gathered strength and corrected the balance the Arab side had won in the early stages of the war through surprise, shock, and skill particularly among Egypt's tacticians in the wars against Israel. What the Egyptians depended on, besides their superiority in aircraft, was the extensive use of missile batteries that the Israelis were hard put to neutralize until the closing days of the war when the Arabs were the least effective.

Gen. Hafez Ismail, President Sadat's security adviser, mistrusted mobile warfare, so potent an attraction for the Israeli general staff, because the average Egyptian trooper was more familiar with slower movements that emphasized the use of missiles from Soviet sources, which had proved to be so effective in the opening stages of this war. It should be stressed that missile attacks helped account for much of the unexpected Egyptian successes on the southern front against Israel.[7]

In any event, while the warfare by land slowly equalized the contending forces that first critical week of the fourth Arab war against Israel, the almost ignored Israeli navy was able to strike the first measured blows for the defense by breaking the tight Egyptian blockade of the Jewish state by air and sea. In addition, beginning on the second day of the war, east Egyptian navigation crossing the Suez Canal in small rubber-hulled kayaks was almost ended when the Israelis brought in small craft of their own, armed with effective missile batteries that already had been used against Arab shipping in the Mediterranean.

Even so, for the opening phases of the war, the Egyptian armed forces and their tacticians still held a considerable advantage over the flustered Israelis and their woefully unprepared government. The myth of Israeli infallibility in Middle East combat, however, already had been shaken and was under destruction. For this war, it quickly became evident, there would be no massive Israeli triumph to humble the Arabs once again. Even if the radical Syrians already were wavering, the Egyptians under the steady guidance of their new leader, Sadat, still were far too tough to be thrown back by an ill-prepared Israeli counterthrust.

This fourth war with the Arabs, however, would not end as quickly or as completely as either side hoped. It was being waged over too large and too important a part of earth, with its huge reservoirs of oil, for either side to conclude that its forces and their reserves eventually would triumph over the foe. For even in its opening phases, this was a different kind of war.[8]

15. Israel Strikes Back

After the disastrous first week of the Yom Kippur War, Prime Minister Meir and Defense Minister Dayan realized they were dealing with a new and formidable Egyptian leader in President Anwar el-Sadat. He had done far more than rearm his troops with Soviet material including an effective array of missiles. He also had instilled such confidence in his soldiers that the Israelis were still on the defensive in much of the Sinai triangle.

The Syrian front, by contrast, now had been stabilized. It also was evident that Hafez al-Assad was making every effort to persuade the Jordanians and the Iraqis to join his beleaguered forces. To Mrs. Meir and Dayan it now seemed that Israel could scarcely count on quickly winning a two-front war that had caught them so unprepared. What appeared to be the better part of military strategy for the Israeli forces was to concentrate on trying to knock Syria out of the war while defending against the surging Egyptians in the Sinai.

It was not particularly adaptable to the Israeli style of martial combat. Also, even at the outset, it seemed to be a long-shot gamble, as Dayan himself was the first to concede, but evidence of continued Jewish weakness on both fronts was found to invite some of the sidelined Arab states to join embattled Egypt and Syria for as long as both kept fighting the Israelis on close to even terms or better.

There was one other factor that the Israeli leadership had to recognize with the resurgence of Egypt as a military power. Sadat's capacity for leadership had been badly underestimated if the performance of the Egyptian military in the opening week of the Yom Kippur War was to be taken at face value. Unlike Nasser, whose classmate he had been at Egypt's leading military academy, Sadat at fifty-five was far more the pragmatist rather than the stiff-necked dictator whom he had suc-

ceeded. Moreover, the new president and premier in Cairo appeared to
rely primarily on freedom of maneuver instead of brute force and his
ultimate purposes could not be easily determined.

From a decidedly unpromising start as a pro-Nazi agent in World
War II who had landed in a British jail, he had escaped in 1944 but once
again was imprisoned in 1946, this time for three years as an anti-
British terrorist. However, by 1952, the still agile Sadat returned to
Cairo with Nasser, helping to overthrow King Faisal. And as Nasser's
vice president, Sadat replaced him at his death but was able within
three years to reform and rearm the lagging Egyptian military with
Moscow's enthusiastic assistance.[1]

Even at a time when the Israelis were inclined to underestimate the
effectiveness of Arab leadership after winning three successive wars
with them, what Sadat already had been able to accomplish in Egypt
was bound to develop respect, if not trust, in Tel Aviv and Jerusalem.
Not that the Egyptian leader was ready to talk peace; he had, in fact,
just begun to fight. But in the United States, even while President
Nixon in 1973 was struggling for his political life in the developing Watergate scandal, his secretary of state, Henry Kissinger, already was
carefully weighing the chances of calling for a cease-fire in the two-
front Yom Kippur War.

What Kissinger contemplated at the early stage in the fighting was
a tricky effort to control American military supplies to Israel in such a
way as to enhance the Jewish state's efforts to resist the Soviet-supplied
Arabs while encouraging both sides to accept a UN cease-fire. It was
often said later in Washington that nobody except Kissinger, with a Nobel Peace Prize to his credit, would have attempted to ration American
war matériel for a smaller ally to end the fighting without either side
being able to claim victory. Yet, as subsequent events surely indicated,
this eventually became a goal of an American secretary of state. He did
not want to take a chance on still another showdown with the Soviet
Union resembling the 1962 Cuban missile crisis.

Even after the Israeli Air Force was able to put enough aircraft in the
skies over Syria in the first stage of the Dayan plan to nullify or destroy
Hafez al-Assad's offensive against the Golan Heights, the pilots reported soon enough that there were too many new antiaircraft batteries
protecting the Syrian troops for effective counteraction. That in turn

called for what amounted to perhaps the first modern missile war that matched American antimissile defenses against the Syrian Soviet-supplied attack missiles.

Losses on both sides exceeded advance estimates and casualties were large, but after more than an intense first week of effort, the Syrians had to give ground. King Hussein of Jordan and his counterparts in Iraq closely followed the missile war and ultimately drew their own conclusions. Neither volunteered to join the ailing Syrians as the American-supplied Israelis now began to use their Phantom fighter aircraft more liberally with effective results.

Within the limits of the eighteen days of intense fighting thereafter, the Israelis could send their combat aircraft against the Syrian missile batteries. They stalled the Arab drive against the Golan Heights and enabled the Israeli ground forces to take a sizable chunk out of the middle of Syria's border elsewhere—a "bubble," as it was called, that indicated Syrian weakness, because it opened the way to an Israeli invasion column headed directly for Damascus.

Necessarily, that was what caused the Syrian commanders to drop the ambitious campaign in which their invasion force had thrust a spearhead column directly toward the heart of Israel. For the Israeli forces on the northern front, the virtual end of the Syrian offensive served as encouragement, particularly when it became evident that nearly half of Syria's Russian-supplied antiaircraft batteries had been knocked out of action with a resultant increase in the effectiveness of the Israeli air arm.

Beyond the battle lines, the Israeli bombers now became effective in destroying a considerable part of Syria's wartime economic strength. In repeated air strikes, the bomber invasion hit Syrian port facilities through which the Soviet-supplied war matériel was transported, knocked out the only big oil refinery in the entire country, and caused an enormous fire that burned the greater part of its oil storage facilities.

What that cost the Israelis was slightly more than a hundred aircraft, but the pilots claimed to have taken with them more than three times as many Syrian fighters and bombers. The net effect was to nullify Syria as a decisive force in the fighting and permit the hard-pressed Israelis to concentrate on the more important and better-armed Egyptian forces to the south. Whatever possibility there had been for a wider Arab war now vanished except for one late thrust by Jordan just before the fighting ended in an uncertain truce.[2]

Next, the Syrians set up an unholy clamor to the Egyptians for a major offensive in the south to take the heart of the northern sector, for an Israeli column now was within striking distance of Damascus. Sadat now was having his own troubles in the southern front. Even though the Egyptian position on the Sinai had seemed defensible in mid-October, everything changed radically within twenty-four hours.

The reason, to put it briefly, was the irrepressible Gen. Ariel Sharon, who had at last won approval for an all-or-nothing Israeli drive across the Suez Canal to the west bank, the African bank, to take the Third Army of Egypt by surprise and knock Sadat's invasion flat on its back. This was the kind of soldier the Israeli people loved for his daring, his selfless courage, his dedication, and his willingness to sacrifice himself if he could bring success to his embattled people.

As could be expected, his was a complicated operation with thousands of Israelis concentrated for a daring crossing of the Suez Canal on the night of October 15–16. Sharon's special problem was that he not only astounded the enemy but also shocked his own Southern Command superiors, who at one point thought he had been surrounded by the Egyptians. However, Sharon's account of his attack, if looked at in sum, shows that he pulled off the decisive offensive of the Yom Kippur War even though he suffered twenty-six hundred deaths in his ranks. Also, he seemed at times to confuse all his superiors except the one who counted most, Defense Minister Dayan, who was at his elbow for the most decisive moves.

This is how the offensive developed: After Sharon's paratroops had secured their landing on the Canal's west bank about 1:00 A.M. on October 16, there was an appalling discovery that not enough rafts existed on the east bank to enable the troops to propel parts of a pontoon bridge across, for the use of the troops, their armor and firepower. Under enemy air attack and ground fire, more rafts arrived just in time to transport and link the pontoon sections for a bridge that was promptly used by the main body of troops and others for the Israeli offensive on the west bank.

As a result, the decisive attack began late on the night of October 17 when Defense Minister Dayan himself gave the order to advance and General Sharon led the drive against the Third Army, one of the three major Egyptian units. The Israelis took heavy casualties—Sharon himself went into battle with a bandaged head—but he succeeded in surrounding and cutting off his Egyptian target in the northwest corner of the Canal area. His forces halted sixty miles from Cairo.[3]

Now it was President Sadat who yielded to a truce proposal that Secretary Kissinger already had presented to the Israelis. The war dictator Brezhnev in Moscow had seen to that, for on October 20 he learned somewhat belatedly that the resurgent Israelis had outmaneuvered the Egyptians, seized the west bank of the Suez Canal, and were within striking distance of Cairo. Brezhnev then invited Kissinger to Moscow for an emergency conference and the American secretary of state just as hastily agreed, mainly because the Arab states sympathetic to Sadat's cause had applied an oil embargo against the United States on October 20.

That was how it developed, at a Brezhnev-Kissinger conference in Moscow on October 21, that a joint U.S.-Soviet proposal for an Egyptian-Israeli cease-fire, placed before the UN Security Council in New York, was speedily adopted by a 14-0 vote, with China abstaining. No matter what Prime Minister Meir may have thought about Kissinger's maneuver just when the tide of battle was turning in Israel's favor, she had to agree to the cease-fire—and so did Defense Minister Dayan.

The joint U.S.-Soviet decision, as a result, saved Sadat from defeat after he had seemed on the verge of a surprise victory at the outset of the Yom Kippur War. Mrs. Meir thereafter never forgave Kissinger for going behind her back to halt the conflict through an alliance with the Soviet enemy. Although President Nixon must have known and approved of Kissinger's actions, the congressional inquiry into the presidential role in the Watergate scandal had reached so critical a point that the White House could not risk a new struggle with the Soviet Union.

That, primarily, was the reason for Kissinger's maneuver.[4]

Even after the cease-fire had supposedly taken effect, the Soviet representatives in the UN continued to complain that General Sharon and his Israelis on the west bank of the Suez Canal were tightening their steel ring around Egypt's trapped Third Army. It was clear enough that what Moscow wanted was the immediate withdrawal of the Israelis and the liberation of their thousands of Egyptian prisoners, something that no American secretary of state could do to oblige the Soviet Union when it was, in effect, threatening an act of war.

What Kissinger then had to do, in what amounted to an emergency, was to inform President Nixon of the Soviet warning and ask for instructions. But the president, at that time, also was facing his own grave internal crisis, so he passed the responsibility for decision making to his secretary of state with instructions "to go to the brink."

The result, as it turned out, was the first nuclear alert in history for the forces of the United States. That was Kissinger's response to a Soviet demand before the Security Council for a joint U.S.-Soviet formation to insure Israeli agreement to the cease-fire. To make certain that his position was understood in Moscow, the secretary of state said in a TV broadcast to the Soviets: "We possess, each of us, nuclear arsenals capable of annihilating humanity. So, both of us have a special duty to see it to that confrontations are kept within bounds and do not threaten civilized life."

The Soviets gave in. Their UN representative, Jakob Malik, who had been just as intractable under instructions from Moscow as his predecessor, Andrei Gromyko, now the Soviet foreign minister, dropped his insistence on a U.S.-Soviet unit to keep the peace. Instead, the Security Council created still another UN Emergency Force under the command of a new UN secretary-general, Kurt Waldheim, with a Finnish military director in the field. Under these circumstances the United States lifted its nuclear alert to its armed forces on October 24 when the first dozen UN observers made certain that the Israeli division blocking the route to Cairo had quit shooting at Egyptian soldiers trapped on the fringes of the Third Army.

Far from agreeing to relieve the pressure on the encircled Egyptians, General Sharon already was insisting that no food or even water would go to the trapped enemy until agreements could be reached on an exchange of prisoners, especially the wounded ones. Worse still for Sadat's troopers, the Israeli position was that not even a UN-operated corridor could be opened to the Third Army until there was an agreement on the prisoner exchange and other details.

Direct negotiations under UN supervision followed when Sadat, to the surprise of Kissinger and his State Department aides, quickly agreed that a deal with Israel would have to be negotiated so that he could regain control of his Third Army and obtain a return from Israel of Egyptian prisoners. For that all-important first meeting, the two sides concluded that the negotiations would be carried on in a small tent city to be set up on the road from the Suez Canal to Cairo.

And so, on October 30, the first Egyptian-Israeli conference on peace took place in this ramshackle tent way station between Maj. Gen. Sharon Yariv of Israel, the retired chief of army intelligence, and his opposite number from Egypt, Lt. Gen. Abd al-Chani Gamazi, with a Finnish general, Ensio Siilasvuo, representing the UN Emergency Force, as the chairman.

Even though the issues were clear enough and the need for an end to fighting and at least a beginning on peacemaking were urgently needed by both sides, as well as the United States, the Soviet Union, and the UN, it took two weeks of hard bargaining before the first modest essentials were agreed upon. For despite Kissinger's pressures on Israel, it took two visits to Washington by Prime Minister Meir to appeal directly to President Nixon and any number of Israeli cabinet meetings before the corridor to the Third Army was opened under Israeli control and UN observation so that prisoners, including the wounded, could be exchanged and food and water could be given to the trapped Egyptians.

In all, eighteen meetings between the negotiators and the UN had to be held in the tent city at Kilometer 101 on the Suez Canal–Cairo road for the barest beginning of the peace process. It was emblematic of the deep mistrust that existed between Israel and Egypt, together with Prime Minister Meir's suspicion of Kissinger, that Israelis had to be given control of even the smallest move toward helping the prisoners and the wounded and seeing that the encircled Egyptians were given food and water, both limited to 250 tons.

More important once these necessary first steps were agreed upon and executed, the negotiators and their Finnish chairman also made a beginning on disengaging their forces—a deal that could not be concluded as quickly. What Israel demanded was the reopening of the Suez Canal to Israeli shipping in return for an Israeli withdrawal from the Canal's west bank to at least ten kilometers into the Sinai from the east bank. The Egyptians countered with a proposal for a thirty-five-kilometer Israeli retreat into the Sinai so that a UN-controlled buffer zone could be set up separating the combatants.

But the Egyptians asked for still more before they would consent to reopen the Canal for Israeli traffic, notably complete evacuation of the Sinai—in a few words, a nullification of all Israeli gains in the Yom Kippur War. That apparently was the signal for all concerned to conclude the preliminary talks and shift the proceedings to a formal peace conference at Geneva, a proposal that Kissinger in particular ardently championed.

For the Israelis, with the Meir government staggered by public disenchantment over its conduct of the Yom Kippur War, the break for Geneva almost coincided with a scheduled election to the Knesset at year's end and a chance to regain some of the public confidence it had lost. Sadat and the Egyptians had nothing to lose no matter when or where the talks resumed.

As for the Syrians, Hafez al-Assad still was holding a number of Israeli prisoners, including some who were severely wounded, whom he hoped to use as bargaining counters in his effort to retain control of the Israeli-occupied Golan Heights. Even more important, the Syrian dictator also was in the embarrassing position of facing up to true negotiations while an Israeli offensive spearhead was holding a bulge in south Syria on the road to Damascus.

But unlike Sadat, al-Assad refused to give the Israelis so much as a list of the names of the prisoners he was still holding and the condition of those who had suffered the most severe wounds. That, primarily, was what stalled the Israeli-Syrian negotiations for months even though the enemy troops on Syrian territory remained at their advance stations. It was hopeless, accordingly, for Kissinger to count on pushing negotiations with Damascus.[5]

In the interim before the Israelis voted on a new Knesset and the fate of the Meir regime, Israel and Egypt agreed to what amounted to only a ceremonial opening of the Geneva peace talks. Nothing much happened there on December 21 at the Palais des Nations except for a fiery Gromyko attack on the United States and Israel that only increased Kissinger's difficulties in seeking an agreement on disengaging the combatants preparatory to peace negotiations. After less combative responses from the United States and Israel, together with a mild statement of the Egyptian position by Sadat, everybody went home to await the outcome of the Israeli election and a resumption of Kissinger's search for peace in 1974.

The election, as expected, only increased Prime Minister Meir's troubles because she won the barest majority in the Knesset on December 31 that enabled her to remain in power. The outcome was based on the public's blame for Dayan's neglect of the country's defenses. The hero of the Six-Day War now was the goat of the Yom Kippur War and he was seldom permitted to forget it from then on.

I stress the lamentable position in which Labor found itself after the year-end 1973 elections because it explains why Kissinger decided to speed up the talks through what became known as "shuttle diplomacy"—flying in his American Boeing 707 between Egypt and Israel instead of returning to Geneva, as had previously been agreed upon. President Sadat, in fact, encouraged the shuttle to avoid the prospect of drawn-out discussions at Geneva.

There also was a certain amount of urgency on the American side for President Nixon, now in an indefensible position in the Watergate scandal, badly needed encouraging news somewhere. He was not about to get it in Vietnam, where Kissinger had participated in negotiating a peace largely on North Vietnam's terms that presently would result in North Vietnam's absorption of South Vietnam. As Nixon's secretary of state, Kissinger hoped to serve his chief more effectively with a pact disengaging the contending armies in the Middle East, or so it appeared at the time.

Kissinger's shuttle began with a trip directly after the new year to the tourist city of Aswan in Egypt, near the newly completed Aswan High Dam as Nasser had planned it. There, he met President Sadat again and showed him a map that projected an Israeli withdrawal from the encircled Egyptian Third Army on the west side of the Suez Canal to a point twenty kilometers east of the Canal. That was fine with Sadat except that the southern part of this withdrawal line was too close, in the Egyptian's opinion, to the Israeli-controlled Gulf of Suez.

At the next stop of the air shuttle in Israel, Kissinger persuaded Dayan to redraw that part of the line so that separating the forces at last had begun early in 1974. As for the size of the armies, further shuttle trips produced an agreement reducing them eventually to no more than ten battalions each when suitably separated with the coming of peace, each with thirty tanks and missiles withdrawn twenty additional kilometers. However, there was no agreement on the end of belligerency, something that Prime Minister Meir did not even propose, because she apparently realized a thoroughly beaten Sadat could not safely be humbled still more. And as for the reopening of the Suez Canal to Israeli shipping, there was a tentative understanding that some Israeli ships could use the Canal although not while displaying the Israeli flag, but complete and undisputed right of passage still was stalled.

The role of the UN Emergency Force separating the combatants, too, caused trouble when Prime Minister Meir recalled that Nasser's sudden dismissal of his own UN guards led to the Six-Day War. More guarantees of the UN's role this time, accordingly, had to be written into the agreement between the always-suspicious Israelis and Arabs. As for the United States, the Arabs signaled a partial lifting of the October 20 oil embargo when the Kissinger negotiations began. The embargo ended on January 17, 1974, with the simultaneous announcement of all agreements concluding the Yom Kippur War from Jerusalem, Cairo, and Washington.

The next day, the Israeli-Egyptian agreement was formally signed, pledging that each would "scrupulously observe the cease fire on the land, sea and air called for by the UN Security Council and will refrain from . . . all military or paramilitary actions against each other." But the agreements with Syria were not as easily concluded.[6]

During the additional four months of negotiations with Syria, in which Kissinger's air shuttle moved repeatedly between Damascus and Jerusalem, Prime Minister Meir and Defense Minister Dayan were forced to resign in a debacle that ended the Labor Party's long reign in Israel. The crisis had been foreshadowed by the December 31 vote in which the Labor majority barely survived in the Knesset. Less than two months later, on February 25, 1974, Dayan announced his resignation as defense minister, because he felt his usefulness to the nation was ended. The public criticism of his neglected responsibilities for national defense, which had led to this decision, had been more than he could bear.

Prime Minister Meir, at seventy-five, was forming a new cabinet at the time, and on March 3 announced in the Knesset that Yitzhak Rabin, the victorious army chief of staff in the Six-Day War and a former ambassador to Washington, would replace Dayan. But at the same time, she tearfully resigned as prime minister.

The Labor representatives in the Knesset who heard her were stunned. They were well aware that their party's coalition with the radical Mapam Party had come close to losing the December 31 election.

And now, without Mrs. Meir and Dayan, who were almost the last of the Israeli old guard in power, the divided Labor coalition itself was marked for defeat as well. Reluctantly, Mrs. Meir reconsidered, agreed to stay on as prime minister, persuaded Dayan to retain his defense post, and continued to work with Kissinger and the Syrians in seeking a companion agreement to the pact with Egypt on the separation of forces after the Yom Kippur War.

But it was too late. The difficulty of dealing with the Syrians, the onset of a Palestinian campaign of terror against northern Israel from bases in Syria, and the rise of a new and powerful right wing Likud Party in the Knesset combined to cause her to resign again, this time on April 11. And now, she made it stick.

Although she remained in high office temporarily until a successor was chosen and installed with a different cabinet, Mrs. Meir gave more power to Defense Minister Rabin and included another Labor veteran, Shimon Peres, in what became known as her "shadow cabinet." Because it was scarcely a secret that the Labor deputies in the Knesset would choose Rabin as their next prime minister, the first of native birth, and Peres as the next defense minister, Syria's Assad decided at last to conclude his negotiations with Israel and take the best settlement he could get. Despite a terrorist campaign by the Palestinians who operated within Syrian borders, a Syrian-Israeli disengagement agreement was signed in Geneva on May 31, 1974. However, except for Israeli troop withdrawals and the release of a limited number of wounded prisoners by both sides, little of permanent value was accomplished.

King Hussein of Jordan, the odd man out in these Israeli agreements with Egypt and Syria at the end of the Yom Kippur War, was left to fend for himself against the influx of myriad homeless Palestinians into his country and in refugee camps around its outer fringes. This would soon become the next major problem to confront the United States and the UN, with Yasir Arafat's development of the Palestine Liberation Organization into a major factor in the knotty public equation presented by the Middle East.[7]

16. Transient Times

A sense of change enveloped Israel with the accession of Yitzhak Rabin as the nation's sixth prime minister on June 3, 1974. The blunt-spoken, fifty-two-year-old soldier did not win by much in the Knesset balloting, only 44 votes of the 552 cast, which was symbolic of the widening public split within the Jewish state.

It may have seemed generous of the new chief of state that he honored his rival, Shimon Peres, who was a year younger, by giving him the most important post in the cabinet, the defense ministry, considering the closeness of the voting, 298 to 254. But that could not temper the tensions between them, which soon developed into a bitter rivalry. Nor did it discourage the upcoming leader of the opposition, the hawkish Menachem Begin, who soon would be boosting his conservative Likud Party in a drive to become the next prime minister.

With the passing of the old guard in Israel after the retirement of Golda Meir and Moshe Dayan, together with the establishment of Sadat's firm rule in Egypt, there was general recognition that the Middle East had entered a period of transition.[1] It was, however, pure coincidence more than anything else that President Nixon within two weeks of the change in Israel's leadership embarked upon what turned out to be his final foreign appearance with Secretary of State Kissinger at his side.

Nixon's fervent desire to get out of Washington at that time was understandable, given the threat to his presidency that was developing in the congressional investigation of the Watergate scandal that summer. It was, furthermore, to Kissinger's advantage to exhibit the president in style among enthusiastic Egyptians in Cairo before escorting him to Jerusalem—a not very subtle way of softening up the critical new Israeli government.

After the buffeting Nixon had been taking from a censorious public and press at home despite his 1972 reelection victory, his reception in Cairo must have been heartening—a delirious welcome by President Sadat and millions of cheering Egyptians. In response, Nixon produced a gift of awesome proportions for Sadat, an American commitment to build a nuclear reactor in Egypt.

The ever-thoughtful Kissinger, in anticipation of a shocked response elsewhere, notified Israel of the American decision to admit Egypt to the ranks of nuclear powers, gently stressing the importance of the peaceful nature of the reactor when completed and activated. But as any bright schoolchild in the latter twentieth century realized, any such moderate nuclear reactor also could be adapted to wartime uses by knowledgeable scientists, which gave the Israeli government something to worry about.

As the outgoing Israeli prime minister, Golda Meir, had learned, the American gift was offered to and grabbed by Egypt with the acceptance of American supervision over the reactor; otherwise, as Kissinger had pointed out, Egypt might well have obtained such a reactor from the Soviet Union—and no guarantee of friendly supervision. That, of course, did not make Prime Minister Rabin any happier when it became his turn to greet the distinguished American visitors on June 17 and had to face up to still another Kissinger surprise.

This time, while accompanying President Nixon on what should have been a festive arrival in Jerusalem, the secretary of state told Prime Minister Rabin of Sadat's warning in Egypt against Israel's neglect of peace talks with King Hussein of Jordan, particularly having to do with the future of the heavily Arab-populated West Bank of the Jordan River that now was under Israeli control. The issue, as Kissinger put it to Rabin, was that the Israelis could not expect to avert a challenge to their rule of the Arab majority along the West Bank now that Yasir Arafat was shaping the Palestine Liberation Organization into a rival for both Jordan and Israel.

The Israeli prime minister did not quibble. If forced to choose between retaining or quitting the West Bank, he told Kissinger, he would hold an immediate national election and let the people decide. The inference was clear enough—the old soldier meant to cling to the West Bank, come what may, through a decision by his people. At one point in the extended argument with Kissinger, Rabin even risked saying he did not believe the assurances that the secretary of state was not trying to pressure the Israelis. For proof, the prime minister cited the sudden slowdown in American arms deliveries that previously had been promised.[2]

Despite all the outward trappings of honor for a visiting American president in Israel, therefore, Kissinger had to leave Jerusalem empty-handed, heading for Jordan to try to reassure King Hussein as best he could through President Nixon's show of interest in enlarging the king's role. But despite all the secretary's stratagems, he wound up talking to himself after the conclusion of the president's tour of the Middle East. For on August 9, 1974, Nixon was obliged to resign amid the congressional inquiry into the Watergate scandal—the first president to do so. And his replacement, Vice President Gerald Ford, issued presidential pardons to Nixon and others in the Watergate scandal.[3]

An Arab summit meeting later that fall at Rabat in Morocco completed the collapse of Kissinger's Middle East negotiations by delegating Yasir Arafat and the Palestine Liberation Organization to represent the Arabs on the West Bank of the Jordan River. Although the decision relieved Prime Minister Rabin of his pledge to call an election, the issue having already been settled, how to restart the Middle East peace talks was, by default of all other parties, left to Kissinger.

It took more than a year for the secretary to resolve the fundamental areas of conflict between Israel and the trio of Arab states involved in the negotiations—Egypt, Syria, and Jordan. As quickly as one or the other of the Arabs showed a slight tendency toward movement to develop a secure peace, there would be discouragement from the Israeli side. And the same proved to be true about any slight Israel wiggle toward compromise. The only one who never gave up was Kissinger, until the collapse that came toward the end of the Rabin government for other reasons.[4]

Although the frequent Rabin-Peres disagreements within the Labor cabinet were troublesome, they did not seem to block all efforts toward resolving the disputes with the Arabs. Mainly, these were matters such as Rabin's appointment of General Sharon as his "personal" adviser although it was obvious that Sharon's advice would be on matters of defense—also the responsibility of Peres as the defense minister. Nevertheless, Peres could not help concluding that the Sharon appointment threatened his own continuance in office.

When Peres thereafter named Prof. Yuval Ne'eman as his "scientific adviser," it was the prime minister's turn to complain and he did so at length. This kind of thing created unnecessary tensions within the Rabin government, which had trouble enough handling more important elements of its responsibilities.

Still another flap came when Peres proposed a small U.S. or U.S.-Soviet presence in two passes that led to the east bank of the Suez Canal, both critical to the Israeli-Egyptian peace talks. Rabin was represented as having pictured this suggestion as a proposal for a Soviet-American military force that, Peres said, was far from his notion. In any event, nothing came of either proposition. When an agreement was reached, the two passes were given to Egypt for supervision but Israelis were permitted a station nearby and both remained under the observation of a small contingent of Americans—the usual solution in circumstances under which neither side trusted the other.

Handicapped by such disagreements on the Egyptian front, the Rabin government also had continued difficulty in settling its differences with Syria and Jordan. During its fewer than four years in office, therefore, the dwindling majority the Rabin coalition was able to maintain in the Knesset over the Begin-dominated minority made it extremely difficult for Israel to make any substantial progress toward peace in the Middle East.[5]

For a brief period, when President Sadat reopened the Suez Canal to Israeli shipping on June 5, 1975, there seemed to be a flicker of hope for more progress in Secretary Kissinger's shuttle service toward peace. But even that turned out to be illusory when it was recalled that the Egyptians had promised to do so the previous year. Beyond that, despite all Kissinger's efforts, nothing further of substance developed to advance the negotiations. As a result, he retreated to the Virgin Islands for a late summer's vacation and President Ford formally notified all parties that the peace talks had stalled.

Prime Minister Rabin then realized he had to do something to distinguish his administration, which up to that time had persisted in its refusal to give ground anywhere. That was when the Israelis drafted an emergency package of Israeli proposals that was delivered to the Virgin Islands for Kissinger's inspection.

The key item was Israel's decision to withdraw a demand for an agreement by Egypt to a state of nonbelligerence. Coupled with that was a pledge by Israel to permit Egyptian use of two disputed passes to the east bank of the Canal, provided there could be guarantees by the United States that Cairo would not again wage war by surprise.

As far as the Soviet Union was concerned, what Israel also sought was assurance that the United States would intervene in the Middle East with armed force in the event of an invasion of the area by a "foreign power," a diplomatic way of meeting a possible threat to the Middle East by Soviet arms.

To compensate Israel for the economic and military aid expended in the Yom Kippur War and the stalled peace negotiations, the negotiating package approved by Prime Minister Rabin requested $2 billion from the United States. On the Syrian front, nothing of substance was proposed by Israel—recognition of the uselessness of any dealings with Hafez al-Assad.

Kissinger evidently found sufficient movement in Israel's final offer to bring it to President Ford's attention, after which the secretary drafted the terms of a compromise to all the parties except Jordan. That, in effect, left it to King Hussein to deal with the Palestine Liberation Organization and the Israelis about the future of the homeless Palestinians within Jordan or at refugee camps on its borders.

The document that emerged from this combined effort was an Egyptian-Israeli accord on the Sinai triangle that was signed on September 1, 1975. There were nine articles illustrated with maps and complicated boundary lines together with a six-part annex of an early warning system to be operated by a small American boundary patrol—Israel's protection against another surprise war. That was the total of Prime Minister Rabin's accomplishment on the international front.[6]

The fractious Israeli government, torn between the continually feuding Rabin and his defense minister, Shimon Peres, did have one other accomplishment to its credit—a brilliant rescue mission of Jewish captives on an Air France passenger aircraft hijacked by Palestinian terrorists. The conflict was enacted before a worldwide audience between June 27 and July 4, 1976.

The French passenger plane, which had left Tel Aviv on June 27, was seized by the terrorists during stopover that day at Athens and flown twenty-five hundred miles to Entebbe in Uganda. There, the terrorists demanded the immediate release of many of their closest associates who were held in prisons in Israel and elsewhere.

It was one time when Prime Minister Rabin and Defense Minister Peres could work together without argument, resulting in the flight of a rescue mission of heavily armed Israeli commandos in a fleet of four Hercules aircraft to Entebbe. The commander was Yonatan Netanyahu, a Harvard graduate with a degree in philosophy as well as a battlefield veteran with decorations for bravery and promotion to colonel.

In this emergency, the Israeli army chief of staff, Gen. Mordechai Gur, had to approve the plan and the cabinet had to be consulted, particularly when a list of the names of the hijacked passengers was issued with implied threats to their safety if the terrorists' terms were not met. As the week passed during the secret preparations for the rescue mission, tension mounted in Israel. On July 1, after about forty non-Jewish passengers were freed in Entebbe, the deadline was set for 11:00 A.M. on July 4 by the hijackers, who by this time seemed to have prevailed upon Idi Amin, the dictator of Uganda, to let them do as they pleased. At any rate, he did not interfere.

However, not until July 3 was the rescue mission in the air, bound for Entebbe, a secret flight as risky as it was daring. Prime Minister Rabin gave the signal for takeoff after briefing Menachem Begin as the leader of the Knesset opposition and obtaining his approval. It was one of the few times during the Rabin regime that all the politicians had rallied behind the military detachment that was taking all the physical risks.

With radio silence in effect, what Rabin and his associates tried to do was to maintain secrecy about the flight because of the very real possibility that Idi Amin might order his Ugandan troops to defend the hijackers if any hint of the rescue operation were broadcast from Israel. However, all went well and Rabin, with others in his confidence, joined Peres in the defense minister's office as the scheduled time for landing approached.

What happened at Entebbe for a little less than an hour beginning about 11:00 P.M. on July 3 was transmitted to Israel in code over an agreed-upon radio channel. The first of the four Hercules transports landed there safely, after which the first band of commandos in their jeeps took off for a nearby building where they knew the hostages were being held. Their orders were to shoot to kill any hijackers who opposed them and they did so.

Within a few minutes, the other three transports followed, protected by other commandos from the first plane while armored cars were unloaded to help in the assault to free the hostages. Once the hostages and the cars were back on the transports, the flight returned north for a refueling stop in Kenya.

As became known later, all but one of the hostages was saved unharmed; the victim died later in an Entebbe hospital. As for the hijackers, all were killed, but there also was a victim among the commandos—their chief, Colonel Netanyahu, who was killed by a bullet fired from a watchtower. He was a brother of Benjamin Netanyahu, who would be the Israeli ambassador to the United States and would become an Israeli prime minister in years to come.

The radio silence ended once the transports and the hostages arrived safety at an Israeli military field. While the nation rejoiced over the success of the rescue operation, there was sadness as well over the fate of the leader of the mission to Entebbe. Other than that, the feuding prime minister and his defense minister could be proud of their role in saving the hostages through the effective intervention of the Israeli commandos.[7]

Once the celebration over the rescue of the hostages faded, the days of the Rabin administration appeared to be numbered. Several of its officials had been involved in scandals and at least two of them already were in prison. The opposition also was accusing others of irregularities, including the prime minister's wife, so that he was in an increasingly difficult position at the onset of 1977. The charge against Mrs. Rabin was possession of a small U.S. bank account, a violation of the law.

Among the opposition in the Knesset, the dominant figure of Menachem Begin already was threatening the current administration, and his Herut (freedom) Party had enlarged to a point at which it overshadowed the steadily weakening Labor Party that had lost its vigor along with its public appeal. When the rejoicing over the Entebbe rescue operation tapered off, one poll showed that Rabin's standing had declined to 35 percent. Clearly, it was time for Begin to make his most forceful bid for power and he did so early in 1977.

As a conservative politician—"a fighting Jew," he called himself—the leader of the Knesset opposition had become a formidable figure in Israel at sixty-four. He had been born in Brest Litovsk in Russia in 1913 to devout Zionist parents and had joined a Zionist youth organization early on, becoming its chairman while still in his teens. However, with the rise of Stalin and his blindness to the threat of Nazi Germany, the Jewish population in the Soviet Union was caught in a pincers movement of their enemies. To try to save himself, Begin and his family fled to Poland.

It was too late. For on August 23, 1939, the Hitler-Stalin nonaggression pact signaled the Soviet leader's attempt to turn Hitler toward the West, France and Britain, in the coming of another world war that now seemed certain. On August 25, the frightened Poles entered into a defense pact with Britain, but as Chancellor Hitler began World War II only a few days later, Poland became the first victim of joint Nazi-Communist aggression. When Hitler advanced from the west, the Soviets invaded from the east and Poland was torn apart between them. In 1940, Begin was caught by the Soviets and imprisoned in Siberia for more than a year as a member of the Polish army. Only after Hitler turned on Stalin and invaded the Soviet Union in 1941 was Begin released and somehow he found his way back to Poland as a freedom fighter before managing to emigrate to Palestine to join his family. His wife already was there.

To understand Begin's militant Judaism and his fervent championship of a strong and forceful Israel, his account of his suffering in that critical period of his life, *White Nights: The Story of a Prisoner in Russia*, is required reading.* He would never forget the pitiless cruelty of the Soviet guards to the helpless creatures in their custody, something that must have prodded him to demand constantly, in his later years, the continual strengthening of the Jewish state regardless of cost.

Beginning in 1942, once he was reunited with his wife and children, this miraculously revived Begin became a sterling pillar of resistance to British rule in Palestine. At twenty-nine, he became the commander of the then-secret resistance movement, Irgun Zvai Leumi; at thirty-five, the cofounder of the Herut Party, its chairman, and a member of the Knesset from the time it was formed in 1948; at fifty-seven, a dominant figure in the conservative Likud (unity) Party that he was determined to lead to power in the Knesset, with the Herut.

The intense nationalist platform of the conservative Likud, and the support it was drawing from an increasingly large segment of Israeli public opinion, demonstrated conclusively the continued decline of Labor, the surviving element of the coalition that once had brought and maintained Ben-Gurion in authority in Israel's earliest years of nationhood. That was the strength of Likud. Its weakness was the disclosure,

*Menachem Begin, *White Nights: The Story of a Prisoner in Russia* (New York: Harper and Row, 1977).

at just about the time Begin kicked off his campaign for prime minister in 1976, that his cherished Herut organization, the heart of his appeal through the Likud Party, had virtually no money left in its treasury. That was damaging in the extreme when it became known, for it was as if a contender for the Republican Party nomination for president of the United States had been told he did not have enough money to buy TV time a few months before election day.

Although it was the law in Israel that votes are cast by the electorate for party slates and not individuals, Begin was damaged by the revelation that he had managed so ineptly that his Herut Party was on the verge of going broke as he sought to be the next prime minister of Israel. While his rivals commented sarcastically on his plight, he took off in a panic for the United States and elsewhere in an appeal for contributions from conservative Jewish supporters of his cause.

The consequences were appalling. Early in 1977, he suffered his first heart attack and was hospitalized. His polls dropped sharply with the May election for the Knesset only a few months away and campaign contributions a dire necessity. Once he felt well enough for his doctors to let him venture from his hospital bed to try to prove his fitness to a dubious electorate, the latter stages of the campaign became his greatest problem. If ever he were to be the guiding force in Israel's government instead of the continual leader of the opposition in the Knesset, he would have to demonstrate his ability to lift Israel to the height of authority in the Middle East.

He had failed four times before his quest for supreme authority. This would be his last chance.[8]

17. After Thirty Years

Labor appeared to be in a decline during the early stages of the 1977 election campaign, but Menachem Begin's Likud Party, too, was far from a majority in most tracking polls. The best Begin could do was his party's 26 percent of the respondents in one leading poll, which did not make even his supporters enthusiastic.

While recovering from a heart attack as he neared his mid-sixties, Begin still was in an Israeli hospital worrying about his future. After being dominant through six administrations over three decades, Labor also was in trouble but few among its leaders worried about the position only once.

The rather timid approach Begin adopted, mainly out of uncertainty about his physical condition, contributed to Labor's overconfidence without doubt. For when Prime Minister Rabin was obliged to retire after hearing his wife charged with violating Israel's foreign bank account law, Begin suggested a coalition government of the succeeding Labor nominee, Shimon Peres. But Peres quickly refused, apparently being sure of becoming the next prime minister.[1]

One other factor came into consideration before the climactic phase of the campaign began. In accordance with accepted Israeli practice at the time, both major parties sought to establish coalitions with various minor parties in the hope of achieving a majority in the Knesset. The upshot was that neither Labor nor Likud could put together a coalition that was likely to bring it a majority in Parliament.

So, in effect, the election was up for grabs although Labor's leaders refused to believe it. They had been so used to winning that they could not concede that Begin had a chance.[2]

And yet, what was happening in Israel over three decades was a radical change in the political and social composition of the electorate.

The Ashkenazim, the refugees from Europe who had been by far in the majority of the early settlers in Palestine, now were outnumbered by an increasingly large proportion of Jewish refugees from other parts of the world, many of them young, vigorous, and resentful of their unchanging elderly top officials. Mainly these refugees were the Sephardic Jews from North Africa and the Middle East, some claiming descent from the Jews who were expelled from Spain in 1492. And they also were the forerunners of a vast new stream of refugees from Oriental and African lands.

To judge from reports of the changing character of the Israeli population, the Ashkenazim, the European Jews and their descendants, still clung to the parties of Ben-Gurion, Labor, and Mapai, but some of the religious parties now were inclined to turn away from Labor for not insisting on retaining every bit of land conquered in the Six-Day War and thereafter. The leading characteristic of the rest seemed to be an almost violent insistence on change.

Then, too, victims of persecution among the Sephardic Jews had a natural affinity for a fellow victim, Begin, who knew how to address their fears and their resentfulness out of his own disastrous experience before reaching Israel. The red flags displayed among others by the Mapam Party, so often a member of the ruling coalition since Ben-Gurion's time, were little more than a danger signal to such refugees—and there were thousands of them.

Finally, and perhaps decisively, the scandals that had overtaken Labor and its predecessor, Mapai, were symptomatic of a political organization that had been in power too long—a condition by no means confined to a small democracy such as Israel. Nor were these faults based merely on talk or suspicion. Jailed officials, together with a suicide of an accused official, told their story and a proportion of the electorate was bound to act accordingly.[3]

It soon became evident to Begin, upon regaining his health and leaving the hospital, that whoever assembled the most competent and otherwise impressive a campaign staff would have the best chance of carrying the election. On that basis, the Likud leader reconsidered a hasty decision he had made in dismissing Gen. Ezer Weizman, the nephew of former president Chaim Weizmann, as the chairman of the Herut executive when the party was broadened to form Likud with alliances from Liberals, the religious parties, and others.

The organization had authority. And it had power. That much was evident from the outset. But instead of being his usual fiery self and defying the enemy at home and abroad with flailing arms and violent language, Begin was curiously subdued for much of the campaign and only rarely fell back on his familiar style as the leader of the opposition.

General Weizman was just as cautious. He had retired in 1970 as the chief of Israel's Air Force—in the words of an admirer, "the founder of the world's best air force"—and was delighted to be associated again with his Herut colleague, Begin, after having left the Meir coalition with him. The general was even more enthusiastic when he learned that he was wanted as the chairman of Begin's campaign organization for the 1977 election. Probably reflecting on past experience, he asked for complete authority to run the show as he saw fit. To his surprise, the candidate gave him what he had sought without a murmur of protest.

It was a sign of Begin's uncertainty that he let his authority slip over what was likely to be his last serious attempt to become the nation's prime minister, having failed so often previously when he had less impressive opponents than Defense Minister Peres. As for General Weizman, having been close to heads of government for years, he had little trouble handling his candidate despite a tendency to wallow in American-style political TV imagery—Begin, the family man; Begin, the devoted husband; Begin, the friend of all children; and so on. Throughout the campaign, it seemed to be General Weizman's notion that the Israeli voter was interested only in commonplaces at home except for opposition to anything the Arabs sought to do to embarrass Israel. The campaign chairman seldom took a chance on any issue of substance or any quotation that had meaning.[4]

As for Begin, when he made decisions as he did in his keynote address at the 1977 Likud convention in January, the drift of his thought was made evident when he inserted a position in the party platform that in effect called for a trade of conquered land for peace with Egypt. Some asked, not bothering to conceal their amazement, "Begin wants to have peace with Egypt so much that he will trade land in the Sinai for it. What next?" The candidate's objective was clear. As a "fighting Jew," he might well have decided to be a candidate who wanted still more wars that changed little or nothing in Israel's position in the Middle East. But instead, after some three thousand Jewish combat deaths in the Yom Kippur War, he seemed to be asking the electorate, "Why not give peace a chance?"[5]

Regardless of Begin's explanation of his purposes, or a complete lack thereof sometimes, his peace plank went into the Likud platform, he swore by it, and took to the road for votes and to the United States for campaign contributions. The kind of candidate General Weizman depicted in his campaign publicity also played down Begin as a hawk and emphasized his devotion to peace, the home, mother, and the kids—a line that may have made him squirm in embarrassment at times but it also was a realistic campaign position for a war-weary public in Israel.

Both in Israeli television and full-page advertisements in leading Israeli newspapers, the Likud Party on the whole avoided the familiar tough Begin sledgehammer approach to slug it out with the Arabs come what may and return no conquered lands either to Egypt, Syria, or King Hussein of Jordan. As for those who believed that Begin's public-relations shock troops would have him leading a campaign to blow up Egypt's American-installed nuclear reactor, that never happened as well.

Labor's public-relations approach was no better, so the rival television and newspaper advertisements probably canceled each other out among a public that had a great many more immediate issues to be concerned about. What the campaign came down to mainly, with both major candidates and their followers matching each other in political *kitsch*, was a TV debate that was arranged between Peres and Begin toward the end of the campaign. Here, at last, the electorate had a right to expect some plain talk between the candidates about their respective parties' positions, but, for the most part, the nation's viewers drew a blank and had to be satisfied with it.[6]

As election day approached, the Likud and Labor faithful realized that two of Israel's greatest military heroes, Moshe Dayan and Ariel Sharon, seemed to be unusually quiet—even dispirited. Of the two, Sharon had been active early in the campaign as the leader of what amounted to a one-man new party that he called Shlomzion, meaning peace for Zion, that he once had counted on for six to eight seats in the Knesset. But Dayan had alternately been reported to be writing his autobiography and trying without much success to rise above his disgrace in the ranks of Labor as the defense minister who had been found wanting in the Yom Kippur War. Neither of these military leaders, however, was regarded as an influential figure in this critical election.

Sharon at least had been mildly active in the contest between Peres for Labor and Begin for Likud. After having at first decided on making his farmland his family home but living elsewhere while housing reconstruction was under way, he set up his Shlomzion Party on a hunch despite warnings from his wife and friends not to try to go it alone in Israel's weird political setup. All too soon, however, he found that he was running out of money to finance all the necessities of party politics and took off for the United States for a one-man money-raising drive.

The adventure ended in disappointment. Worse still, he learned from polls he had commissioned that Shlomzion at best could win only two seats in the 120-seat Knesset; presumably, one would be his so he could count on one other member in his party to support his cause in Parliament. He decided he would have to seek cover and, as a first move, consulted Begin, who still was in the hospital getting over his preelection heart attack. Although the Likud leader was sympathetic, he asked the discouraged general to see his party organization chief, Yitzhak Shamir, about becoming a candidate for the Knesset pledged to that party.

However, the deadline for the submission of each party's lists of names for its candidates passed without anybody, including Begin and Shamir, approaching the becalmed Sharon. That was how he went into the election as one of the two candidates of his frayed Shlomzion Party basically because there was no other place for him to go. But he took heart despite that when he read in a newspaper that he and General Weizman were under Begin's consideration for defense minister in the event of a Likud victory.[7]

Dayan, despite his brilliance as an Israeli military leader, did not have even that bit of encouragement. He spent much of his time, according to friends, defending himself from charges made against him in the formal commission of inquiry into the cause of Israel's unreadiness when the Arabs launched their sneak attack in the Yom Kippur War. Those who knew him became familiar with his passionate arguments that he had never failed the nation, that it all seemed to be somebody else's fault. He also was inclined to argue that the Egyptians, having failed to halt Israel's military when Sharon's troops crossed the Suez Canal and trapped the Egyptian Third Army just before the ceasefire took effect, now were bound to be in a more conciliatory mood.

Thus, the Israeli military leader seemed to be edging away from his allegiance to Labor and the associates in the Meir and Rabin cabinets who had been making him the goat of the failures in the Yom Kippur War. It was a point of view that was bound to be noticed by the opposition Likud crowd in general, and Begin was the likely new prime minister if Likud could upset the ruling party in the election for the new Knesset.[8]

One other factor in the decisive period before the election was bound to have important consequences—the shifting allegiance of the National Religious Party, the largest organization of Orthodox Jewry in the nation. Having been a partner of Mapai/Labor since the time of Ben-Gurion, the fount of orthodoxy in Israel had been troubled since the major acquisition of former Arab territory during the Six-Day War by the tendency of more recent Labor politicians to be willing to trade parts of that unexpected treasure trove in return for an Arab-pledged peace. To the Orthodox, to surrender any part of what it called Eretz Israel (land of Israel) amounted to treason, and both Rabin and his Labor successor, Peres, lost Orthodox support because of it.[9]

Now, owing to Begin's hawkish reputation, even if he were acting the part of a more reasonable Likud leader, it appeared that he might very well get most of the votes of the National Religious Party and perhaps some of its smaller affiliates as well in the upcoming election. The question, however, was whether the totals would be sufficient to give Likud a victory and make Begin the next prime minister. And on that score, the uncommitted public vote, as the late polls indicated, was shifting to Begin and the Likud-allied organizations on the basis of mounting charges of corruption within the Labor government hierarchy. True, just before election day, some polls still were indicating another in Labor's thirty-year string of victories, but the tallies were not conclusive.

However, the position was desperate enough for a prominent figure in the Labor Party to be told by a friend that the election would result in its first defeat in three decades. That, finally, was what happened that dreary election day of May 17, 1977.[10] When Sharon and his wife voted in Rehovot, the home of the Weizmann Institute of Science and a Labor stronghold, the general observed that he saw few friendly faces and that appeared to be the case in most other areas that had traditionally given their allegiance to Labor. But overall, the general did get the two delegate seats he had expected in the Knesset and he calculated he had, at the end, just about broken even on late contributions and expenses.

Once the votes were counted, Labor had lost 19 of its 51 seats in the

Knesset for a reduction of its pledged deputies to only 32 in its worst defeat in 30 years. Likud meanwhile added 6 seats to its 39 for a new total of 45, bearing out the basic political lineup in Israel that gave neither party a majority entirely of its own making. What put Likud over the top was a shift of 16 deputies from the National Religious Party and one affiliate to give the new Begin coalition 61 votes of the 120 in the Parliament. But added to that were the 15 deputies of the new political organization called Movement for Change for a probable working majority of 76 votes. The remaining dozen scattered votes included Sharon's two deputies for his Shlomzion party.[11]

Peres, Labor's losing candidate, blamed the defeat on the series of scandals by leading government officials in the party, but argued that the deeper cause was the outcome of the Yom Kippur War that followed. It was, the party's chairman conceded, a massive loss of public confidence that had ended the party's thirty-year string of victories from the founding of Israel and the election of Ben-Gurion in 1948.

The scandals on which he elaborated included a five-year prison term for the party's nominee for governor of the Bank of Israel on charges of bribery and embezzlement, another prison term for the head of the Israel Corporation and a former director of the Ministry of Trade and Industry, the suicide of a housing minister who was under a police inquiry, and the resignation of the prime minister himself on charges of association with his wife's small foreign savings account.

Peres concluded:

> Our three years in office had ended badly. Our party was deeply depressed; the corridors of its headquarters in Tel Aviv echoed emptily as I settled into the chairman's office, and into the daunting task of rebuilding morale and confidence. But the outgoing government's record, seen in more dispassionate historical perspective, was by no means negative. We had made major progress on the road to peace with Egypt, the strongest of the Arab nations. We had restored and greatly expanded Israel's war-battered military might. The economy had been carefully husbanded back to health after the trauma of war. But the single most memorable feat that history would record to our credit was, without a doubt, Operation Yonatan—the IDF's daring rescue mission to Entebbe.[12]

One of the most important consequences of the 1977 vote, which seemed to have been largely overlooked in the excitement of Begin's triumph and the downfall of Labor, was the major role that had been given to the National Religious Party and an affiliate in deserting its alliance with the left wing. Now, firmly planted on the Right with the more conservative factions of the electorate, the most devout faction in Israel would soon be able to exercise veto power over any prime minister who flouted its passionate belief in retaining claim to what once had been biblical Israel.

What that appeared to mean, at least for the present, was that the bargaining power of the incoming Begin administration would be severely limited in the growing reliance on trading land for peace. There already was a tendency among the new religious addition to the right wing to call the conquered West Bank area of the Jordan River by its biblical identity—ancient Judea and Samaria. As such, the emphasis increasingly was on retaining all that territory acquired in the Six-Day War even though its million or so population was mostly Arab, particularly in its largest cities.

As Judea and Samaria, therefore, it was considered by the religious right holy and an intrinsic part of biblical Israel—a legitimate area for the founding of new colonies of lately arrived Jewish refugees and others akin to them. The same attitude persisted to an ever stronger degree when it was applied to East Jerusalem, the part of the city that had been principally settled by Arabs, who worshiped at their ancient mosque within its walls just as the Jewish majority in the modern city prayed near the Temple Mount. Inevitably, such clashing attitudes between Jew and Arab in themselves were bound to become a source of bitter warfare unless the new government could develop a compromise satisfactory to both sides.

But nobody, particularly the latest converts to conservatism, the religious right, appeared to be willing to talk compromise in the house of victory for Begin and his associates in the Likud Party. That meant the West Bank and all Jerusalem, as Israel's capital, had to be placed beyond negotiation by the incoming government, which then would be limited to yielding the conquered Sinai Peninsula, in whole or in part, in return for any deal for peace with Egypt and Jordan; as for Syria, the Israeli military was bound to insist on retaining the area to deny terrorists a base from which to continue to raid and kill Jewish settlers in the north of Israel.

Such considerations as these, although they may not have figured in the voting except for the religious right, were bound to have an impact on the new Begin government once it was organized. For that, too, was among the major elements that emerged from the election of 1977. Even after thirty years and a massive rebuke to Labor's governments during that period, no peace was in sight either for Israel or the rest of Palestine.

PART THREE | **Between War and Peace**

18. Begin Takes Over

Instead of seizing control of Israel with a whoop of defiance for his enemies after the surprise victory of his Likud Party, Prime Minister Begin suffered a relapse that delayed his recovery from a heart attack. Slowly, almost painstakingly, he let his colleagues know during brief hospital visits with him in Tel Aviv that the first objective of his administration would be peace. Peace with honor, to be sure, which meant to him peace without giving up an inch of the reconquered area of Judea and Samaria—the West Bank of the Jordan River—but peace nevertheless. This, he insisted, would be the goal of the conservative government of one who had been denounced as a rabble-rouser, a troublemaker, even a warmonger.

The first non-Labor chief of state in twenty years seemed particularly anxious that his aim should become known to Samuel Lewis, the American ambassador to Jerusalem, who had been among the first to convey the congratulations of the new American president, Jimmy Carter, on the triumph of the Likud leadership in the recent election. For President Carter, too, so Ambassador Lewis emphasized, was interested in attaining a just and honorable peace in the Middle East and had so informed President Sadat of Egypt as well.

For Prime Minister Begin, the onset of American pressure to deal with Egypt, Jordan, and Syria had been expected and he was prepared for it even in his sickbed, thankful at least that he did not have to deal with the sleight-of-hand diplomacy of Henry Kissinger, whose term as secretary of state in Washington had ended with the defeat of the latest Republican president, Gerald Ford, in the 1976 American election. Just what could be expected from Jimmy Carter, the first Democratic president since the unfortunate Lyndon Johnson, no one in Begin's entourage was quite sure, but it seemed reasonable to expect that

American policy in the Middle East would continue to oppose Soviet intrusion in the area, maintain the flow of Arab oil across the Atlantic, and seek thereby to promote a lasting Arab-Israeli peace. That, as far as Prime Minister Begin was concerned, meant that the Americans also would soon be busy in Cairo expressing their interest in peace to President Sadat if they had not already done so.

This was the position when Begin left the hospital for the prime minister's office in Jerusalem, to which the president of the Israeli republic had appointed him by law as the leader of the winning political party in the 1977 Israeli election. And here, he put together the cabinet through which he would rule the land to which he had devoted the greatest part of his life. His intent, so he assured his family and friends, was to serve six years until his seventieth birthday, then retire to write his memoirs, barring an outbreak of still another war with the Arabs.

No matter how desirable and necessary peace had become for all the distressed nations of the Middle East, war had become alarmingly close to a way of life in the region and a sudden recurrence of armed conflict there could never be completely discounted. This was the mood in which the victorious Likud chieftain began putting together his government in June after surmounting his most recent heart attack, and his appointments reflected the kind of people he wanted at his side to help him adapt Israel to the changing needs of the times.[1]

There was no trouble whatever about selecting the defense minister. It had to be the prime minister's campaign director, the general who also had created the Israeli Air Force, Ezer Weizman. To observe that General Weizman was pleased when he learned of his appointment would be putting it mildly. As a retired military commander, he was overjoyed to be so amply rewarded for running a safe and sound winning drive against the hitherto unbeatable Labor/Mapai coalition for as long as it could satisfy the religious right that had shifted to Likud with disastrous results. The prime minister could be sure, therefore, that he had a firm, even a devoted, ally in the defense ministry.[2]

Another whom Begin wanted with him among the first appointments was Gen. Ariel Sharon, and it was not only because of the two additional delegates Sharon brought with him to enlarge the strength of the Likud coalition. Sharon had become the only truly heroic figure to emerge from the Yom Kippur War by reason of his leadership of the troops that crossed the Suez Canal and surrounded the Egyptian Third

Army just before the truce took effect. The problem was that he did not want the internal security post the prime minister offered him, because it was outside the realm of policy making. Instead, what he suggested was a cabinet post as minister of agriculture together with responsibility for establishing new Israeli settlements on the West Bank and elsewhere, possibly in East Jerusalem if the new government dared attempt it.

The suggestion pleased the prime minister, not only because he had filled the troublesome agriculture ministry but also because he had a brave and experienced military leader in charge of setting up Jewish defenses in the massively Arab-populated West Bank, now called Judea and Samaria by the incoming Likud coalition. Begin felt strengthened with two military leaders among the first to be selected for his cabinet and now confidently prepared to announce his third, a resurrection of the politically dead, the Labor Party's goat of the Yom Kippur War, Gen. Moshe Dayan.[3]

The appointment of General Dayan to the key cabinet post of foreign minister, complete with his black eye patch, touched off an exciting demonstration of public support for the old war hero who had been so maligned by his own people in the Labor Party for the nation's initial losses in the Yom Kippur War. It was, so Begin exulted long afterward, as if he had named the likes of Gen. Charles de Gaulle to the new Likud cabinet.

The new minister-designate, too, was proud of being called back to the service of Israel by the leader of what had been the wartime opposition and accepted the office of foreign affairs as recognition of his extensive services to the nation on and off the field of battle.[4] For now it had become his responsibility to try to bring peace to Israel as it once had been his duty to insure victory in combat.

The public's enthusiasm for that appointment was long and loud, so much so that Begin filled the rest of his cabinet posts quickly with friends, allies, and holdovers, confident that he had formed a government that could withstand the worst barbs of the Labor opposition. And so it turned out for the immediate future, particularly when his reward for expressing an interest in Middle East peace to the American ambassador was an almost immediate invitation from President Carter to visit the United States at his earliest convenience.

It was flattering no doubt for the new prime minister of Israel to be taken so seriously by the latest occupant of the White House, but, to an essentially cautious soul like Begin, for all his tough talk while in opposition to his government, the bid to present himself in the United States also carried an implied warning with it. If Israel, for example, were offered some concessions by the American president, there was little doubt that Israel also would be called upon for some sacrifices in the interest of peace. And if such a suggested give-and-take were to materialize in the forthcoming visit, Begin and his advisers agreed that Israel might very well offer President Carter a resumption of the Geneva conference with the Arabs.

Under such circumstances, the Israeli leader's consultants seemed agreed, Prime Minister Begin in due course also could offer to grant Egypt a few parts of the conquered Sinai Peninsula, some concessions to the Arab peoples of the West Bank (Judea and Samaria) such as autonomy, a buzzword if there ever was one, and a guarantee of ironclad Israeli safeguards for the holy places of Jerusalem that were sacred to Christians, Muslims, and Jews.

Such preparations as these were not based on guesswork. Begin's predecessor, Prime Minister Rabin, already had been given a thorough grilling by both the new American president and his secretary of state, Cyrus Vance, without yielding anything. Rabin's visit, President Carter had concluded, was disappointing; it followed, therefore, that the heat would be turned on for the American visit of his successor.

Jimmy Carter, thirty-ninth president of the United States, had assumed his high office at the onset of 1977 when he was fifty-two after defeating his Republican rival, President Ford. The former Democratic governor of Georgia had singled out Middle East peace as a leading issue for his administration, already had discussed it repeatedly with his security advisers during and after the presidential campaign, and was anxious to move forward, not only in the interests of the Arab and Israeli peoples directly concerned but also because the stakes were high for the United States as well.

President Carter could not conceive of any reason for the damaging Arab boycott against trade with the United States and already had stimulated antiboycott legislation in Congress. But he also had failed to understand why both the Israelis and their Arab neighbors would not even talk to each other in an effort to settle their differences. And as for the continual threat of warfare over the possession of Old (Arab) Jerusalem, now under Israeli control, and other issues that were left over from four Arab-Israeli wars in twenty-five years, these were continuing threats that the American president refused to tolerate.

As Carter pointed out, the United States at the beginning of his term in 1977 was becoming increasingly dependent on oil from Saudi Arabia and associated states—a continual source of trouble and potential blackmail—so that it now became very much in American interests to get Middle East peace talks started again. Early in March, when he went to New York to address the United Nations, he ran head-on into the question of recognizing the Palestine Liberation Organization, something that apparently made him important, for he shook hands with anybody who came along at the UN including a representative of the PLO. Such details as these had become mountain peaks of disorder in Israeli-Arab relations whether Carter appreciated it or not and he slowly realized that he could not make much progress toward Middle East peace unless he and his American associates took the time and trouble to unravel such knots that seemed continually to block progress toward peace.[5]

The American president doggedly proceeded to sound out every other leader in the Middle East who would come to the White House early on and even ventured abroad to talk to those who, for one reason or another, did not find it in their interest to come to Washington. When President Sadat of Egypt appeared, he seemed to the American president to be a "shining light" who almost at once inspired trust, although the visitor was frankly quite dubious about eventual Egyptian diplomatic recognition of Israel. When Begin's conservative Likud Party unexpectedly routed the Labor government after the Egyptian president's departure from Washington, however, Sadat apparently "accommodated himself," to use Carter's phrase, to the new order of politics in Israel.

The American president later was informed from Cairo that Sadat had been given a favorable impression of the new leader of Israel as a strong, honest personality.

As for others, Carter left no doubt that he enjoyed meeting King Hussein of Jordan at the White House, seemed confused by President Assad of Syria, whom he saw in Geneva, and showed interest in welcoming Crown Prince Fahd of Saudi Arabia to Washington. But, Carter concluded, "The more I dealt with Arab leaders, the more disparity I discovered between their private assurances and their public comments." That, quite naturally, was always par for the course in many a discussion of Middle East issues at the United Nations and elsewhere.[6]

With all that behind him, the American president now prepared for a forthcoming meeting with Prime Minister Begin at the White House by replaying a tape of the Israeli leader's interview on "Issues and Answers." In his notes on the tape in his dairy for May 23, Carter called the Begin position on difficult Middle East issues "frightening." To prepare himself for the Israeli's arrival at the White House on July 19, the president made it a point to try to explain his position on Middle East issues to a number of American Jewish leaders, including members of Congress—a backup effort, apparently, in the event that he and his Israeli guest did not get along.[7]

However, when Prime Minister Begin and Mrs. Begin arrived, the president found him to be "congenial, dedicated, sincere and deeply religious" but concluded it would be difficult for him to change his hostile position on most issues affecting Israel's relations with its Arab neighbors. What they settled on during the relatively brief visit of the Israeli leader, as Carter noted, was the necessity for truly comprehensive Middle East peace but there was clearly no agreement on how that desirable goal could be attained.

From the president's summary of his conversations with his guest, it would appear that what Begin did on such inflexible Israeli positions as yielding Old Jerusalem to the Arabs and also avoiding new Jewish settlements on the West Bank was to duck a direct response, for when he arrived home, he insisted that he gave not an inch as far as Jerusalem and the West Bank were concerned, although he did talk about giving up parts of the Sinai.

When Carter finally realized what had happened, he concluded glumly that his optimistic feelings about Middle East peace "had a short life."[8] And as for a Geneva conference, there was no reviving it that summer or fall, or was there any way in which the Arabs and the Israelis could be persuaded to meet for the kind of negotiations that Carter deemed necessary for a settlement of outstanding issues.

The only ray of hope that he perceived, despite all his efforts, was the interest he had aroused in President Sadat of Egypt for a thorough discussion of all the issues affecting Egyptian-Israeli relations. During a White House visit early in October by the Egyptian foreign minister, Ismail Fahmy, the American president had been given a letter from President Sadat assuring that nothing should be done that would prevent Egypt and Israel from negotiating directly. Sadat was willing to accept the United States as an intermediary before or after a Geneva conference (which by that time no longer was a possibility) but not as a dominant influence in any new move toward peace in the Middle East.

In conversations with Foreign Minister Fahmy, however, Carter gained the impression that only Sadat was interested in a prospective one-on-one meeting between the leaders of Israel and Egypt. Fahmy himself was cold to so revolutionary a prospect, which seemed to him both risky and even counterproductive. Still, it was evident that Carter himself had taken heart from Sadat's desire to talk about the issues directly with someone from the Israeli side, preferably the prime minister himself.

However, there seemed to be no yielding on the Israeli side. Foreign Minister Dayan already had been at the White House to talk about diverse matters with President Carter after the visit from Prime Minister Begin. But in no instance had the one-time Israeli war hero seemed willing to endorse the notion of a one-on-one Israeli-Egyptian conference on outstanding issues. His attitude, like that of his opposite number in Egypt, remained detached, formal, cold, even discouraging about any future prospect for direct talks between the two great enemies in the Middle East.

What seemed to bother Dayan more than anything else was a recent joint Soviet-American statement, issued October 1, in which the two great powers agreed to the principles under which they would act as cochairmen of a new Geneva conference on peace in the Middle East. The Soviet foreign minister, Andrei A. Gromyko, at a White House meeting with President Carter the previous week, had agreed that the objective of such a session should be to negotiate the end of warfare in the Middle East and the normalization of relations between Israel and Egypt. That, of course, also implied Egyptian recognition of Israel—an enormous goal in itself—plus an exchange of ambassadors and a joint agreement on boundaries that almost certainly would mean the return of the Sinai Peninsula to Cairo's control.

That the Soviet Union would join the United States in proposing so momentous an objective was in itself a considerable feat of diplomacy by the American president and his secretary of state, Cyrus Vance. But it failed to impress Dayan as Israel's foreign minister and, when the Americans carried the issue to Cairo, the Egyptian foreign minister, Fahmy, was so disturbed that he resigned.

So it turned out that the only major figure in the Middle East who was willing to move in the direction of peace talks with Israel was President Sadat—and he seemed so lonely a figure among all those involved in the Middle East negotiations that President Carter felt sympathy for him. In a meeting with Dayan early in October at the White House, the American chief of state repeatedly urged the necessity of compromise on the Israeli foreign minister. But although the old war hero reluctantly conceded both sides would have to give ground on all major issues, he warned Carter that the Israeli government— meaning Prime Minister Begin himself—would be bitterly opposed to compromise either on the issues affecting the West Bank or Jerusalem.

In the White House discussions, as Carter noted in his diary, there was scant mention in these preliminary dealings with Egypt and Israel about the position of the Palestine Liberation Organization and its leader, Yasir Arafat, that became so difficult a problem in later years. It almost seemed as if the Americans were taking the position of the Palestinians for granted if the Egyptians and the Israelis could be brought together at Geneva or anywhere else for an exhaustive examination of all the issues dividing them. As events would demonstrate for years to come, nobody could take the Palestinians for granted; nor was their spokesman, Arafat, to be ignored when it came to settling the terms on which his people could live at peace with the Israelis in the narrow stretch of land that had at various times belonged to both of them.

Yet, strangely enough, President Carter could not bring himself to be diverted from his interest in trying to bring Egypt and Israel together for discussions either by considering the problems of the Palestinians, the Syrians, the Jordanians, or the outright foes of the United States in the Middle East, such as Iraq and Iran. As late as October 21, his diary demonstrated that he had written to President Sadat seeking the Egyptian leader's support for the "common search for peace in the Middle East."

What Carter boldly suggested was that Sadat should publicly agree to the American proposals to bring Israelis and Egyptians together for a discussion of all outstanding issues. Next, several Democratic senators, learning belatedly of the president's correspondence with Cairo, endorsed his effort to resume Middle East peace negotiations with or without a Geneva conference under the joint chairmanship of the United States and the Soviet Union.

Suddenly, the idea being talked about in the White House had assumed a more elaborate form. On the basis of President Carter's entries in his diary, the notion of a Geneva conference now had been set aside and with it there had been an apparent postponement of a discussion of the Palestinian issue—a separate state for those people—in any forthcoming conference. What the Egyptian president's latest suggestion called for was a summit conference in, of all places, East Jerusalem with the "disputing parties" and the five permanent members of the UN Security Council attending. (East Jerusalem lay between Old and New Jerusalem.)

Of course, the project was impossible to begin with, as even Carter conceded privately. He admitted to second thoughts about trying to put together a conference table for representatives of the United States, the Soviet Union, Britain, France, China and the Arabs, Israelis, and possibly even the Palestinians but he did not want to discourage Sadat. Without doubt, the Egyptian leader now was willing to take enormous chances for peace; in a talk with Secretary of State Vance, he had even mentioned a desire to meet soon with Prime Minister Begin.

President Carter noted, too, that Vance had notified Jerusalem privately of Sadat's suggestion but there was no immediate response from the Israeli leader. Tension was rising now at the White House. The international stage was being set for dramatic developments that conceivably could change the tumultuous course of history in the Middle East. In this extremity, the center of attention was not Washington, Moscow, or even Jerusalem. In that fateful early November of 1977, the initiative for peace had shifted to Cairo.[9]

19.   Sadat to Israel

The scene: the Parliament of Egypt in Cairo. The date: November 9, 1977. The speaker: President Anwar el-Sadat. The issue: war or peace in the Middle East.

For the fifth time in a little more than a quarter of a century, the bitterness between Arabs and Israelis had been stirred to such all-consuming hatred that still another war could have resulted at any time. And now, with the Soviet Union arming the Arabs and the United States protecting the Israelis, this was no longer a struggle that could easily be confined to the smaller client states of the great powers.

The larger danger was global conflict, a third world war, in which the leading participants would be prepared to fight and perhaps use the destructive power of the atom. To those who believed that such fears were exaggerated, consider how World War I began because the crown prince of Austria-Hungary and his consort were murdered by a Serb nationalist at Sarajevo and how a hate-obsessed anti-Semite led Germany and much of the world into World War II.

No, while even little Israel now was known to have a limited nuclear capability, it would have been madness to invite still another conflict of arms in the Middle East without an effort to save peace, no matter now uncertain it might prove to be. And this, at last, was why the world listened that day in early November when President Sadat, seemingly acting on sheer impulse, cried out that he would go to the ends of the earth to avert wounding a single Egyptian soldier. He added, almost as if it had been an afterthought, "I'm ready to go even to the Knesset of the Israelis to talk to them."[1]

So that was it—the open arms of an Egyptian leader, the successor to the brutal Gamal Abdel Nasser, who was offering to Israel what many Arabs still believed unthinkable: a negotiated peace beginning

160

with a visit to the heart of the enemy. Ismail Fahmy, his foreign minister, already had protested against his dealings with Israel, slight though they had been. Major Arab leaders of other Middle East nations, too, would be rebuking him, some such as even Syria threatening to break diplomatic relations. Still, Sadat, now in his sixtieth year, was taking an enormous chance for peace—and he doggedly stood by his effort.[2]

It remained to be seen how and when Begin would respond—Begin, the hawk, the braggart, the howling nationalist while in opposition to the Labor Party's thirty-year rule of the Jewish state. For he, too, had been talking of peace, but with strong reservations; to be sure, Sadat also wanted some guarantees, agreements that were better than mere assurances, but that was all in the future. For now, the question was "What will Israel's response be?"

The first response that night in Jerusalem came from Begin's press secretary, Eliahu Ben-Elissar, a journalist with a Ph.D. but very little faith for the opposition either in Israel or the Arab world. It so happened that he was first in line for press comments from the government when a reporter phoned to tell him about Sadat's offer to come to Israel. "Well, let him come," snapped the press secretary, either being bored or thinking the whole business a grand joke. He dismissed it immediately, apparently believing it a waste of time even to inform the boss.

It so happened, therefore, that Prime Minister Begin found out about Sadat's bid for a trip to Israel and the Knesset the next morning when he switched on his radio to catch the early news broadcasts. The working press thought much more of the story than the press secretary, and played it heavily. But at first, the prime minister, too, pulled a negative response out of his psyche. After consultation with his press secretary, he issued a brief statement from his office inviting the Egyptian president to Israel if he felt like it. The indifference of the Israeli response was so obvious that Cairo insisted impatiently that Sadat in all truth had been serious. Added to that, both Ambassador Lewis and official Washington took up the Sadat offer to visit Jerusalem with enthusiasm after Begin reconsidered his position.

The result on November 10 was a formal invitation, dictated for immediate radio, TV, and press use, for the Egyptian president to visit Israel. It was issued in Arabic, Hebrew, and English so nobody could complain, as some already were beginning to do, that the Israeli government had tried to brush off the Egyptian president. That, however, did not cool off Sadat. He was so fired up that he had Ambassador Lewis telephone the prime minister with an Egyptian proposal for a letter of invitation written and signed by Begin as prime minister.

That at last was when Begin and his cabinet decided that Sadat meant business, as Ben-Elissar, the press secretary, admitted. And this time there was no delay about having a typed invitation quickly prepared on the prime minister's stationery, which he duly signed with a flourish and dispatched at once to Cairo. Next day, Ambassador Lewis, the indiscreet go-between, notified the Israeli government of Sadat's decision to accept.

By that time, even Begin became impressed with the possibilities of hearing the most important Arab figure among his enemies, coming from Cairo soon, to stand before the Kneeset to propose peace. So it came to pass that the leading accused Jewish terrorist and warmonger among the one-time Israeli opposition was being honored by the president of Egypt as his partner in seeking peace in the Middle East. The Laborites who had inherited the mantle of David Ben-Gurion now would be the opposition.[3]

Although President Carter in Washington was pleased with the tentative arrangements, he was under no illusions about an expected adverse reaction to Sadat's initiative among other Arab leaders in the Middle East. That same day when Sadat had informed his Parliament of his desire to visit the enemy, Carter had met the Shah of Iran who had warned him that the Saudi Arabian king among others would be mighty displeased.

That, as final arrangements were being made between Cairo and Jerusalem, amounted to an understatement. Syria, Jordan, and the Palestininians, in one way or another, criticized Sadat for betraying his Arab brethren and accused him of dealing with the enemy merely to bring about the return of seized Egyptian territory instead of holding the line against the new Israeli attacks. For such developments as these, Carter concluded, well in advance of Sadat's appearance in Jerusalem, his bid to Israel for peace had made him vulnerable to the Arabs whom he was accused of having deserted.[4]

Sadat seemed cheerful and enthusiastic when his big Egyptian Boeing touched down at Ben-Gurion airport late on Saturday, November

19, directly after the end of the Jewish Sabbath. Begin, his somewhat nervous host, with an entourage, was at the runway to greet his distinguished visitor who appeared eagerly at the aircraft's cabin door, then clambered down the stairway to shake hands with his erstwhile enemies.

The Egyptian leader was in high spirits, a broad smile on his swarthy, moustached face. Those in the welcoming party noticed, as well, a dark patch on his forehead, most likely the heritage of Muslim prayers five times a day during which heads were lowered to the ground. An Israeli band was at the runway for the occasion to salute the leaders of Israel and Egypt respectively with the "Hatikvah," the Zionist anthem, and the national anthem of Egypt. Then there were greetings and handshakes all around with the new arrival very much at ease, slapping shoulders now and then as he recognized old soldiers in particular.

The brightness, even the gaiety of the occasion, was not exactly what Prime Minister Begin had expected, being a somewhat formal type himself; however, noting the relaxed manner in which President Sadat was taking charge of his arrival, the Israeli leader managed to relax but he did not seem to be enjoying himself while his guest remained the center of attention. Sadat was particularly attracted to Begin, of course, as the head man who greeted him first of all, but quickly enough he singled out others, particularly former Prime Minister Golda Meir—"the old lady," as he referred to her in a good-natured thrust, then followed up by saying he had thought of traveling to see her while she was in high office.

For the defense minister, General Weizman, President Sadat also had a special greeting when he saw the founder of the Israeli Air Force in a wheelchair because of a recent traffic accident. Weizman, however, was well able to handle himself, for he used crutches to stand up, then elevated one crutch in salute as if it had been a rifle. The Egyptian chief applauded the effort, then asked the defense minister to see him the next morning at the King David Hotel in Jerusalem where he was staying.

Still another old military opponent, General Sharon, now the agriculture minister, also won a special greeting from the Egyptian president, a reminder of how close Sharon's troops had come to the Nile after crossing the Suez Canal and trapping the Third Army: "We were waiting for you in Cairo," so the new arrival remarked with a grin. Then Prime Minister Begin rounded up his delegation, saw to it that

Sadat was suitably escorted to his suite at the King David Hotel, and put off the rest of the celebration for the morrow.

It was, all in all, a spectacular landing for a one-time enemy on Israeli soil. Only the Labor opposition, headed by Shimon Peres, seemed neglected and somewhat out of sorts. Also, Moshe Dayan, the strongman of the Begin cabinet as foreign minister, appeared to hold himself apart from the lighthearted proceedings probably out of judicious concern over the shape of things to come. Evidently, he still could not get over the way he had been treated by his Labor colleagues and his former Likud opposition while he was being blamed principally for Israel's unpreparedness for the Yom Kippur War, a failure of which President Sadat and his Egyptian armies took full advantage at the outset of the conflict.[5]

In stark contrast, it was of peace, not war, that Sadat addressed the Knesset on Sunday afternoon while confronting the leaders of his enemies. As the world watched and wondered at the calmness and the courage of this slender, elderly Egyptian, he began so quietly on television that his words in themselves conveyed a sense of high drama:

> Every person who meets his end in war is a human soul, irrespective of whether he is Arab or Jew.
>
> You want to live with us in this part of the world? In all sincerity, I tell you, we welcome you among us, with full security and safety. This, in itself, is a tremendous turning point. We used to reject you. We had our reasons and our claims. . . . Yet today I tell you, and declare it to the whole world, that we accept to live with you in permanent peace based on justice.

The emotion in the Knesset chamber just then was overwhelming. Menachem Begin's biographer reported that the usually boisterous Knesset was fascinated, that some of the audience shed tears. But then, this was an extraordinary moment in the tumultuous history of Israel's first thirty years of rebirth in the Middle East while the leader of Egypt, its greatest foe, suddenly swept prejudice aside to propose terms of peace.

For openers, as might have been expected even under these fortunate circumstances, Sadat stated unflinchingly the familiar positions his country had taken against Israel's conquests: a return of all non-

Israeli lands seized in 1967 and thereafter, justice for the Palestinian peoples remaining within Israel, and all the rest of the demands the Israeli government repeatedly had rejected. At that juncture, even the least hawkish of the Israelis in the Knesset chamber, the defense minister, General Weizman, scribbled a note that he showed to Prime Minister Begin: "Prepare for war," at which Begin nodded.

But Sadat's earnestness, which came through so impressively over television both in the Middle East and abroad, could not be dismissed so simply—and quickly. For the Egyptian immediately followed up, raising his voice slightly. "I did not come here to sign a separate peace between Egypt and Israel. A separate agreement between Egypt and Israel cannot guarantee a just peace. Furthermore, even if peace is achieved between Israel and all the confrontational states, without a just solution of the Palestinian problem, it will not be that just and stable peace for whose attainment the world is pressing."

Still, Sadat also stressed the penalties for failure, the worst being Israel's isolation, forever threatened with annihilation by its hostile Arab neighbors backed by the power of the Soviet Union.

"We were together in international conferences and organizations," he reminded his grim-faced audience now, adding, "but our representatives did not—and still do not—exchange greetings."

The Egyptian president did not have to add that such steadfast nonrecognition among all other Arab states in the Middle East would not be as easy to surmount; everybody who heard him was well aware of the difficulties that lay ahead if Sadat's offer of friendship could be accepted through a negotiation of his terms. Arab prejudices were not to be changed overnight.[6]

In this altogether charged atmosphere as Sadat concluded and stepped aside, Prime Minister Begin came forward to answer him. There had been no advance text from the Egyptian side; the translation from Arabic, too, had been halting and flawed so that the Israeli leader could not be entirely sure his distinguished guest had been completely understood. Anyway, Begin began with a mild compliment:

> Until last night, the distance between Cairo and Jerusalem was not only geographical. President Sadat showed courage in crossing this distance. . . . He knows, as he knew from us before he came to Jerusalem, that our position concerning permanent borders between us and our neighbors differs from his. However, I call upon the president of Egypt—and upon all our neighbors: do not rule out negotiations on any subject whatsoever. I propose, in the name of the over-

whelming majority of this parliament, that *everything* [here the emphasis was shattering] will be negotiable. . . . No side shall say to the contrary. No side shall present prior conditions.

The atmosphere in the Knesset now was electric. Sadat, who had found a seat at one side of direct view of the TV cameras, was leaning forward with an expression of intensity as if to anticipate the voice of the translator. His dark features softened visibly as he heard the rest of the equally generous response of the prime minister of Israel:

> We will conduct the negotiations with respect. If there are differences of opinion between us, that is not exceptional. . . . [here there was a wisp of a smile as the Israeli leader concluded] We shall conduct the negotiations as equals. There are no vanquished and there are no victors. All the peoples of this region are equal, and we will all relate to each other with respect. In this spirit of openness, of readiness of each to listen to the other—to the facts, reasons, explanations, with every attempt at mutual persuasion—let us conduct the negotiations . . . until we succeed, in good time, in signing a peace treaty between us. [7]

Now, no one was whispering of war, not anywhere in this remarkable scene in the heart of Jerusalem was there a sneer, a cynical smile, a derogatory wave of the hand as if to brush aside all these unprecedented assurances of goodwill as a kind of barefaced diplomatic vaudeville routine. No, here in this chamber, among the diverse peoples of the Middle East, there appeared to be a possiblity for real peace between Arabs and Jews for the first time since Israel once again had declared itself a nation on May 14, 1948.

For the vision that an otherwise pedantic prime minister of Israel had conjured up out of the fullness of his spirit that November Sunday was of blessed mingling of the diverse people of the Bible, of boundaries that all could cross without hindrance or fear, of parents universally teaching their children to love their neighbors, and of children, born amid mixed races and beliefs, being reared to shun hatred of humankind.

Such was the response of the prime minister of Israel to the president of Egypt in that emotion-charged scene, done without a prepared text because he had no advance notice of what his guest would say before the Knesset of Israel. Perhaps there would come, in the stillness of the night at some future dark hour, a sudden gasp of dismay from one or the other who had spoken that Sunday afternoon at what had been said—or left unsaid—that altogether historic day. But for now, for the moment of truth in an ancient land whose peoples had suffered so much, the dominant feeling was of hope that a new era had come to pass when peoples truly could dare to enjoy the peace of a togetherness that never before had existed in the land of Palestine since the era of King David and King Solomon.

Alas, reality in the livid faces of struggling journalists suddenly intruded on the two chiefs of state as they emerged from the Knesset late that day after their agreement before a worldwide television audience to seek peace with each other in a part of the earth that had all too often known only of prejudice, hatred, and war. Instead of the almost prayerful acceptance of the willingness of Sadat and Begin to seek an accord between their peoples and themselves, which distinguished the spirit of that rare afternoon inside the Knesset, the reporters of leading news organizations in the world—besides the local Israelis and their Egyptian neighbors—now demanded to know how this latest approach to a peaceful Middle East was to begin, and when, as well as how it could be expected to proceed.

For those who turned aside in disgust at the clamor of the journalists, let it be said here by one of their number for much of this century that few could be fairly judged by their manners, which usually were atrocious in a pack such as this one, but by the results they were able to achieve in clarifying the meaning of a momentous event such as this one.

As Israel's highest official, standing with Sadat as his honored guest outside the Knesset, Prime Minister Begin began fielding questions that were shouted at him from the pack in a babel of languages that would have affronted many another world leader save for the likes of a Churchill, a Franklin Roosevelt, or an austere de Gaulle. It was apparent, from the outset of this impromptu challenge by the assembled global press, that Begin's first instinct was to shield his guest who had risked so much to stand before his enemies and propose peace, regardless of whether peace ever could be attained.

What Begin decided to do on the spur of the moment was to handle the one question that a dozen or more voices were directing at Sadat: "When will Begin be invited to Cairo?" The responses, interspersed with more questions from different voices, ran something like this from the Israeli prime minister:

"Yes, I'd like to see Cairo. . . . But at this stage, I can understand why no invitation has been issued so far."

Interruption by the unworried Sadat: "Of course the prime minister has a right to visit."

Begin resumed, again trying to spare Sadat more belligerent outbursts: "You heard the president say I had a right . . . so we've only postponed exercising that right. . . . But maybe, because the time is so short, I'd better invite President Sadat to Jerusalem for a second time."

To that, Sadat in effect said amen with this observation that gave the newsmen and women still more reason for admiring the Egyptian's calm and his initiative: "May God guide the steps of Premier Begin and the Knesset because there is great need for hard decision. . . . I already did my share of making decisions by coming here and I'll be looking forward to those decisions."

With that, the news conference, such as it was, broke up and the members of the Knesset realized, if they had not already done so, that they were now embarked on a long and dangerous journey toward peace in the Middle East with an Egyptian partner who already was being denounced far and wide by his Arab neighbors for daring to talk of peace with the Jewish enemy in the legislature of the state of Israel. [8]

To President Carter, who had publicly prayed for peace that Sunday morning while attending a special early service at the First Baptist Church in Washington, President Sadat's visit to Jerusalem and his speech before the Knesset were ranked with the most dramatic events in modern history. The American chief executive and his family had heard and watched Sadat on TV at the White House.

Although Carter was thrilled at Sadat's symbolic gesture and the fervor of his address, there was also a somber realization by the American chief of state that the Arab response otherwise had been disastrous. For one thing, it was now evident that there was no hope whatever for a Geneva peace conference under the joint chairmanship of the United States and the Soviet Union. As for the Israeli negotiations in response to Sadat's visit to the camp of the enemy, that also was something over which the United States now had no influence.

In his diary for November 23, President Carter wrote: "There is general confusion in the Middle East about specifically what we [the United States] should do next. The same confusion exists at the White House."[9]

20. Begin to Washington

Within a month, Prime Minister Begin hastened to Washington with his own peace proposal, which he presented to President Carter at the White House. It was the Israeli leader's response to the worldwide admiration that had come to President Sadat after the eloquent Egyptian pleaded for an end to war before the Parliament of his enemies—an unexampled act of bravery in the bloody history of the Middle East.

Regardless of the mounting rage Sadat had aroused among most of his fellow Arabs through his brilliant initiative, he already had won President Carter's support as well as the attention of the American Jewish community, which had been so important a factor in the thirty-year development of the Jewish nation. Sadat's willingness to open negotiations with Israel, therefore, could scarcely be ignored, much less brushed aside with a mere casual show of interest.

By the Israelis, too, there was an entirely different outlook toward war and peace in this new partly conservative, partly religious Likud Party that had brought the Begin administration to power after a three-decade rule of the Mapai/Labor coalition that had begun with David Ben-Gurion. Gone was the reckless Arabs-be-damned attitude that had been so characteristic of Begin and his hawkish followers while they were in opposition to the established Israeli governments. Now the subdued peace talk that had been heard from Likud orators headed by Begin himself, became of first importance to this new administration in Jerusalem. Peace at last had to be given a chance.

As President Carter noted in his diary, Prime Minister Begin's expressed willingness to yield part of the Sinai area the Israelis had seized from Egypt in the Six-Day War was far in advance of anything that had previously been heard from Jerusalem. What Begin had asked in return from Sadat was to demilitarize a part of the Sinai closer to the Israeli border to strengthen the defenses there.

That, however, was the limit of the concessions the American president had noted with approval. He still did not believe that President Begin should maintain the right to build Israeli settlements in the heavily Arab West Bank or the Sinai, nor was there any considerable American support for something Begin called his "autonomy" plan affecting the West Bank and the Arab majority in Old Jerusalem.

Still, from Carter's point of view, the Begin package was at least a beginning toward what was likely to be a prolonged series of negotiations between Egypt, the largest and strongest of the Arab states that were Israeli's neighbors, and the Israeli government itself. For December 16, 1977, the American president confided to his diary: "We had a thorough discussion. I expressed my concern that his [Begin's] proposal was inadequate and that the inadequacy of it might lead to the downfall of Sadat. I urged him not to make any public statement about it until after Sadat has a chance to assess it. He promised to do this."[1]

In the Middle East, meanwhile, Defense Minister Weizman and President Sadat conducted entirely separate although related meetings that began, curiously enough, almost immediately after Sadat's speech to the Knesset. That Sunday night, Weizman and others from the Begin cabinet had been invited to a ceremonial banquet at the King David Hotel in honor of the Egyptian president's visit to Jerusalem and his appearance before the Israeli Parliament. Two other retired Israeli generals, Foreign Minister Dayan and Deputy Prime Minister Yigael Yadin, joined Weizman at the festive Egyptian tables but the two sides had little in common except mutual suspicions. Although Sadat and Begin meanwhile had a brief private conversation elsewhere at the hotel, their associates confined themselves mostly to formalities.

Later in the evening, the Israelis settled down in another private session with Boutros Boutros-Ghali, the Egyptian foreign minister succeeding two colleagues who had resigned in protest, and Mustafa Khalil, the head of the Arab World Bank and the secretary of the Socialist Union, Egypt's ruling party. In an altogether cautious manner, the participants agreed on further meetings in which to discuss joint problems when and if the atmosphere brightened. However, communication across the Sinai and the Suez Canal turned out to be even more difficult than had been expected; in so short a time, the doubts each side had about the other could not be easily overcome. In fact, what did happen at the first few Egyptian-Israeli sessions consisted mainly of reminiscences of past wars and battles in which the participants had been on opposite sides.

Still, the effort persisted. As Weizman wrote at one point: "In Israel, we were at a crossroads although I had yet to find a name for the new situation." And he added, "One route leading off from the crossroads was a little footpath winding its way into the unknown; its direction was indicated by an arrow . . . 'seek peace and pursue it.' "

Weizman's meeting with Sadat followed the next day in Jerusalem, their first, but little was accomplished except an exchange of greetings and a resolution by both to find some way, as Sadat put it, "to stop killing each other." The Egyptian president then made certain to invite Weizman and other Israelis to Cairo so that they could seek a better relationship with the Egyptian people. And with that, Sadat dismissed the Israeli defense minister and received an Arab delegation representing the people of the West Bank and Old Jerusalem, the shutouts to date in this developing effort of Egypt and Israel to find common ground for peace.

Although Weizman now took precautions to warn his military commanders against relaxing their vigilance over Arab border incursions, he soon found himself at Ismailia, Sadat's residence outside Cairo, for still another meeting with the Egyptian president. This time what Sadat suggested was the negotiation of mutual overflight rights, the exchange of ambassadors, the onset of talks about Israel's withdrawal from occupied territories, and acceptance of Palestinian rights.

All this was too much for the Israeli defense minister in the absence of the prime minister. It was evident then, after that second meeting for Weizman, that the route to peace with Egypt, as he put it, would be long and tortuous. There were no simple solutions to all the problems that continued to separate the peoples of the Middle East, including the Arabs themselves.[2]

In presenting his new draft of a peace plan with Egypt to President Carter, Begin emphasized Israel's willingness to hand back part of the Sinai Peninsula to Egypt while reserving the right to keep the Gaza Strip along the Mediterranean, which had never been Egyptian territory. He had also given much thought and argument to his proposal for "autonomy" for the large majority Arab population of the West Bank and, to a lesser extent, Old Jerusalem.

Upwardly, what "autonomy" could be taken to mean, from the American or even the Egyptian point of view, was the willingness of the Israeli occupation forces to withhold any claim of sovereignty over the West Bank but only for the time being. Meanwhile, the proposal contemplated yielding to residents of the occupied territories authority over their domestic affairs. But as for permitting the Egyptians to take over the West Bank or grant the area independence to be run by a proposed new Palestinian state, that was beyond anything that Begin would contemplate. So, in effect, the position of the West Bank still was a problem without a solution. And that was even more true of the Arabs in Old Jerusalem, for here the Israeli position remained that the Holy City, new and old, was Israel's capital and should so remain.

As for Palestinian rights, the Begin draft for a treaty with Egypt had been prepared at a time when the Israelis were not ready to grant Yasir Arafat and his Palestine Liberation Organization the right to be heard as a separate entity that was prepared to represent the second and still unborn state contemplated in the UN partition resolution of November 29, 1947. If the PLO could not be admitted to the bargaining table under Israel's terms, as Begin brought them to Washington, it was evident that much more discussion was in store for all parties.

What President Carter finally elected to do, in this troubling situation, was to recommend Begin's submission of his draft treaty to President Sadat at a forthcoming Egyptian conference in Ismailia. The Israeli prime minister won a relatively small concession from the White House when he indicated, in an amendment to his draft, that he would be willing at some unstated time in the future to discuss the sovereignty of the West Bank. The amendment read: "Israel stands by its right and claim of sovereignty to Judea and Samaria and the Gaza District. [But] in the knowledge that other claims exist, it proposes, for the sake of the agreement and the peace, that the question of sovereignty in these areas be left open."

Questioned on American television about this concession, the Israeli prime minister ducked the possibility of a Palestinian state being carved out of Israel's conquered areas, saying, "The first man to hear from me should be President Sadat." With Sadat's agreement to receive the Israeli draft treaty for review, a request made to him by President

Carter, the way was now open for Begin to attend a summit conference at Ismailia with his draft treaty as the issue under discussion.

For better or worse, what the Israeli prime minister had been able to accomplish in his journey to Washington was to divert emphasis from Sadat's version of Middle East peace to the amended Begin draft. Just how much that would mean to the parties concerned, however, depended on the acceptance of the main portion of the latest Israeli proposal. And as Begin departed for Jerusalem, that was just as unlikely a possibility as Sadat's plan for peace that already had been rejected by his former Arab allies, now for the most part his enemies.[3]

That, however, seemed not to bother the Israeli prime minister. What he seemed to want to do more than anything else at that point in the dealings between Egypt and Israel, as supported by the United States, was to establish himself as an equal partner with the Egyptian president among the other rulers in the Middle East who had deliberately reduced themselves to onlookers and, with few exceptions, foes of the peace process.

While he was in Washington, Begin had sent his public-relations representative, Eliahu Ben-Elissar, to Ismailia for a preliminary talk with the Egyptians, who were planning the larger session there later in the month. This was in effect a precautionary move, for by this time the prime minister was wary of still more Egyptian surprises. He was as a result impatient with Ben-Elissar upon the latter's return to Jerusalem with a grandoise tourist view of the Nile, the Sphinx, and the Pyramids. The prime minister never had been much of a tourist.

At Christmas that year, Begin organized an imposing Israeli delegation for the Ismailia summit, including Foreign Minister Dayan and Defense Minister Weizman, which he led into the glamorous resort city beside the Suez Canal. To make certain that his draft treaty would not be ignored in the proceedings, the prime minister persuaded Sadat at a one-on-one meeting behind closed doors to create two committees, one political and the other military, through which the decisions expected from the Ismailia conference would be analyzed and prepared for practical use by the participating governments. In a brief discussion that followed, Sadat accepted Jerusalem as the headquarters for the political committee in return for Begin's agreement on Cairo as the site of the military committee.

Once the conferees went along with both their leaders' proposals, the summit settled down to the intricate business of peacemaking, with Begin plowing through a clause by clause reading of his proposed provisions of the peace treaty text he had already submitted to President Carter. Sadat and his fellow Egyptians seemed bored on the whole although they raised no objections to the Israeli prime minister's performance.

That, however, turned out to be only a part of Begin's presentation. He followed up with an elaboration of his proposal for "autonomy" in the domestic affairs of the Arab majority of the people inhabiting the Left Bank and Old Jerusalem. It was, on the whole, a somewhat muddled proposition that aroused opposition among the Palestinians because it did not really give them enough of what they wanted and at the same time drew criticism from the Knesset opposition amid charges that the prime minister was giving away too much.

President Sadat's response to Begin was relatively brief. What he stressed, instead of bit-by-bit progress toward the problems separating Egypt and Israel that his opponent had favored, was the acceptance of several broad principles, such as Israel's agreement to withdraw from areas occupied during the Six-Day War, the right of the Palestinians to self-government beyond mere "autonomy," and other issues on which Israel's draft treaty failed to elaborate. With that, after a listless discussion among the respective delegations at the Ismailia summit, the president of Egypt proposed an automobile tour of the altogether pleasant Ismailia area—a favorite not only of vacationing Egyptians but also of international tourism.

Once the summit resumed in the afternoon, Sadat seemed in a good-humored mood even when he elaborated on his objections to the Israeli position. Although the Egyptian leader seemed to appreciate Begin's willingness to give up parts of the Sinai in return for Egyptian concessions on the Palestinian issue, the West Bank, and Old Jerusalem, the original Sinai offer simply was not good enough. In a few words, Egyptian security from Israeli incursions was as important as Israel's insistence on protection from Arab raids. "If I tell my people that my friend Begin said the Israeli settlements will remain in Sinai, with a defense force," Sadat continued, "they will stone me. Believe me, they will stone me."

It was a forcible way of presenting to the Israeli delegation the sensitivity of Sadat's deteriorating position in the Arab world. Because he was willing to talk peace with the Israelis, Arab leaders from Damascus to Baghdad and from Tripoli to Algiers increased their attacks on him and some were even demanding his assassination. If ever a seeker after peace needed support, it was this Egyptian president after having proposed an end to murder in the Middle East before the Parliament of his enemies.

Predictably, what Begin replied with were references to the 6 million Jewish deaths in the Holocaust. And so the two sides, each with valid concerns for the future, merely talked past each other far into the night that first day at Ismailia and part of the next until the summit broke up in painful disagreement. All that was accomplished for the record was the creation of the two study committees but they were given nothing to do. As Defense Minister Weizman concluded, the road to peace seemed to have turned into a blind alley.[4]

Within the Israeli government after the Ismailia summit, there also were disagreements although Prime Minister Begin had such a large majority in the Knesset that he had no fear of being overthrown. On what amounted to a vote of confidence that was forced by his critics in the Labor Party, he won by a large margin by insisting that his detailed peace proposal now was the principal basis for negotiation. If this were an exercise in self-delusion, as it appeared to be from the outset, it also emphasized the haplessness of Sadat's position despite the high regard in which he was held by President Carter and a substantial part of the American public.

As for Carter, he did try during a year's end trip to the Middle East to win the support of King Hussein of Jordan and the Shah of Iran for the embattled Sadat, both of whom agreed tentatively to try to change Arab opinion in the Egyptian leader's favor. But, despite such fair words, nothing happened in the Arab world to make the president of Egypt more acceptable while pursuing his peace initiative. Only the American president himself could do that and, at the beginning of 1978, he was reluctant to try.

In Israel meanwhile, Prime Minister Begin had turned to Sharon, the hero of the Yom Kippur War in its final stages, who now had been given permission to strengthen Israeli strong points in the Sinai Peninsula including airfields and to expand new settlements in defensible areas nearby. As if that had not been alarming enough for the Egyptian leadership, which now included Hosni Mubarak as Sadat's most dependable executive, Sharon also was building new Israeli settlements on the West Bank, adding to fortifications of existing bases, and even planning similar action in East Jerusalem, like Old Jerusalem an area the Arabs considered their own.

Such aggressive movements as these already had drawn objections from Begin's two chief ministers, Dayan for foreign affairs and Weizman for defense, both of them moderates who favored negotiation rather than confrontation with the Egyptians. Dayan in particular had argued for concessions his chief could easily have made from the vast Sinai area, which was larger than Israel itself, while retaining a few major strong points. But Prime Minister Begin, having already heard still more criticism of his dealings with Egypt from the Knesset, now could not yield to the softer line urged by Dayan and Weizman. The Labor minority's attacks on the prime minister in the Knesset were having an effect on his view of Israel's relations with Egypt. And that in turn caused Dayan, now grown older and less venturesome, to join Sharon in his campaign to strengthen the Israeli position in the Sinai by building more settlements near Israeli-held airfields—a procedure Sharon called "setting facts in the ground."

Sharon, in Weizman's view, had "lost sight of the distinction between his own personal good and the good of the state." But now, the prevalent Israeli move in the negotiations with Egypt, as enunciated by the prime minister, was the building of new settlements in the Sinai. These actually were armed camps, that would either force the Egyptians to agree to colonization or at worst set up a bargaining position to win an Israeli retreat.

All this was duly reported to President Carter when his aircraft stopped for about an hour at Aswan on his new year's flight from the Middle East back to Washington. So it happened that his first concern upon returning to Washington on January 6, 1978, was the deterioration in the Sadat-Begin relationships—this, as a result of the American president's priority in the conduct of foreign affairs mainly because of the risks any new Middle East war would create to the most immediate American interests.[5]

Secretary of State Vance, who had been sent to Israel with an urgent request to try to keep the negotiations going between Israel and Egypt, returned before month's end with a warning that a breakdown was imminent. What had happened while he was in the Middle East was a new flare-up in which President Sadat had threatened to end the peace talks without further delay. The reason had seemed trivial—Begin's remarks at a dinner in Israel in Vance's honor had offended the Egyptian president, causing him to withdraw his negotiators. Instead, he was persuaded to let Israeli negotiators come to Egypt, but no one could predict how long that patchwork truce would last.

President Carter thenceforth took counsel with his shrewd foreign policy adviser, Prof. Zbigniew Brzezinski of Columbia University, who had a bit of a temper himself. Next, when Secretary Vance returned to Washington with the gloomy forecast that the peace talks were doomed, Carter was sufficiently concerned to ask the retired Republican secretary of state, Henry Kissinger, for a counseling session at the White House. Out of all this, the president decided that he would invite President Sadat and Prime Minister Begin to the White House separately during the winter and early spring on the supposition that they might be more amenable to reason on neutral ground.

As to Carter's role in these emergency proceedings to avert another Middle East war, he decided—although not in so many words—that he would try to mediate the differences between them.[6]

21. Carter as Mediator

Although Jimmy Carter had the best of intentions, he had to sidetrack his Middle East peace campaign early in 1978. The American president was obliged to postpone a crucial meeting with Prime Minister Begin in the United States after a Palestinian terrorist attack in Israel provoked a violent response. With Israeli troops surging across the Lebanese border to wipe out Palestinian strongholds there, Carter was unable to complete his plan for what amounted to a peace conference between Begin and President Sadat of Egypt either at the White House or perhaps at the more remote and guarded Camp David retreat that had served as Franklin Roosevelt's rustic hideout in World War II, called "Shangri-La."

Carter was well aware that bringing the two Middle East leaders to America for make-or-break peace talks out of reach of the press amounted to a major personal risk for him and his Democratic administration. Coming so soon after President Nixon's forced resignation over the Watergate scandal, the Georgian's determination to act as a mediator between the Middle East combatants also led to a lot of head shaking among his White House intimates.

But this, President Carter had determined after long conferences with his advisers, was the only alternative left to him and to the United States if still another and even more damaging Arab-Israeli war—the fifth in a quarter century—was to be averted. Growing Soviet influence in the Middle East and the necessity of safeguarding American oil imports from the area—now amounting to more than one-third of the nation's foreign trade—had been the decisive factors in his decision along with humanitarian efforts to avert still more killing and even greater tragedy.

The damaging assault by terrorists affiliated with the Palestine Liberation Organization had occurred near Tel Aviv just a few days before Prime Minister Begin had been scheduled to leave for his White House meeting at which President Carter intended to broach the American-initiated private peace conference with President Sadat. The Egyptian leader, sadly discouraged, already had been persuaded to postpone his withdrawal from all further contacts with Israel during a previous meeting with President Carter at the Camp David retreat.

So now, the American president and his advisers at the White House had to await the outcome of this latest small war between Israel and the PLO terrorists before proceeding with the Begin conference in the hope that the Israeli prime minister, too, could be impressed with the necessity of participating in one more attempt to save the last chance for Middle East peace.[1]

What had happened in Israel early in March was a midnight landing of a PLO terrorist band from a rubber raft on the coastline north of Tel Aviv. Unopposed, the invaders stormed across the countryside, hijacked a bus and its passengers outside Tel Aviv, and then ran head-on into Israeli roadblocks barring their entry into the nation's largest city. At least thirty-five Israelis were shot to death in the gun battle that followed and almost a hundred others were wounded, some severely.

At once, and with good reason, Prime Minister Begin announced that he would be delaying his scheduled visit to President Carter at the White House for a week, then ordered his army to wipe out the PLO sanctuaries across the northern border in Lebanon. (With Israel in control of the Golan Heights in Syria and a Syrian army patrolling southern Lebanon elsewhere, the unfortunate Lebanese, divided as always with their 3 million people split between Maronite Christians and Muslims, seldom could defend themselves.)

Israeli forces responded with disciplined vigor to the demand of the prime minister before the Knesset: "Gone are the days when Jewish blood could be shed with impunity." When Israeli jets laid down a bombing attack in advance of the invading ground troops on March 15, the campaign to wipe out PLO bases in southern Lebanon took form with savage intensity. Within a few days, the Israeli mission of revenge was complete with several hundred PLO guerrillas on the run before them and thousands of otherwise peaceful Lebanese civilians routed from their homes.

On March 21, when Begin felt it safe to depart for his date with President Carter in Washington, the Israelis had advanced as far north in Lebanon as the Litani River but showed no sign of early withdrawal. Nor did either the Syrian regulars or the small and ineffectual Lebanese police force try to challenge them. This is the way people had to survive somehow on the Israeli-Lebanese border and this was the kind of attack President Carter hoped to avert in future years if he could persuade Arabs and Israelis to seek peace instead of living under constant alerts for wars large and small.[2]

Early in February, some six weeks before Prime Minister and Mrs. Begin arrived in Washington, President and Mrs. Carter had received President and Mrs. Sadat at the White House and flown with them to Camp David in the Catoctin Mountains in Maryland. That snowy weekend, aside from snowmobile racing and tramping together over the wintry landscape, Presidents Carter and Sadat evidently reached an understanding for a final appeal that was to be made to Prime Minister Begin, once he came to the United States, to try to accommodate his aims for Israel to the overwhelming need of all the peoples of the Middle East for at least a chance to live in peace with one another. To avert the suspicions of those who would undoubtedly charge that Carter favored the Egyptian cause, and had conspired with Sadat to the disadvantage of Begin, who was to meet the American president separately, no attempt was made to avoid publicizing the basic purpose of the meeting: to convince Sadat not to withdraw from the peace process as he then was threatening to do.

That in itself had not been a concession that was easy to extract from the Egyptian leader. From the time of the failed Ismailia summit in Egypt, Sadat's relations with Begin had gone downhill to a point at which the Israeli prime minister reversed his agreement to reach a deal on sovereignty over the West Bank, contending it rested solely with Israel, and also insisting on retaining intact all settlements created by Israel in the conquered Sinai region.

Begin's rejection of all bargaining principles later was supported by the Knesset, 306 to 206, which caused Sadat to withdraw from the political committee set up at the Ismailia summit and threaten to quit all other efforts to reach a peaceful agreement with Egypt. During the Camp David winter visit, he was so despondent over the chances for reviving Israel's interest in real negotiations that it was with extreme difficulty that President Carter persuaded him to delay announcing Egypt's withdrawal.

What Carter gained thereby was his chance to try to persuade Prime Minister Begin, upon his arrival at the White House late in March, to reconsider the harshness of Israel's position in the Sinai, the West Bank, and Old Jerusalem. Few would have given much for the American's chances then.[3]

There was a mystic charm about the effectiveness of Camp David as a meeting place for the decisions of the great, the near great, and even the ungrateful from the time it had first come to public notice as the spot where Winston Churchill and Franklin Roosevelt had conferred on the first American landings during World War II on the Normandy beaches against Nazi-occupied France. There, too, President Eisenhower had discussed American-Soviet problems with Premier Khrushchev on the latter's version of "the spirit of Camp David." (Camp David was incidentally named after Ike's grandson.) President Nixon, too, had used the camp as a retreat before the Watergate crisis forced him to resign, mainly when there had been private talks on international problems with the Soviet's Premier Brezhnev.

It was a measure of President Carter's confidence in President Sadat that the Egyptian leader and his wife were given a thirty-five-minute ride by White House helicopter to Camp David for their weekend visit to the United States. In the solitude of that mountain retreat, Sadat unburdened himself to his American host about the hopelessness of further dealings with Prime Minister Begin, particularly because he had so heavily backed Agriculture Minister Sharon's policy of building and arming new Israeli settlements in areas of Arab majorities—the West Bank, the Sinai, even East Jerusalem, which, though scantily occupied, was still claimed as Arab territory to the same extent as Old Jerusalem.

In a speech Sadat delivered before the National Press Club in Washington before his departure with Mrs. Sadat for Cairo, he showed flexibility in his bargaining position by agreeing in effect to demilitarize most of the Sinai area. He also suggested joint sovereignty with Israel over religious sites in Jerusalem and tried to avoid commitments on other disputed points except for his continued opposition to new armed settlements in the West Bank and Sinai under Israeli rule.

In the considerable period before Begin's delayed visit to Washing-

ton, President Carter tried to familiarize leaders of the American Jewish community with Sadat's moderate position in the downsized peace
negotiations apparently to try to build support in the United States for
the resumption of efforts to reopen the deadlocked dealings between
the Israelis and the Egyptians. It did not work. For when the Israeli
prime minister and Mrs. Begin arrived at the White House on March
21, he told President Carter he had been "wounded in the heart" when
his initial offer of withdrawal from the Sinai had been brushed aside
despite initial praise.[4]

After that, the exchanges between the Israeli and American delegations went downhill rapidly, culminating in President Carter's description of the Begin position as "the six no's"—no West Bank Israeli
withdrawals, no halt to new or expanding settlements, no Sinai withdrawals, no application of UN Resolution 242 to the West Bank or
Gaza, no self-determination for Palestinian Arabs, and no changes in
any of the above. Begin's dry response was that the American president
had a negative way of expressing the Israeli position, to which Carter
observed in his diary that it was a "heartbreaking development."

Nobody on the American side said anything about taking Prime
Minister and Mrs. Begin to Camp David for the kind of weekend the
Sadats had enjoyed. The Begins, having had a somewhat strained experience at a White House dinner, did not seem anxious to prolong
their session at the White House. And with that, the Israeli part of the
mediation process broke up in complete failure, Democratic fund-rais-
ing took a spectacular nosedive, and the Democratic Party itself was
otherwise damaged by the president's failed venture into Middle East
diplomacy.

Four months passed without any fundamental change in the position—either in Washington, Cairo, or Jerusalem. Nor did the Israelis
pull their troops out of Lebanon for as long as the PLO had a chance to
reorganize, rearm, and start terrorizing Israel's northern border settlements all over again. As for the Americans, they sold a much-prized
fleet of new F-15 fighter aircraft to Saudi Arabia with much publicity
that made the Israelis all the more resentful.[5]

At long last, on July 31, President Carter realized he was in a dread-
ful position both at home and abroad and decided on the only option
that was left to him. He wrote long and well-nigh identical letters to
President Sadat and Prime Minister Begin, then sent them to the Middle East with Secretary of State Vance acting as a private postman to
hand deliver the envelopes—each of which contained a personal invi-

tation from the president of the United States to confer with him at Camp David at their earliest convenience. Until both Begin and Sadat responded, Carter swore all hands at the White House and the State Department to secrecy because he now had no idea whether this last effort for a Middle East peace would succeed or fail.

To the immense relief of a beleaguered White House, both Sadat and Begin accepted quickly so that a public announcement was made on August 8 that meetings would start at Camp David for an indefinite period beginning September 6. Now Carter decided to go for broke rather than temporize, as his advisers almost unanimously proposed, when they recommended as a goal a joint declaration of basic principles for a durable Middle East peace. Instead, Carter scrawled in his diary the most difficult of challenges in a less than perfect world: "I directed our negotiating group to assume as our immediate ambition a written agreement for peace between Egypt and Israel, with an agenda for implementation of its terms during the succeeding months."[6]

It should not be taken for granted that the American public as a whole approved of their president's gamble that peace between Israel and Egypt could be attained through a private conference at a hideaway in the Catoctin Mountains. Particularly after the embittered experience through which the nation had passed during the Vietnam War, the almost instinctive response of much of the public to any new foreign venture was extreme caution. The long period of isolation before World War II that ended at Pearl Harbor had not been an accident of history. Except for the foreign-born, relatively few Americans at the time had much interest in foreign affairs outside the universities across the land and such views had not substantially changed with the coming of peace later in the century.

Whatever balance there was to rural America's characteristic resistance to most foreign ventures could be found mainly in the big cities along both coasts and sometimes in a few large centers of population in the Midwest. Consequently, members of Congress from such areas, particularly Democrats, were inclined to follow President Carter's moves toward a Middle East peace with an increasingly critical attitude if he seemed to be favoring the Arab cause, an accusation that now was being increasingly heard on the air and in print as well.

Such positions as these made it impossible for the White House press office to fulfill the president's fervent desire to keep the press away from Camp David during his conferences with President Sadat and Prime Minister Begin. Even if he had tried it, the hundreds of news people and photographers from every major American and other world centers would have laid siege to Camp David around its perimeters with devastating public results. Fortunately, he listened to reason in good time so that Jody Powell, who was running his press office, was able to set up an adjunct operation to service the Camp David news force, which was enormous and extremely active.

Regardless of results, good or bad, a nearby American Legion hall was rented by the White House as a press center, complete with offices, a briefing room, and a filing operation with two hundred phone lines, eighteen Teletype machines, and direct communications to both Cairo and Jerusalem. Beside the gate that marked the entrance to Camp David, a dozen phone lines also were hooked up so that any reporter on deadline could flash his office in a hurry—that is, if the opposition could be held off. These were not merely picturesque arrangements. Anybody who has ever covered a major news break for national and international audiences could appreciate the necessity of creating dependable communications systems close to the center of operations.

At Camp David, the three principals—Sadat, Begin, and Carter as mediator—could hardly be pinned down to a particular point at any time during the period set aside for the conference.

Each of the three, moreover, had a large and influential body of advisers. For Sadat, the Egyptian team was headed by Mohamed Ibrahim Kamel, his foreign minister, and Boutros Boutros-Ghali, his minister of state, plus five others in the foreign ministry and the ambassador to the United States. Begin was accompanied by Moshe Dayan as foreign minister, Ezer Weizman as defense minister, the ambassador to the United States, and five others. Carter had the largest staff, ten people including Secretary of State Cyrus Vance, Zbigniew Brzezinski, his foreign adviser, and the ambassadors to Israel and Egypt.

As for the press, the State Department had issued nearly five hundred special badges but these were restricted to the general area not including the compound itself except for special briefings. That was mainly because the principals and their staffs were distributed across the landscape in cabins, each with a distinctive name, and conferences small and large were operating long into the night as a rule.

Carter, as the only permanent resident, occupied a lodge called Aspen near the helipad at which he had arrived. Nearby were Dogwood, where Sadat was assigned, and Begin's abode, Birch.

Mrs. Carter, as the hostess, often worried that the cabins were too crowded but there was not much she could do about it. In Red Oak, for example, Dayan occupied one of two beds but three other Israelis had to crowd into a second bed. Holly, a center for the peace talks, was rarely used because the three principals seldom aired their problems together.

From the camp commander's office, where the Secret Service operated, other cabins dotted the mountainside, including Linden, Elm, Witch Hazel, Maple, Hawthorn, Hemlock, Chestnut, and so on, plus a dispensary, barracks, a waterworks, a tennis court, putting greens for golf, a swimming pool, and a bowling alley. At Laurel there was a large conference room that also was seldom used because Begin and Sadat preferred to meet in Carter's cabin the few times they were together.

Under the circumstances, dress was nearly always informal with blue windbreakers lettered CAMP DAVID in gold for the delegates and everything from sweaters and jeans or khakis for the rest. For relaxation, Sadat led the walkers with long hikes during the early morning hours while Carter favored tennis, usually with Mrs. Carter. Begin apparently never relaxed, maintaining formal attire throughout. The rest diverted themselves with everything from chess, for Brzezinski—when he could find a partner—to viewing a daily change in films, bicycling, billiards, or golf. All this was usually off-limits to the press.

Dining nearly always was a problem but the Camp David chefs seldom were at a loss in the frequent emergencies. Sometimes, Sadat was choosy about his food. Other times, because the Israelis wore *kippahs* and ate kosher, golf carts filled with kosher food could be seen racing across the landscape to fill a sudden demand from the members of their delegation. That never happened to the Muslims, however, because Sadat thoughtfully brought along his own chef who met all emergencies without trouble. As for the Americans, most of them ate together at the big camp dining hall at Laurel.

Special provisions, too, had to be made for prayers. At Hickory, which was set up as an emergency chapel, the Israelis and their accompanying rabbis used it for their Friday night and Saturday morning services while the Christians followed them on Sundays. Sadat, as the leading Muslim, prayed with the others in his delegation in private and there were no complaints.[7]

That was how affairs were conducted at Camp David for the thir-teen days from September 5 to 17, 1978. The theme was agreed upon by the three principals as a joint statement at the outset:

> After four wars, despite vast human efforts, the Holy Land does not yet enjoy the blessings of peace.
> Conscious of the grave issues which face us, we place our trust in the God of our fathers, from whom we seek wisdom and guidance.
> As we meet here at Camp David we ask people of all faiths to pray with us that peace and justice may result from these deliberations.[8]

22. Camp David I

Prime Minister Begin arrived at Camp David on September 5 with the doleful observation that there had not been any agreement between Egypt and a Jewish nation for two thousand years. Consequently, all he asked at the outset of President Sadat, who had preceded him, was a modest attempt to settle a few basic issues separating them.

As the host to the two embattled executives, President Carter could hardly have been surprised by such limited aims. But in any event, he solemnly repeated that the American purpose at Camp David would be to reach agreement on a durable peace for both parties. Begin, nearly always ready for the kind of uproarious debate at which he excelled in the Knesset, was all for starting at once but had to be told diplomatically that President Sadat was not available, that he had expected to start work the next day.

Even so, the Israeli leader then proposed to take on President Carter, after which Carter patiently explained to him that the purpose of the mediator was to encourage Israeli agreement with the Egyptians, not so much the United States. The American goal, he repeated, was peace in the Middle East.

After supper, however, Begin returned to Carter's cabin for a preliminary talk on the issues that included repeated assurances of American goodwill, an observation intended to allay Israeli suspicions that the United States was favoring the Egyptians in this effort to attain peace. Carter also pointed out that the Israeli and Egyptian delegations both had strong leadership, experienced personnel, and a frequently expressed longing for peace. It was, as the American president frequently emphasized, the American aim to make peace by establishing agreement on all outstanding issues from control over the Sinai and protection of the West Bank to the guarantees for Jerusalem while maintaining the security of all holy places.

If there could be no immediate agreement on all points, as the mediator explained, the issues could at least be defined and the positions of each side established so that the remaining problems could be attacked with vigor and goodwill in the concluding days of the Camp David meeting. The American also pledged that there would be no secret agreements, no unofficial United States positions on the issues unless both sides first were notified and every effort would be made to encourage compromises.

I doubt if anybody could have accused President Carter or his principal guests, Messrs. Begin and Sadat, of devilment and bad faith at the outset of the Camp David adventure. Yet, feelings between the three became so intense that Sadat and Begin never spoke to each other during the last ten of the thirteen days they spent together at Camp David and both on various occasions publicly expressed their doubts of the American president's good faith. On the American position alone, before the conclusion of the talks, twenty-three different versions of the key framework for peace were prepared.

Still, when the two principals and their mediator retired that first night at Camp David, all sincerely and honestly sought peace and all expressed hope that it could be achieved. But privately, both the Israelis and the Egyptians still believed from day one that the Americans were tapping their telephones and spying on them in other ways, grievous breaches of good faith that never occurred. As for the Americans, they began suspecting after a few days at Camp David that their guests somehow were leaking information on the proceedings to the newspaper, news magazine, and television correspondents, some of whom soon were proclaiming that they had exclusive insights into the negotiations. It all turned out to be a part of the saga of Camp David once it was completed.

Carter took voluminous notes that first night on all Begin's positions for retention of bases and territory in the Sinai, "autonomy" but not independence for the Arab majority in the West Bank, and complete maintenance of Israeli authority over Jerusalem as its capital. All these, as usual, also contained particular conditions to which Israel also demanded agreement from the Egyptian side. And despite Carter's continual questioning of the refusal of all Israeli compromises, Begin insisted the Egyptians would have to give in to his views or no deal was possible.

On the West Bank, for example, Carter insisted on knowing from the Israeli prime minister how much freedom he truly expected to allow the Palestinian residents there. The disarming response was total freedom except for measures affecting the security of Israel and the regulation of the immigration of Palestinian refugees. However, as the discussion continued, it turned out that the Palestinians would have very little freedom under the Israeli proposal, for Begin contended he had the power of veto over almost all local West Bank decisions, such as even road construction and the supply of drinking water that might affect Israeli security.

When Begin left Carter's cabin and the American president finally fell into bed, it was past midnight and the first of the long days at Camp David had ended with a sharp reminder of how far the combatants would have to go before they were even within reaching distance of an agreement. At the outset, there was no disposition on either side to yield an inch to the other side. The difference in method alone was frustrating, for Sadat believed in agreement on bold principles while Begin was all for inching along by considering each detail separately. However, when Carter challenged the Israeli leader on whether he was so bound up in detail that he could not bear to discuss the big picture, the quick response was: "I can go either way."

That remained to be seen.[1]

The grimness of the opening hours at Camp David softened perceptibly as the participants became used to one another and their influential staff people mingled with the Americans whom President Carter had brought with him. If the atmosphere became friendlier, that did not mean either side was yielding very much to the other at the outset. But as the influence of Rosalyn Carter and Aliza Begin made itself felt (Jihan Sadat had to remain in Paris with a sick grandchild), there also were times when a more relaxed air graced the proceedings.

At one time on the second day at Camp David, Sadat led off before a diverse audience of Egyptian and Israeli advisers and American staff people with his extremely tough opening position paper. President Carter could feel tension building as he watched Begin's hardening fa-

cial expression. In an effort to save the situation, the American president suggested cheerfully that if Begin would sign Sadat's document,
once the Egyptian finished reading it, all hands would be saved much
effort.

The whole room suddenly burst into laughter. Begin caught the
spirit of the occasion and asked slyly, as Sadat looked on, "Would you
advise me to sign, Mr. President?" Carter grinned, said no, and suggested that both the Israeli and Egyptian leaders might want to consult
their staffs. After that, in a more relaxed atmosphere, in which the participants seemed more at ease, everybody finally got to work in
earnest. It was time to put away the hard and fast Egyptian and Israeli
positions and negotiate, not so much on issues that still provoked pro-
found disagreement, but on those matters where a deal was possible.
Not that there suddenly were chances of instant agreement; far from it.
But the task of President Carter as mediator was made considerably
easier when, through tacit approval by the parties, such completely un-
resolved issues as the occupation of Jerusalem were set aside in favor
of matters, such as the Sinai, that might result in agreement however
difficult the bargaining might become.

This kind of a break in the toughness of the Israeli and Egyptian
positions, coming at unexpected times, permitted the participants to
review each other with a friendlier attitude. During a hard-nosed debate between Begin and Sadat at one time early in the sessions, one or
the other recalled kissing the TV journalist, Barbara Walters, and mus-
ing over what his wife might have thought if she had seen the affec-
tionate salute on the small screen. That brought laughter, as did an
observation about the hashish smuggling business across the Sinai between Egypt and Israel during which there was speculation over which
side was responsible.[2]

On the first Sunday, September 10, the sixth day at Camp David,
President Carter once again felt something had to be done to relieve the
continual tension between the participants that threatened so often to
cause the talks to deadlock in fear of ultimate failure. As a break for the
entire party, Carter proposed a trip to the battlefield at Gettysburg,
Pennsylvania, only a few miles from Camp David, for an afternoon at
the site of the decisive battle of the Civil War and the scene of Abraham
Lincoln's Gettysburg Address.

Because it was Sunday, a working day for the Israelis and the
Arabs, Carter made arrangements to spend the afternoon with them on

the expedition to Gettysburg. However, he specified before departure that there were to be no discussions about the peace talks during the trip mainly because much of the press corps would be at Gettysburg, too, for interviews and pictures. Once everybody agreed, President Carter planted himself firmly between Sadat and Begin in the back seat of his limousine and led the motor cavalcade out of Camp David.

The American president had escorted his guests to Gettysburg earlier during a tour of the countryside in general but this time he elaborated on Abraham Lincoln, the Civil War, and the meaning of Gettysburg in American history. As he proceeded with an account of the strategy of the Union and Confederate commanders, pointing out the positions of the combatants at various times, he noticed that the Egyptian and Israeli military experts were thoroughly familiar with the decisive movements on the battlefield—a part of their studies at their respective military academies.

Prime Minister Begin appeared mildly interested throughout, but President Sadat became enthusiastic when he stood at the site where Lincoln had addressed the nation on the meaning of Gettysburg and even quoted its more celebrated passages. While his guests could still reflect on the terrible sacrifices that war had imposed on a divided United States, President Carter decided to take advantage of the occasion upon their return to Camp David by unveiling the first American position paper for a Middle East settlement.[3]

Carter realized he was taking chances with the ever-suspicious and sometimes brusque Israeli leader, so he made elaborate arrangements for the presentation of the document by assembling the entire American and Israeli staffs for the occasion at their Camp David briefing center. Sadat, having already given his position paper, would receive a copy of the American proposals later that evening. But for now, the American president almost pleaded, it was to Begin first that the mediation paper was addressed with the hope, as Carter expressed it, that he would "be flexible and minimize any proposed changes."

There was one caveat about this first American position paper. As Carter phrased it, for the time being, three issues were not being covered—the Sinai withdrawal arrangements, the Israeli settlements, and the sovereignty of the West Bank and Gaza. If it were at all possible, he added, the first two would be handled at Camp David later but he doubted that the questions affecting sovereignty could be resolved at the current meeting.

There was an eerie quiet in the forum at which the American proposal was distributed. Except for the rustle of turning pages, no one spoke until Begin solemnly announced he would defer judgment on the American position and asked Carter to defer issuing it to Sadat that evening. The reason, the Israeli prime minister explained, was that Sadat's paper and the American draft now were before the conference but Israel had not yet given its view for the future of Egyptian-Israeli relations.

"I have already told Sadat that his is unacceptable," Begin concluded. "Therefore, we will produce our own because all three should be published. I will leave this room deeply worried."

Carter did not want to quit on so troublesome a note. He explained that the only document to be published after the Camp David meeting would be the final version that was acceptable to Egypt and Israel. Moreover, he emphasized that what he wanted both sides to agree on was full diplomatic recognition and the exchange of ambassadors, a status that could only come about—and this he did not have to explain—if the two nations settled all outstanding issues.

The American president argued once again that UN Resolution 242 had to be the basis for any agreement between Israel and Egypt, for it stressed the inadmissibility of the acquisition of territory by war, a just and lasting peace, withdrawal of Israeli forces from territories occupied in the Six-Day War, gave guarantees a territorial inviolability and the political independence of every state in the area, plus a just settlement of the refugee problem.

To Carter's amazement, Begin became so upset during their discussion that he would not even consider Resolution 242 as the basis of any agreement with Egypt. At that, the American lost his temper, warning that the deletion of Resolution 242 from the agreement would negate any basis for negotiation "now or in the future." The Israeli prime minister replied in kind.

That led, fortunately, to an immediate adjournment until later that night at 9:30. During the dinner break, President Carter had a chance to inform Sadat of what had happened, but the Egyptian, having had no part in the argument, kept his cool and went to bed at his usual early hour. But for the embattled Israelis and Americans, there was no sleep for most of that night.[4]

Begin led off the night session by introducing his attorney general, Aharon Barak, who led off with a proposal to delete all references to Resolution 242 from the American document. Carter at once fired back, "If you had openly disavowed 242, I wouldn't have invited you to Camp David nor called this meeting."

The Israeli prime minister observed coldly that he had been against 242 for eleven years. That flap continued for some time while tempers became overheated and neither side made any progress until Weizman suggested, "Let's move on." For hours on end, in a point by point discussion of the American document, Begin knocked down Carter's well-meant proposals and sometimes seemed to be trying deliberately to outrage the American president with such trivial suggestions as eliminating the words *Palestinian people* and changing the text to *Palestinian Arabs*. They also debated interminably the meaning of such words as *sovereignty, rights,* and *autonomy.* Nor did mere dictionary definitions suffice. Toward the end of the proceedings at 3:00 A.M., nobody in the room could be sure of either the Israeli's or the mediator's agreement on anything. Even the Israelis themselves became tangled up in confusion when Begin wanted to insert in the American document the phrase "Jerusalem, the capital of Israel," and Dayan, his minister of state, observed wearily that Sadat would not sign a document containing that definition of the Holy City. Evidently so tired that he could no longer object, Begin did not insist on his proposal.

Somehow, with help from Barak as the reader and calming suggestions from both Dayan and Defense Minister Weizman, the point by point analysis of the American document concluded and the meeting adjourned. It was probably the low point of the Camp David conference and it would require forbearance on all sides to preserve the amenities from then on. Sadat, after all, also had a temper, a passionate devotion to his country, and an often unreasonable desire to have his own way in any negotiation. And that night, he was peacefully asleep.[5]

Dayan, with his black patch so prominently displayed over his left eye and held by a black cord circling the back of his head, was among the last to leave the conference room when he was asked by President Carter to walk back to the Aspen cottage with him. Although the president appreciated Dayan's loyalty to Prime Minister Begin, he evidently needed reassurance that the disastrous evening did not mean that the Israelis would soon be leaving Camp David in a huff.

In any case, as they walked toward the Carter cottage, the president unburdened himself to the Israeli foreign minister with doubts about Begin's commitment to a possible Camp David agreement. Dayan assured him that his prime minister did want an agreement but retaining some hold on the Sinai was crucial to Israeli interests. What Dayan suggested was an Egyptian agreement to allow Israeli fortifications to exist in the Sinai for a short time after title to the settlements reverted to Egypt. The president was dubious, but said he would try.

The two men quietly talked of other problems in the darkness outside Carter's cabin while an Israeli guard with a golf cart waited at a distance to drive Dayan to his abode. By the time the impromptu conference ended, it still was dark among the trees surrounding Aspen although daybreak was near. As they shook hands and Dayan turned to walk back to his golf cart, he was so weary and the sight of his one good eye was so limited that he walked head-on into a tree.

"My heart went out to him," Carter wrote later.

The first streaks of light could then be seen in the black skies over Camp David as Dayan was driven away from the president's cabin.[6]

23. Camp David II

When the conference was well into its second week and pressures were constantly increasing among both the Egyptians and Israelis, President Carter could not sleep one night because of his concern about the problems facing all of them at Camp David. The prospect of a peace agreement seemed to be fading. The delegation leaders were rejecting even the mildest American suggestions for compromise. And sometimes, rumors swept across the camp that either Sadat or Begin was leaving.

That night, September 13, a Wednesday, Carter recalled that he had interrupted a heated argument among Sadat's advisers on the porch of his cabin the previous morning, an incident that was both unusual and worrisome because the Egyptian president was not one who allowed back talk in his presence. To the American, so angry a discussion appeared to indicate a breakup among the Egyptian advisers and probably foreshadowed the delegation's departure.

The more Carter thought about that entirely accidental encounter the following night, the more troubled he became. It seemed obvious to him that some of Sadat's more militant advisers, as he put it, were deeply committed to the cause of the PLO and other radical groups that might be adversely affected by decisions being taken at Camp David. Even more disturbing, when the American president had telephoned to Sadat earlier that night, the brusque response had been that the Egyptian leader had gone to bed early and could not be disturbed.

Carter, now wide awake, concluded that Sadat might be in danger and promptly telephoned the Secret Service, then got Zbigniew Brzezinski out of bed at 4:00 A.M. and sent him scuttling in his pajamas to the Sadat cabin to check on the Egyptian president. Within a few minutes, Brzezinski reported all seemed normal at the Sadat cabin except that the president still was more upset over a late meeting with Dayan than any fancied danger to his life from some of the hard-liners around him. He had misinterpreted what Dayan had told him about the importance of Knesset ratification of Prime Minister Begin's decisions to mean that all the work at Camp David had merely been an exercise in perpetual motion.[1]

Both Carter's sleeplessness and Sadat's tantrums were more than sufficient evidence, if any more were needed, that nerves were on edge at Camp David as what appeared to be the final week of negotiations there was drawing to a close. Prime Minister Begin, being both negative and combative by nature, seemed less affected outwardly than either this Egyptian rival or the American president, but he also had been making threatening motions about breaking up the conference prematurely.

The previous night, the Israeli leader had warned he would reject any final document calling for the removal of Israeli settlements in the Sinai, to which Carter had responded that he would refuse to prepare any document without such a formula. Both, however, apparently were so tired of shouting at each other that they departed with a handshake. That, too, was the way things were at Camp David that final week.[2]

The Israeli tactic of colonizing present and former Arab territories with families of Jewish settlers, something for which Ariel Sharon had been responsible as a Begin cabinet minister, now became the sticking point of the entire negotiating process. Through Carter's persuasiveness, supported by the formidable American panel of experts headed by Vice President Mondale, Jerusalem and the West Bank seemed to have been settled for the moment as issues and even the problem of the refugees had been bypassed. However, Begin still struggled to hold some of the final fortifications and the settlements that had been planted near them, a no-no for Sadat.

For the morning of the tenth day, September 14, Carter joined Sadat for Sadat's walk of about an hour and fired suggestions at the Egyptian president while they covered more than four kilometers. What the American started with was a proposed new highway to connect the Sinai Peninsula with Jordan, which moved Sadat to suggest that he would permit use of an air base at the Sinai terminus provided it was operated exclusively by Egyptians. Between that and a discussion of the American Civil War, Sadat had no further contributions to the Middle East peace process for the time being.

However, when the Israelis followed that morning with a request for a better deal on the settlement issue, the best Carter could do was to offer to put off the issue for future resolution without preconditions, something Sadat quickly vetoed. He wanted to know when the Israelis intended to withdraw without preconditions from the Sinai—and that was that. There appeared to be no way in which the American president and his staff now could avert failure of the peace conference.[3]

The next day, September 15, which was the eleventh day of the conference, Carter was at work drafting a speech to Congress in explanation of his failure when Secretary of State Vance rushed in with the announcement that Sadat and his delegation had packed, were ready to move out, and wanted a helicopter. Carter's first response was to order all hands to defer the arrival of the helicopter until he approved. Then, after taking a brief refuge in prayer, he joined Sadat at his cabin for a showdown.

Sadat, fortunately, was amenable to reason. While his staff waited for him on the porch of his cabin, he listened silently while the American reminded him of how his hard-line Arab enemies would respond with scorn when he returned empty-handed from Camp David after his bold venture into Jerusalem and thereby forfeited the worldwide renown he had won. Even more convincing and more important, Carter also stressed how close he had been to an agreement on all points with a tough Israeli prime minister. Such issues as Jerusalem and the West Bank already were settled, he said; the minor issues also had been agreed upon and all that remained was the question of Israeli settlements. Even here, he insisted, there still was a chance of movement.

When Sadat seemed to be wavering, the American president suddenly asked him to stay put for another day or two. And then, Carter concluded, it would be time for all of them to quit at once if conditions did not improve, in place of an Egyptian withdrawal before the session was over.

Clearly, Sadat was moved. He explained his sudden decision to pull out by blaming Dayan for announcing Israel would sign no agreements at the conclusion of the Camp David meeting. It had angered the Egyptian because it put him in the position of being the only one to sign a United States document bearing on peace in the Middle East and thereby giving away any bargaining position he might have reserved for later use against the Israelis. Carter's answer, given promptly, was that if either nation rejected any part of the agreement, the whole thing would be invalid.

With so firm an assurance, after considerable hesitation, Sadat agreed to stick, the request for a helicopter was canceled, and Carter returned to his cabin to continue to work on his speech to Congress in which he still undertook to explain his failure. Except for Sadat's deferred walkout, nothing had changed. And the Israelis, having observed the proceedings from afar, held their ground in anticipation of an American diplomatic setback at Camp David.[4]

During the evening, Carter and a few members of his staff joined Sadat and the Egyptians in watching Muhammad Ali beat Leon Spinks in their televised professional heavyweight boxing match. Having rooted for Ali, Sadat was pleased. But Carter's assistants who had spent the evening with the Israelis returned with a gloomy report. There was no change in the Israeli position on retaining a few settlements near the remaining Israeli bases in the Sinai as well as the West Bank.

It had been difficult for Carter to persuade Sadat to proceed as far as he already had gone toward meeting the positions outlined in the continually changing American drafts. But after the third day, during which Sadat and Begin had shouted at each other with bitterness and anger for hours on end, the Israeli prime minster had been such a problem for even the mildest consultation that the Americans had usually talked instead with either Dayan as the foreign minster, Weizman as the defense minister, Aharon Barak as the attorney general, or others among their fellow delegates.

Through concessions laboriously worded and agreed upon in a kind of shuttle diplomacy between the Israeli prime minister and his associates, Carter and the Americans had managed until now in the last days at Camp David to bring the two sides to within just a few steps of reaching a major breakthrough in their relations. But Sadat had come to the limit of the concessions he felt he could make and Carter understood his last chance rested with Begin. The Israeli leader meanwhile also seemed to have realized that his refusal to make the slightest concessions in his tough original position had obliged his cabinet people to work around him in an effort to preserve some semblance of cooperation with the United States.

Begin, of course, could have swept it all away in a grand gesture that would in effect have weakened the Jewish state's relationship with both the United States and eventually with America's Jewish community as well. That, as far as some of his associates were concerned, appeared to be what made the prime minister more amenable to compromise as the Camp David experience was winding down. Under such changed circumstances, Begin, accompanied by Dayan and Barak, proposed to meet Carter for a final accounting on September 16, a Saturday, which was the next-to-last day before the Sunday closing.

The American president was skeptical that last-minute Israeli changes could save the crusade for a Middle East peace. He had made an attempt that day to loosen up Sadat on the question of Israeli settlements in the Sinai but without result. The Egyptian president had consented to accept UN forces in the area, replacing the Israelis as they withdrew, maintain all buildings and airfields, and allow the remaining Israeli settlers three years to leave after the completion of an agreement. But, he insisted, the Israelis did have to go without an exception.

Dayan, preceding Begin's arrival, found no hope on the Sinai issue but, to settle a similar problem on the West Bank, he suggested to President Carter an exchange of letters between the United States and Israeli to which he believed Begin would agree. That worked when the argumentative Begin joined them, showing a new front of reasonableness.

The Israeli prime minister then proposed that, if all pending issues except the Sinai settlement problem were to be resolved, he would put that issue to a vote of the Knesset within two weeks. Seeing a dim ray of hope, the American president wanted to know if Begin would remain neutral on such a Knesset vote and received in return a pledge that the prime minister would release all his majority members of the Israeli legislature from a pledge of party loyalty.

Well!

That was the closest thing to a breakthrough the American leader had been able to pry out of the Israeli prime minister during the entire Camp David experience and the American delegation made the most of it. The switch in the Israeli position was a reminder of Ben-Gurion's observation that, to be a realist in Israel, one had to believe in miracles. President Carter, being desperate while teetering on the brink of failure, was in no mood for philosophy.

While a seemingly changed Begin now was orating proudly about making history, his American host feverishly produced the twenty-third of his drafts of the proposed agreement and went over the text paragraph by paragraph to be sure of no further differences from the Israeli side. Now a beaming, friendly Israeli leader was standing aside to let Barak and Dayan handle whatever arguments remained over the final American text.

There seemed to be a hitch at one point about accommodating the Palestinians in Israel during the pending negotiations toward an Israeli-Egyptian peace treaty once the Camp David accords were signed. Dayan handled that one, proposing to let the Palestinians be represented along with the Jordanians for whatever benefits were given to neighboring Arabs. The Begin delegation, too, responded to a last-minute plea from Sadat who, for some obscure reason, did not like the phrase "self-government for the Palestinians." What the Israelis suggested instead was "how the Palestinians shall govern themselves," a reshuffle of words without a difference, but the Egyptian leader accepted the change without comment.

The Camp David solution for Jerusalem was another story entirely. Here, when the Israelis seemed at a loss for bridging their position with the United States text, Carter announced that Sadat had accepted a proposed exchange of letters with the United States to emphasize the Egyptian differences. Begin and the Israelis jumped at the letter of exceptions and that deep divide had been crossed. Unlike the Knesset vote that had been accepted as the deciding factor in the last remaining difference, Begin now agreed that no new settlements would be built on the West Bank after the signing of peace accords. That left the issue of new settlements there to be resolved between the parties—and it would be so recorded in a letter from Begin to Carter.

As of Sunday morning, the final day at Camp David, there existed a shaky facade of last-minute agreements covered by exceptions, letters of intent, and various other devices to paper over the deep divisions between the Israelis, the Palestinians, and the Egyptians. As President Carter was painfully aware, all the work he and the rest of the American delegation had done during the thirteen days of their mountain retreat still could be nullified by a few bad-tempered words on either side.

Right off, as the American leader was going over the final draft of the Camp David agreement, he was informed by Secretary of State Vance that the Israeli prime minister had reread the proposed Egyptian letter about Jerusalem, which was to be incorporated in the compact, and refused to sign it or let it be linked to the negotiations in any way.

What Begin objected to, Vance said, was an impression conveyed in the Egyptian letter that the United States would be criticizing Israel for occupying East Jerusalem, which, like Old Jerusalem, was considered Arab territory as distinct from the Israeli majority in modern Jerusalem.

The remedy, as usual, was to rephrase the letter the Egyptians and Israelis were supposed to exchange with regard to Jerusalem so as to give no offense to either side. After several attempts, that crisis was resolved by reviewing all the statements about Jerusalem that had been made by American ambassadors and UN representatives about the Holy City. But within the morning hours, all was lost again when Begin and Sadat could not agree on a letter calling for Knesset approval within two weeks about the removal of Israeli settlements if all other issues in the Camp David accord had been resolved.[5]

This was the difference as Carter was given to understand: What Begin insisted upon was a statement that peace talks would commence after the Knesset had voted approval of Israeli withdrawal of settlements. But the way Carter worded it, such negotiations would not begin until after the Knesset had voted to approve the settlement withdrawal. This difference of words with the same meaning, after a considerable argument, was resolved in Carter's favor by Attorney General Barak for the Israeli side, whereupon the American president hustled off with the approved text to be sure that Sadat agreed. There, he encountered Begin, who had just ended a visit of reconciliation with Sadat and seemed very pleased at the prospect of a successful outcome at Camp David.

However, even after Sadat assented to the text in question, President Carter took no chances on his changeable collaborators. He had his secretary type final copies of the agreed texts of the three extra letters to be incorporated with the Camp David agreements, sent a copy to each leader and to each member of the American delegation, and called it a day. The accords, patched up as they were and still dependent on a Knesset vote within two weeks, at last were ready for signature at a White House ceremonial that evening as a preliminary to the negotiation of a peace treaty at a later date between Israel and Egypt.[6]

In front of Carter's Aspen cottage, just before leaving for the White House in a helicopter, President Sadat and Prime Minister Begin embraced each other and President Carter in a ceremonial love match. As Carter recalled their departure from Camp David, all three were euphoric and even the usually ascetic Begin seemed to have been lifted to a fantastic emotional high. It was after 10:00 P.M. that Sunday when the trio arrived at the White House to be greeted with congratulations from both the Democratic and Republican leaders of Congress as well as Rosalynn Carter and Aliza Begin among many others.

The signing of the Camp David peace accords, together with a nationally televised news conference, was conducted immediately from the East Room of the White House with a momentarily transformed Prime Minister Begin proclaiming to the outside world that the Camp David talks henceforth should be known as "the Jimmy Carter conference." While everybody was still applauding, the Israeli leader continued proudly: "We still have a way to go until my friend President Sadat and I sign the peace treaties. We promised each other that we will do so within three months [but] I would like to say a few words about my friend President Sadat. We met for the first time in our lives in Jerusalem. He came to us as a guest, a former enemy. And during our first meeting we became friends."

The far more realistic Carter concluded: "For a few hours, all three of us were flushed with pride and good will toward one another because of our unexpected success. We had no idea at that time how far we still had to go."

As for Sadat, always the realist, he broke up the party as quickly as possible by departing for bed and a much-needed rest after another eighteen-hour day. With his unprecedented venture into the center of a former enemy he had made possible the first and most important peace treaty with Israel in the history of the Arab world.

While the bitter-enders in Egypt and Israel shouted death threats amid cries of "Traitor!" President Sadat and Prime Minister Begin shared the 1979 Nobel Peace Prize while President Carter, their host at Camp David, led the applause for the risks they had taken at home and the sacrifices they had made. The Israeli Knesset, as expected, ratified the proposed Israeli withdrawal from the Sinai and thereby confirmed Begin's unexpected contribution to peace in the Middle East.[7]

24. The Price of Peace

"Blessed are the peacemakers: for they shall be called the children of God," said President Carter, with an apt quotation from St. Matthew, in concluding his report to Congress that Monday night about the Camp David accords.* In the balcony of the House chamber, as all the members of Congress burst into applause, were the most honored among the peacemakers, President Sadat of Egypt and Prime Minister Begin of Israel. Together with the American president, both would long remember the impressive scene that September 18, 1978, for it marked what then seemed like the foretaste of an all-embracing Middle East peace.

In the friendly tumult that rocked the sedate congressional precincts that night, all things seemed possible beginning with the soon-to-be-concluded peace treaty between Egypt and Israel, the first formal recognition of the Jewish state by an Arab power that already had been pledged to negotiate such a compact including joint recognition of the right of each state to exist together with an exchange of ambassadors. Scant wonder that the great American legislature had saluted the enterprise—and the risks—of the kindly and hardworking Georgian who was the nation's thirty-ninth president and shortly would be seeking reelection!

Carter had earned this night and his expectedly high standing in the unofficial national polls that it had brought his presidency after he, in common with the leaders of the Egyptian and Israeli delegations, had expected to be tumbled unceremoniously into the abyss of political failure after their Camp David experience. Now, within three months or less, so the prospective Nobel Peace Prize winners and their host

---

*The quotation is from the Beatitudes in the New Testament of the Bible.

had pledged each other, the great milestone of the first peace treaty—once a seemingly impossible goal—would be reached and exceeded.

The sense of anticipation both on the floor of Congress and in the public balcony was virtually without precedent that Monday night in the nation's capital. And President Carter, having concluded his report on a note of triumph, had every reason to expect that his chief partners in the Camp David accords would do their share to achieve the first peace in the Middle East among Arab and Jews in more than two thousand years.[1]

But even before the last echoes of an applauding Congress faded, there was an uncomfortable awareness among the political realists there and elsewhere overseas that the anticipated forward movement of the peace process was already striking unexpected snags. Some seemed innocuous, such as slight misunderstandings between the parties, to be sure, but there also had been published and broadcast reports in a newsworthy press and occasionally on the air that differences still existed between the Egyptian and Israeli delegations.

This was not the backfire of a mean-spirited and malicious White House press corps—always the first target of abuse when any American president undergoes criticism that seems unwarranted to his supporters. It already was being reported from Israel, for example, that the religious right, a part of the Begin ruling coalition, was rebelling against ceding the Sinai to Egypt and undercutting the new Jewish settlements among the Arab majority in the West Bank.

Nor was President Sadat any better off, according to first reports, for he was being insensibly attacked by his fellow Arabs outside Egypt for making common cause with a detested Israel.

To be sure, the royal family of Saudi Arabia remained in his corner, as might have been expected of an American ally that sends billions of dollars' worth of oil to the United States annually. But the once-dependable King Hussein of Jordan, surrounded both within and outside his borders by enraged Palestinians faithful to the leadership of Yasir Arafat, now held himself aloof from the support of Cairo's daring initiative at a time when Jordan's support could have made a real difference.

Such bits and pieces of unfavorable news at home and abroad made it mandatory the day after the congressional report that President Carter give President Sadat a courageous send-off before his return to Cairo at which the Egyptian leader counseled him as always: "My friend, you take care of the Israelis and I'll take care of the Arabs."[2]

But the farewell to Prime Minister Begin was something else again. It began with an irreverent note, the American president's presentation to his departing guest of a poster reading "Shalom, you-all," a greeting forwarded to the White House from friends in Georgia. Then, retaining a positive attitude, the American president cautioned his Israeli guest against permitting rumors to circulate about supposedly disruptive comments including denials of approving the three letters to which he had agreed along with the Camp David texts. Of Begin's embarrassment, there was no doubt, for his comments, so Carter noted, were evasive at best.

However, in New York City the next day, there were confirming reports of further disruptive comments by the Israeli leader, so President Carter was forewarned and determined to send Secretary of State Vance to Israel to try to forestall what seemed to be a buildup toward an outright rebellion. The reason, if this was what Begin then had in mind, was self-evident, for if the Begin supporters on the religious right were likely to withdraw their support of his administration, it was entirely possible that the still-powerful Labor opposition could make a comeback and take over the government.

It was such considerations as these that President Carter faced as the days lengthened into weeks without any indication that Prime Minister Begin and President Sadat were ready to meet again at the White House to formalize their peace treaty with agreements on mutual recognition, the realization of the blessings that St. Matthew had accorded to the peacemakers in the dim and distant past.[3]

Before year's end, there were some striking changes in both the Egyptian and Israeli positions.

To President Carter, American diplomats familiar with an Arab meeting in Baghdad reported that the Saudi dynasty, far from supporting the United States, had joined in condemning the Camp David agreements. Moreover, King Hussein of Jordan turned up there as a spokesman for radical Arabs, a group that presumably also represented the PLO.

Nor was Prime Minister Begin exempt from physical attack in Jerusalem, the city that he repeatedly referred to as his capital throughout, including the Arab-occupied areas. Even so, reports from the Holy City now confirmed that even Begin had faced extremist attacks, hav-

ing been set upon by militants in his private automobile while on his
way to a conference. It was splattered with pelted eggs and tomatoes
while stones were hurled at his windshield, smashing it although he
himself was unhurt.

In a telephone call to Sadat, however, the American president
learned the Egyptian president, who had been in direct communication
with the Saudis, was undismayed about the reports of a change of front
by them at the Baghdad conference. But when Vice President Hosni
Mubarak visited Washington shortly before the new year of 1979, he
took seriously the continued failure of the Israelis to resolve such con-
tentious issues as the disagreement over Jerusalem, the West Bank settlements being created by Israel, and the security of the refugees
represented by the PLO. For the new year of 1979, therefore, final
agreement on the treaty draft remained to be achieved, although it still
generally coincided with the Camp David accords. To compound the
problems being created for the treaty, Yasir Arafat let it be known that
he was boycotting all talks affecting the pact.

As an additional handicap that neither Begin nor Sadat had
counted on, Arabs and their sympathizers at most UN meetings in the
new year opened an anti-Israeli campaign in which resolutions were
adopted condemning the Jewish state's position on Jerusalem, Arab
sovereign rights, and the creation of settlements in areas with Arab majorities. Although such measures accomplished nothing, what they did
make it appear to the uninformed that the UN was condemning Israel.[4]

Almost six months had passed since the completion of the Camp
David accords, but President Carter still had not obtained final treaty
approval from the infuriating Begin, who continued to avoid agreement on the remaining issues. Sadat, however, appeared ready to sign
and the American president determined to try to complete negotiations
with him and the Israeli prime minister in a visit to the Middle East.

The American president had reason for concern. He reflected that
he had spent more time on trying to bring peace for the Middle East
than on measures more closely linked to the well-being of the American people. Until that early March of 1979, his failure had cost him
dearly, for his standing in the opinion polls had slumped from its high
directly after his success at Camp David, mainly because of the delays
in treaty talks that had not been his fault.

In this extremity, feeling desperate and badly let down in Israel if not in Egypt, Carter determined to visit both countries with Rosalynn in a climactic effort to save the Middle East peace for which he had virtually sacrificed his presidency. Upon their arrival in Cairo early in March, President Sadat arranged a triumphal welcome for them and immediately tackled all the troublesome issues that Prime Minister Begin had used to stall the peace treaty he had promised so fervently to approve in the name of Israel.

If the Israeli leader had acted out of fear of his Orthodox opposition to the proposed treaty, the course Sadat had followed was almost exactly the opposite, although he, too, had been bedeviled by his bitter conservative foes. In only about an hour, the Egyptian president accepted President Carter's position on all outstanding matters so that the solution of the last issues blocking the treaty now rested with Israel.

President Carter, for his part, also was anxious while he was in Cairo but not for himself or for Rosalynn mainly because of the magnificent reception the Egyptians had arranged for their visit. What worried the American chief executive far more than any second thoughts he may have had about the time and effort he had lavished on the treaty was the intensity of the Arab opposition that still confronted President Sadat. However, in response to his distinguished guest's concern, the Egyptian leader merely echoed his frequent response: "My friend, you take care of the Israelis and I will take care of the Arabs."

Even so, Sadat remained the practical politician when he and Carter analyzed the remaining problems facing approval of the treaty in Israel. The Jewish opposition would be unrelenting, the Egyptian said, and Begin might well try to stall through 1980 in the expectation that Carter might not be reelected and his Republican successor might ditch the treaty completely. But as for Egypt, he emphasized, approval of the compact was essential because he believed his country would be best served if he cooperated fully in all respects with the United States. And this, Carter later reflected gratefully, was a most welcome attitude because it came at a time when the Soviet Union seemed to be making inroads in the Arab world, particularly in the Middle East, by courting the rising Arab opposition to Egypt's dealings with Israel. As a result, both Presidents Carter and Sadat concluded that it was important to finish the Israeli-Egyptian treaty negotiations as soon as possible.

The rest of the Carter visit to Egypt, accordingly, became memorable for the elaborate style in which it was conducted. The American president was asked to address the Egyptian Parliament and did so to resounding applause. Then he was given a grand tour of the Nile delta with his wife that concluded at the pyramids of Giza and a tumultuous welcome at Alexandria. That, Sadat said proudly, was an experience he hoped to provide for Prime Minister Begin after the peace treaty between their nations was signed.[5]

Curiously, despite encouraging advance notices from Foreign Minister Dayan and Defense Minister Weizman, the Carters' visit to Jerusalem began in a disappointing manner. Upon their arrival at Tel Aviv airport, Prime Minister Begin and an official Israeli government delegation greeted them, then escorted them toward what had been billed as an elaborate reception at the outskirts of Jerusalem. However, a mob of protestors had taken over by the time the cavalcade arrived with the distinguished American guests, so the reception had to be canceled.

After being taken to Prime Minister Begin's home, President Carter had another unpleasant surprise when his host announced a point-blank refusal to sign anything unless both his cabinet and the Knesset approved of either changes in the proposed treaty text or the three accompanying letters that had been a part of the Camp David agreement. Even the Israeli president, Yitzhak Navon, had not expected such difficulties. When a puzzled Carter asked him privately about such checks on the prime minister's authority, Navon confirmed that Begin of course had the unquestioned right to negotiate a treaty on behalf of Israel and intimated that difficulties were being raised that did not exist.

What had motivated the prime minister's change of front apparently was his enlarged concern that the Orthodox parties in his ruling coalition would break ranks if he went too far toward meeting Egyptian positions in the proposed peace treaty that had become so sensitive an issue to the religious right. And yet, the Labor Party opposition in the Knesset, as led by Shimon Peres, himself a former defense minister, was wholeheartedly for completing the Israeli-Egyptian peace treaty as soon as possible. As Peres explained his position, he was against the government but not against peace.

To President Carter, stalled by a fearful and even reluctant Israeli prime minister, such assurances from the loyal opposition were heartening even if they seemed, for the time being, to have made an insufficient impression on the prime minister. And yet, it was understandable that the heartiness of the Egyptian response to the visit of the American leader and his wife, as opposed to the mingled atmosphere of hesitation and even outright fear in Israel when they arrived there, was bound to lead to rising media reports of the anticipated failure of treaty talks in Israel. That, at any rate, is exactly what happened on the basis of Jody Powell's daily briefings of the news media at the White House. It followed that the American press, radio, and TV strongly indicated the probability of failure for the Israel-Egyptian peace treaty.[6]

On the morning of March 13, preceding their departure, the Carters invited the Begins to breakfast. Then, as their wives left them at the table of the King David Hotel, the president decided on a last appeal to the prime minister to save the peace treaty by pointing out how few issues separated the parties. In return, Begin dropped his irritating manner and admitted that only a few remaining issues were of concern to him.

President Carter tried to resolve these doubts in his response. He guaranteed the United States would provide Israel with Sinai oil at prevailing prices if the supply were to be interrupted for any reason and asked only for an early Israeli withdrawal from the western Sinai.

Begin, suddenly matching the American's cooperative attitude, announced that he would permit the Palestinians to engage in peaceful political activity and would minimize restraints on Palestinians within the West Bank and Gaza areas. He also disclosed that Israel now held only 32 Arab political prisoners without trial.

Carter raised the stakes then, demanding Begin's decision on the entire Israeli/Egyptian treaty, but the Israeli leader refused to do so. Dayan joined them just then and, upon being asked the same question, took the American side. So did Weizman, who dropped by shortly afterward, but Begin still would not budge.

In the lobby, in what amounted to a last fling of the dice in this exceedingly tense situation, Carter offered to omit all proposals about the Gaza strip if Begin would accept the rest of the American package for the Israel/Egypt treaty. It was then that Begin gave in and made possible Sadat's unqualified approval later in Cairo; the Carters' mission to the Middle East ended in success.

Upon the Carters' arrival at the White House, the president was inundated with congratulations led by Speaker Thomas P. ("Tip") O'Neill for the Democrats and Henry Kissinger for the Republicans. As O'Neill put it, "Mr. President, you're not a deacon any more. You're a pope." The only sour note came from the White House press corps when the reporters complained they had been misled into believing that the Egyptian/Israeli peace treaty had been killed.

In a huge tent that was erected on the south lawn of the White House, President Sadat and Prime Minister Begin once again visited Washington together on March 26 for the signing of the Egyptian/Israeli treaty and a banquet in the evening in celebration of their success. The great gamble for peace, American style, lasted this time for several months before the nay-sayers on both sides once again slashed holes in this agreement as they had in the previous one for the Camp David accords. After that, Carter said toward the end of his presidency, "We did the best we could to bridge this wide gap and won a partial victory."[7]

Long after the Camp David accords and the Israeli-Egyptian peace treaty had become history, the leader of the Israeli opposition, Shimon Peres, concluded that the negotiations resolved only one issue, peace between the two enemies in the Middle East, and all other problems were left for later resolution—Jerusalem, the Palestinians, and peace between Israel and other Arab nations. These, Peres argued, were treated in what he called "cosmetic accords" and side letters that, in reality, settled very little. He discounted the pledge for Palestinian "autonomy," for one thing, and he called the appeal to other Arab countries for peace a "sop" primarily to Syria.

As to the rest, Peres held that Begin had given up "every grain of sand" in the Sinai, failed to keep his pledge to live out his life among the Israeli settlers there, and even had removed the last settlers by force, adding, "Perhaps only a right wing government can take such action." Nor did he believe Camp David provided a solution for the Palestinians. And as for Jerusalem, that key issue, he contended, was summed up in the exchange of letters that showed the partners had agreed to disagree.

Peres, a latter-day prime minister of Israel, was more generous to Jimmy Carter, and wrote: "Without the unique contribution of Jimmy Carter, there would have been no Camp David accord. . . . That success became his greatest achievement as president."

As for the Egyptian/Israeli treaty, the opposition leader had this to reflect on for succeeding generations: "The great breakthrough in the agreement with Egypt consisted in the fact that this was our first treaty with an Arab country. But the peace with Egypt also was the easiest. The Sinai is not the Holy Land, the historic homeland of the Jewish people. The Sinai, moreover, is virtually empty; once it is demilitarized by agreement, the question of sovereignty over it becomes less important. The other fronts, I always realized, would be tougher to resolve."

That became the problem for the Israeli government of Menachem Begin as well. But before the end of the dream, he had the satisfaction of being given a grand welcome in Cairo by his erstwhile foe, President Sadat, something the Israeli leader never forgot. As he shouted into a telephone to President Carter in Washington, "The people of Egypt opened their hearts to me. . . . I am very moved. I left by car for a while . . . went into the crowd, which was crying, 'We like you, we love you.' It was absolutely wonderful!"[8]

But for President Carter, and the leaders of Egypt and Israel who became his chief beneficiaries, the price of peace soon became discouragingly high. From Palestine to Iran, raging Muslim fundamentalists for some time had been trying to arouse the Arab world in turn against all "foreign" influences, including Israel and the United States, with grave consequences for both. Each dispute, whether it involved Egyptian dealings with Israel, or the religious sanctity of the rights of the Palestinian or Iranian peoples, became a cause that was fought for with violence that often burst all bounds.

So it happened, while Egypt and Israel were trying to build a cautious peaceful relationship through American patronage, a fundamentalist mullah seized control of Iran from the shah, Mohammad Reza Pahlavi, and took ninety hostages, including more than fifty Americans, from the American embassy in Tehran. On November 4, 1979, an otherwise quiet Sunday morning in Washington, D.C., President Carter learned of the demands of the mullah, Ayatollah Ruhallah Khomeini, soon after having approved the admission of the shah to a New York hospital for urgent medical treatment.

For the United States to have returned the shah to the ayatollah and his followers in Tehran was out of the question, but so was an immediate armed response, particularly after the president had presided over so long and difficult a negotiation to restore peace between Egypt and Israel. Instead, Carter froze several billion dollars' worth of Iranian assets in the United States while directing the State Department to make efforts, possibly with help from Israel, to obtain the release of the American hostages. As for Egypt, President Sadat already had been warned of the possibility that fundamentalist Arabs might be trying to harm him and was in military alert.

Surmounting all of Carter's trouble at the onset of the presidential election year of 1980 was the challenge that already was being flung at his staggered administration by the forceful and attractive Republican candidate, Gov. Ronald Reagan of California, the movie star turned politician. From the high point the president had reached in his polls directly after the completion of the peace treaty between Egypt and Israel, his standing had slumped considerably and there seemed to be very little that he could do about it.

For the American people, the detention of Americans seized in Iran, together with rising terror spread by Palestinian intruders from Lebanon on Israel's northern borders, constituted a twin blow against the way Carter was handling American foreign policy—a situation of which Governor Reagan took full advantage. That, together with the declining American economy and rising unemployment figures, also struck hard at the president's chances for reelection. For all his efforts in the cause of peace, this kindly and devoted American leader deserved something better for his future prospects but it simply was not turning out that way.[9]

For Jimmy Carter the price of peace in the Middle East came very high.

25. War on Terrorism

Regardless of the handicaps Jimmy Carter had to face as president, he never lacked for courage.

On a lovely spring morning in 1980 when he was making his secret effort to rescue the American hostages in Iran, he learned that an Israeli with experience in the field happened to be paying a courtesy call at the White House. The visitor, Shimon Peres, chief of the Labor Party's opposition to Prime Minister Begin, was widely known as the Israeli defense minister who had headed the successful effort in 1976 to rescue hostages who had been held in Uganda.

Acting purely on a hunch that otherwise pleasant April 24, the president welcomed Peres at once to the Oval Office and, without explanation, asked him what he would do, if he were in the president's position, about rescuing the American hostages who had now been held captive in Iran for five months and twenty days.

The tough-minded Israeli, not knowing that an American effort already was under way to save the hostages, hesitated not one moment in urging such action regardless of risks. He argued that his government had taken far greater chances in far-off Uganda and thereby saved many lives. In response to the president's apparent concern about the penalties for failure, the visitor responded that such hazards had to be faced by any responsible government, that in fact the Israeli regime had been obliged to work against time and operate almost entirely in the dark in its hostage crisis.

Against terrorism, the Israeli concluded, there could be no guarantees of success in an emergency rescue operation, but, unless the cause seemed hopeless, the enormous gamble involved would have to be taken. That, at least, as Peres explained, had been the reasoning of the Israeli government behind its rescue operation. Just as abruptly as the

213

Oval Office session had begun, the care-worn president dismissed his caller with thanks and said he had been helpful.[1]

Not until that afternoon, while waiting at National Airport to board a New York–bound plane, did Peres hear the official radio announcement of the disaster that had wrecked the American rescue effort at a lonely assembly point in the Iranian desert outside Tehran.[2]

Later, asked to comment on the Barbara Walters TV news program that day, Peres praised the president's courage, said he had made the right decision, that the effort to save the hostages had to be made. It was about the best that any outside observer could do under the circumstances, as the White House acknowledged with thanks to the Israeli visitor.[3] But neither then nor later was it possible for the Carter administration to conceal the severe blow it had suffered in public opinion, for from then on the Ayatollah Khomeini and his mullahs separated the American hostages from the rest, scattered them around Tehran in secret hideaways, and made it virtually impossible for any new rescue attempt to be made.[4]

But meanwhile, for the rest of that presidential election year in the United States, the freeing of the hostages became so important an issue in Governor Reagan's successful Republican campaign that he consistently led Carter in the polls through election day, when he scored a landslide victory in the electoral college, 489 to 49, and a massive plurality of about eight million votes in the popular tally. When Reagan moved into the White House on January 20, 1981, the Ayatollah Khomeini obliged him by releasing the sixty-two American hostages who had been held in Iran for 444 days. The price for the United States was the return of Iranian frozen assets valued at $8 billion plus a secret weapons deal that was not publicly disclosed for years thereafter and even then never affected President Reagan's enormous personal popularity.[5]

While the United States was tied up during that presidential election year, and for some time afterward even with President Reagan in the White House, Prime Minister Begin and his Israeli army generals planned an assault on Palestinian terrorists who had been operating in northern Israel from strongholds across the border in Lebanon. As a test of possible objections from the United States, the Begin government announced in July 1980, during the American presidential campaign, that all of Jerusalem from then on would be the nation's capital and a part of East Jerusalem would be annexed for the building of more Jewish settlements in former Arab territory.

President Carter at the time was so preoccupied with the Iranian hostage crisis and the Reagan challenge that he offered no serious objection to support Arab complaints that Israel was violating the Camp David accords.[6] That was when the Israeli attack began in earnest on terrorism. Nor was President Reagan overly concerned, once he took charge in 1981, when the Israelis extended their anti-Arab offensive as their bombers destroyed a nuclear reactor near Baghdad in Iraq on June 7, charging it could have been used when completed in the building of atomic explosives. Iran and Iraq at the time had been locked in the first year of what developed into a long war that hurt both of them.[7]

Four months later, on October 6, President Sadat was shot and killed in Cairo by assassins while he was viewing a military parade and was succeeded at once by his vice president, Hosni Mubarak, also a trusted American ally. Even though President Reagan could not risk appearing in Cairo upon the advice of his Secret Service guards, he sent three former presidents—Carter, Nixon, and Ford—to the funeral of the slain Egyptian leader. Another among the eighty chiefs of state who attended, Prime Minister Begin, came from Jerusalem to pay his tribute to the Egyptian leader who had given his life for peace.[8]

The previous June, Begin and his Likud coalition had defeated Shimon Peres and his Labor Party once again and now were well started on a second term in high office. Accordingly, upon returning to Jerusalem after the services for President Sadat in Cairo, the Israeli prime minister saw no reason to hesitate any longer about an all-out offensive against the Palestinian terrorists who were steadily increasing their raids across Israel's northern borders from bases in Lebanon.

To lead the assault, Begin chose the hero of the Yom Kippur War, Gen. Ariel Sharon, as defense minister with full authority to invade the Lebanese countryside, including an assault on the capital, Beirut, if it became necessary to do so. As allies, General Sharon was authorized to cooperate with the Lebanese Christian militia, known as the Phalangists, who were the traditional opponents of the Muslim Palestinians. Unlike the 1978 border conflict against the Lebanese terrorists that was halted at the Litani River, there were no limits to this one (and Sharon, on his own initiative, extended his orders once he and his troops crossed the Lebanese border).[9]

There were thirty thousand Syrian troops in Lebanon at the time, together with the Palestinian guerrillas, and a series of Syrian antiaircraft batteries were in the Lebanese Bekaa Valley. However, the Israeli commander had permission from the outset to attack the Syrians as well as the Palestinians who operated against Israel from Lebanon. And once all was in order for the assault, the ever-cautious Begin made a special trip to Washington, D.C., for something more than a courtesy call on President Reagan. During skirmishes with the Palestinians on the Lebanese border in the opening year of the Reagan administration, the American president had reason more than once to warn the Israeli prime minister against too much hostile activity against Lebanon and Syria along their borders with the Jewish state. But this time, Reagan showed little patience with Begin's talk of Palestinian guerrillas as Communist allies and Syria's ties to the Soviet Union. Instead of pursuing the subject, the American president merely referred the visiting Israeli leader to various White House deputies who would clear up whatever differences there were between them.[10]

Upon returning to Jerusalem, however, Begin was in a rebellious mood because Palestinian border warfare had been on the increase. Then, on June 3, 1982, Palestinian guerrillas were blamed for an attack that day on the Israeli ambassador in London. That, Prime Minister Begin decided, was the signal for the all-out attack on the Palestinians that he had been planning for so long. As a result, he gave General Sharon permission to move across the Lebanese border and on June 6 the Israeli invasion began by land, sea, and air.

Three days later, while heading for the capital of Beirut under General Sharon's command, Israeli forces were held up in the Bekaa Valley where Israeli jets attacked and destroyed seventeen Syrian antiaircraft missile batteries in the valley. With nearly all resistance contained thereafter, the Lebanese capital was encircled and cut off on June 14 by the Israeli invaders amid cautionary messages from both the White House and the Pentagon. But the Christian leader of Lebanon, Bashir Gemayel, allied himself and his Phalangist (Christian) militia with the invading Israelis, so it became difficult to stop General Sharon and his forces.[11]

The White House now took a stronger position, demanding a cease-fire of Prime Minister Begin. He temporized, agreeing sometimes but later holding off. An impatient White House worried with good reason about the possibility of a much larger war if this conflict of interest continued and demanded restraint. But General Sharon, as defense minister, seemed to have burst out of control to the consternation of a divided Israeli cabinet and a Knesset in which the majority leader,

Peres, criticized what he called the government's "misguided approach." That, of course, was putting it mildly.[12]

What had happened was that an Israeli cabinet-approved decision to clear southern Lebanon of the Palestinians to a depth of twenty-five miles, a logical proposal to limit incursions into northern Israel, had been brushed aside by a defense minister eager to make a showing and a prime minister who seemed genuinely afraid of interfering with him. What the Israeli offensive had developed into went far beyond twenty-five miles, concentrating as it did on the military encirclement of Beirut, normally a city of about a million people—almost one-quarter of the population of the entire country.

President Reagan let it be known that he disapproved of shelling a virtually defenseless Beirut, as General Sharon already was doing. Now more proposals for a cease-fire emanated from Washington while Prime Minister Begin seemed unable to make a decision that would undercut his defense minister. This kind of stop-go war continued for much of the summer with part of General Sharon's activity shifting to the support of Gemayel's Christians in East Beirut while concentrating on punitive measures against Muslim West Beirut with its two large camps of Palestinian refugees.

All the while, the White House was leaving no doubt of its disapproval of the entire operation, particularly when American TV carried the most tragic illustrations of the deaths of little children in the Israeli bombing attacks on Beirut. Still, Prime Minister Begin evidently could not decide to shut down the offensive and General Sharon insisted on maintaining it even though whatever resistance there now existed in Beirut was so weak as to be completely ineffective. Only passing notice was taken during the 1982 summer of the election of the Christian leader, Gemayel, as president of Lebanon, although he could scarcely have functioned under the circumstances.[13]

But on September 14, after a disastrous summer for Lebanon, President Gemayel was assassinated. Two days later, the Lebanese Christian militia swept into West Beirut and was blamed for the slaughter of many Palestinian refugees in the two camps there. The consequences were so shocking that protests from the United States as well as the Labor opposition in the Knesset overwhelmed a weakening prime minister. Now the Israeli opposition was furious, demanding an inquiry into the entire military operation amid proposals in the Knesset for the immediate removal of Sharon as defense minister.[14]

At first, Prime Minister Begin swept aside all the opposition's clamor for Sharon's removal. But eventually, Sharon's position could not be maintained in the face of well-nigh worldwide criticism of the slaughter in West Beirut's refugee camps, although he was retained as a minister without portfolio in the cabinet after having been relieved as defense minister. As for the Israeli army, although its mission against the Palestinians had long since been completed, it remained in Lebanon for about three years while the tormented nation tried as best it could at successive elections to solve the problems that had been created by its government and the Israelis.

To Peres, still Labor's opposition leader in the Knesset, the entire Lebanese episode had been a blow to the nation's reputation and he tried as best he could to counteract it. But Begin fought back, refusing to concede wrongdoing. To resolve the conflict, the Knesset authorized the formation of a commission of inquiry into Israel's responsibility for the massacres in West Beirut, with Supreme Court Justice Yitzhak Kahan as chairman. Even so, the prime minister remained defiant, responding with a letter in which he argued that no one could have predicted such a catastrophe and disclaimed fault.

In the commission's final report, however, Begin was held responsible "for not having evidenced . . . any interest in the Phalangists' activity in the [West Beirut] camps." In self-justification, he continued to insist the war against terror had been necessary, called it a victory, and refused to abandon General Sharon to their critics. Together, they defeated a Labor attempt in the Knesset to force through a vote of "no confidence" that would have toppled the government.[15]

As months passed, the prime minister's emotional and physical decline became evident even to some of his most loyal supporters although his personal popularity dropped only marginally in the polls. He took to staying by himself, particularly after the death of his wife after a long illness. Thereafter, the White House tactfully suggested a visit with President Reagan, but no reply came from Jerusalem. And on August 29, 1983, offering no advance notification to anybody, Begin called the cabinet into an emergency meeting and submitted his resignation without explanation except for a soft-voiced exit line: "I cannot go on."

Still, because the prime minister had designated no successor and his term did not expire for a year, he was thrust in the always difficult position of a chief executive who had to remain in power temporarily despite his insistence on retiring from the cares of high office. And so it turned out that his sharply divided nation still looked to him for decisions as the head of state that he refused to make, and no one, not even the president, could intervene for him by law.

In this extremity, the Likud coalition had to face up to its responsibilities as the nation's ruling political party and designate a successor to the prime minister. The appointee was to rule through the forthcoming 1984 elections for which the eager Laborites already were preparing under Peres's leadership. After anxious consultations with the remaining representatives of the Likud group—Herut, the Liberals, and the smaller religious parties—the outgoing prime minister was replaced by his foreign minister, the sixty-nine-year-old Yitzhak Shamir, a still active founder of the nation from Ben-Gurion's era.[16]

Shamir was both a safe and a credible choice to lead the nation through another tense and uncertain period in its history. Born Yitzhak Jazernicki in Poland in 1915, he had climaxed his schooling in Poland with a law degree from the Hebrew University upon his immigration to Palestine, where he became a member of the Irgun Zvai Leumi and a founder of the Stern gang. Upon his arrest by the sovereign British in 1941, he was exiled to Eritrea but resumed activity when he returned to Palestine in 1948 as one of the founders of the new nation. He became successively a member of the Knesset, its speaker, a trusted adviser of Begin's as foreign minister, and now the state's prime minister.[17]

There was relatively little the new executive could do to soften the emergency across the land as the 1984 election approached and it became clear that he would have to fight a resurgent Labor coalition headed by Peres as the opposition leader. In vain the cabinet members closest to Begin pleaded with him to take an active part in the campaign against Labor, a move he quietly rejected, although he did make it a point two days before the vote to endorse Prime Minister Shamir for election.

The polls indicated well in advance that the tally would be very close, but no one—least of all the candidates themselves—could guess how evenly the nation's electorate was divided, because of the difficult circumstances under which the voters cast their ballots. The result, with a majority of 61 of the 120 Knesset seats being required to form a new government, was Labor, 44; Likud, 41, with minor parties as supporters respectively of both leaders making up the bulk of the Parliament. The Israeli electorate had demonstrated a loss of confidence in both its major political parties, for Labor's forty-seven seats won in the 1981 election had now declined by three and Likud's loss had consisted of seven seats from its 1981 high of forty-eight.

The new totals, therefore, put both major parties at the mercy of the most influential of the minor parties, the religious right. Had the rabbinical leadership chosen to return to Labor, Peres undoubtedly could have formed a government as the new prime minister but the rabbis decided to stick with Likud. The outcome, as a result, amounted to a virtual tie so that neither major party could summon a majority of the Knesset votes to form the next government.[18]

There ensued a long and discouraging period of barren discussions between Peres and his Labor supporters, matched by Shamir and the rest of the Likud leadership, with both refusing to yield ground to the other. When the discussions of the top group widened as days passed without a decision on the formation of a new government, Ezer Weizman, having resigned as the Likud defense minister, urged both major parties to form a government of national unity with each in turn serving half of the fifty-month term of the next prime minister. Particularly in Israel, where political partisanship could become violent at times, this was scarcely a perfect solution but it was the only one possible under the discouraging circumstances.

By Peres's account of the proceedings, he was the first to assent to share the government with his rivals but Shamir would not agree until General Sharon urged both the leaders to do so in the interests of national unity. That finally was how Likud bowed upon the urging of a defense minister who had been removed after being blamed by a commission of inquiry for the excesses of the Israelis' Christian allies in the martyrdom of hundreds of defenseless Muslim refugees. Accordingly, Sharon was promptly rehabilitated in the new Labor ministry that took over the first half of the government of national unity as minister of commerce, together with Yitzhak Rabin as defense minister.

These were the strange circumstances under which Peres became the prime minister for the first half of the union government in 1984 that sought the withdrawal of the Israeli army from Lebanon—the sorry end of an adventure for Israel against terrorism greater than the one he had advised President Carter to undertake that lovely spring morning in 1980.[19]

PART FOUR | **Israel and the Middle East**

26. How Much Unity?

It took Prime Minister Peres four months to win a consensus in his cabinet of national unity for the withdrawal of Israeli troops from Lebanon. Even so, he was lucky because the Likud opposition was stubborn and lost only because one of its number, David Levy, the housing minister, changed sides and supported the removal of the invaders.[1]

By that time in 1984, an election year in the United States, Lebanon still remained a trap for unwary foreigners, as had become evident on October 23, 1983, when a suicide bomb loaded with TNT killed 241 United States Marines and sailors, members of a multinational peace-keeping force, as it exploded in their headquarters at Beirut International Airport. If the Israeli forces had been able to avoid so great a tragedy, it was only because their presence around mainly Christian East Beirut was not as exposed to such danger.

Nevertheless, both President Reagan and the American Congress were relieved when the Israeli pullout was completed except for a security zone of only a few miles of depth north of the Lebanese border. There, a close watch was maintained against the partisan Hezbollah, the "Party of God" that was allied with the Palestinians, who still managed to conduct raids into northern Israeli.[2] The limited extent of the remaining conflict mainly eliminated it as a worrisome factor in the American presidential election that November when President Reagan crushed the opposition, forty-nine states to one, in the greatest American victory at the peak of government up to that time.

With the United States launched on a massive spurt of prosperity in a continuation of the Reagan administration's defense-spending and tax-cutting policies, dissension in the Middle East, like most other foreign policy issues, seemed to be of comparatively little interest to the

American public. Just about the only issue of concern abroad amid this Reagan boom was, as always, the president's continued anti-Communist campaign. But even here, with a weakening Soviet Union, there was little to disturb the serenity of the White House.

It followed, with Soviet financing vastly reduced, that Arab attacks on Israel had to be funded with ransom payments that came to public notice now and then even though few such outrages yielded substantial returns for piracies.

In the first year of Reagan's second term, 1985, for example, there were two of consequence. A TWA jet was taken over by terrorists on June 14 after takeoff from Athens, after which 153 passengers and crew remained hostages for seventeen days before being released. The only casualty was an American serviceman. Four months later, on October 7, four Palestinians captured the *Achille Lauro*, an Italian cruise liner, in the Mediterranean off Cairo and held 400 passengers for ransom, but only for two days. Again, an American was killed.

There often was speculation that Israel's aggressive attitude toward the Palestinians in Lebanon had reduced the possibility of other Arab attacks from different directions, but proof of such convenient theories was hard to come by. Nevertheless, in Prime Minister Peres's half of the government of national unity, he was spared from calling upon the national defense in another major armed struggle and thereby was able to devote himself to a far more important war—inflation that had reached 20 percent in June after he took office and an even worse 28 percent in the following month.[3]

Amid signs of panic among many of Israel's wage earners in such straitened circumstances, Prime Minister Peres's duty, upon completing arrangements for the return of the troops, was to assemble a panel of the most practical-minded members of his cabinet, industrialists, labor leaders, and economic experts from the academic community to decide how best to bring down the inflationary spiral. He had been in and out of public office in Israel for more than thirty years and now, as prime minister at sixty-one, was as capable as anybody in the land—perhaps better prepared than some—to put into effect the draconian measures necessary to stabilize the economy.

Having been born in Poland and emigrated to Palestine with his parents, Isaac and Sarah Persky, he had known the country from age eleven and studied there except for a concluding period at Harvard. With the founding of Israel, he served in the Mapai secretariat and later the defense department for thirteen years, half of them as the minister in charge. Thereafter, he either was high in the government of the Labor Party or the leader of the opposition, so that, as prime minister, he realized he had to act—and quickly—to rescue the economy.[4]

Before a hastily formed Economic Council consisting of members of the Histadrut (the labor unions), the employers' organizations, the academic community, and the cabinet, he called at once for a freeze on prices and wages for six months. But by the spring of 1985, that did not work because inflation was still running at the rate of 15 percent and soon would be worse. The stabilization program that he had hoped to create by decree simply was not the solution to the nation's ills and the public was growing desperate with the purchasing power of the shekel sinking by the day.

The prime minister then tried a more deliberate approach, a series of working papers from the various constituencies he had assembled— together with weekly progress reports from the lot. That took an enormous amount of time and effort without developing any "sure thing" program to soothe a public that now was thoroughly alarmed. In an economy that was shot through with Socialist-tinged ideas and practices (meaning much more dependence on government than in the United States), both the distress and the fear of worse to come were very real.

It was June 28, 1985, before the prime minister could present just the semblance of what he called an Economic Stabilization Plan, or ESP, to all but a few of the leading members of the loyal opposition. This time the conservative Likud members opposed the deal that was presented for the government by General Sharon. Prime Minister Peres thought it might help if he announced he was slashing government costs, knocking down every office that cost the taxpayers $100,000 or more, but even that did not sway the opposition. The Likud people clearly wanted to kill the Labor ESP and struggled more than twenty-four hours without a rest to try to do it.[5]

In the end, the ESP was approved but, once it was applied in July, the trials of both the government and the Israeli public were just beginning. Before the crisis was eased, Peres concluded, there had to be a currency devaluation of 33 percent, prices had to rise by up to 28 percent, and permission was given to raise wages only by 15 percent.

The outcry was terrific because the average citizen was suffering a steep drop in purchasing power, that is, if he still had a few shekels in his pocket. It did not help the average citizen to realize that government bureaus also were being hard hit because the previous government subsidies for basic commodities such as milk, bread, eggs, and sugar also had been dropped for the time being. Moreover, government subsidies for public transport were wiped out.

Still, the very toughness of the ESP was what saved the country. Within a month, in August, inflation had dropped to 2.5 percent in a prime minister's report and the monthly inflation figure declined still more to 1.5 percent before year's end.[6] To give the prime minister his due for having addressed the problem and taken his chances, this is how he explained the outcome:

> The Israeli ESP was not revolutionary. It tackled the key issues simultaneously across a broad front: exchange rate policy, wages, government spending and monetary policy. But ultimately, ESP worked because it won the trust of the Israeli public. People recovered their confidence in the economy because they believed the government knew what it was doing. They were prepared to accept the need to sacrifice not just because the government, not least in its dialogue with the unions and the employers, demonstrated a new determination and a new capacity for bold but rational thinking.[7]

There was one other major factor, however. That turned out to be a most welcome $1.5 billion package of American aid to Israel, which was spread over that critical two-year period. It was an addition to the regular American grant of $3 billion in civilian and military aid and credits that had become a regular part of the Israeli economy at the time, all of which came with a bow from grateful sections of the Israeli public to Uncle Sam.[8]

Along with getting the army out of Lebanon and grappling successfully with inflation, Prime Minister Peres also managed to conciliate President Mubarak of Egypt in resolving a dispute over a part of the Red Sea coastline called Taba, south of the port city of Elat. Peres's political twin and eventual successor in the national unity cabinet, Foreign Minister Shamir, clung to the small stretch of Taba although he had not seemed worried about yielding the whole Sinai Peninsula to the Egyptians. However, before Peres's term as prime minister ended, he agreed to Mubarak's proposed solution of the Taba argument by submitting it to international arbitration—a case the Egyptians ultimately won.[9]

With that exception, the Peres record of accomplishment for twenty-five months as the director of Israel's government was so impressive that he wound up with an 80 percent approval rating in the polls—a status that few believed his elderly successor, Shamir, could match. The enthusiastic Laborites, for a time, did not hesitate to suggest to Peres that he withdraw at once from the national unity compact and cause the Likud opposition to struggle along by themselves. But Peres argued that he had given his word and refused to poke a hole in the national unity package at that juncture. He probably figured he would have a better chance later if he kept his part of the bargain—an eminently correct decision as it turned out.[10]

T oward the end of Peres's relatively brief term in high office, he also managed to inaugurate a promising relationship with the mercurial king of Jordan, Hussein, who had a Palestinian problem that sometimes became almost as difficult for him to handle as that of the Palestinian Liberation Organization in Israel. Of Jordan's 4 million people, perhaps as many as 20 percent were Palestinian refugees and others camped on the country's borders—a problem in itself particularly when the PLO became the main agency to represent them.

What brought King Hussein and Peres together when Peres descended from prime minister to foreign minister in the second part of the national unity cabinet in Jerusalem headed by Prime Minister Shamir was a growing belief that a Jordanian-Palestinian state might well be the answer to both their problems. At successive individual meetings with touring American envoys in the Middle East, they managed to so promote the idea of such a joint representation that even a usually suspicious American State Department was inclined to listen for a time.

Advisers and friends of both the Israeli and Jordanian leaders, too, became so intrigued that what was intended to be a secret meeting was arranged for them on April 11, 1987, at the home of a mutual friend in London. King Hussein then was fifty-two and had inherited his throne at sixteen from his father; Peres, also with well-nigh a lifetime of public service in Israel, was sixty-four; even more important, each thoroughly respected the other and enjoyed the prospect of trying to develop a joint policy for their respective constituencies that would in effect arrange for a nonviolent Arab representation for their Palestinian peoples other than the infuriating Yasir Arafat, the PLO leader. Arafat, of course, was not supposed to know about these arrangements, which accounted for Peres's brown wig and a single trusted foreign minister assistant, Yossi Beilin, matched by the king and his prime minister, Zaid Rifai, in mufti.

After lunch, the four proceeded to explore the possibilities of an accord between their respective governments and found themselves in agreement on many points with regard to the PLO, although there were divergences here and there on other matters. But as their discussions continued through the evening until a late hour, the possibilities of forging an eventual Jordanian-Israeli agreement seemed to impress both parties.

The chief difference was that King Hussein wanted Palestinian representation to be resolved at a broad international conference based on the twin UN Resolutions 242 and 338 as adopted by the Security Council, which had to be the council's basis for any UN intervention in Palestine. Even though Peres recognized that the PLO would thus be barred from the talks for refusing to recognize Nos. 242 and 338, he was not at all sure so many-sided a meeting would be able to agree on anything of substance.

What Peres suggested instead of a full-dress international meeting was an agreement by Jordan to initiate the creation of a Palestinian-Jordanian delegation with Israel's backing that would, by its very nature, exclude all representation for the PLO to participate in Israeli-Jordanian peace talks aimed at a peace treaty like that of Israel and Egypt. No matter how much Arafat objected, the two hoped, the non-PLO Palestinians would not want to be left out of a peace conference, so it followed that they would accept the nonviolent delegation offered them.

When Peres and the king separated for the drafting of their respective position papers, what seemed likely was a broad international one-day meeting at the onset of a sponsored peace conference that would bring Jordan and Israel together for their long-awaited talks with another major step toward a Middle East accord as the objective. The international session, both emphasized, would merely be the framework, the actual negotiating being limited to Jordanian and Israeli envoys. All this was then incorporated later into two documents that were prepared by the Israelis, Peres, and Beilin, and later accepted by King Hussein. The understanding at the end was that these working papers would be presented to the United States through the State Department in the hope that the project would eventually emerge as an American proposal.

Peres also saw to it that copies of the two approved drafts of his discussion with King Hussein reached an assistant to Secretary of State George Schultz, who was stopping off in Helsinki at the time on his way back to Washington from a Moscow conference. That, however, was as far as the démarche ever traveled. When Peres made his report of the secret proceedings to Prime Minister Shamir, Shamir at once sent a special envoy to Washington to disavow the whole procedure as improper and lacking the approval of the Israeli government. And so, in the end, King Hussein was disappointed, too. However, he would find other means in succeeding years to reach a somewhat more formal peace accord with Israel, although not as the head of a Jordanian-Palestinian state.[11]

As if this diplomatic foul-up had not been sufficiently embarrassing to all concerned, it soon was exceeded by the disclosure of the Iran-contra scandal in the United States, in which well-meaning Israelis also shared a part of the responsibility. A congressional report eventually blamed President Reagan for the affair, which involved the sale of arms to Iran in exchange for Iranian help in obtaining the release of American hostages held in Lebanon, a part of the money for the arms deal going to the support of the anti-Communist Nicaraguan contras.

Israel's part in this secret operation began in the latter part of Peres's term as prime minister when he agreed to help Robert McFarlane, President Reagan's security adviser, complete a deal for the covert sale of American arms to Iran, the proceeds being used to help release American and Israeli hostages being held in Lebanon. Arab terrorists until that time had been seizing foreign travelers in Lebanon and holding them for ransom, a practice that continued into the 1990s despite the growth of the secret American operation.

During Peres's term as prime minister, both Foreign Minister Shamir, who succeeded him, and Defense Minister Rabin cooperated in carrying out the American initiative, sometimes even providing shipments of Israeli weapons to Iran if it was not immediately convenient for Americans to supply Iran's needs. What the Iranians wanted principally was the American-made TOW antitank missiles and Hawk antiaircraft missiles, Peres said.

The American-Israeli part of the operation worked so smoothly that the first Lebanese hostage, the Reverend Benjamin Weir, was freed in Lebanon on November 14, 1985, and was quickly reunited with his family in the United States. In the following year, two more American hostages followed him, the Reverend Lawrence Jenco on July 26 and David Jacobsen on November 2. What the Israelis managed to do through Mossad, their secret service, was to maintain contact with both Iranian and Lebanese elements involved in the operation to expedite weapons in one direction and the release of hostages in another.*

On a 1986 visit to Washington, the then–Prime Minister Peres was received at the White House, and noted with pride that a grateful President Reagan "poured out his gratitude" for the help the Israelis were giving the United States in this extraordinary venture. All this time apparently, without the Israelis' knowledge, a part of the Iranian arms money unused in the hostage exchanges was being forwarded through other secret means, presumably the CIA, for use in the payment of the anti-Communist contras who were attacking a Nicaraguan Communist government. An angry Congress long since had barred the use of United States money for the support of the contras, which was later given as the reason for the subterfuge once it was exposed.

The disclosure of the scandal came originally from a leak to a small publication in Beirut, which was soon followed by a formal statement from the speaker of the Iranian Parliament that he had received a Bible inscribed by President Reagan from the president's security adviser, Robert McFarlane, who was reported to have also brought Iran military equipment. At first, there were furious White House denials but eventually President Reagan assumed full responsibility for the operation except for paying the contras.

Among those the White House dismissed in connection with the Iran-contra operation were a national security adviser, Adm. John Poindexter, and a marine, Lt. Col. Oliver North. McFarlane, the Israelis' contact, attempted suicide but recovered. In four days of testimony before Congress in 1987, North testified the scheme had originated with the late CIA director, William Casey, and named others already identified as leaders. A subsequent congressional report blamed the Reagan

---

*The attempt to extort ransom for kidnapped foreigners by radical Arabs in Lebanon tapered off in the early 1990s when fewer that forty were listed in custody there and most were released or rescued by 1992.

administration for allowing "pervasive dishonesty" and "disarray at the highest levels of government."[12]

With Shamir as prime minister, replacing Peres, who by that time had become foreign minister, the Israelis no longer were active in the Lebanese hostage crisis because they had all they could handle beginning January 15, 1988, with enormous Arab riots in Jerusalem centered about the Dome of the Rock in Arab East Jerusalem. An uprising that had begun on December 9, 1987, had claimed at least thirty-eight Arab lives. The Dome, one of the holiest places in Islam, had to be put under the heaviest Israeli guard while the violence lasted well into the new year.[13]

The prosecutions in the Iran-contra scandal continued meanwhile in the United Stats for the rest of President Reagan's two terms, the last six years of which were marked by what was then regarded as a record stock market boom. On December 24, 1992, toward the end of President Bush's succeeding administration, that chief executive formally ended the Iran-contra prosecutions with presidential pardons for six high officials headed by the secretary of defense, Caspar Weinberger, all of whom had been charged with misleading Congress in the Iran-contra inquiry.[14]

Peres admitted he paid a heavy price for the fiascoes in which he had participated, beginning with the Jordanian deal that failed and the Israeli role in Iran-contra. However greatly unity was necessary in a prosperous and rapidly growing Israeli nation toward century's end, it remained to be achieved.[15]

27. Conflict with Iraq

With Israel very much on the defensive, Saddam Hussein's Iraq became a major threat in the Middle East at the opening of the century's last decade. Without warning, the dictator's Soviet-made tanks led his army across their southern border with oil-rich Kuwait on August 2, 1990, and seized control within twenty-four hours.[1]

The disapproval of the United States did not bother the revolution-minded Saddam, nor did he seem overly concerned about Israel, one of his foes in the Middle East, which had destroyed a nuclear reactor he began building early in the 1980s. It was Israel instead that had more reason to be worried now that Saddam might decide to spray his Soviet-made missiles in its direction once he finished absorbing Kuwait.

As former prime minister Peres had good reason to know, the French had contracted in the 1980s to build the nuclear reactor Israel had destroyed. The French also agreed to provide the Iraqis with fifty-three pounds of enriched uranium in two deliveries, enough to build an atomic device. Although Peres had depended on a secret French pledge not to fulfill the second delivery of uranium, one of his successors as chief of the Israeli government had not been as trustful and sent aircraft to destroy the nuclear reactor before it was completed.

With Saddam Hussein now in control of Kuwait and in a strategic position to strike at either Saudi Arabia or Israel—perhaps both in time—no one in Jerusalem could be comfortable over the future even if President Bush had sent American warships and an aircraft carrier into the Persian Gulf while leading a UN move to condemn Iraq's conquest of a tiny ally, smaller than the state of Vermont. Whatever Bush was planning as reprisal at the time, the Israelis already had been informed they would not be asked to participate in any UN move against Saddam. The reason was plain enough. To fight Saddam, the United States would be appealing for Arab support, something that could not be easily realized if Israel became a part of a United States-led opposition force.[2]

Saddam was not likely to be a pushover, no matter what happened. He was then fifty-three, having been born and reared in the town of Tikrit in Iraq on August 28, 1937. He had qualified for a law degree at the University of Baghdad; at the same time, however, he also had acquired a reputation as a revolutionary, having participated in a plot to overthrow the Iraqi government that failed in 1959. Later, he was jailed, served two years in prison in 1964–66, and escaped in 1966.

By 1968, he had become the chairman of what was called a revolutionary council in his homeland and was leading another attempt to capture control of Iraq. And this time he succeeded, for in 1979, when he seized control in Baghdad, he gave himself the title of president and termed the country a "republic," although he exercised dictatorial rule. Now, judged by his actions, his aim was to establish himself as the new force in the Arab world and a challenge to the leadership of the Western powers.[3]

In almost everything that Saddam did while in control of Iraq, which is almost as large as California and has an oil reserve of its own, he had been influenced by his bent for war. During his time as chief of government in Baghdad, he had led the eight-year war against Iran that ended in 1988. And just before that, on May 22, 1987, his aircraft had attacked an American warship, the USS *Stark*, in the Persian Gulf, firing Exocet missiles that killed thirty-seven American sailors, then contended that the attack had been a mistake. Still, President Reagan had accepted the excuse without a murmur of protest.[4]

As for the Iran-Iraq War, Saddam was not the one who had ended it. On July 20, 1988, it was the Ayatollah Khomeini in Iran who accepted a cease-fire proposal drafted by the United Nations after an estimated one million people had died in the eight-year conflict. True, as the Ayatollah had recognized in a radio address, he had at the outset promised to fight Iraq "to the last drop of my blood" but he now had decided on peace in the best interests of his country.

If he and his followers in his Islamic nation had learned any lessons from their long and useless struggle, these had made an impression on their enemy, Saddam. Within a year, he was planning his attack on tiny Kuwait and, in effect, also threatening the largest of American foreign oil suppliers, Saudi Arabia. It remained to be seen

how many would now follow his attempt to dominate the Arab world
as Nasser of Egypt and Khomeini in Iran had previously attempted at
the cost of so much hardship to the respective peoples.[5]

This time, Egypt, for one, refused to support Saddam in what
amounted to a challenge to the United States at a time when the Soviet
Union was clearly in decline. And with Egypt and Saudi Arabia immediately at odds with Saddam's Iraq, it was a foregone conclusion that
Iran also would do whatever it could to make life uncomfortable for
the Iraqi strongman. Even in careworn Lebanon, the hard-hit Muslims,
who had been so dreadfully wronged by the Christian Phalangists during the recent Israeli invasion, were rejecting whatever appeals came to
them from Baghdad.

Of course, in the timeless routine of the remaining despots of the
Arab world, there still were a few supporters of the Iraqi dictator who
had dared affront the United States, Britain, and the Western democra-
cies by grabbing a key part of the Western oil supply network. He was,
to use the phrase most often heard among intellectual Arab youth, a foe
of the "colonialist West" that had deprived them of the right to growth
and expansion in a highly competitive world. The fabled notion of Pan-
Arabism, "Arab oil for Arab peoples," was raised once again after Saddam's conquest of Kuwait but, as nearly as could be judged at the time,
there was only one distinguished convert, King Hussein of Jordan. Like
the much harder-hit leader of the Palestine Liberation Organization,
Yasir Arafat, King Hussein made common cause with the Iraqi dictator
mainly because both were then in opposition to Israel.[6]

Somehow, neither the king nor the PLO leaders understood that
Saddam could succeed only if the Arab dynasty he headed could expel
the Western powers from both the Persian Gulf and the oil-rich Arabian peninsula.

As an Arab journalist summed up the position in the trying period
of indecision before the United States and its UN supporters struck
back at Saddam:

> There were deadly if half-baked ideas floating in the Arab world
> when Saddam overran Kuwait—ruinous concepts of Arab national-
> ism that flew in the face of political realty . . . wild notions about how
> to break the impasse between Arabs and Israelis, resentments toward
> the West born of the very attraction to it, and then that desire to place
> the blame on the gulf states for everything wrong under the sun. The

Iraqi dictator plucked these ideas and resentments and turned them into monstrous instruments. The military means to check him were principally in the hands of the United States and the coalition it soon fashioned. But the battle to exercise the dreams and the delusions that led Saddam was, at its heart, a battle for the Arabs themselves.[7]

As a supposedly pro-Western Arab leader, King Hussein became an almost immediate international question mark when he decided to support the outrageous conquest of Kuwait by Saddam's reinvigorated army only two years after his long war with Iran following the Ayatollah's agreement to a UN cease-fire. In a quotation from the king that was carried in the United States by NBC News, he called Saddam "a person to be trusted and dealt with" as well as "an Arab patriot in the eyes of many." To complete the bargain into which he had thrust his ailing nation, the Jordanian people, and himself, the king seemed to place little stock in an American-supported UN resolution calling for economic sanctions against Iraq.

What he apparently was trying to do to demonstrate his interest in peace was to advocate withdrawal of American and other Western troops from Saudi Arabia in return for Saddam's retreat from Kuwait; in addition, there also appeared once again the king's favorite notion of an international peace conference that would resolve Israel's position on the West Bank in favor of the PLO.

The king had let it be known in the West that Jordan considered Iraq its best market for its limited exports. He also had not been making much headway in the Arab world with his reputation as the most American-minded of Arab leaders and a supporter of the American alliance with Israel. For the moment, he seemed to be testing the possibility of a change of front.

There were financial interests at stake to a certain extent. In a report published at the time, it was said that Jordan had requested UN aid to make up for the potential damage to its economy estimated at $2.1 billion annually. If true, that was calculated to boost unemployment to prohibitive figures in a nation of only 4 million people without an oil reserve of its own.

It would seem, therefore, that the king was not turning aside for the moment against his American-Israeli relationship because he feared economic trouble. On the contrary, it was evident already that a commitment by Jordan to the economy of the Arab world might well prove far more costly for the Jordanian people than if the king had remained committed to his pro-Western course. As he and his advisers struggled to stabilize income with outgo, it appeared probable that his main troubles for the future would be more political than economic. He already had been forced to dismiss one prime minister; in the following more liberalized administration, he had been obliged to grant more freedom to his restless public, particularly to a parliament dominated by fundamentalist Islamic forces and to the few surviving newspapers in Amman that he had tightly controlled.[8]

Basically, King Hussein's problems seemed to have been intensified by the astonishing growth of his Israeli neighbor; with the decline of the Soviet Union in the century's last decade, an estimated seventeen thousand Russian Jews now were emigrating monthly to the Jewish state in fear of the revival of pogroms. That not only intensified the fears of the Palestinian Liberation Organization along with the loss of whatever money the PLO formerly had received from Moscow but it also made Jordan's own large Palestinian population increasingly restive.

The king's relations with the United States, too, had markedly declined when two successive presidents, Reagan and Bush, failed to be impressed with his proposal to make himself the spokesman for a joint Jordanian-Palestinian state. This idea had been repeatedly rejected by the State Department in Washington, D.C., even if it did attract support from a former Israeli prime minister, Peres. The key factor, however, turned out to be Yasir Arafat's understandable hostility to the notion that he should step aside in favor of the king of Jordan in his control of the PLO.

Apparently angered by the failure of all his schemes to make himself the leader of the peace process in the Middle East, therefore, King Hussein now was angling toward support of the latest aspirant to Arab nationalist leadership, Saddam Hussein, and intensifying his own difficulties in the process. Having lost an American arms shipment through a negative vote in Congress, he seemed to be considering a shift of protectors to the onrushing Arab dictator from Baghdad who had challenged the United States and was heading for a showdown in the Persian Gulf. At the height of the cold war, it is doubtful that the Soviet Union would have permitted a client state such as Iraq to interfere with United States interests in the Persian Gulf through the takeover of

Kuwait. But with the cold war at an end and the Soviet system itself on the very verge of collapse, adventurers like Saddam Hussein felt free to threaten the oil-based economy of the richest and most powerful nation on earth. Perhaps he had gambled that the Americans would not respond. He was bound to be surprised.[9]

Saddam did not have long to wait for President Bush's response. A savage American air war blasted his Iraqi capital of Baghdad beginning January 16, 1991, six months after his conquest of Kuwait. He fought back with Soviet-made Scud missiles that also hit Israeli cities, although their forces were not involved.

Within two weeks, at least twenty-six Scuds had struck Israeli cities with wide estimates of damage, four deaths, and hundreds of others injured, all of which led to an Israeli offer to destroy the Iraqi Scud bases but the proposal was declined with thanks. What concerned President Bush more than anything else was the possibility that the use of Israeli troops would alienate the Arab forces under the American commander in chief, Gen. H. Norman Schwarzkopf.

The general, backed by President Bush and the chairman of the Joint Chiefs of Staff, Gen. Colin Powell, was pounding Baghdad and other Iraqi cities with wave upon wave of allied aircraft, including more than a thousand from the United States and others from Britain, France, Saudi Arabia, and Kuwait. He also was ready for an extensive land war with nearly 500,000 troops, including 350,000 Americans and allies from Britain, France, Saudi Arabia, Egypt, Syria, and others.

The Israelis were not alone to suffer damage in the war against Saddam, styled "Operation Desert Storm." An Iraqi attack on Saudi territory resulted in three days of border ground fighting at the onset of the war that General Schwarzkopf dismissed as having as little effect as "a mosquito on an elephant." However, the Iraqi Scuds took a toll in the Saudi cities of Dhahran and Riyadh despite an American defense with Patriot missiles.

In response to the Israeli and Saudi attacks, the United States opened up with Tomahawk cruise missiles launched from American warships in the Gulf that hit Saddam's palace, his communications center, and the headquarters of his defense ministry. The Iraqi Air Force of MiG-29 Soviet fighters was wiped out early in the conflict and the Iraqi air defenses were silenced. During the weeks that the war lasted, it was estimated that 150,000 Iraqi troops were killed in action and tens of thousands of others were captured or surrendered.

The American-led coalition of ground forces, all told, was in action only four days before Saddam surrendered after what he called "the mother of all battles." The cost to the United States in troop fatalities was 141 killed in action and others among the allied troops lost no more than 60. When President Bush announced the war's end on February 28 over national TV he said: "Kuwait is liberated. Iraq's army is defeated. I am pleased to announce . . . that exactly 100 hours since the ground action began and six weeks since the start of Operation Desert Shield, all United States and coalition forces will suspend offensive combat operations."[10]

In the euphoria that spread through Washington thereafter, the great error was that Saddam Hussein was permitted to remain in power. It turned out to be a mistake because he was soon enough breaking his pledge to his conquerors not to be selling his oil for secret arms deals. It did not take him too much time before he had managed to reassemble an armed force that was prepared to create more trouble for Israel, Egypt, Saudi Arabia, and others in the Middle East against whom he had grudges because of his past adventures that had turned out badly.

Besides the damage the Israelis suffered, Saudi Arabia cities also took some direct hits over the six weeks of combat from Saddam's air operations. But it was Kuwait City, the capital of the Saudis' neighbor, that suffered the most damage by far. When Saddam's forces moved out after the cease-fire, the wealthy town's center was in ruins. Most of its banks and many of its homes were looted, business was wrecked, the entire power network had been severed, and fires were blazing in more than seven hundred oil wells—damage that could not be repaired for a long time and at great cost.

Dealing with Saddam, as the Israelis had learned to their cost, had been much more than a nuisance. He had shown himself to be a menace and he would continue to be a problem for the allied negotiators who were left behind to see that he lived up to the UN terms of his surrender. He had survived his old enemy, the Ayatollah Khomeini, who had died on June 3, 1989, after a long illness, but that scarcely meant Saddam was at peace with Iran. On the contrary, while hobbled by his peace agreements that purported to put him in a box between a southern "no fly" zone and other northern impediments, he still proved himself to be a wily operator who knew how to make his oil work for him regardless of the problems of international supervision.[11]

In the post–Gulf War world, regardless of Israel's considerable losses while sidelined through agreement with President Bush, the continued American support of the Jewish state was never in question either then or later. What did become an uneasy United States objective was to fashion a realistic policy for dealing with the two so-called rogue states, Iraq and Iran. It did not even take a year's experience until the State Department discovered, to its embarrassment, that the flawed policy called "dual containment" of Iran and Iraq did not work.

Even before the Ayatollah's death, the Israelis had learned that they could, under favorable circumstances (that is, something of benefit to Iran), cooperate marginally with the Iranians on matters of mutual interest. Such deals, particularly those having to do with commercial trade, continued to develop now and then after the Ayatollah's death. Differences with the Iraqis, however, remained to separate the two nations, primarily because the Iranians are Persian at the core and retain Persian interests and the Persian language even if 98 percent also share the same Islamic religious beliefs as the Iraqis.

In the post–Gulf War era, however, the United States never did establish even the limited relationship of the Israelis with the Iranians. The basic reason, of course, was the attitude of mutual hostility between Tehran and Washington that was even more exaggerated in American efforts to contain Iraqi evasions of the UN peace accords that helped Saddam Hussein with his wily rearmament despite all the American measures to keep him in his box.

The longer the policy of "dual containment" continued in the Bush era and later under the Democratic administration of President Bill Clinton, the less effective it became mainly because American trading partners in Europe and elsewhere saw no harm in dealing with both rogue states regardless of the failure of the United States to improve relations with either of them. Of the two, Saddam's Iraq found even more numerous ways of evading the peace agreement imposed by the United States. On the evidence provided by journalists as well as diplomatic observers, Saddam soon managed to be as well armed as some of his rivals for power in the Middle East.[12]

All this in turn reflected on the Saudi Arabian oil trade with the

United States, for the Islamic fundamentalist movement in time presented such a threat to the Saudi royal family that the United states found it expedient to increase the American armed strength in the Persian Gulf area until long after the end of the Gulf War. It did not help matters that the Saudis from time to time also were involved in disputes with smaller units of the almost-outmoded council of the oil-producing states—arguments that seldom were settled among the aggrieved parties but remained to sour relations between important elements of the industry. If the Soviet decline had any influence on this process, it was simply the effect that the removal of a major competitor, temporary or not, may have on the pricing structure in any large and complicated industry such as the domain of oil.

In Israel's relations with other nations in the Middle East, therefore, the changes in the oil empire after the Gulf War also had a decided effect on the United States as the leading force in the area. Freed of the tensions induced by the cold war, successive American presidents were being drawn into the search for peace there to a greater extent than ever before. To some among Israel's influences in government, this suggested renewed opportunities for a better life for its people; to others, it eventually came to represent unexpected dangers.[13] That was particularly true when Saddam Hussein once again defied the United States by forcing UN inspectors to leave Iraq when they sought proof of charges that he was using human beings in his alleged experiments in preparation for "germ warfare" against his foes. The United States at the time was assembling huge armed forces in the Persian Gulf area, but Saddam disregarded the threat.

28. A Changing World

In a brutally combative Middle East, many an Arab foe of Israel must have wondered how it was possible for such a small state to survive while the massive Soviet Union, an Arab protector, collapsed toward century's end.

For a destined Israeli prime minister of the 1990s, Yitzhak Rabin, the answer came in a short, sharp burst: "Moscow had all the military power and all those missiles, but look what happened to it in the end because of the economy."[1] For Mikhail Gorbachev, the first and last Soviet president, the answer was in his final broadcast on December 25, 1991, after the failure of his six-year reform movement: "The old system fell apart before the new system began to work."[2]

There was much more to the Soviet failure after seventy-three years than such conclusions, of course, although it is true that Communist theory and the realities of the marketplace did not mix. But that was scant comfort for the Arab states that had profited from Soviet support—Iraq, Iran, Syria, the Sudan, and Libya among them. Such outlaw governments, so considered by the United States, now had to shift for themselves. And so did the most persistent of Israel's enemies on the home front, the Palestine Liberation Organization. To most Israelis, the Soviets had been the PLO's foremost protector.

As Rabin would have been the first to agree, that did not mean the Jewish state could relax its vigilance or reduce its defense forces. It was far more likely that Israel's Arab enemies would become reckless in throwing off restraint in their desperation to find a substitute for the support in money, weapons, and advice that the Soviets had provided for them in Moscow's better days. To fight with Israel, the extreme Arab opposition now brought a ruthlessness that it sometimes had tried to conceal in the belief that the United States might eventually slacken its support of the Jewish state.

While he was dismantling the Soviet system beginning with his assumption of authority in 1985, Gorbachev appeared anxious to cooperate with the United States and seemed to make it a point to confer with representative Americans whenever possible beginning with President Reagan. At one time early in 1986 in a conversation with a black leader, the Reverend Jesse Jackson, the Soviet chieftain expressed concern about the flight of Soviet Jews to Israel apparently because they feared a resumption of persecution through revived pogroms. But little happened to stem the panicky exodus to Israel among those who could do so.[3]

In Moscow meanwhile, Gorbachev's course ran downhill, so that, even if he had tried, he could not have been of much use to his former Arab allies. While trying to reform the Soviet system with "glasnost" (openness) and "perestroika" (restructuring), he became the last of a processional of failed leaders including Leonid Brezhnev, Yuri Andropov, and Konstantin Chernenko.

During his six years as the Soviet's leader, Gorbachev fired opposition chieftains, including the veteran Andrei Gromyko, agreed with President Reagan and reduced the nation's nuclear armaments, sharply cut the size of the Soviet armed forces, dissolved the Warsaw Pact and on September 5, 1991, dissolved the Union of Soviet Socialist Republics as well.

What emerged on December 21, 1991, was another union of eleven former Soviet republics as a collection of independent states dominated by the Russian republic with Boris Yeltsin as its leader. All Gorbachev had left to do on December 25 after being mocked, derided, and threatened by tumultuous Moscow demonstrations was to yield control over the former Soviet nuclear arsenal to Yeltsin, lower the Red flag over the Kremlin, and resign from an office that no longer existed in a form of government that had vanished. As a memento to the swiftness of change in so difficult a world, the city of Leningrad, so named in honor of the founder of the Soviet system, Nikolai Lenin, resumed its pre-Communist identity, St. Petersburg, a monument to the czars whom Lenin succeeded.[4]

To those who still hoped that the new Russia in some miraculous way could exercise the terrifying authority of the Communist system as it existed from Lenin through Stalin, there was a chilling response from George F. Kennan, a student of history who had represented the United States in Moscow in the last years of the cold war.

In an analysis published just before Gorbachev's downfall and the emergence of Yeltsin as the leader of Russia as well as the collection of other newly independent former Soviet states, Kennan demanded to know what sort of example was being set for the new order by a country marked by a "decay of the inner cities, declining educational levels, a crumbling substructure and a deteriorating environment."

It was, Kennan concluded in response to his own question, "a hard and low moment in the historical development of the Russian people." He saw relatively little immediate change for a public beggared by seven decades of economic hardship and low living standards while also being deprived of the political power to seek peaceful change. The Russian people, he pointed out, had been exposed "not only to the exactions of a pitiless dictatorship but also to the ferocious petty frictions of daily life in a shortage economy."

How short that economy really was, the outer world only now realized, he went on, saying: "Nor can we ignore the social effects of all these upheavals. Political persecution and war left tragic gaps in the male parental population, particularly in the villages. Family structure was deeply destabilized, and with its stability there were forfeited those sources of inner personal security that only the family can provide."

Kennan had a dubious outlook for the Russian Federation's future, as a result, as enormous masses of people suddenly were being thrown on their own resources to change their government from a ruthless dictatorship to a democracy, shift the economy from centralized authority to a free enterprise system, and transfer their political loyalties to a string of untried republics that had replaced both the czarist and Communist empires of the past three centuries. Viewing a people so poorly prepared for change and a youth without memory of anything better, the best the American diplomat could suggest was an extended period of hardship for the newest Russian venture in government that was inevitable for the unfortunate people concerned.[5]

That so unfavorable a judgment had been reached among the masses themselves also was evident in the spectacle of rising emigration among those who had relatives elsewhere, particularly among Jewish families with ties to Israel—a stunning development that spread conflicting emotions among the Jewish state's Arab neighbors.

Although the exodus seemed not to have been particularly aimed at arrival in the United States by others in the Soviet successor states who had the means to depart, it coincided with a rising protest mainly among working-class Americans against any increase in immigration—a curious response to the Statue of Liberty on her pedestal in New York Harbor, beckoning with her lamp in her outstretched right arm to the dispossessed in a gesture of welcome to a land of promise.[6]

While the Arab opposition in the Middle East was trying to change and strengthen its lagging offensive against the growth in Israel's population in the early 1990s, King Hussein of Jordan quietly drew back from his temporary attraction to Saddam Hussein's Iraq after the thrashing the Iraqi dictator suffered in the Gulf War. During the early 1990s, the king took care to change his image once again to that of the benevolent statesman who had been considered, next to the Egyptian leadership, the most dependable Arab ruler the Israelis could count on for support.

In effect, what King Hussein's turnabout amounted to was a kind of weather vane in the stormy Arab world of the Middle East. For in this crisis after the loss of Soviet protection for dictators from Hafez al-Assad of Syria to Saddam Hussein's Iraq, the king appeared to be signaling that the radical Arab cause no longer either attracted or deserved his attention. For the sake of his people, and undoubtedly himself, he left no doubt that he was returning to his former comfortable role as an Arab chieftain facing westward—a friend of the United States and a supporter of Israel who soon would be ready to conclude a recognition agreement with the Jewish state modeled after that pioneered by Anwar Sadat.[7]

The king's return to his former allegiance did not, by any means, check the rise of the fundamentalist Muslim movement that still was gripping huge masses of peoples from Pakistan on the east to Algeria on the west. Even if the Russian and associated republics now had much more to worry about than relations with outlaw states in the Middle East, the United States had to reinforce its armed protection for friendly Arab states from Egypt to Saudi Arabia at the same time that former Soviet targets such as Poland, Hungary, and the Czech republic were clamoring for admission to NATO.[8]

These shifting tides of influence were also producing pressures in high places that might at one time have been considered a sign of conflicting interests but now were accepted as temporary accommodations—in effect, signs of changing times. Having lost Moscow's financial support with the collapse of the Soviet Union, the Palestine Liberation Organization was reported to have struck a better bargain with the Saudi Arabian regime despite the Saudis' dependence on American oil patronage and armed support.

True or not, the Israelis apparently realized that such Saudi investment was in effect a hedge against a future challenge from fundamentalist Muslim rebels temporarily headquartered in Britain and elsewhere. Whatever the Egyptians were doing to temporize with the Muslim threat, they had reason for concern as well as the Saudis, being surrounded by such fundamentalist havens as Libya and the Sudan.

Change also made the once-docile PLO far more violent in the declining years of the century. The reason was the activities of a number of other Islamic extremist groups, including Hamas, Hezbollah, and the Muslim Brotherhood, all of whom depended on stirring up hatred of Israel in order to raise money from a distressed Arab leadership. Between Iraq, the oil-rich emirates of the Gulf, and sometimes Saudi Arabia or an even more doubtful Iran, the terrorists plied their bloody business whenever they saw an opportunity and took their chances at being mowed down by Israeli guns.[9]

Of the Arab gangsters, which is what much of the PLO opposition amounted to, the oldest and among the most violent was the Muslim Brotherhood, which had begun in Egypt by trying to make a living out of violence with whatever propaganda could be used to attract money and popular support. Before there was an Israel, quite naturally, the Brotherhood assassins operated against their own government, but that did not work very well against bloodier dictators such as Nasser. Accordingly, the Brotherhood branched out, used Muslim hatred of Israel as a strengthening device, and eventually attracted the patronage from time to time of such moderates as King Hussein of Jordan. However, in the modern world of Islam, the Brotherhood could not contend with the superior appeal of the PLO and the organizing ability of Yasir Arafat, a much underrated Arab leader.[10]

Hezbollah, a latter-day strong-arm group of the Shiite Muslims, centered its efforts against Israel from outposts in Lebanon, took regular attacks and huge losses from Israeli invaders, but seemed to have enough support and patronage from Syria, Libya, and probably Iraq and Iran as well to maintain hit-and-run thrusts against northern Israeli settlers. Like the Muslim Brotherhood, however, Hezbollah's effectiveness was limited and had neither the arms, numbers, nor political support to become a major threat to the Israeli army. But just as the Brotherhood seemed a well-nigh permanent problem from its bases in and around Egypt, Hezbollah also could inflict serious injuries at times with its sudden raids on outlying Israeli villages and farms.

The newest in this growth of terrorist factionalism among the Arabs, Hamas, burst upon the surprised Israelis almost entirely by accident. It was preceded in the spring of 1985 by the exchange of more than a thousand Palestinian-imprisoned terrorists for three Israeli soldiers captured by the PLO and held in Lebanon. As might have been expected, the freed Palestinians at once resumed sporadic violence against their former captors in the West Bank and Gaza, where most of them lived.

During the next year to eighteen months, Hamas, with its fundamentalist suicide bombers and its uncompromising campaign of death and destruction against the Israelis, made its first fanatical impression on the PLO's drive against the Jewish state. The offensive was called by a new name—the *intifada* (Arabic for "shaking off")—that became the embodiment of terror itself to its victims in Israel.[11]

On the afternoon of December 8, 1987, an Israeli truck driver accidentally killed four Arab day laborers when he smashed into a car in which they were riding home on the Gaza Strip. Their neighbors in the Jabalya refugee camp there at once became suspicious, then vengeful, because of a fast-spreading rumor that the killings had been deliberate. Before the night was over, raging mobs of angry Palestinians were stoning Israeli soldiers on patrol, invading a camp bristling with Israeli reservists and flinging firebombs with wild abandon.

That was how the *intifada* began out of a Palestinian rebellion born of hate at what they believed to be Israeli oppression—only it was not called that at first. And Hamas, the latest Arab fundamentalist organization that swore a never-ending struggle against Israeli rule, was not then identified with its suicidal course to offer up life itself as a sacrifice to overthrow the Jewish state.

Even though the rioting at Gaza rose in mass attacks on the Israeli military the next day, forcing a call for reinforcements, the defense ministry seemed disinterested. That afternoon, when the disorders mounted in savagery and spread to the Egyptian border at another large Palestinian refugee camp, then cropped up in widely separated spots across the land, all was still calm in Jerusalem. Yitzhak Rabin, then the defense minister in the Shamir government on national unity, showed so little interest that he departed that weekend on a trip to conclude some not very urgent business in Washington, D.C.

By the time Rabin returned on December 21, the *intifada* had burst all bounds. By then, the Palestinian deaths throughout the land had exceeded three hundred and units of the Hamas commandos were leading suicide units of young Palestinians against the Israeli armed forces—the defense ministry's delayed response to the emergency.

Now it was the Israeli government that surged to excesses with Rabin's order to the troops to use force whenever necessary to break the back of the insurrection. On televised film seen in America, Britain, Europe, and much of the rest of the world, horrifying scenes of torture and inhuman combat led to rising protests that flooded into the Israeli government's offices. In Tunis, the headquarters of the PLO, there were daily denunciations of the Israeli campaign to restore order. Even more serious, terrorist groups headquartered in Lebanon, Syria, and Jordan all were joining the fray with reckless abandon, and Saddam Hussein in Iraq soon would be boasting that he would kill Israelis in the mass with chemical weapons.[12]

By January 20, 1988, Defense Minister Rabin was reporting to the Knesset that he was still relying on "might, power and beatings" to knock down the *intifada*. Hamas, with its fundamentalist fanaticism, had induced a far more forceful role on Arafat and the PLO in their distant headquarters in Tunis. What had happened, as Rabin himself was among the first to realize, was that he would be engaging in an almost permanent state of war with the most radical elements of the PLO if he continued to trade blow for blow, bomb for bomb, gunshot for gunshot.

All manner of Israeli strategies had failed as the *intifada* stretched out for two years. Houses had been burned, Palestinians had been expelled in masses. All manner of other punishments had been tried but failed to halt the spread of the *intifada*. As a result, Rabin proposed negotiations with the Palestinians once there was a serious move toward the restoration of peace within Israel. But meanwhile, with whatever

time he could spare, he set up a relatively quiet routine of talks with local Palestinian leaders and others with the fixed notion, which had
been growing on him, that all this violence required both a political and
an economic solution.

But it would not come easily, nor could it be worked out in a matter of days or weeks between experienced negotiators. This was a
movement that would have to start simultaneously at the bottom as
well as at the top, because the Palestinians, through the PLO and the
various terrorist organizations, could not be placated with promises of
better times. What this amounted to as the *intifada* at last wound down
was a make-or-break situation for the Israeli government.

At that critical period, Rabin, the crusty old soldier, tried as best he
could to seek peace with a modest plan that he began circulating first of
all among the faithful of the Labor Party. What he had formulated was
not a result of any high-level approach; on the contrary, his proposal
had originated in his quiet inquiries among local Palestinians wherever
he could persuade them to discuss their problems with him. He had
come upon some as activists roaming the streets and disorderly neigh-
borhoods. Others were mostly nonmembers of the PLO he interviewed
at places where they dared talk freely of their hopes and fears. And
then, as a climax to his efforts, he and a few he trusted had sought out
the most radical Arabs, who gave their opinions in the prisons where
they had been confined.

Out of this consensus of opposites, Rabin had put together a program that called for Palestinian self-rule beginning with the West Bank
and Gaza Strip, the installation of a Palestinian government upon a
withdrawal of armed Israeli forces, and the periodic conduct of free
elections of, by, and for the Palestinians.

Prime Minister Shamir seemed to be so impressed at the time in
January 1989 that he adopted the Rabin program as his own, always
provided that the *intifada* itself was halted. At that stage, with the uprising in its final phase, the Palestinians themselves were ready for negotiations and there was no interference then from the headquarters of
the PLO in Tunis.

Unfortunately, within two months, Shamir continually stalled the
first meetings with the Palestinians, and it became clear even to Rabin
as his defense minister that this government of national unity no longer
was functioning. However, Rabin did not bring it down; the movement
in the Knesset to end Shamir's half of the national unity regime came

instead from Rabin's old rival in the Labor Party, Peres, the prime minister for the first half of the term. The difficulty, however, persisted because there were not enough votes in the Knesset to put anybody else
in power, so Shamir and the Likud Party had to be reappointed by
President Chaim Herzog to serve until new elections could be held in
June 1992.

The result of all this maneuvering was that Rabin resumed the sole
sponsorship of his peace proposal to the Palestinians, but he lost his job
as defense minister when Shamir went back as prime minister with an
all-Likud membership. It was typical of the way Israeli politics operated at the time with the two major parties so closely matched and so
dependent on the maneuverings of the minor parties in their coalitions,
particularly the religious right wing.[13]

After the American-led Gulf War that knocked Iraq's Saddam Hussein out of his conquest of Kuwait, President Bush's secretary of state,
James Baker, came to the Middle East to try to revive the stalled peace
process with the Palestinians. His method was to assemble a peace conference in Madrid at which there was great goodwill, much passionate
speech making, the acceptance of a four-track peace-negotiating apparatus between Israel and, each separately, Syria, Lebanon, Jordan, and
the Palestinians, but at the end of October 1991 it was evident that no
progress could be made through so unwieldy a diplomatic apparatus.[14]

It was, however, a meeting that instilled hope for the future—and
for Rabin's plan for peace with the Palestinians—that he was certain to
revive if he ever came to power again.

That happened in 1992 after Shamir and his Likud government lost
out to Labor's triumphant revival with Rabin as its standard-bearer for
prime minister. Once again, the old soldier's dramatic comeback was
played out against the background of the last of his picturesque strug-
gles against his lifelong rival, Peres. What Rabin had to do in effect was
to change the way the Israeli party system operated by managing to
create a majority within Labor for a direct primary by the party membership on the choice of a candidate for prime minister. Once that was
accomplished, Rabin defeated Peres as the party's candidate at the
peak of government, although the vote was very close.[15]

Leading up to the national election on June 23, 1992, Rabin ran on a
rousing platform of peace with security for Israel, more money for education, the absorption of immigrants (four hundred thousand Russians now were citizens), reducing unemployment, and putting more

money back into the nation's infrastructure instead of the losing policy of creating new Jewish settlements in Palestinian territory. At one point, Rabin trumpeted his battle cry, "The electorate must choose between stagnation and hope."[16]

The listless Shamir, again seeking reelection, was no match for his former defense minister. In that struggle, Labor won almost a million votes out of the 2.65 million cast, enough for 44 Knesset seats to Likud's 32 and an additional 17 seats from allied parties for a majority 61 of the 120 Knesset seats. It was by far the largest election ever held in Israel and it foreshadowed a future in which American-style direct primaries and the direct election of prime ministers would be the rule rather than the exception.[17]

Besides the usual problems of a prime minister–elect in picking and choosing among Labor and minority party candidates to form a workable government, Rabin faced one more contest in his long rivalry with Peres. For although Peres had lost out in the primary voting within the party, he still retained much influence among the rank and file. But now Rabin was seventy, Peres was sixty-nine, and the nation was teetering on the brink between peace with the Palestinians or a continuation of the long and so far intractable civil war.

Rabin made the first move. He offered Peres the foreign ministry, in which he would obviously have a leading role in the renewal of the peace process with the Palestinians and their supporters in the Arab world. Peres never wavered this time. He accepted. And so the bitterness of the long contest between them faded as Rabin led the way to a new effort to achieve peace with Peres as his foreign minister.

Together, at last, they were committed to serving their troubled nation in a changing world.

29. Rabin and Peres

"Our face is toward the rising sun," Rabin proclaimed in his second inaugural as Israel's prime minister.

He meant it, too. For in again taking the helm in Jerusalem, he sought day by day and week by week to stress the guidelines for peace with the Arabs that had been preserved despite a failed Madrid conference. As he put it on heading the government once again after fifteen years: "Many here and abroad wish today for a new road, for impetus, for a new page in the history of the state of Israel. We shall change the national order of priorities."[1]

Despite such fanciful flights of language in 1992 to mark his second beginning as prime minister, fifteen years after his first term, Rabin at seventy was usually solemn and plain-spoken, unsentimental in the extreme. Beneath a militarily correct exterior, the mark of nearly three decades of army service, he was deeply devoted to his family—his wife, children, and grandchildren—and almost fanatically loyal to his colleagues in a cabinet that now included his erstwhile rival, Foreign Minister Peres.

Rabin's parents, Nehemia and Rosa Cohen Rabin, had been early arrivals in Palestine, settling in Jerusalem soon after World War I—the city of his birth on March 1, 1922. Like many other children in British-ruled Palestine, he drifted into farming after his primary education and spent the years from sixteen to eighteen in an agricultural school. But evidently that line of work did not appeal to him, for during the next six years he underwent military training, including a year's experience at a staff college in England. When he was twenty-six, he met and was married to Leah Schlossberg, another Palestinian, a little more than three months before Israel was declared a nation in 1948.

With their two children, the young Rabins took the risks inherent at the time among military families in an Israel that was almost always under fierce Arab attack, but luck was with them. They survived and prospered. From chief of the Israeli training command at thirty-two, Rabin progressed to chief of the Israeli northern command, deputy chief of staff, and, at forty-two, he became the army's chief of staff from 1964 to 1968.

Then came a major change for him and for his family—his un-looked-for appointment while a member of the Knesset as the Israeli ambassador to the United States and life with Leah and the children in Washington, D.C. It was a critical time in American political affairs, for it marked both the ascent and the downfall of one of the most enig-matic figures in American history, President Nixon. That Washington experience inevitably included some of the harshest lessons in self-government for any free people—matters that Rabin never forgot.

Once he returned to Israel to become the leader of the Labor Party from 1974 to 1977 and his first term as prime minister, he had ample oc-casion to reflect on the pitfalls in democratic government that trapped the unwary—but he and his cherished wife survived that experience, too. It was just as well that they did not let his resignation discourage them toward the end of that term.[2]

In the fifteen years before Rabin won his second term at the head of government, he served in two of the national union regimes from 1984 to 1989, first for two years in the government of his old rival, Peres, and the remaining three years under the elderly Likud prime minister, Shamir. Rabin's reelection as prime minister at last settled the long po-litical struggle with Peres when Peres accepted appointment as a Labor foreign minister in the Rabin cabinet—a union of effort that would be of inestimable benefit to a nation that desperately needed it.

Given Rabin's skeptical nature and his instinctive mistrust of deal-ings with Yasir Arafat and the Palestine Liberation Organization, how else could Israel have changed its history except through Foreign Min-ister Peres's assumption of personal risk in advocating a policy in favor of the PLO? Certainly, that was not what Rabin had in mind when he promised to give peace a better chance in his inaugural broadcast to his fellow Israelis and the world: "We will initiate vigorous steps to put an end to the Arab-Israeli conflict. We shall do so on the basis of recogni-tion, by the Arab states and the Palestinians, of Israel as a sovereign state with the right to live in peace and security. We wholeheartedly be-lieve that this is possible, that this is necessary, that this will come"[3]

From the close contacts Peres had maintained with local Palestinians during the long and uneasy negotiations that began with his membership in two national unity administrations in Jerusalem, he had become convinced that Rabin's faith in such talks was misplaced. On the basis of available evidence, the foreign minister was certain that Arafat and others in the PLO offices at Tunis were pulling the strings for the local talks. If true, that demonstrated nothing was to be gained by continuing so meaningless a charade—but the problem was to convince the prime minister his policy would lead nowhere.

However, the alternative—to place the government's trust in a new round of talks with Arafat and the PLO—also was difficult for Peres to advocate, particularly because of the long history of the foreign minister's differences with Rabin. Still, a flawed policy could scarcely be dropped without offering some reasonable alterative—and no one in the new government, Peres included, was ready to conclude the conversations in Washington.

The resolution of the issue involved something more than brushing aside mere personal quirks of judgment. Both the background and the outlook of the prime minister and his foreign minister were markedly different. For Rabin, having spent most of his life in the military, the security of the nation always was uppermost among his sense of values; for Peres, even though he had worked for years in the defense department, his motivation was that of a politician first and, latterly, an economist, someone who did not believe in absolutes.

True, there had been times in their long rivalry for primacy in government and the Labor Party during which Rabin had tried to dismiss Peres as a wheeler-dealer while Peres in turn had worried that Rabin was just another stiff-necked militarist. But as they both seemed to realize in their seventh decade, such judgments seemed out of character with the kind of leadership that now was expected of them. The Polish-born Peres had been in Palestine since age eleven when he arrived with his parents as immigrants; here, he had obtained his education save for a year at Harvard and here, too, he had been a Labor Party official since 1947, a part of the government on and off since 1953, including the prime ministry.

Whatever was done to bring a long-delayed peace and perhaps prosperity as well to the struggling state of Israel was not likely to depend on any individual, not even the prime minister nor foreign minister; in a self-governing country that was approaching a population of 5 million in the Middle East, whatever was done now would perforce have to win the support of a majority of the public. If ever there was to be a new deal in the Middle East, this was it.[4]

For Peres, the way to go was to experiment with Palestinian control of the Gaza Strip just to determine if any semblance of a Palestinian regime could be trusted to exist side by side with a thoroughgoing Israeli government. He had been advocating some such approach since the early 1980s but neither his government nor the PLO had paid much attention to him. Gaza was so much trouble by itself, given an impoverished and often desperate population of almost a million Palestinians, that neither the PLO in Tunis nor any of the successive governments in Jerusalem wanted to consider it. Refugees, overcrowding, poverty, hunger, squalor, and crime—every shameful product of a neglected civilization existed on the Gaza Strip, and nobody, including the PLO and the Israeli government itself, seemed to want to do anything about it.

What enabled the Palestinians in Gaza to exist mainly was the employment they received daily in nearby Israeli towns and settlements together with such local enterprises as commercial fishing in the Mediterranean. But whenever there were Israeli crises with the PLO, which were frequent, the Gazans were the first to feel the consequences, because their travel credentials then were deemed unacceptable, with hunger and suffering as a result. The pain, the slums, the crime, and the shantytowns produced only shame for Israel, which was why Peres over the years always put forward Gaza relief—he called it "Gaza first"—as the first subject for experimental Palestinian rule.

In the atmosphere of mingled tension and suspicion that clouded Israeli-Arab relations at the time, as Peres was the first to realize, he had to contend with the PLO's refusal to move from Tunis to Gaza mainly because an Israeli politician had suggested it. On the Israeli side, there also was a reluctance to act because any sign of a softened Jewish position toward the Arabs was likely to increase the demands the PLO would make for any accommodation.

However, once Peres became Labor's foreign minister in the Rabin government and again tried the Egyptians on the "Gaza first" experiment, there was a change of front in the Mubarak government in Cairo. Amid signs of interest, a few Egyptian diplomats close to President Mubarak inquired cautiously about any response the Israelis had received from the PLO in Tunis. At that, Peres had to sigh once again, because he realized the PLO would not move for the convenience of a new Israeli foreign minister.

But fortunately, President Mubarak and some of his advisers in the latest Egyptian government apparently realized that Prime Minister Rabin's dependence on local Palestinian cooperation could not in itself force the PLO from a leading part in the peace process. That, at least, was Peres's conclusion when Cairo signaled interest in the "Gaza first" option. Although Rabin reserved judgment, he approved Peres's experiment.

It was typical of Peres's operation in the foreign ministry in Jerusalem that he now sent an appeal to President Mubarak's advisers to persuade Arafat and the PLO in Tunis to reconsider the "Gaza first" option. Although he was cautious enough not to admit the failure of Prime Minister Rabin's dependence on a local Palestinian solution to Israel's troubles with the Arabs, that was not necessary. Once the Egyptians agreed to try "Gaza first" as a testing ground for peace, the next step depended on favorable action in Tunis.

Over a period of months toward the end of 1992 and early 1993, President Mubarak together with other Arab moderates in the Middle East were able to move Arafat and the PLO toward renewed negotiations with Israel through the Gaza option. It then became Peres's task to try to convince Prime Minister Rabin that the local Palestinians in themselves lacked the power to halt rising Arab violence against the border areas of the Jewish state. No matter how adamantly Rabin was opposed to dealing with the PLO as an "outside" Arab force, this—in the opinion of his foreign minister—was the only realistic course for the future.[5]

As Peres summarized the private talks he had with Rabin at the time, the local Palestinian delegation in Washington had neither the authority nor the strength to suggest an area within Israel's jurisdiction where the specifics of a proposed peace agreement could be tested; hence, there was no prospect that a mere local agreement could bring about an end to the continued violence that was draining the resources that otherwise could have stimulated a developing Israeli economy. Much as the prime minister objected to dealing with the PLO, the foreign minister contended, Arafat's organization and its financial supporters among the Arab states had to be a part of any settlement the Israelis hoped to achieve with the Arab world.

Still, Rabin clung to his prejudices even though the eighth meeting of the local Palestinians in Washington had failed to produce any forward movement toward a Middle East peace. However, at about the same time, the Israeli authorities had rounded up 415 accused Hamas terrorists and expelled them in connection with an investigation of the killing of an Israeli policeman. In retaliation, the local Palestinian delegation called off the rest of their scheduled peace operations in Washington.

Rabin's last chance to make good on his political campaign pledge for peace was to try his foreign minister's approach, much as he disliked it. And although he mistrusted secret diplomacy, that was the course on which he now embarked when the Washington talks resumed without any tangible result.

During the latter part of 1992 and early 1993, the Norwegian government already had made an offer to both Israel and the PLO of its facilities for an entirely confidential discussion of the issues separating them. Partly by chance, partly by design, there also had been preliminary soundings between trusted intermediaries of the principals through the good offices of a Norwegian deputy foreign minister, Jan Egeland. An initial meeting between low-level people in the confidence of the Israeli government and the PLO already had been held in London merely to make contact and start the action.

Then, on January 21, 1993, both sides got down to business with another secret meeting at Sarpsborg, near Oslo, that brought together an Israeli history professor, Yair Hirschfeld, who enjoyed Foreign Minister Peres's confidence, and Abu Ala, a PLO representative who turned out to be an Arab economist, Ahmad Queri. Their go-between for the arrangements was a Norwegian trusted by his government, Terje Larsen.

The surprised and delighted Foreign Minister Peres learned only after that meeting of the PLO's interest in his proposal of "Gaza first" as a testing ground for a future settlement of some of the most immediate issues separating the two adversaries. The Norwegians kept faith, as did the participants in the talks for as long as they lasted. And Prime Minister Rabin, despite all his reluctance to deal with the PLO, eventually became a participant in this unique exercise of secret diplomacy as did Yasir Arafat.[6]

Truly, as Rabin had said in his second inaugural, "Our face is toward the rising sun."[7] Now, however, he would have to take care not be burned.

Abu Ala was not at all bashful in putting forward the PLO's demands at that first business meeting in Norway. What he suggested was an immediate Israeli troop withdrawal from the Gaza Strip together with what he called a "mini–Marshall Plan"—a multibillion-dollar financial operation paid for by the United States—to keep close to a million Arabs alive during the transition to home rule. It followed that further negotiations would decide just how intricate and costly home rule in Gaza would be and the extent of Israeli participation in it. To the Israeli representative at that first meeting, Hirschfeld, it seemed to be a promising start.

By indirection, all the major issues affecting the PLO's ultimate objective of a twin Palestinian state, as provided for in the UN General Assembly resolution of November 29, 1947, were set aside—including the settlement of such major disputes as the status of Jerusalem, Palestinian refugees, description of borders, Jewish settlements in Arab areas, and so many others. This was, as Peres and Arafat seemed to have agreed at the outset, an exploratory discussion of a "Gaza first" solution that would create precedents for an eventual negotiation of larger issues.[8]

However, after a second meeting the following month that tried to spell out specifics in a seven-page paper called "The Sarpsborg Document," even Peres backed off and Rabin's skepticism increased. What the PLO now proposed was for the Israelis to yield control over the Gaza Strip to the UN with enforcement power presumably falling directly to the PLO or another Arab affiliate. That was moving too far too fast for an Israeli government as conservative as Rabin's. What he approved of instead was an Israeli proposal, put forward by Peres through Professor Hirschfeld, for the PLO to move its headquarters from Tunis to Gaza for more direct dealings with Israel, which intended to retain control of Gaza despite the enlarged role contemplated by the PLO.[9]

Subsequently, as winter edged into spring and the Norwegian talks centered in Oslo beginning in March 1993, the exchanges between the parties became much more frequent. Suggestions also came from President Mubarak in Cairo and Prime Minister Rabin in Jerusalem—a testimonial to the usefulness of the exchanges now that all other avenues of communication had been abandoned. The Oslo channel, however, still remained secret as far as the outside world was concerned.

Upon the insistence of Arafat, who had forwarded a map of the area under consideration to Cairo, the "Gaza first" proposal now had become "Gaza-and-Jericho-First," which meant that the PLO wanted to broaden the negotiation to include at least one city in the West Bank of the Jordan River, Jericho. That was not at all to Rabin's liking, for he still apparently refused to give up hope that in some as yet undetermined manner a non-PLO Palestinian program could emerge from this secret discussion between Israel and the PLO.[10]

However, the prime minister also realized these discussions in Oslo might well be an alternative to the continued outbreak of PLO-sponsored violence within Israel. That spring, there already had been a series of terrorist attacks that had caused at least ten Israeli deaths within three weeks, as a result of which the Israeli government had issued its usual order barring more than one hundred thousand Arab workers from jobs in Israel, most of them from the Gaza Strip.[11]

Rabin suspected that Arafat was not above ordering spurts of terrorism to encourage Israel's continuance of the secret discussions in Oslo, which also could eventually cover the Israeli position on the West Bank as well as the Gaza Strip. For that reason, as Rabin once described his position to an aide, he saw to it throughout the secret discussions that Israeli armed strength remained at the peak. "If you want to make drastic concessions for peace," he once said, "you must show the public you can take drastic measures for security."

Although former rival leaders of the Labor Party, Rabin and Peres developed a close working relationship in which they frequently reviewed the Israeli objectives and made whatever changes seemed necessary to both without too much further consultation. Once the prime minister concluded that there was no further hope in establishing a breakthrough for peace by way of the local Palestinians, who had failed so dismally in the Washington talks, he accepted the relationship with Arafat and his PLO leadership group in Tunis for as long as the secret conversations lasted.

The West Bank did provide difficulties, particularly the negotiations that had to do with Jericho paralleling the arrangements that were being made for the eventual governance of the Gaza Strip. However, the prime minister had a ready response for those who warned that the Israeli public might well rebel against any West Bank giveaway that recurred during the secret talks. To that, Rabin commented that an incorporation of the entire West Bank within Israel would mean accepting 1.3 million West Bank Arabs as Israeli citizens, which would amount to a drastic change in Israeli population figures—not to overlook Israeli political parties and their reason for existence.[12]

One other factor was of major importance to the prime minister as the secret Oslo talks with the PLO continued through the late spring and summer. He conceived his responsibility to include the most painstaking means to be certain, not only that President Clinton and Secretary of State Christopher were informed in the United States but also that whatever questions they raised were given a satisfactory answer.

As a result, Rabin's relations with the American chief of state and his foreign minister remained a source of strength to him and to his government. Such close cooperation also made it possible to eliminate the usual misunderstandings that sometimes bedevil the most sensitive foreign relationships. Christopher, one of the most traveled of all American secretaries of state, became a frequent night stopover guest at the Rabin ménage as the secret diplomatic adventure of many months surged toward a climax in the fall.[13]

30.   The Oslo Process

Everybody concerned seemed prepared for the failure of the secret peace talks in Oslo between Israel and the PLO, which is why there was such astonishment and even jubilation over their success far outside Norway. The difficulties thereafter—which were serious—took a while to develop.

During the nine months of the Oslo meetings, the urge for confidential relationships was so great that even Prime Minister Rabin and Yasir Arafat, the PLO leader, worked with what they both cheerfully referred to as a "hot line." That was the term they applied to their secret contact through Yossi Genosar, a former General Security Service (Shabak) director, who had weekly meetings with Arafat through much of 1994 and 1995.

The uses of the go-between made a sufficient impression in his regular visits to PLO headquarters in Tunis to cause the PLO director to let the Arab press know, in a moment of self-importance, that he had a "hot line" directly to Rabin. Quite naturally, when the prime minister wanted to know more about the "hot line," he asked the somewhat mystified Genosar, who in turn put the question to Arafat at their next meeting.

"You're the hot line," the PLO's chief responded, adding that he had not wanted to name the Israeli and let his cabinet in on the secret. Anyway, the incident did not seem to bother Rabin, who still had little faith in Arafat at the time but who thereafter referred to Genosar as the "hot line" as well.[1]

The exchange occurred at about the midpoint of the negotiations, when Rabin and Arafat had never met, saw no reason to do so, and continued to be deeply suspicious of each other. At the time, there had been seven inconclusive negotiating sessions, the last five in Oslo through the courtesy, even the sponsorship, of the Norwegian government. Even so, Rabin did not like what was going on and sent York Singe, a lawyer, to the eighth meeting with instructions to reject all Arab proposals and start all over with a new all-Israeli document.

When Singer did so, the Arab delegate and his Israeli counterpart went through the new text word for word—a session that took thirty-six hours—and ended suddenly when neither side could agree on how and why Jericho and environs on the West Bank should be given the same status as the Gaza Strip in the negotiations. By that time, the delegates and their assistants were so weary and their tempers had been so sorely tried that a monumental argument virtually destroyed all hope of compromise. The session concluded in a massive shouting match—and that was that.[2]

They tried again a week later after rest and reflection, but now the Palestinian side weighed in with its own new document plus twenty-five additional demands, taking a turn at Israel's game and getting nowhere, too. After that debacle, it seemed for a time that the cause of the Oslo sessions had ended in complete discord. But now, the host for the secret sessions, Foreign Minister Johan Jorgen Holst, took up the role of a "hot line" emissary with a delegation of his Norwegian countrymen he had led to Tunis to confer with Arafat and the flabbergasted Palestinians.

Holst refused to accept the breakdown as final. He had a long and brilliant record as a diplomat and now he made use of it in a letter to Foreign Minister Peres that emphasized the seriousness of the Palestinian position and suggested Israeli reconsideration. Coming from such a source, Peres was immediately impressed—so much so that he supported the Norwegian proposal in his own appeal directly to the astonished prime minister.[3]

That at last made Rabin hesitate. And no wonder! Foreign Minister Holst, at fifty-six, had the respect of the United Nations and the international community. From the time he had finished his education with postgraduate studies at Harvard after undergraduate work at Oslo University and Columbia University in New York City, he had been in the service of the Norwegian Institute of International Affairs, becoming its director in the 1980s. His appointments followed as minister of defense and foreign minister.[4]

Not content with having sponsored the secret Oslo talks, Foreign Minister Holst now was in effect suggesting that the failure of the negotiations under current circumstances would be Israel's responsibility. While Rabin still hesitated, he received word from his minister of health, Haim Ramon, who had met with another Arab source in Jerusalem, that PLO concessions were possible, that Arafat did want to bring about a better arrangement with Israel.

Reluctantly, the prime minister sent Singer back to negotiate with the PLO in Oslo late in July. Nothing much happened, however, because the Arabs' proposed sharing of Jerusalem as always became the sticking point. What Arafat wanted was a part of Jerusalem that he could call the capital of an Arab rival state in Palestine—something no Israeli leader would grant.

But at just about the time in August when the deal might have fallen through, Arafat yielded, postponed all further discussions of the future of Jerusalem, and maintained his position when three of his delegation members resigned in protest. A climax now was at hand, for which Foreign Minister Peres, with his prime minister's approval, flew to Stockholm and met Holst to try if at all possible to wrap up the negotiations. The Israeli then made the point that only a few details remained to be settled, that further delays could only imperil an agreement, and that both sides would benefit through the Norwegian diplomat's intercession.[5]

With Rabin's approval, the Norwegian foreign minister organized an eight-hour telephone negotiation between Stockholm and Tunis, beginning soon after 10:00 P.M. on August 17. With the cooperation of Swedish authorities who were involved, Holst acted as mediator from Stockholm with Foreign Minister Peres and also the Oslo negotiator, Singer, representing Israel. At the Tunisian end, the responsibility for the Palestinian side was exercised by Arafat and his chief of foreign affairs, Abu Mazen. Whenever necessary, Rabin also was consulted while abed in Jerusalem.

Somehow, despite all the pressures involved, the consultation ended in a final agreement. On the morning of August 20, after Holst, Peres, and Singer returned to Oslo, they were joined there by the Oslo negotiator for Tunis, Abu Ala, and an assistant; after that, typed copies of the Israeli-PLO agreement were signed by the parties at the Oslo Plaza Hotel. With that, both sides moved the Oslo process toward self-rule for 2.3 million Palestinians in the Gaza Strip and the West Bank.

But there still was a long way to go because both the Israeli and Arab peoples had yet to be notified of this agreement and the various letters of intent that were to be exchanged between the parties. And no one then could say what the response would be—but for the moment much had been accomplished that few, if any, had thought possible at the beginning of that crucial year.[6]

The world learned toward the end of August, in formal announcements from Jerusalem and Tunis, that Israel and the PLO had completed a working agreement for peace between them in which the PLO recognized Israeli's right to exist in peace and security while Israel recognized the PLO as the representative of the Palestinian people in negotiations to activate the Middle East peace process. A sweeping commitment against further violence by both sides was a part of the deal, but it did not come about until the most stubborn resistance by Arafat was overcome.[7]

Nor was there any assurance in the printed texts eventually released or elsewhere that either side might not reconsider its options. In the unsettled and often unpredictable Middle East, however, the pledges made in the compact in themselves were enormously reassuring, always dependent on how responsibly they were regarded and carried out.

"It is time," both sides agreed at the outset of the document, "to put an end to decades of confrontation and conflict, recognize their mutual legitimate and political rights, and strive to live in peaceful coexistence and mutual dignity and security and achieve a just, lasting and comprehensive peace settlement and historic reconciliation through the agreed political process."

What the pact sought to do was to establish "a Palestinian Interim Self-Government Authority, an elected Council for the Palestinian people in the West Bank and the Gaza strip for a transitional period of not exceeding five years, leading to a permanent settlement based on Security Council Resolutions 242 and 338." It was specified that the Council would be elected under international observation and safeguarded by a Palestinian force.

The Israeli military government was pledged to withdraw from Gaza and the Jericho area and transfer its authority for civil administration to the Palestinian Authority to promote economic development and progress in education, culture, health, social welfare, direct taxation, and tourism. A number of special authorities would also be created, including an electricity Authority, a Gaza Sea Port Authority, a Palestine Development Bank, and so on. For public safety, the Palestinians were given their own police force, and both parties were pledged to promote a "Marshall Plan" for the area (probably meaning an effort to raise more American loans).

The most meaningful part of the agreement, however, came in the letters given by Rabin and Arafat granting mutual recognition and pledging peace.

Like the Camp David accords, the exchange of letters covered issues of great importance to both parties who simply did not want to commit themselves in the main text of the agreement. It remained for an always-doubting public outside the Middle East to evaluate the importance of these pledges of mutual recognition, an end to violence, and promises to publish violators.

Arafat led off as follows in his letter to "Mr. Prime Minister," a salutation that characterized his feelings:

> The signing of the Declaration of Principles marks a new era in the history of the Middle East. In firm conviction thereof, I would like to confirm the following PLO commitments:
> The PLO recognizes the right of the State of Israel to exist in peace and security.
> The PLO accepts UN Security Council Resolutions 242 and 238.
> The PLO commits itself to the Middle East peace process, and to a peaceful resolution of the conflict between the two sides and declares that all outstanding issues relating to permanent status will be resolved through negotiation. . . . Accordingly the PLO renounces the use of terrorism and other acts of violence and will assume responsibility over all PLO elements and personnel in order to assure their compliance, prevent violations and discipline violators.

The response from Rabin was equally formal:

> Mr. Chairman,
> In response to your letter . . . I wish to confirm to you that, in light of the PLO commitments included in your letter, the Government of Israel has decided to recognize the PLO as the representative of the Palestinian people and commence negotiations with the PLO within the Middle East peace process.

The exchange of letters in effect marked the beginning of what turned out to be a miasma of doubts and misgivings over the entire process of the negotiations that now committed both parties to resolve all issues in dispute within five years. These included the fate of Palestinian refugees, Jerusalem, border problems, statehood, and, first of all, Palestinian self-rule in the occupied territories.

Nevertheless, President Clinton was so enthusiastic about the agreement that he telephoned Rabin in his Jerusalem office on September 8 to congratulate him, but the president was decidedly uncomfortable about the prospect of inviting Arafat to Washington for a ceremonial signing of the compact. Arafat at the time was not on the list of accredited diplomats either for the White House or the State Department.

Although Rabin enjoyed Clinton's tribute, the Israeli leader also wondered whether he could put up with Arafat's presence at the White House ceremonial. The prime minister's staff suggested that perhaps the signing could be performed by Foreign Minister Peres and Abu Mazen of the PLO, but nearly everybody in the office soon concluded that would not do. If Rabin and Arafat both stayed away from President Clinton's signing ceremony, it would be considered just another political charade with little meaning and even less validity.

For the rest of that week, both Rabin and his advisers changed their minds several times, not really knowing what to do, until Secretary of State Christopher telephoned late on September 10 with word that President Clinton had invited both the prime minister and Arafat, which settled everything, or so Rabin's intimates believed. But by the next morning, there was another crisis when Foreign Minister Peres was threatening to resign because he had not been invited. To avert a resumption of rumors about the old Rabin-Peres feud, the White House staff enlarged the guest list to include Secretary of State Christopher, Foreign Minister Peres, and the PLO's foreign expert, Abu Mazen.[8]

Before such dignitaries as these together with a distinguished group also invited by the White House, the signing ceremony took place on the afternoon of September 13 on the White House lawn—an auspicious sunny day for all concerned. President Clinton, Arafat, and Rabin thereupon signed the Declaration of Principles that professed to end "confrontation and conflict" between the State of Israel and the PLO to achieve a "comprehensive peace settlement."

Then Rabin's response fairly burst from him. At that moment after the signing of the document to applause from the crowd, he turned to

President Clinton and rumbled with the earnestness of an old soldier on parade, "This is a very important moment in all our lives." To that, the president nodded smilingly in gracious acknowledgment.

But Arafat was not to be outdone. A smaller figure in military uniform topped by his customary Arabic headdress, the speckled *keffiyah*, he turned toward the president and added, "This is truly an important moment," then said with great emphasis, "Mr. President, it is now your role to support the peace process and it will be up to you to make it work."

As the distinguished audience applauded all three participants, Arafat turned slowly and walked toward his former enemy with outstretched hand. Long afterward, recollecting so picturesque a confrontation between the Palestinian outsider and her husband, Leah Rabin wrote of that scene:

> The look of discomfort on Yitzhak's face was unmistakable. He looked as if he'd swallowed something large and painful. He was shaking the hand of a man he had said he would never dignify with a direct contact. He was breaking a vow. How could he forget the victims of terror even at this historic moment? Had it not been before the eyes of the world, he might not have felt so deeply conflicted. . . . I imagine he was thinking, "The whole world has heard me say *never* and now I am."

At the decisive moment, while Rabin hesitated, President Clinton gently nudged him to respond. Then only did the prime minister of Israel move to clasp the outstretched hand of the chairman of the PLO. The handshake was brief and mechanical, each of the old foes fearlessly facing the other. Then, when it was over, Rabin turned to Foreign Minister Peres beside him and muttered with grim humor, "Now it's your turn."

Rabin addressed the delighted audience in celebration:

> Today here in Washington at the White House, we will begin a new reckoning in the relations between peoples, between parents tired of war, between children who will not know war.
> We have no desire for revenge. We harbor no hatred toward you [with a nod to Arafat]. We, like you, are people—people who want to build a home, to plant a tree, to love, to live side by side with you in dignify, in affinity, as human beings, as free then.
> We are today giving peace a chance and saying again to you, "We who have fought against you, the Palestinians—we say to you today in a loud and clear voice: 'Enough of blood and tears. Enough.' "

With the last round of applause on the White House lawn Arafat and Rabin left President Clinton's side and joined the audience, shaking hands and greeting friends and acquaintances as they went. Among the elite of Washington whom the president had invited, there were others they saw and recognized individually.

For Rabin, there were a few of the surviving families of victims of Arab terror whom he had brought with him as symbols of what he hoped would be the past. And for Arafat, there was a joyful reunion with Hanan Ashrawi, his Palestinian spokeswoman during many a crisis of the past. For these also had been guests of the president of the United States on this great occasion.

It all had happened just two days before Rosh Hashanah, the Jewish New Year, as Leah Rabin recorded in her memory book—the peak moment of her long and happy marriage.[9]

After the elaborate peace ceremonial in Washington, it was difficult for all concerned to resume the daily grist of what was meant to be a vastly changed relationship between the State of Israel and the Palestinians. Of course, it could not happen quite so easily, for half a lifetime of the bitterest opposition between Arab and Jew could not be changed overnight with the signing of a document on the White House lawn.

Even in their personal relationships, Rabin and Arafat found it difficult to unbend later while they attempted to develop a working relationship. It helped that the PLO did try in the early weeks of the new order to refrain from either confrontation or violence; the Israeli military, too, held its fire instead of charging headlong at a suspected enemy at the first sign of disorder in the streets of a town or the nearby countryside.

The prime minister of Israel and the chairman of the PLO were coolly courteous during their formal meetings in connection with their new relationship. To Arafat, Rabin was always "Your Excellency." To Rabin, his Arab counterpart invariably was "Mr. Chairman." In their discussions, each pressed the other for greater activity to suppress dissension in the ranks and seek a less confrontational relationship. Rabin sought Arafat's help in suppressing continued Arab violence against Israel outside Palestine as well as in the land where both peoples now tried to live together in peace. And Arafat tried to encourage Rabin to limit the incursions of the Israeli military against the border areas, particularly the Golan Heights of Syria and the northern Israeli border with Lebanon.[10]

This did not necessarily mean, in the beginning at least, that major differences remained between the two leaders. In the opening weeks of the new relationship, Arafat sometimes would respond in the Israeli prime minister's defense against continued Arab criticism from abroad, saying at one point, "With Rabin, you always know where you stand." And the prime minister, on his part, once was heard to defend Arafat against doubts of his sincerity in controlling terrorism, saying, "Even *we* don't stop all the terror in areas *we* control."

Even so, behind the scenes, hopes already were being raised among the Arabs of Palestine for schools, hospitals, businesses, police forces, and homes for an Arab nation in Palestine that would live side by side with Israel. And such hopes could not forever be denied.

31.   New Deal in the Middle East

Encouraged by the Oslo agreements between Israel and the PLO, the United States moved quickly to persuade Prime Minister Rabin to include the neighborly kingdom of Jordan in the latest accords.

However, neither the Israeli leader nor King Hussein needed much persuasion. The day after the celebrated handshake between Rabin and Yasir Arafat on the White House lawn, it so happened that emissaries for Israel and Jordan had concluded weeks of secret talks with their initials on a draft treaty linking their two nations.

What remained to be done, therefore, was to extend the responsibility for the newest treaty proposal to the respective heads of state. Suiting deed to thought, Prime Minister Rabin bluntly asked the king at their next meeting, "Do you mean business?" To which the king responded that the business of extending the peace process in the Middle East was very much on his mind.[1]

In this manner the new deal in the Middle East was advanced another important step, although both were well aware of the bloodthirsty mood of the opposition in both countries, Israel and Jordan, and elsewhere in the region. Still, with the collapse of the Soviet Union, it no longer was possible to blame Communist plotters for the savage efforts of both Israeli conservatives and Arab radicals to destroy peace.

Eight months before the Israeli prime minister and the king of Jordan signed the completed treaty they had negotiated on the basis of the agreement initialed the day after the Israel-PLO pact, a Jewish extremist, Baruch Goldstein, had massacred twenty-nine Arabs at prayer in a Hebron mosque on the West Bank of the Jordan River. He had been an American-born settler in Israel, who had put on a military uniform to carry out his criminal act, and was himself killed as a result. It did not take long for the Arabs to strike back for the murders that were committed on February 2, 1994. In a little more than a month, on April 6, an Arab suicide bomber murdered six Israelis in a northern village. A week later, another Arab blew himself up with a bomb and took five more Israelis with him in a nearby village.[2]

This was the appallingly familiar pattern of violence and terror that had accompanied most advances toward peace in the Middle East, but Prime Minister Rabin refused to be deterred from his faith in the Oslo process. He recognized that there were frantic extremists among both the Arabs and Israelis who would try to stall all attempts at peace. True, both would invariably invoke religious beliefs to try to excuse their callous disregard of human life, a position that pained more principled believers.

But terrorism, too, was the inevitable risk that had to be undertaken on an almost daily basis by Prime Minister Rabin, Foreign Minister Peres, and their opposite numbers among the Arabs with whom they strove to extend this new deal in the Middle East to Jordan—and beyond. To someone as secular as Rabin, and as unemotional in the face of danger, these were the risks that came with holding high office. All he could do to protect himself and those about him was to hope for the best and continue to rest his faith in the protection of the Israeli military, the police, and the undercover Shin Bet organization.

The prime minister, more than most others, knew perfectly well that there were no easy answers to his problem. Whatever the danger, he had to face it.[3]

There were grave risks, too, in King Hussein's position, for he had been obliged to assume responsibility for almost a million Arab refugees from Palestine who either had fled to his kingdom after the Six-Day War with Israel in 1967 or sequestered themselves in hovels directly outside his capital, Amman. As he was to admit some thirty years later, the war itself had been his mistake, and he freely confessed as much to his people at the time he was preparing to sign the peace treaty he had negotiated with Israel, the next Arab state after Egypt to do so.

Much of Hussein's faith in his association with Israel, as well as his concern for the Arab refugees created by the Six-Day War, stemmed from his disastrous experience at the time. For in 1967, acting through what he called too great a belief in propaganda for a huge Arab uprising against the infidel newcomers, he had ordered his Jordanian army to join the troops of Egypt, Syria, Lebanon, Iraq, and Saudi Arabia against the Israeli army.

What happened in those six days of conflict, as he conceded, was a massive defeat in which the superior Israeli forces subdued the Arab opposition in short order with its superior air force and its tanks, causing at least six thousand deaths. As a result, the king said, he entered upon a commitment to peace with Israel and a long-term responsibility for the welfare of the Palestinian refugees.[4]

The proposed peace treaty between Jordan and Israel, already initialed by the negotiators, meanwhile had been stalled mainly because of the response to the Goldstein murders at the Hebron mosque and the various Arab slayings of Israelis in retribution. Meanwhile, the first results of the Oslo agreement between Israel and the PLO had taken effect with the retreat of Israeli forces from Jericho, the heart of the West Bank and most of the Gaza Strip except for the homes of forty-five hundred Jewish settlers there.

Arafat, too, had taken advantage of the lull in diplomatic activity by moving his headquarters from Tunis to the Gaza Strip and, in a subsequent appearance on the West Bank, making a triumphal visit to Jericho.

With the lull in the activity of vengeful Arabs determined to take Israeli lives in return for the Goldstein murders, King Hussein and Prime Minister Rabin met secretly in London to resume negotiations on what turned out to be a much broader peace agreement than the one their deputies had initialed. What they decided to do there, and later that spring and summer of 1994 during a series of meetings mainly at the Jordanian palace in Aqaba, was to come to economic as well as political terms with each other.

What that meant immediately was a complicated agreement by Israel to share its water resources with water-starved Jordan, which included a commitment to raise jointly at least $200 million for the creation in both nations of an intricate system of dams that would be supported by a desalination process. As a feature that must have appealed particularly to the Israeli farmers involved, the king and the prime minister worked out a deal under which the Israelis would continue to tend their accustomed fields in Jordan, although that particular land would be returned to Jordanian sovereignty.

Much of these and other economic details of the Jordan-Israel treaty were handled by Foreign Minister Peres, who, far from trying to outdo his old rival, the prime minister, now was working closely with him as a friend and ally. In fact, during the development of this relationship, Peres found it necessary to fly to Amman for the first time to broaden the water development proposal with an additional canal joining the Red Sea and the Dead Sea. The objective was to turn the desert in between into what was called the Peace Valley, an Israeli tourist and industrial center.

This was the break that finally concluded the basic Jordan-Israel negotiations, for on July 25, 1994, President Clinton arranged a three-way summit with King Hussein and Prime Minister Rabin at the White House. The Israeli and Jordanian leaders brought with them a still more important addition to the draft of the treaty over which they and their associates had labored for so many months—a document of non-belligerence by both parties to be added to the text of the peace pact.

But though President Clinton was satisfied, as well as the American ambassador to Israel, Martin Indyk, both the king and the prime minister wanted to go over the complicated document in such detail that the president realized the ceremonial signing would have to be put off. And so, amid goodwill on all sides, the Jordanian and Israeli delegations as well as their leaders returned to the Middle East for a final effort to resolve their remaining problems.

There were more ceremonials, to be sure. In the turgid atmosphere of the Middle East, such details were important for the peoples involved as well as their leaders. To rush into an agreement meant only that too many questions would be raised later; therefore, besides the completion of negotiations, including a painstaking delineation of their common borders, several more meetings took place between the king and the prime minister.

One of the most important was the first Jordanian overflight of Israeli territory, accomplished by the royal Jordanian jet piloted by King Hussein, who celebrated the event in a radio conversation with Prime Minister Rabin on the ground. Soon afterward, both participated in the dedication of their first open-border crossing near the Red Sea coastline followed by a lunch to commemorate the operation at King Hussein's palace at Aqaba. Both had deemed such deliberate measures necessary to allay the suspicions of the hostile minorities among their respective peoples.

At last, on October 26, 1994, the Jordanian-Israeli treaty was signed at the Jordanian-Israeli border crossing in the presence of President

Clinton, who flew from Washington to participate in an event that promised, in the words of Prime Minister Rabin, "to make the desert bloom." To that, King Hussein added his accolade, becoming the second Arab chief of state to come to terms with Israel.

Unfortunately, the same month, an Arab suicide bomber in the Middle East had shocked both nations and the Middle East as well by killing twenty-two people in a torched Tel Aviv bus. In the attack on the Israeli government's peace policies that followed from the opposition leader, Benjamin Netanyahu, Prime Minister Rabin retorted bluntly that the Likud politician was "dancing on the blood" of the victims. That, too, was a part of life in Israel in that critical era.[5]

The leaders of the outside world were far more receptive to the peace initiative in the Middle East. President Clinton's interest had been evident throughout his first term in the White House, surely an important sign of continued American support for an extension of the Israeli compact with Anwar el-Sadat's Egypt. But now the movement to celebrate the newest Middle East agreement spread significantly to other important international areas—notably the 1994 award of the Paris Peace Prize of the United Nations Educational, Scientific, and Cultural Organization (UNESCO). That summer, Prime Minister Rabin, Foreign Minister Peres, and Chairman Arafat of the PLO appeared together at a UNESCO ceremonial in the French capital to accept the organization's award for extending to Jordan their effort against continued war.

That fall, the two Israelis and the Palestinian again were honored in Spain with a prize for international cooperation in honor of the Prince of Asturias, bestowed at an elaborate ceremony by King Juan Carlos. At just about the same time, the most cherished honor of all, the Nobel Peace Prize, came to Messrs. Rabin, Peres, and Arafat while they were sharing renewed congratulations with King Hussein of Jordan for the signing of the Israeli-Jordan peace treaty.

Then came the Nobel Peace Prize ceremony on December 10 in Oslo in which the two Israelis and the Palestinian chairman became the guests of King Harald V and Queen Sonja of Norway. However, to Prime Minister Rabin, it was scarcely a time for rejoicing because the opposition at home already was trying to portray him as a "traitor" for dealing with the Palestinians and ceding areas in the Gaza Strip and West Bank that formerly had been occupied by Israeli troops—territories in which Arabs outnumbered Israelis sometimes by as much as 10 to 1.

Although others may well have been intent on celebrating the honor that had come to the prime minister and his two associates, he was in a somber mood for his response. Recalling how he had been handed a gun at six—a time when most children the world over are more interested in play—the prime minister reflected on his life as a soldier here in the halls of peace saying, "The profession of soldiering embraces a certain paradox. We take the best and the bravest of our young men into the army. . . . Yet we fervently pray that day [of duty] will never come—that the planes will never take flight, the tanks will never move forward, the soldiers will never mount the attacks for which they have been trained so well."[6]

In that frame of mind, so different from most of those about him who were celebrating (except Arafat, who still was in uniform with his usual headdress), the prime minister joined Foreign Minister Peres in contributing their share of the generous Nobel Prize to serve the interests of preserving peace. Rabin never commented on why he was so obsessed with images of war at a time when he had every right to be enjoying the fruits of peace, however briefly, but perhaps he recalled the tragic sacrifice of an Israeli corporal on the day of the Nobel Prize announcement in Jerusalem.

The corporal, Nachshon Wachsman, had been kidnapped and held for ransom that day by Palestinian terrorists who threatened his life if the Israelis failed to release some two hundred Arab prisoners. In a gun battle with Israeli troops at the house in Jerusalem where Wachsman was being held, he was killed along with all the terrorists and an Israeli soldier. Even to an old soldier like the prime minister, it was a terrible price to pay for peace—one of the bitter experiences that came with the honor of the Nobel award.

He had assumed full responsibility for the outcome, knowing perfectly well that his opponents would make political capital over what had been, for him, an unavoidable outcome to an encounter with terrorists.[7]

Far from appeasing the opposition, the honors that had been bestowed on Prime Minister Rabin and Foreign Minister Peres fairly goaded their enemies into almost nightly demonstrations of outrage in Jerusalem.

The Likud leader, Benjamin Netanyahu, went so far as to make an issue of the ceremony of the Nobel Prizes and other honors to the leaders of the government of Israel, belittling the awards and calling the recipients "traitors" to the Jewish state.

"We can overcome Peres and Rabin," he proclaimed to tens of thousands of demonstrators who invariably responded to his call for rallies against the government's efforts to promote peace with the Palestinians. To the Likud, with its hard core of religious extremists, the decision to yield parts of the heavily occupied Palestinian areas of the Gaza Strip and the West Bank of the Jordan constituted the Labor government's "surrender" to Arab terror. What was happening in Jerusalem, therefore, amounted to a mobilization of a Likud-sponsored operation to try to bring the Rabin government to its knees.

At the heart of the opposition were the religious parties, which were small in terms of the number of seats they held in the 120-seat Knesset, but powerful in the fanatical response their membership could produce in the antigovernment demonstrations that were now reaching a climax. In the attack on the post-Oslo agreements that the religious far right opposed with all its strength, they were estimated to amount to at least 60 percent of the voting-age population of Israelis.*

To illustrate the intensity of the hatred that Netanyahu directed at the government, he told Foreign Minister Peres during a Knesset argument that he was "threatening the security and freedom" of the government of Israel, a charge that also was regularly hurled at Prime Minister Rabin. In newspaper ads, it was customary as well for the Likud people to charge the government itself with treason. It was also a part of Netanyahu's political strategy to link Arafat and his Palestinians with the Rabin government as twin forces to be opposed—something the far right accepted to such an extent that they marched under a banner reading "Death to Arafat."

It followed that the Palestinian terrorists, far from cowering in the shadows, struck hard at their opponents by attacking outlying settlements of Israeli farmers. In one instance, on October 29, 1993, a settler named Haim Mizrahi was kidnapped and murdered by Arab terror-

---

*By contrast, the extreme Orthodox in the Jewish community in the United States amount to only about 15 or 20 percent, the majority being members of either Conservative or Reform congregations.

ists, who then burned his body. In reply to that outrage, a citizens' army of settlers attacked a nearby Arab village, stoning its houses and their inhabitants, and shooting some of them. Thereafter, on succeeding days, the settlers blockaded roads throughout the West Bank area in an effort to bring all life to a halt—and they nearly succeeded with the help of officials in what was called the Council of Settlements.

This was the impromptu engagement that shaped the lines of battle for most of two succeeding years and, in effect, caused the able-bodied settlers to mass in self-defense against Arab depredations while at the same time striking back at nearby Arab villages. The result was a maelstrom of trouble on both the West Bank and the Gaza Strip even though Arafat, to give him his due, did try as much as he dared to maintain his part of the various agreements he had reached with his Israeli counterparts.

But in so tumultuous an atmosphere, intensified through the encouragement of numerous Orthodox rabbis to organize defensive strikes by besieged settlers, it was often impossible to maintain order in the countryside for any lengthy period. True, there were moderates among the Israeli rabbinate as well who did their best to try to preserve order. But with so much pressure by the Likud leadership to continue the antigovernment demonstrations in Jerusalem, a return to normalcy in the mid-1990s became difficult if not impossible. At one point, even Netanyahu himself was appalled at the disorder in the Holy City and counseled restraint, but most crowds by that time were beyond control.

If Netanyahu did try now and then to soften the passions of extremists among his followers in the nightly demonstrations, no one came forward to testify that such concerns, however delayed, could also have been attributed to the outstanding rebel on the radical right, Gen. Ariel Sharon. As a potential member of a Likud government that could conceivably come to power, Sharon stimulated the nightly protest marchers in Jerusalem by also accusing the government of "collaborating with terror." Others went to extremes in scattering Likud literature, including one leaflet that depicted Rabin decked out in the uniform of a Nazi SS officer.

Under the circumstances, Rabin apparently came to believe it would be useless for him to try to demonstrate to the Knesset that he really had taken account of the need to protect Israeli settlers in areas where Arabs were in the majority. To have resorted to such technicalities in so supercharged an atmosphere, so his associates argued, would have created even more confusion among friend as well as foe.

At one time in 1995 during a Knesset debate, the prime minister did refer briefly to a few of the Israeli boundaries he regarded as final in his continued negotiations with the Palestinians. These included the Jordan River as the final eastern boundary of Israel, an extended border for the city of Jerusalem, and a provision that included fixed areas of Jewish settlements within areas on the West Bank where Palestinians were in the majority. But inevitably, the critical response was that not enough was being done to satisfy the families of the settlers, which once again reopened the issue to partisan debate before Rabin was ready to submit maps of the positions he wanted to maintain in any final agreement with the Palestinians.

The attacks headed by Netanyahu and further encouraged by Sharon therefore continued without letup until both Rabin and Peres felt besieged. But the extreme Right among the Likud opposition still was not satisfied, maintaining both its hatemongering and its exaggerations of Labor's supposed excesses. Probably the low point was reached in this campaign of mingled desperation and deceit when a Knesset member identified as a far right-winger, Rechavam Ze'evi, announced to all who were willing to listen, "This is a government that has decided to commit national suicide."

It was scarcely a sentiment that anybody in the Knesset would have dared apply in his era to David Ben-Gurion, who rode roughshod over his enemies. But with Yitzak Rabin shoved on the defensive through a disorderly opposition that sought to overthrow his government through the most peculiar tactics, it seemed that the Likud leader, Netanyahu, had decided on rule or ruin.

If the American-sponsored new deal in the Middle East was to be discarded, that apparently was the price that Israel would have to pay for a change in its government.[8]

32. The Sacrifice

Now well into his second term as prime minister of Israel and very likely to seek his third in 1996, Yitzhak Rabin had become an impressive figure in the international community. Strong of body and energetic in mind, he fairly towered over his dismayed opposition while his government enjoyed the recognition of 155 nations headed by the United States, Britain, and the other great ones of Europe plus Japan, China, India, and even the once-hesitant Vatican.

It must have given Rabin particular satisfaction at seventy-three, as an old soldier, to realize that his small nation of 5 million souls, viewed a little less than five decades after its rebirth following two thousand years, no longer could be considered an intruder among 350 million Arabs in the Middle East. For at this time in 1994, Israel had not only won recognition from Egypt and Jordan but was doing a brisk business as well with Morocco, Tunisia, and the Arabian peninsula oil states of Oman, Qatar, and Bahrain.[1]

In the prime minister's world tour that followed his shared award of the Nobel Peace Prize, of particular importance to Israel was Japanese cooperation in the development of the highest techniques in industrial efforts. And on the Korean peninsula, probably to Rabin's surprise, President Kim Young Sam of South Korea was so interested in Israel's ability to cooperate with Yasir Arafat and the PLO that he asked his guest to stay over another day to talk about it. Kim Young Sam still had his own problems in getting along with his ever-threatening neighbor, the surviving Communist hermit state of North Korea.[2]

Despite the efforts of the Likud Party to undermine the Rabin regime and besmirch the prime minister's character once he returned home, the admiration of the world at large remained unchanged, and his people, save for the radical right, responded to the designs for living that his government proposed. It was of the first importance to Rabin, both politically and personally, to continue to develop his relations with King Hussein of Jordan as well as President Mubarak of Egypt—his two closest Arab neighbors.

For this reason, in celebrating Israel's forty-seventh Independence Day on the eve of May 14, 1995, Israeli TV broadcast the prime minister's discussion with King Hussein on the growth of the Israeli-Jordanian relationship as well as its effect on neighboring Arab states. In Rabin's continued efforts to arrange for another suitable accord with Syria in return for an Israeli proposal to vacate its Golan Heights outposts, this was somewhat more the problem of Syria's Hafez al-Assad.

On a happier note, the relationship with the United States, Jordan, and the PLO was strengthened when President Clinton, King Hussein, and Yasir Arafat joined both Rabin and Foreign Minister Peres for another landmark broadcast, this one on the Cable News Network's "Larry King Live" program. To emphasize his position on Jerusalem for the home front that night of June 8, 1995, the prime minister took this unequivocal position: "For me, Jerusalem [is] united. It will [remain] under Israel's sovereignty, it will be the capital of Israel and the heart of the Jewish people. . . . At the same time, we are committed to free access and free practice to the members of the two other religions, to the holy shrines in Jerusalem, to the Muslims and to the Christians."

Despite such concerns for the home front, Israel's foreign relations were never far from Rabin's thoughts because he, like Ben-Gurion before him, realized how important it was for this small nation, clinging to the extreme western edge of the Asian continent, to expand its relations with foreign trading partners. One of the most promising opportunities came with the prime minister's first visit to the struggling new republic of the Ukraine, once known as the granary of the Soviet Union, on September 12 and 13, 1995. Here, the problem of Prime Minister Yevgeny Marchuk, in his liberated part of the new Russian federation, was to stimulate his country's vast agricultural economy—a project with which the Israeli leader was familiar.

But beyond the demands of commerce, there also was a very special reason for Rabin's visit to the Ukraine, a two-hour flight from Israel, for on a trip to Babi Yar, near Kiev, the scene of the Nazi massacre of thirty-four thousand Ukrainian Jews in 1941, the prime minister mourned the tragedy in words that had a significant warning for the excesses among his own people at home, had they been willing to listen: "The Jewish people were shot and killed here, but out of the trenches of death we were reborn, and now we must tell the entire world: let our tragedy be a warning sign to every human being that danger has not yet passed over the land."[3]

Only a little more than two weeks later, on September 28, 1995, there was another significant broadcast in which Prime Minister Rabin participated, this one to mark the realization of the extended Oslo accords, which so outraged the right wing at home because it gave self-rule to tens of thousands of West Bank Palestinians. The ceremonial took place at the White House in the presence of President Clinton, President Mubarak, King Hussein, and Yasir Arafat, with Rabin as the concluding speaker. This was, in all probability, the most important of the many collaborations in the Israeli government between Foreign Minister Peres and the prime minister, who now took special pride in the achievement, saying:

> Here we stand before you, men whom fate and history have sent on a mission of peace: to end, once and for all, one hundred years of bloodshed.
>
> Our dream is also your dream, King Hussein, President Mubarak, Chairman Arafat, all the others, and above all President Clinton—a president working in the service of peace—we all love the same children, weep the same tears, hate the same enmity, and pray for reconciliation. Peace has no borders.

Despite the tumult raised by the opposition on October 5, including chants of "traitor" in Jerusalem, the Knesset approved the latest –accord that was the product of the calm efforts of the Labor Party's leaders. On a later night, when the prime minister came home to his distressed wife and children, who had witnessed the televised scenes of protest in Israel and expressed their concerns, he responded in seeming resignation: "What's to be done? We're living in a democracy."[4]

Although there is no credible evidence that the prime minister knew of it, something already had been done. It was not much. But there is a record in the Shin Bet agency, Israel's CIA, that in the summer of that year its director, Carmi Gilon, had met Rabin and also Netanyahu to warn both that the threatening political exchanges between the Labor and Likud speakers in the Knesset and elsewhere could produce a violent result. The Shin Bet leader also urged both to try to tone down the viciousness of the dialogue.

The record includes a notation that Gilon made the same observation before a panel of Israeli journalists who had covered both the prime minister and his opponent, but nobody appeared to pay much attention to the Shin Bet leader's concern. The record remained unnoticed for the time being, probably because it was attributed only to a mysterious figure identified as K, the Hebrew letter *Kaf*, which was easy for busy agents to ignore.

Even before that, in January 1994, there also is a record made by two persons identified as associates of Ben-Gurion University that "Rabin will not die a natural death" because of the inner-party violence over the peace that was being arranged with Arafat and the PLO. The speaker was identified as a former professor dying of cancer, Yehoshafat Harkaby. But that prophecy of the prime minister's doom was even easier for busy officials to ignore, for it was never heard of again until it was published in an investigative book.

Everybody seemed particularly concerned about not offending the right-wing zealots, so the anti-Labor campaign continued unchecked regardless of what Netanyahu himself did or did not do. In the most recent record given to the authorities, there was what amounted to an anonymous tip to the Shin Bet, a letter naming an anonymous right-wing extremist and former student at a university in Tel Aviv as a plotter against the prime minister's life, but it would have taken a mind reader to identify the target.

If Rabin or his closest associates knew of these fragmentary tips, there was no sign that he or his party leaders took them seriously. He never wore a bullet-proof vest, carried a gun, or did anything more than walk with his assigned bodyguards, most of whom preceded him in crowds with only one of their number, as a rule, staying behind him to protect his back. That kind of security did not deter a determined assassin, who, as it turned out, was even then on the trail of his victim.[5]

What Rabin did do, months before this climax approached, was to be certain that his party would not lack for immediate leadership if he should suddenly be removed from power by illness, accident, or outright assault by a gunman. There was a distinct understanding among his intimates in the Labor Party that Foreign Minister Peres, being a former prime minister, would step in at once if the office was vacated for any reason, temporarily or permanently. And Peres knew that and was prepared to exercise the authority entrusted to him.

Beyond that, Rabin also had let it be known that he favored two younger people, both close to him and deeply in his confidence, as his eventual successors beyond Peres's term of service. They were a former Israeli army chief of staff, Ehud Barak, who had become a member of the Rabin cabinet in July 1995, as interior minister, and Haim Ramon, who left the line of succession about that time to become the president of the Israeli labor federation, the Histadrut, always a powerful force in the Israeli government even though it was not technically a part of the organization. With these appointments and the continued service of Foreign Minister Peres, it would seem that Rabin, at the very least, had tried to protect both his government and his party from chaos in the event that something tragic should happen to him.

For his family, he had the utmost confidence in his wife, Leah, to whom he had been married for forty-seven years, and their two grown children, who now were well able to take care of themselves. Beyond that now, he was ready for anything that might happen to his country, his people, or himself.[6]

Despite the opposition of the extremists in Israel, there had been a series of popular peace rallies sponsored by the Labor Party that year, and Prime Minister Rabin had made it a point to attend most of them, usually as the concluding speaker. But there was one planned for November 4, a Saturday night, about which he was not too sure, because he seemed to have a feeling that it would not attract many people. That, at least, was his wife's conclusion, because he had to be certain first of all that the turnout would not be so low as to discredit public interest in the peace process.

The convincer came shortly before the date set for the rally when one of its chief sponsors, a former mayor of Tel Aviv named Shlomo Lahat, assured him the audience would be both large and enthusiastic. And so, reluctantly, the old soldier prepared to do his duty that Saturday night after the Sabbath ended at sundown. He had just one meeting at his Tel Aviv home before departing, a session with one of his favorites, Haim Ramon, now the chief of the Histadrut labor federation. Then, he joined his wife, Leah, and headed for his official car, an armored Cadillac of silvery hue, that was waiting for him outside their apartment complex because he had promised to be on the platform by 8:00 P.M.

Everything seemed to be in order. Except for the missing Cadillac emblem atop the radiator hood that had been wrenched off, something that happens more often than not to annoy Cadillac owners, the car was well outfitted, safe, and eminently comfortable. The prime minister and his wife sat together as usual in the back seat with an open curtain behind them so that the small following escort car with two security people could be seen through the broad back window. In the front seat beside the usual driver, Menachem Damti, there was the prime minister's usual personal security guard, Yoram Rubin.

For a change, there were no anti-peaceniks out tonight in the neighborhood to be gawking at the passengers in the Cadillac and shouting such familiar epithets as "Traitor" and worse. And for that, to be sure, the prime minister must have been thankful as the Cadillac sped smoothly from the apartment house entrance and headed for the scene of the peace rally, a huge stage in front of the city hall of Tel Aviv called Kings of Israel Square.

So far, so good, but the security guard, Rubin, usually so calm and certain of both the prime minister and himself, now was quite nervous, even a trifle upset, as he shifted around on the front seat beside the driver. The run to Kings of Israel Square normally took only about ten minutes and there seemed to be no cause for concern en route, but suddenly the security man swung around and turned his head toward the prime minister. Keeping his voice down, he muttered,"Yitzhak, I want you to know there is a serious warning that a suicidal Islamic terrorist may try to infiltrate the crowd tonight."

There was no response. Rabin knew his security man so well and for so long that they were on a first-name basis, but neither pretended to foresee the future nor did they flinch from it. Such warnings simply came with the job. There was nothing anybody could do about them beyond making certain the prime minister was well guarded and protected from harm by the usual ten bodyguards that were customarily assigned to surround him in any crowd as large as the audience expected tonight in the Kings of Israel Square.

Even Mrs. Rabin, as she recalled long afterward, felt helpless when she heard the warning. As she put it, "I allowed it to drift to the back of my mind: You're going to a peace rally, you have a fleeting vision of what could happen, and then you file it away."[7]

The peace rally was a great success with more than a hundred thousand people jamming the square before Tel Aviv's City Hall. It celebrated the signing of the second and last of the Oslo peace accords, so there were representatives of Egypt, Jordan, and Morocco on the massive stage that faced the VIP parking lot where the silvery armored Cadillac was stationed to pick up the prime minister and his wife at the end of the rally. A few steps along, a ladder from the square to the open stage was all that separated the huge crowd from the speakers.

Despite the oratory in which Foreign Minister Peres was the lead-off attraction, the rally turned out to be a tribute for Prime Minister Rabin, the concluding speaker. Long before he addressed the audience, however, there were continual roars of applause for him, cheers whenever his name was mentioned, an uproar as he approached the podium for the windup. In a moment of sheer joy, he paused and then suddenly embraced his old foe, now his devoted ally, Peres—the high point of the rally.

Although Rabin warned of violence during his concluding remarks, it did not seem to be the gist of his message that night. Instead, what he emphasized—a quotation that his wife treasured for years thereafter—was a declaration of faith in the destiny of the State of Israel, his last words in a life devoted to the service of his country: "I have been a military man for 27 years. I fought as long as there was no chance for peace. I believe there is a chance now, a great chance, and we must take advantage of it for the sake of those who are here and those who are not, and there are many."

To top the enthusiasm of the evening, there was singing with a rusty-voiced prime minister following the huge audience and the orchestra as best he could, first in a "Song for Peace" that included such lines as: "Let the sun rise and give the morning light" and "So sing only a song for peace, with a great shout."

Once that was over, evidently not knowing what else to do with the printed sheet of lyrics that had been passed out during the evening, Rabin folded the single page neatly and preserved it in his inner coat pocket just above his heart.[8] And then, for the finale, there was a tumultuous, crowd-led singing of the Israeli anthem, "Hatikvah." After that, there was utter confusion on the stage as Rabin's security people formed about him to lead him to the few steps down to the pavement directly behind Foreign Minister Peres. But at least a score of strangers, accredited or not, no one could possibly know, darted to the stage and nobody stopped them.

In the melee, Mrs. Rabin had all she could do to stay within reaching distance of her husband and his security people. What she recalled afterward was that her husband seemed to have forgotten something, turned, and went back to the stage, then swung about with his escort of guards and was still slightly ahead of her as he reached the pavement apparently to head for the parked Cadillac.

By that time, Peres was no longer in sight. As an amateur photographer named Ronni Kempler was able to prove, with a film he shot from the crowd that night, Peres had gone on during Rabin's turnaround (to thank the sponsors of the rally) and shaken hands with supporters, then spoken briefly with the driver of the prime minister's Cadillac. And all the time, the Kempler film photographed a squat youth in a black skullcap standing almost directly in the path of anybody coming off stage as Peres drove away in his own car.

When the prime minister came down the stage stairs the second time, there were no ten guards in sight around him. There were four directly ahead of him and the lone straggler was in no position to guard his back in the melee.

It was then that the youth in the black skullcap whipped out a 9mm Baretta, whirled quickly to thrust it right against Rabin's back, and fired three shots, two of which hit their mark fatally while the third struck a bodyguard. Somebody yelled, "They're blanks," just as Rabin fell forward with some of his bodyguards piled atop him.

That much Mrs. Rabin saw, then she herself was whisked from the crowd by security people while the guards somehow were able to recover sufficiently to carry the fatally wounded prime minister to the parked silvery armored Cadillac. But with so many other cars and literally hundreds of people milling around to get out of the huge square before the City Hall, there were inevitable delays because no one had thought to make sure the prime minister's car could move rapidly from the square if necessary.

By that time, the youth in the black skullcap and his weapon were in custody, identified as a former student of religion at a local university with a brief record of military service, twenty-five-year-old Yigal

Amir, a member of a Yemenite immigrant family in Tel Aviv, with three brothers and four sisters.

"I aimed at the center of his back,"Amir was quoted as having told the police later. "I'd been planning to kill him for a long time."[9]

None of this was known at the time to Mrs. Rabin, who had been picked up by a police escort from the crowd that surged about her husband when he fell with his bodyguards atop him. She did not know then, nor was she told, that the bullets had hit their mark; perhaps, in the confusion, even her informants did not know and there was no way for her to determine whether her husband of forty-seven years, the father of her children, was alive or dead. All she did know was that all the vaunted arrangements for the security of the prime minister had been utterly scrambled even to the extent of clearing the route of the Cadillac that presumably had borne him to a hospital—what hospital she did not know.

From the square before Tel Aviv City Hall, she had been driven eventually to the headquarters of the General Security Services of the Israeli government, the Shabak, the country's equivalent of the American FBI. And there at last, when she still was being given no information, she telephoned her daughter, Dalia, who joined her at Shabak headquarters at just about the time that the authorities admitted the prime minister had been taken to Ichilov Hospital in critical condition.

It was there at last that Mrs. Rabin and her daughter learned that the prime minister was undergoing emergency operating procedures with frequent blood transfusions, but the frantic efforts—through no fault of the physicians or the hospital—had come too late. Before the night was over, Yitzhak Rabin, twice prime minister of Israel, had died after being shot by a youthful assassin—a sacrifice to the turmoil that now threatened to consume his struggling nation as well as himself.[10]

In the breast pocket of his bullet-riddled coat, just above his heart, the crimsoned folded sheet of the "Song for Peace" he had sung with his own people that night was found with the lines so well remembered:

"Let the sun rise and give the morning light" and "So sing only a song for peace, with a great shout."

33. Reviving Israel

When President Clinton flew to Jerusalem in *Air Force One* for the Rabin funeral, the preservation of peace in the Middle East remained a key objective of American foreign policy. And yet, as the president stood beside the leaders of more than eighty other heads of state in Israel's national cemetery, the strength of the Israeli people themselves attracted him.

As others paid tribute that chilly November 5 to the assassinated prime minister in the presence of his immediate predecessor, the seventy-two-year-old Shimon Peres, Clinton's attention centered on the stoic composure of so many of the people of Israel who stood near the closed coffin. All seemed to have the urge not only to pay their final tribute to a fallen leader but also to show a doubting world their resolve to carry on.

In the American president's eulogy while standing beside the coffin, which was suspended over its open grave on Mount Herzl, it was evident that the gallant response of Israel's ordinary citizens also had moved him, for he spoke earnestly of hope for the future as well as the inspiring record of the assassinated prime minister. In so doing, he praised the people of Israel for what they already had accomplished in less than fifty years by building a "thriving democracy"—as he put it—"in a hostile terrain."

The president recalled the wars the Israelis had won for their freedom and the efforts they already had made for peace with their Arab neighbors—"the only enduring victory" in his words. He termed Prime Minister Rabin "a martyr for peace . . . a victim of hate." Then, raising his voice, he concluded with an appeal to reason there in the cemetery, an effort to revive the spirit of the people of Israel in their dark hour, saying:

>   Surely, we must learn from his martyrdom that if people cannot
>   let go of the hatred of their enemies, they risk sowing the seeds of ha-
>   tred among themselves. I ask you, the people of Israel, on behalf of
>   my own nation that knows its own long litany of loss from Abraham
>   Lincoln to President Kennedy to Martin Luther King Jr., do not let that
>   happen to you.
>   In the Knesset, in your homes, in your places of worship, stay the
>   righteous course.

In so doing, he pledged, the Israeli people would continue to sustain
the support of the United States. And he concluded, "May our hearts
find a measure of comfort and our souls the eternal touch of hope."

With a final prayer from the presiding rabbi, the prime minister's
coffin was lowered gently into the grave as his tearful widow and their
children watched. President Clinton murmured his own farewell as he
passed the black-draped casket, using the Hebrew "Shalom, haver," as
befitted a last salute to an old soldier, with the translation "Peace, my
friend."[1]

Now it was a more settled Israel—mourning but firm, saddened but
closing ranks—over which Peres presided as prime minister, first as the
unanimous choice of his cabinet colleagues on the evening of November 4 to lead the nation temporarily, then later confirmed in a Labor primary election in his own right as prime minister for a second time.[2]

From the outset, however, Peres seemed to assume that the united
support the nation had given to Yitzhak Rabin would come to him automatically, a grave error in any self-governing nation where a government's purpose and performance often are of almost daily concern.
Led by Benjamin Netanyahu, the Right now began making a determined bid for power against what it conceived to be a faltering government, curbing the Labor regime's policy of trading land to the
Palestinians in return for an uncertain peace and stalling where possible the gains the PLO already had won. But this internal dispute by no
means undercut the union of the Israeli people against any foreign ag-
gressor, as the Syrians and the Hamas raiders in Lebanon soon discovered when they launched new attacks from the north.

However, the national political discourse on policy soon became so
abrasive that Prime Minister Peres felt obliged to do what Rabin had always rejected—consult a domestic opponent such as Netanyahu,

"Bibi" to friend and foe alike, about ground rules for always-tough political arguments during Israeli election campaigns.

It did not work. As might have been expected, what "Bibi" did in
response to Peres's appeal was to hedge, adopting a position of virtu-
ous morality in which he denied his support for the violence of the extreme Right, agreed to a gentlemanly discussion of the issues, and
rejected any votes from those who dared rejoice over the Rabin assassination. In another counterthrust at the Labor regime, the Likud leader
argued that his enemies were trying to "dehumanize" him and his
party, something he bitterly resented.

In effect, therefore, very little changed in the 1996 Israeli political
campaign, the first to be decided by popular vote, in which a listless
Peres tried to hold off a surging right-wing foe. Before the campaign
was well under way, Labor saw its usually comfortable lead sharply reduced from a 70 percent high in the polls during Rabin's last week as
prime minister. Nearly all parties agreed that the election was bound to
be close, with Labor on the defensive, charged by the foe with yielding
too much land and too many privileges to the Palestinians.[3] The hap-
less response was, "What does Bibi want? War?"

Likud's major issue was security for the Israeli people, matched
against the growth of a Palestinian state, and Peres was hard put to justify the concessions Labor already had made. What Likud proposed in
the campaign was to reverse the Labor Party's policy of creating a
larger democratic rule for Palestinians, including a chairman, Arafat, a
legislature for governance, and a growing territorial base for what was
called a Palestinian Authority, with police bearing arms given to them
by the State of Israel. As portrayed in the Likud drive backed by the religious right wing parties, the prospects of a Palestinian state within
the areas now occupied by Israel amounted to an attempt to disfran-
chise the 150,000 Israeli settlers on the West Bank and Gaza Strip who
already were outnumbered by the Palestinians there.[4]

The way Likud's campaign for prime minister developed was in itself
a negation of the Palestinian peace process upon which the Labor government had embarked to combat the rising violence of terrorist Arab
groups such as Hamas, Hezbollah, and others. The right-wing Israeli
operators were mainly trying as best they could to weaken, even disavow wherever possible, agreements that previous Israeli govern-

ments had made with the PLO or neighboring governments of Arab states, sometimes both.

As this election drive developed, leading to the vote for prime minister, it was in itself an illustration of the conservative position in Israel involving grants of territory that had been made to the PLO. Organized Israeli opposition protest rallies began soon after Rabin's burial, which was when an orderly Israeli troop withdrawal was already under way in some West Bank and Gaza Strip cities. One of these early movements, in which the West Bank city of Jenin was involved, drew little attention in the country at large. But it was quite different when Israeli forces retreated on December 11 from the largest city in the West Bank, Nablus, after which Palestinian police took control of law enforcement there.

In response to Likud protests throughout Israel, Prime Minister Peres came to Washington on December 12, saw President Clinton, and addressed Congress to explain the policy of Israeli withdrawals with emphasis on the need to organize for war.[5]

As if that had not been sufficient provocation for the aggrieved Israeli settlers who were making such an issue out of Peres's retreat before the now-aroused PLO, they were infuriated within ten days by their government's even more symbolic West Bank pullout from Bethlehem on December 21. Facing still more fervent protests from inside by Sharon and the Arab terrorists in the pro-Iran Hamas organization, the besieged Peres regime now became so concerned that it demanded a showdown with the Palestinian Authority in advance of the critical 1996 election year.

The outcome, however, satisfied neither side, for the disruptive pro-Iranian leadership of Hamas refused to stop attacking the Israeli regime while insisting its membership was not voting in any Palestinian election or trying to disrupt the forthcoming Israeli vote for prime minister. The PLO took such encouragement from the confrontation that its champion, Arafat, was elected chairman on January 20, 1996, of what was called the Palestinian Authority. It then was taking control of West Bank and Gaza areas as they were vacated by the Israelis.

Arafat had no serious rivals for Palestinian leadership, having won 88 percent of the vote for what was widely construed as the beginning of the Palestinian state that had been envisaged with its Jewish counterpart in the UN General Assembly resolution of November 29, 1947. The Israeli government, perhaps unwittingly, contributed to the outcome by releasing 812 Palestinians from jail ten days before the PLO vote in which the pro-Arafat Al Fatah group won 75 percent of the seats in the first election for a Palestinian legislature.

With such an impressive vote, Arafat tried to show concern over a resumption of terrorist activity by Hamas, Hezbollah, and other proponents of Arab violence early in that decisive election year. Prime Minister Peres, however, had to close Israel's borders temporarily with both the Gaza Strip and the West Bank on February 25 when an Arab suicide bomber killed twenty-five people on a West Jerusalem bus, followed two days later by another bus blast in Ashkelon that took the lives of an Israeli soldier and the latest suicide bomber.

The Arab terrorists enlarged their battlefront inside Israel with the approach of spring, regardless of the army's defensive measures. There were nineteen deaths on a West Jerusalem bus March 3, and fourteen more Israelis died the next day when another bomb wrecked a Tel Aviv shopping center, both of them suicidal operations in which the bombers themselves were killed.

It was not much satisfaction for the Peres government that the confessed killer of Yitzhak Rabin was sentenced to life imprisonment March 27 after being found guilty by a three-judge panel. To the dismay of the assassinated prime minister's family, the unrepentant killer, Yigal Amir, also was offered the privilege under Israeli law of participating in voting from his prison cell.

It took almost six months for the wavering Peres regime in Jerusalem to strike back at its tormentors. The first target on April 11 was a haven for Hezbollah guerrillas inside the Lebanese frontier, which was shelled by Israeli warships off the Mediterranean coastline. Two days later, a fleet of Israeli helicopters fired rockets at the enemy but also, unfortunately, struck an ambulance, causing six civilian fatalities. As the attacks continued, there was another disaster on April 18 at a UN refugee camp near Tyre in which Israeli artillery shells took an estimated one hundred lives.[6]

Although Prime Minister Peres then claimed substantial progress in the Israeli offensive against the terrorists, an effort to demonstrate firmness well in advance of his scheduled election at the end of May, the polls showed the nation was badly split between Labor and the surging Likud opposition. Peres was nervous enough about the outcome to hustle off to Washington for another session with his chief patron abroad, President Clinton, who thereupon signed an agreement with him committing the United States to oppose terrorism.

That, however, by no means stopped the uprising within Israel that did so much damage to what was construed as a weak government when contrasted with the assassinated Rabin's accomplishments. Prime Minister Peres had a chance to demonstrate his ability to tighten national security in his debate with Netanyahu before the election, but failed to advance his cause in the last polls before the voting. In consequence, his slender lead at the end of so hard-fought a campaign could scarcely be regarded as a sign of the coming victory that he claimed would be his when almost 3 million people voted on May 29.

For hours during the voting, the usual polls based on the decisions given by individuals after they had cast their ballots that day demonstrated how the Israeli public had changed sides after the assassination of the old soldier, Rabin, whom the vast majority had trusted so implicitly. Even though Peres did manage to maintain a thin polling majority during the early voting hours, as the Israeli government radio carried periodic announcements, it was evident that neither he nor Netanyahu would win the commanding majority that was so necessary to any Israeli government at so perilous a time.

But gradually, during the early evening hours, Netanyahu and his Likud partnership crept ahead of the hard-hit Labor government and somehow managed to hold the advantage even though the election had not yet become conclusive. The best evidence of the coming reversal that would mean the last of Peres and his Labor government came from the White House in Washington, where President Clinton—himself a candidate for reelection that year—in effect conceded the probability of Netanyahu's election as prime minister.

This was the way the American president tried to show his goodwill for the Likud candidate, to whom he had failed to give the stout support he invariably offered to Prime Minister Peres: "Whatever the results [of the Israeli election], the United States will continue its policy of support for the people of Israel, for the democratic process there, and for the process of peace. And our policy will be the same. If Israel is prepared to take risks for peace, we are determined to do our best to reduce the risks and increase the security of those who do that."

Before the final tally, President Clinton obviously could not have publicly conceded Peres's defeat but his White House aides (as quoted in the *New York Times* datelined May 30) admitted the president had been disappointed in Peres's showing and was expecting the prime minister's loss to Netanyahu. In fact, "crestfallen" was the way the president was described at the outcome of the Israeli vote even before it had become final.

The final totals, reported by the Israeli election commissioners, gave Netanyahu victory over Peres by less than 1 percent of the total vote, only 29,457 out of nearly 3 million ballots that had been cast. The standings gave Netanyahu 1,501,023 to 1,471,566 for Peres.'

Under the circumstances it took considerably more time for the victorious Likud candidate to form a workable government even after a saddened Peres conceded defeat and inevitably faced a struggle to maintain his leadership of the Labor Party. The problem arose because, as usual, neither major party was strong enough by itself to form a majority in the 120-seat Knesset that was necessary to sustain a prime minister regardless of the outcome of the election.

In the Knesset, the 1996 vote gave Labor thirty-four seats and Likud thirty-two, both very far from the sixty-one-seat majority the victor would need to keep Netanyahu in power. The electoral victor then had to bargain for cabinet posts with the nine other parties that shared the rest of the fifty-four seats in the Knesset, a mind-boggling operation even by Israeli standards that eventually came down to the support of the small religious parties, each vigorously opposed to sharing parts of Israel with the Palestinians even in the face of agreements entered into by previous Israeli governments.

With their support more than a week after he had won the election for prime minister, Netanyahu signaled that he was close to the formation of a new government. He also announced his opposition to a Palestinian state and Palestinian control of East Jerusalem, but sought retention of Israeli-occupied Golan Heights on the Syrian border. By June 16, when he was assured of the backing of sixty-one votes in the Knesset, the new prime minister put his government in place with the inclusion of the far Right's Ariel Sharon in the cabinet as minister in charge of the infrastructure, the 150,000 settlers, made the difference for the Likud victory over Labor.

By summer's end, the Palestinian legislative organization was threatening a general strike because the new Israeli regime was expanding its areas for settlement in what Arafat had come to believe was a virtually all-Arab West Bank. That was not to be Netanyahu's policy, however. It was almost certain that he would be delaying, avoiding, or even canceling previous agreements on sharing any settled areas for Israelis with the PLO.

Rather than permit what seemed like such renewed strife to be projected into the American presidential election, in which Clinton was being opposed by the leader of the Republican-controlled Senate, Bob

Dole, the president asked both Netanyahu and Peres as the rival Israeli leaders to reopen peace talks with the Palestinians that had been frozen since the Likud's victory in the prime ministerial election. Little, however, was accomplished in September, when the American presidential campaign was in full swing, beyond a tentative proposal by Netanyahu to permit more Palestinians to obtain daily work with Israel— a sore point since the Labor Party's loss.

Before the month's end, there was savage fighting affecting both sides in the heart of Jerusalem. While the White House was trying to arrange for a meeting of the opponents with an American mediator, Dennis Ross of the State Department, fifty-four Palestinians and fourteen Israelis were killed inside the Holy City, a hundred were wounded, and Netanyahu became a target for abuse.

Despite his fervent denials of fault, he had to accept his share of the blame—and there was more than enough to go around.

Jerusalem's newest crisis had begun mildly enough on September 24, 1996, when Bibi ordered a new entrance opened to an existing archaeological tunnel under the al Aksa Mosque on Temple Mount—a revered Muslim shrine. At once, the Arabs labeled it "Bibi's fault" and the rock throwers took to the streets to face Israeli rubber bullets. By September 25, the Israeli troops and the new Palestinian authority police were exchanging volleys amid charges that the mosque was being damaged.

But had it been "Bibi's fault" as claimed? Unfortunately, his apologists had to admit there was a certain amount of truth to charges that he gave the go-ahead to the tunnel work to bolster Israel's position that the entire city, including the Arab portion in the old section, now had to submit to Jewish rule. The Arab resistance became more frantic than ever.

Having involved himself so often previously in efforts to preserve peace in the Middle East, President Clinton interrupted the final month of his own reelection campaign to bring Bibi, Arafat, and their staffs together again in Washington with King Hussein as a bystander. And though the tunnel fighting tapered off, Bibi became adamant in his refusal either to admit fault or to take any reasonable part in restoring discussion over the future of Jerusalem. He also refused to close the new tunnel entrance under the Al Aksa Mosque or even to go through with the scheduled Israeli evacuation of the city of Hebron on the West Bank.

To make matters worse, the Iraqi army secretly and otherwise violated the conditions under which Saddam Hussein had been permitted to retain control of his country after losing the Gulf War. And that, even to Bibi's touchy conservatives who had been so insistent on blaming Labor's "treachery" for grants of Israeli land and authority to the Palestinians, now became another problem of concern toward century's end. Keeping Saddam in his box, the position in which he was placed by the American military, became an additional burden on Israel, Egypt, and Jordan as well.

Regardless of the new Israeli government's efforts to ease the plight of its people, peace remained discouragingly elusive.[8] Fighting terrorist organizations such as Hamas and Hezbollah did not seem to be acceptable to the new Palestinian Authority under Arafat's control except as a sometime thing, so the entire burden for holding off both Palestinian pressures and the terrorist guerrillas fell on the Jewish state. The Arabs did not seem to want it any other way.

34. Likud's Hard Line

Before Benjamin Netanyahu had been in office nine months, he and his Likud government faced the same problem as their predecessors, Shimon Peres and his Labor regime. It was, as always, security from attack by Arab foes.

After Netanyahu's razor-thin victory at the polls on May 23, 1996, and his formation of his Likud coalition government, he had adopted a hard-line policy toward Yasir Arafat and his Palestinians in Gaza as well as their fellow Arabs in East Jerusalem, the Old City, and elsewhere within the Jewish state's borders. Whether or not this supposedly tough policy had anything to do with it, there had not been any Arab suicide bomber attacks within Israel since March 1997.

No one in authority, however, had any illusions about Arafat's supposed efforts under the Oslo peace accords to fight a renewal of Arab terrorism. In the past after a suicide bombing outrage, he had his police seize some alleged terrorists but all had been quietly released after a while. What the Palestinian Authority chairman was doing now had no effect on terrorism in particular; instead, he had been boycotting the peace talks with Israel since March 1997.

During this period Netanyahu had developed the Likud hard line. It consisted primarily of an attempt to outflank the Arabs in East Jerusalem by pushing a building program among them to house more of the thousands of Russian immigrants who were fleeing from their country. The housing offensive, in consequence, already had aroused protests from Arafat as well as an accusation from King Hussein of Jordan that Netanyahu was "destroying peace."

By sheer accident, at about the time the king's letter was made public, a crazed Jordanian soldier had run amok on an island in the Jordan River, shared by Israel and Jordan, where he gunned down seven teenaged Israeli girls on a school trip. Nor did it blunt criticism of the prime minister when he joined the king in visiting the bereaved parents to express sympathy.[1]

The public condemnation from Jordan's king only increased the mordant atmosphere in which the latest Israeli regime tried to operate. While the bulldozers were clearing land for new Jewish housing in East Jerusalem, Arabs still were protesting Netanyahu's project of tunneling under the Temple Mount that seemed to them to threaten the safety of their sacred Al Aksa Mosque.

In effect, therefore, the current scene was disturbing to all Jerusalem as the capital of Israel with a population of almost six hundred thousand as well as its enormous importance as a commercial, cultural, and religious center. The hard line had its disadvantages, but Likud's policy persisted.

This was not at all what the security-conscious Israelis had expected of the Netanyahu government. By a narrow margin, they had turned away from Peres's Labor regime mainly because they had hoped Bibi would provide increased security for a sorely tried people. Now with his bulldozers in East Jerusalem and his housing drive for new immigrants, he was upsetting the Arabs of East Jerusalem and their associates, Arafat's Palestinians, which was—so some said—too much of a risk and could bring a forceful response.

But the Netanyahu argument was both practical and logical. How else could he as prime minister provide for such a surge of fresh immigration than to increase the already burdened construction industry in an expanding nation? It was, therefore, difficult for the Labor opposition to argue the case for halting the necessary expansion of home building although, even in the Likud coalition, there were some who believed it might have been wiser to have found a less controversial area than East Jerusalem for resettling the latest immigrants. In a narrowly divided Knesset, the prime minister more often than not had to work hard to rally the support of the nine other political parties allied with Likud to maintain his government in power.

The Labor opposition meanwhile had been preoccupied with the rise of the former army chief of staff, Ehud Barak, who was challenging the fading leadership of the seventy-three-year-old Peres now that Peres had lost control of the government. Until that struggle was settled, Bibi once again could buy time to strengthen his administration, although there was no indication that the usual patronage demands made upon him within his party would be blackened.

Had the prime minister been able to carry a large Likud majority with him into the Knesset, there is no doubt that he could have worked his will in policy matters with greater certainty. But with only thirty-two Likuds in the 120-seat Knesset and the other twenty-nine members of his coalition scattered among the nine other parties, he soon learned that any of the non-Likuds who had put him in power could demand his support by threatening to desert him in a no-confidence vote.

This kind of political blackmail would have been hard enough for a more wily politician to take, but the principled Netanyahu's temper sometimes flared under such pressures. He knew perfectly well, from the outset, that the desertion of just a few delegates might be disastrous. And right off, he was in the middle of an argument with David Levy, his foreign minister, and his defense minister, Yitzhak Mordechai, who made no secret of their mistrust of sixty-nine-year-old Ariel Sharon, the self-appointed champion of the outraged displaced Israeli settlers in Arab territories of Israel.

Directly after the first of Bibi's cabinet crises, caused by the abrupt resignation of Finance Minister Dan Meridor, Sharon touched off a storm by demanding publicly to take over the Israeli treasury together with his current responsibilities for the Israel Land Authority and the Israel Public Works Authority.

During the fuss that followed, it was widely reported in the Israeli press that Levy had threatened to resign if Sharon was given Finance, which might have caused Bibi the loss of the few delegates he needed to stay in office. That time, he was able to satisfy all parties and retained the services of Foreign Minister Levy mainly by keeping Finance temporarily vacant.

However, while still stalling on Finance, Bibi also suffered another cabinet resignation, that of the usually dependable Ze'ev Begin in a less important post. No sooner had that crisis been laid to rest than the conservative champion of the mass Russian migration to Israel, Natan Sharansky, the minister for industry and trade, boycotted all cabinet meetings until he forced Bibi to give him more money to aid more Russian immigrants.[2]

The most imposing threat of all, as months dragged by for Bibi's increasingly nervous administration, appeared to come mainly from the impatience of the few critically needed Knesset delegates of small religious parties in his lineup. They had been demanding stronger Israeli action against the other Arabs left in Jerusalem, mainly in the old section just north of the scantily occupied and hilly East Jerusalem that also was claimed by the Arabs.

Bibi's first move to satisfy the religious people supporting him had been the tunneling expedition under the Al Aksa Mosque on Temple Mount, which had been stalled amid forceful threats of worse still to come from the outraged Arabs and their supporters in the revived Islamic fundamentalist movement in the Middle East. That line of action, even to the Jewish religious faction, now seemed hopeless.

Instead, Bibi had decided to increase the Jewish colonization movement in East Jerusalem where there appeared to be enough open space for several thousand new Jewish homes. But, like nearby old Jerusalem, any problem of Arab counteraction in East Jerusalem almost immediately threatened the prosperity, as well as the stability, of modern West Jerusalem directly opposite—and that was risky, too.

Nevertheless, this is what Bibi undertook when he maintained his bulldozers in East Jerusalem to work in a hilly area called Har Homa just inside the West Bank of the Jordan River. Right off, Arab women, children, and a few stragglers among elderly men gathered to resist in the area that was known to them as Abu Ghneim. At once, a detachment of Israeli soldiers in uniform took over in battle gear and set up machine guns. At that, the residents from a nearby Arab village came running amid screams of defiance.

The confrontation grew in intensity that February 28 as evening approached—Friday evening, as it turned out, the end of a day of prayer for the Muslims and the onset of the Jewish Sabbath at dusk. That, perhaps, more than anything else, persuaded both sides to pause. Amid hesitation by the Israelis to force the issue mainly against women, children, and elderly men, the threat of another bloody miscarriage of the colonization movement eased for at least that day.

But it by no means disposed of Bibi's program for building Jewish settlements amid Arab homes in East Jerusalem. Apparently in an attempt to respond to cautionary signals from the Clinton administration, Bibi withdrew a few Israeli settlers from various West Bank areas in an apparent effort to show that he was trying to comply with the Oslo peace accords.[3]

Bibi's stopgap measure failed because the bulldozers kept right on operating and the government's service people continued to develop plans for more Jewish housing projects in areas the Arabs had designated for themselves in the East Jerusalem hills. Finally, Chairman Arafat decided he had to do something in connection with the Oslo peace accords and issued a round-robin plea to all the project's foreign supporters to intervene.

"What we are facing today from the settlements in holy Jerusalem," Arafat said in a statement issued from his headquarters in Gaza City on March 15, which extended to the rest of his Palestinian areas, "is a plan to destroy the peace process."

Addressing representatives of the United States, Russia, various European nations, Japan, and Arab countries at Gaza, Arafat sponsored a resolution that criticized the Israeli government, but the American consul general in Jerusalem, Edward G. Abington, objected and halted passage. As a result, the Arab delegates at the international conference in Gaza accused the United States of refusing to stand up for the Oslo peace.

Chairman Arafat had tried, with his international protest rally, to force the Israelis to abandon their attempt to encircle the Jerusalem Arab community beginning with the East Jerusalem building program for sixty-five hundred new Jewish homes in the area that would very likely outnumber the Arab villages nearby. It did not help the Israelis when Bibi tried to mollify their opponents with a slight withdrawal of Israeli settlers from the nearby West Bank.

That, too, was criticized this time as "too little and too late." Even so, a UN Security Council resolution condemning Israel, which came up at about the same time, died under an American veto. That was followed by a UN General Assembly resolution that was unanimously passed except for opposition by the United States and Israel.

All that was left for Bibi was to blast off at the Arabs beginning with Chairman Arafat and including King Hussein of Jordan for accusing him of scuttling the Oslo peace, something he denied. The Israeli leader's response was made in Moscow on March 12, when he was concluding a meeting there with the Russians, in which he said he was "fed up with criticism."

In his denial that he was destroying the Oslo peace accords, the Israeli prime minister argued, "If the Palestinians are serious about peace, let them sit down with us. If they are serious about airing their differences, let them sit down with us."

But Chairman Arafat was not about to dignify the new Israeli building project by discussing it. Nor did the United States representatives, despite their support of the Israelis under renewed Arab attack, relax their own efforts to try to persuade the Netanyahu government to postpone its East Jerusalem building project. The suspicion was abroad, therefore, that Bibi feared his coalition would fall apart if he did not do something to show he was deeply interested in restraining Palestinian influence in Jerusalem.

In a retort to the critical letter King Hussein addressed to him, the Israeli prime minister called it "doomsday talk" and suggested that the Arabs instead were damaging the Oslo peace accords, saying, "The whole historic attitude toward obvious disagreement is in itself not conducive to progress."

So the bulldozers kept rolling along and the crisis kept building.[4]

For the next three months, Bibi felt obliged to answer both the Arabs and his own domestic opposition in the slowly reviving Labor Party to a series of cabinet crises about everything from General Sharon's pitch to take over the Finance Ministry to a threatened vote of no confidence in the Knesset at a later time. Even the prime minister's extramarital love life became a part of the debate when Bibi's wife had to field a question about it during the taping of an Israeli TV interview.

But throughout, nothing happened to ease his government's troubles or satisfy his critics at home and abroad. Even when Chairman Arafat temporarily deferred his efforts to restrain the Israeli home construction program in East Jerusalem, Bibi had to try to blanket the continual hostility between angry members of his cabinet, notably the alliance between Foreign Minister Levy and Defense Minister Mordechai, to prevent General Sharon from taking over the Finance Ministry.

Now and then, it all began to sound like a faint echo of the proceedings in Washington, D.C., with the Republicans accusing China without proof of financing President Clinton's reelection, except that there was no current attempt in Jerusalem to rent out a David Ben-Gurion bedroom to buy a few more votes for a strapped candidate for prime minister.

What seemed to gripe Foreign Minister Levy more than Arab protests was the internal activity of General Sharon, who, so it was disclosed by the Israeli press, looked up an emissary of Chairman Arafat's named Mahmoud Abbas for secret talks that seemed not to have produced any tangible result. However, the mere disclosure of such undercover politics by a fellow member of the cabinet so offended foreign Minister Levy that his resignation once again was rumored and denied.

All Levy said about the matter was that he was, in effect, considering his options. As for General Sharon, never one to back away from a fight either at home or on the battlefield, he was completely unrepentant about his undercover operations and his ambitions to enlarge his cabinet status in the Likud government.[5] None of this inner turmoil, of course, contributed to easing the almost daily ritual in which stone-throwing Arab youths and Israeli troops firing rubber bullets continued to duel with each other on Jerusalem's streets as well as in critical spots such as Hebron on the West Bank, from which the Israelis also were refusing more withdrawals.

The apparent purpose of all this obfuscation and delay in enacting agreements previously negotiated by Labor governments with the Palestinians was to mollify the extreme conservatives in the Netanyahu coalition. They conceived of all Jerusalem, and all Palestine as well, as the traditional home of Israel from ancient times.

In view of the energetic presence of so many Palestinians in the area, this was a difficult position for the Likud cabinet to justify, but that was Bibi's problem in his deeply troubled first year as prime minister and nothing he did or tried to do made life any easier for his disturbed administration.

The only other Israeli casualty in this strained relationship became the unhappy septuagenarian. Peres, who lost his leadership of the Labor Party to Barak, the former army chief of staff, who had been, with Haim Ramon, now a Knesset member, Yitzhak Rabin's designated favorites among his proposed successors.

What happened on May 13, amid Bibi's developing crisis of leadership as prime minister, was a Labor Party vote in which Barak's majority killed an effort by Peres to become the party's president—a preliminary to his failed effort to retain his party's leadership in the following month.

Barak tried to put the best face on his victory over the elderly Nobel Prize winner, saying he would continue to consult with him, then added, "A man like Shimon Peres needs no title to have an influence and he will be able to have a great influence. He is a giant." But all such fine words could scarcely disguise the eclipse of one of Israel's distinguished elders as the Labor Party's leader, an event that took place the following month when Barak formally replaced him.[6]

Another of Israel's great ones, the Israeli president Ezer Weizman, also was widely criticized, once Labor lost power. Somehow, his opponents blamed the president for not having supported the powers of the Rabin government with greater vigor and to defend the Oslo peace accords from violation by both sides, Arafat with his continued failure to realize his pledge to fight terrorism in his Palestinian territory and the Likud conservatives for their housing construction in Arab East Jerusalem. It had been a position that some of the nation's press commentators on the Labor side had deplored at the time, which added neither to Weizman's prestige nor Netanyahu's staying power at the peak of government.[7]

While Netanyahu was attempting to hold his Likud coalition together with his delayed troop withdrawals from areas ceded to the Palestinians by previous administrations, there was a dawning realization that nothing whatever had been done recently to renew the deadlocked peace accords, and that Arafat and his Palestinians appeared to have no intention of seeking negotiations in the foreseeable future.

The Clinton administration had been attempting fitfully to try to bring the Arabs and Israelis together but without encouragement from either side. And while Netanyahu's government had not suffered a major terrorist act for many months, such a much-desired measure of security could not last forever no matter how great the government's efforts might be.

In the Middle East toward century's end, violence was a way of life, not only in Israel but also in adjacent Arab lands—even Saudi Arabia, the source of so much American imported oil, where still-unsolved explosions traced to truck bombs killed five American soldiers at a military training center in Riyadh on November 13, 1995, and nineteen additional American troops stationed at their own base in Dhahran on June 25, 1996.

What price security for Israel?

35.   Bombs in Jerusalem

When the suicide bombings resumed in Israel during the midsummer of 1997, fifteen people including both Arab carriers were killed in Jerusalem and almost two hundred were hurt—the worst outbreak in months. The shocked Israelis struck back at once with threats of sanctions against the Palestinians and commando raids against terrorists in their country.

Although scores of suspected Palestinian terrorists were arrested mainly by Israel, even President Clinton conceded that resumption of the American-sponsored peace talks—an objective of his government—had been put off. As for the enraged and frustrated Prime Minister Netanyahu, all he could do at first was to blame the tragedy on the failure once again of Chairman Arafat of the Palestinian Authority to fight the pro-Iranian Hamas terrorists in his own area, Hamas having claimed responsibility for the attack. Arafat as usual was all injured innocence as he set about leading his minimal share of arrests—his usual response to such outrages.

As for the people of Israel, who had been approaching a record 6 million population that summer amid a promising lift of prosperity, their anger and their frustration were evident on every side after the twin blasts on the early afternoon of July 30.[1] Only a little more than a year had passed since they had turned out of office a Labor government that had failed to protect them from such disasters. And now the Netanyahu regime, after all its tough promises for better security, also had failed them.

The Arab minorities of almost 2 million in the Gaza Strip and the West Bank of the Jordan River were far worse off after the bombings, and their economic condition had never approached that of the Israelis, now in the fiftieth year of their reborn nation. As usual in these fre-

306

quent assaults—called a "barbaric act" by President Clinton—it was al-most an automatic response for the Israeli army to close off all crossing points between the areas ruled by the Palestinian Authority. That at once excluded the Palestinians from their regular work in Israeli busi-nesses, factories, and homes with a consequent heavy loss of income and, eventually, regular employment.[2]

This time, in addition, Chairman Arafat was under criticism by his own Palestinian legislature, which had only recently issued a devastat-ing report accusing members of his cabinet of corruption in the appar-ent loss of more than $300 million by his Palestinian Authority in 1996. So merely going through the motions of arresting alleged terrorists on his side of the border with Israel was unlikely to reduce the tensions that were tightening about him.

Terror may have caused the Israeli haters on the Arab side to rejoice and the Arab haters on the Jewish side to fight back, but such conflicts settled nothing. If still more proof in the modern world were needed, one had only to see that the second most populous nation on earth, Hindu India, could scarcely claim to have improved the lot of its people with four wars against Muslim Pakistan in this benighted century.

Even so, the Palestinian leadership and their Arab supporters in the Middle East still were not prepared for peace with Israel even though President Clinton continued to talk hopefully about reopening peace negotiations through a State Department mediator perhaps be-fore the conclusion of a period of mourning in Israel for the latest vic-tims of Arab terror. The Americans, however, with good reason now had cause to examine their own internal safeguards against terror after the arrest of two Arabs in Brooklyn, each wounded in a shoot-out by New York police with the ingredients for a homemade bomb that was meant, according to an informer, "to finish the job begun in Jerusalem."

The United States had its own share of problems with homegrown fanatics without suffering Arab immigrants to try to add to them.[3]

The details of the twin suicide bombings in Jerusalem added horror to the tragedy in a particularly crowded section of the western city called Machane Yehuda, jammed together in an area of narrow streets lined with covered markets and shops mainly of fruits and vegetables as well as cheap clothing and odds and ends. As always, that kind of bargain center inevitably also attracted tourists and a number of

Americans were scattered among the regular customers that hot July afternoon.

In retrospect this time, it also appeared that the suicide bombers themselves and their supporters had added a few details from a late movie to the crime they were about to commit. For people in the crowd later recalled seeing the bombers—two men in somber movie-type black suits and dark eyeglasses who stood together only about ten or fifteen yards apart. They carried black attaché cases. That was followed within a few seconds by another explosion from the second man with even more horrifying results.

Bodies, arms, legs, and severed feet mingled with produce and bits of wooden stands as smoke and flame obscured the tragic scene. The screams of the injured and the shouts of volunteer rescuers dominated the wreckage of the market and its shattered stores until the distant sound of fire and police rescue squadrons could be heard approaching the maelstrom. A few of the injured staggered and fell to one side just as the rescuers took over. And for the rest of the afternoon there was only pandemonium and mourning at what once had been a peaceful tourist attraction as well as a center for produce freshly marketed each day for the people of Jerusalem.

In the Orthodox burial rites, the last of the rescuers to leave were the bearded rabbis in long black attire and wide-brimmed black hats, painfully scraping up human remains including flesh and bones to add to the corpses being prepared for a funeral.

There were eyewitness accounts of how roofs fell in on the dead and injured, of a severely burned victim whose flaming clothes were ripped from his body in an effort to save him, of people without feet, others with legs or arms torn off by the twin blasts. And yet, curiously, when the two bombers were discovered with their bodies almost shredded with burns, their faces were unharmed but there was no means of immediately identifying them or linking them to a paper found elsewhere that attributed the crime to Hamas and demanded the immediate release of Palestinian prisoners from Israeli cells.[4]

The only possible clue to an impending mass attack of such brutal nature had been reported to Israeli police headquarters a few days before by Palestinian police after they had battered down an apartment door in a village near Bethlehem and found the body of a Palestinian beside what seemed to have been the ingredients of a bomb he had been preparing that had blown up. The Palestinian police apparently did not attribute great importance to their discovery, which was re-called only with the wisdom of hindsight.

Prime Minister Netanyahu's investigators later reported after the twin blasts that they had interrogated a Palestinian family from which two men had been missing for some time, but there were no links be-tween them and the Jerusalem bombers. Nevertheless, Prime Minister Netanyahu, in announcing his immediate countermeasurers against the Palestinian terror, also expressed confidence that his investigators would be able to identify the bombers and the organization that had prepared them for their mission of death.

In a TV interview carried in the United States on "Larry King Live" by CNN, the prime minister remarked bitterly that the two bombers had not come from the moon or Mars but were part of what he called a large organization in which these and other suicide bombers were trained for their work, given instructions how and when they were to destroy their victims and themselves, and in return were promised that their families would be cared for after their sacrifice for the Palestinian cause.

"These people," Bibi went on for American TV, and later for his home radio service, "operate in Palestinian Authority areas and we therefore must demand that the P.A. abide by its most fundamental commitment under the Oslo agreement to fight terror."[5]

It was widely reported that the Israelis also were threatening to cut off the source of money the Palestinian Authority receives from the United States and the European Union among others. Should this kind of financial freeze-out take effect along with all the other threats of Is-raeli counterattacks to halt further bombing, the Palestinian Authority could not very well operate in its accustomed style for the benefit of some of the ministers accused of improper conduct, a few also of in-volvement in corrupt practices.[6]

All this, however, followed Netanyahu's immediate outburst when he received Chairman Arafat's telephone call of condolences after news of the twin bombings spread to the world. The text of the prime minis-ter's reproaches, not all of which reached the American public by TV or radio, included charges that the Palestinian leader had failed to carry out his pledges under the Oslo peace accords to fight terrorism within his own areas. Specifically, what Netanyahu contended was that Arafat should have been seizing 150 alleged bombing conspirators and jailing them instead of permitting them to continue to operate against Israel.

"You have encouraged the violence and incitement," the prime minister said in his telephone reply to Arafat. "You have not arrested Hamas and Islamic Holy War activists, and you have not fought the terrorist infrastructure. Worse than this, the senior elements in the Palestinian police have been involved in terrorist acts." He added later, "There will be no forgiving and no absolving. We are not ready to accept that murderous acts will be a part of our daily lives every few weeks and months."

In his "Larry King Live" interview, the prime minister's anger was even more apparent when he recalled, at an unspecified date and under apparently different circumstances, he once heard Chairman Arafat running among his people in the Gaza area shouting, "Jihad! Jihad! Jihad!" The meaning of *Jihad* is, of course, "holy war." In that respect, too, Netanyahu rebuked the Palestinian leader and demanded once again strong action against the perpetrators of terror whose headquartes remained within Palestinian police areas.

When he had pulled himself together later, Arafat's office issued a response that protested he was doing the best he could to "confront these terrorist activities as we have done in the past and will do in the future." He also termed the bombing attack an assault aimed "against the Palestinians, and against the Israelis." He next was quoted as having said Netanyahu should not abandon the peace process, although there was no suggestion from anybody on the Palestinian side that they were willing to resume peace talks in the foreseeable future, much less make concessions to try to safeguard the Israelis.[7]

The Israeli cabinet suggested, with regard to the deadlocked peace talks, that the Palestinians first honor "all of its commitments, first and foremost against terrorism." When Secretary of State Madeleine K. Albright later telephoned Arafat, he assured her that he really did want to make it possible for both sides, his and the Israelis, to operate in a secure atmosphere. But publicly, in the immediate aftermath of the tragedy, he seemed anything but accommodating. It was a case of showing the United States his best side and confronting the Israelis with a much sterner image—only he impressed neither.

As for President Clinton, he was decidedly edgy about getting into the center of this confusing diplomatic scene until both sides had become less aggressive publicly and more willing to listen to reason. It seemed to Washington insiders that the White House's people, on the whole, were conscious of the enormous risks the president was undertaking if he tried to enforce a peace in so dangerous a situation. For if there were a misstep and if a conflict resulted between aggrieved Israelis and their Palestinian foes, then the would-be peacemakers very likely would have to share the blame.

This, evidently, was the reason for the extreme caution that was attributed mainly to Vice President Al Gore in the reports circulated in Washington about the frequent White House conferences on American policy in so difficult a situation. What the president appeared to be doing, in the main, was to listen to all the advice he was given and take his time before plunging into another attempted White House lawn meeting for the Middle East principals.

He was, however, firm in condemning the bombing attack, saying, "There is no excuse and there must be no tolerance for this kind of inhumanity. The slaughter was aimed directly at innocent Israelis. And make no mistake, it was aimed at the majority of Israelis, Palestinians and Arabs who wanted a lasting and just peace."[8]

Although Secretary of State Albright was ready to make her first trip to the Middle East, the president saw no reason to send her on the mission until the mediator, Ross, had determined that her presence could help put the peace process back on track. Having only lately discovered that her grandparents were Jewish and had died in the Holocaust, it was not by any means going to be an easy assignment for her to undertake. Still, she knew perfectly well what was the first requirement before she was willing to undertake the direction of a major American peace effort, for she commented: "Arafat said he would make a 100 percent effort to get the security situation under control but he can't guarantee 100 percent results."[9]

In the threats and recriminations that poured nightly from Israeli radio in the tense period directly after the bombings, it was difficult to assess the position of the Netanyahu government with the people of Israel who had so narrowly elected him fourteen months before the Jerusalem blasts. The Labor opposition in the Knesset had withheld criticism during Likud's immediate response with its broadcast over Israeli radio of threats to raid Palestinian areas for bombing suspects and other military undertakings as a warning of sanctions against the Palestinians.

But it was noteworthy that there was only grim silence when well-meaning national figures took to the air to suggest that Labor should not join Likud in a program to form a national unity government. That apparently was not likely to happen as long as General Barak, the new leader of Labor, was determining the opposition response to the Netanyahu government's failure to provide better security for the people of Israel.

Earlier that summer, Prime Minister Netanyahu already had had a close call in a no-confidence vote when he heard General Barak say for the opposition, "The government will not fall in the Parliament today, Mr. Prime Minister, but the countdown has begun to the end of your rule. Today, you are being saved by the skin of your teeth, by promises that will not be kept, by agreements that will not be honored."

That warning had touched off another lively argument between supporters of the rivals for power, after which Barak's forecast of the outcome was realized—a 55 to 50 vote in the prime minister's favor with two abstentions and thirteen absences or blank votes in the 120-member Knesset.

Despite all the wheeling and dealing which Likud people had to do for the favorable vote, it turned out that the damage to the prime minister's coalition probably was greater than he had expected—enough to make him concerned about his campaign to house more Jewish immigrants in Arab East Jerusalem that Arafat was opposing with such vigor. No politician in Jerusalem at that juncture would have seriously considered renewing his assault on the Arabs in Palestinian sectors while holding off the Labor opposition at home.

To be specific about the damage in the ranks that Bibi already had sustained, the principal defector had been his foreign minister, David Levy, and some Knesset members he controlled. In addition, two former members of the governing coalition, Zeev Begin and Dan Meridor, who had resigned from the Bibi cabinet, also had given up on the prime minister, as had a Knesset committee chairman, Uzir Landau. A small coalition group called the Third Party had stuck with the prime minister, however, when he apologized for a personal affront to General Barak of the opposition. And finally, boycotting cabinet minister Natan Sharansky had asked for and received a government promise of more than $60 million in new housing for the thousands of Russian immigrants.

Barak was not the only one at the time to predict that the prime minister's number was up. To Meridor, the defecting former minister of finance, it was a sign of the times that the ruling coalition seemed weaker even though it had survived that first test vote of the summer.

He said, "This is only the beginning."[10] But after the confusion and re-sentment of the Palestinians stirred by the double suicide bombing of Jerusalem, the public tendency was to rally behind their government. How long that heartening development would last depended on so many changing factors that both major Israeli political parties were looking first of all to Washington rather than the Palestinian Authority, which now had been thrown thoroughly on the defensive.

What Prime Minister Netanyahu did to shore up his position on the home front, besides his continual attacks on the resentful Arafat, was to tone down his home-building program for Arab East Jerusalem, but try quietly to keep it going. That temporarily pleased the White House and at the same time lessened one irritant in the tenuous rela-tionship with the Palestinians.

The turning point had come when Bibi, instead of backing a build-ing permit for Irving I. Moscowitz, an American millionaire, permitted the prime minister's office to block his planned home construction in East Jerusalem—a reversal for the Likud program. One of the prime minister's officials, David Bar-Illan, explained that the East Jerusalem home construction project now "may be considered provocative by the Arab population of Jerusalem," a concern that previously had not been shared by Bibi himself.[11]

Indeed, in Israel as well as the Middle East as a whole, the times they were a-changing.

There was a decided change, too, in the easygoing attitude of Amer-ican immigration officials toward at least one of the two wounded sus-pects in a Brooklyn shoot-out with police who seized them July 31, the day after the Jerusalem bombings, as they apparently were trying to ac-tivate several pipe bombs allegedly to blow up Brooklyn's Atlantic Av-enue subway station.

The prisoner, seized with an associate in their Park Slope apart-ment with the bombing apparatus, was identified as a Palestinian with a Jordanian passport, Ghazi Abu Maizar, who had twice tried to enter the United States illegally from Canada, was caught a third time, but received permission to remain in this country until August 23 when he was slated for deportation.

A third alleged confederate of Maizar and his fellow Arab, Lafi Khalil, weakened on what he called their bombing plot and notified police, who broke into their apartment with guns blazing, put them un-der arrest, and took them to Kings County Hospital in Brooklyn for treatment for their wounds and arraignment. The pipe bombs were seized as evidence, particularly after the tipster contended one of the arrested pair had said they were about to finish what the Hamas terrorists had started in Jerusalem. The accomplice, too, was held.

Police said Maizar had told them Israeli authorities had wrongly called him a terrorist, all of which led the New York head of the FBI, James K. Kallstrom, to conclude: "I think we were close to a disaster and it didn't happen, and that's the good news." In the alleged conspirators' Brooklyn flat, police said they found a picture of the blind Sheik Omar Abdul Rahman, a militant Egyptian cleric who was convicted in a New York bomb plot and is serving a life sentence in an American prison.[12]

What the Brooklyn adventure amounted to, in sum, was that the United States may not have had a security problem comparable to that of Israel's but to ignore it would have been the greatest folly of all. The tragic experience of Jerusalem had a meaning for America, too.

36. The Trials of Peace

Five weeks after another suicide bombing killed sixteen people in Jerusalem, three more Arabs sacrificed themselves with bombs in the Holy City and took four more Israelis with them on September 4, 1997.[1]

It was the thirteenth sacrificial attack in Israel since 1994, bringing the total of mainly Israeli deaths by such bombings to 153. In the latest blast on Ben Yehuda Street, a shopping thoroughfare, at least a dozen Israelis were reported seriously wounded and almost two hundred suffered lesser injuries. Like the July 30 attack, the bombers were unidentified. Their victims were two young women, a twelve-year-old girl and a middle-aged man, none having any military role.

The day after the latest blast by terrorists, Israel suffered an even greater tragedy when twelve naval raiders were ambushed and killed in Lebanon by an Arab column. Nearly nine hundred Israeli troops had been slain in Lebanon in recent years for no good reason, causing cries to be raised in Jerusalem to abandon Israeli outposts.[2]

Both setbacks occurred shortly before Secretary of State Albright's Middle East visit between September 9 and 15 to try to resume Israeli-Palestinian peace talks and improve relations with Syria.[3] Mrs. Albright was gracious and stern by turn, but upon her departure she admitted quite candidly that her mission had been a failure. However, it was clear enough she had not expected any better to begin with, for she had waited eight months after taking office before arriving in Jerusalem. Upon leaving Damascus, she said: "I will come back to the region whenever the leaders have made the hard decisions and I can make a difference. But I am not going to come back to tread water."[4]

She referred here to the failure of her predecessor in President Clinton's first-term cabinet, Secretary of State Warren Christopher, who made twenty-five trips to try to produce a stable peace in the Middle

315

East and also failed to make progress. The difference, in fairness to Christopher, was that his concern was the likelihood that another Arab-Israeli war might touch off a major conflict involving the United States, but the collapse of the Soviet Union and the end of the cold war already had eased that possibility for the Pentagon.

For Mrs. Albright, although American sources did not refer to any danger to her in her shortened Middle East visit, her security was an obvious concern to those assigned to accompany and safeguard her. In any event, having delayed her visit for such a long time and gotten nowhere in her own estimation, she let it be known upon her departure that she would confer again with Israelis and Palestinians in Washington.

Referring to her program for such meetings, she told reporters before departing, "I wish that this trip was able to provide larger steps because they are needed. I'm not going to pretend to you here that I have accomplished a great deal. I am not going to make more, out of this than it is. These [the Washington visit program] are small steps and they may prove useful in getting the peace process back on track. . . . It's quite evident that the crisis of confidence is very severe, and it requires a great deal of work to try to rebuild trust."

When the Secretary of State left the Middle East, what she expected from Israel was a slackening of Prime Minister Netanyahu's efforts to grab more territory claimed by the Palestinians and to persuade him to return to the Palestinians the $500 million the Israelis annually collect from Palestinians in taxes that are supposed to be passed on to the Palestinian Authority—a transaction that had been suspended for weeks before Mrs. Albright's visit.

Once Mrs. Albright departed, Netanyahu did make the first move to renew payment of the tax money owed the Palestinian Authority, which had been unable to pay its employees during the interim and was trying to raise a loan from European countries meanwhile based on the withheld money that rightfully belonged to the Authority.[5]

Although the secretary of state made no secret of her sympathy for Israel and for the aims of the Jewish state, she also was sharp in her criticism of Netanyahu's extreme methods in opposing the Palestinians. What she quite candidly and openly expected him to do, she said, was to cease the expansion of Jewish settlements in Arab areas, which she called provocative, the confiscation of Arab land and the demolition of Arab homes that were claimed to be on Jewish territory.

What she was trying, she explained, was to "create a climate in which accelerated negotiations can succeed." These negotiations were

understood to be an immediate approach to final arrangements between Israelis and Palestinians for the creation of a Palestinian state under conditions acceptable to the Israelis—a mammoth project in itself.

Given greater cooperation by Israel, what she then proposed was
to insist—as she later did—that the Palestinians in general and Yasir
Arafat, in particular as the Palestinian Authority chairman, take major
steps in striking against Arab terrorists. The target here, as she stated it,
was the opposition to Hamas, the leading terrorist organization, which
operated from bases in Palestinian territory as well as southern
Lebanon and even inside Israel itself.

What she expected of Arafat, she said in uncompromising fashion,
was a sustained and vigorous effort to stamp out terrorism and terrorist bases in the Gaza Strip and the West Bank of the Jordan River, the
Palestinian Authority's territory. Until that happened, as far as the Israelis were concerned, there could be no progress toward peace.

In her visit to the Palestinians, however, Mrs. Albright was careful
to emphasize her sympathy for their troubles, saying, "The Palestinians have suffered a great deal, including the human costs of closures,
on restrictions of movement and of housing demolition and land con-
fiscations. Your frustrations are understandable. This is not what peace
was supposed to bring."

As she left Jerusalem, she emphasized to Netanyahu that the battle
against terrorism was vital but it could not be used as an excuse for
putting off negotiations with the Palestinians. For Arafat, she concluded that he could not expect much progress until he made a vital effort to control and defeat terrorists and their bases in his territory, a
prerequisite for the negotiation of political issues with the Israelis.[6] Before her departure, Arafat did move against terrorist bases and locked
up some suspects, but not nearly enough to satisfy the Israelis.

It was obvious that both sides would have to give ground before
there could be a settlement between them. The United States, at least at
the conclusion of Mrs. Albright's visit, was not prepared to force the issue. How long the stalemate would last remained conjectural. And as
for the possibility of war, neither side could afford it even if the doves
were not very much in evidence toward year's end.

President Clinton, having been on his summer's vacation, took no part
in the negotiations conducted by his secretary of state but he was firm
in his denunciation of the latest suicide bombings in Jerusalem. He said

that the attack was intended to "kill innocent people and the peace process itself." He added, "This must not be permitted to happen."[7]

Hamas, the terrorist group that claimed responsibility for the July 30 bombings, also issued a similar communiqué after the September 4 blasts. In the latter crime, eyewitnesses said the three bombers came to Ben Yehuda Street pushing handcarts containing suitcases and steered the carts a short distance from each other before setting off the explosions that tore the bombers apart and felled the four victims. The Hamas communiqué was located in Ramallah by a telephone caller. It specified that the bombers were part of a "Martyr's Brigade for Freeing Prisoners" and demanded the release of members of Hamas held in Israeli jails. The attack, the communiqué added, was a response to an Israeli rocket blast in south Lebanon in which several Palestinians were killed.

Prime Minister Netanyahu, conscious of the approaching visit of the American secretary of state, justified his position against what he called Palestinian terror by saying there could be no political progress while Israelis are "being blown up in the streets"[8] but he added, "Instead of fighting terrorists, we see Arafat hugging and kissing them."

This time, however, it was reported that Arafat had arrested about a score of Hamas members who were held in Palestinian jails. The Palestinian chairman had done as much in the past but released his prisoners quietly once the inquiries dribbled off.

Still, in other past incidents, he did have both the will and the power to punish extremists if he believed it expedient to do so. Early in 1996, after the first Palestinian elections, Israel was pulling out much of its armed forces from Gaza and the West Bank and the regular entry of about one hundred thousand Palestinian daily workers in Israel also was improving relations. Given such favorable conditions, the Palestinians responsible for several bus bombings that winter were suitably punished.

These, however, were different times when a softer Labor regime was in power. Labor was encouraged then by what seemed like a heartening show of force that the Israeli government appreciated, thereby stimulating its policy of trading land for peace—something that Netanyahu's Likud coalition opposed then and now.

Recalling such performances that they applauded at the time, Israeli government people faithful to Netanyahu remained convinced that Arafat could do as much again, probably more, if he were given the incentive to do so. In this mood, just before the bombings in

Jerusalem, both the United States and Israel were trying to bring Arafat to the conference table with suggestions that he might be able to win support for a new airport and seaport on the Gaza Strip, together with access roads across Israeli Territory to the West Bank, provided he agreed to return to the deadlocked peace negotiations.

However, the Jerusalem blasts disposed of such inducements until the argument over responsibility for the rise of terror came to a head and the Palestinians and the Israelis were willing to resume their long-stalled negotiations for peace. Pending such arrangements, the outlook for peace was even dimmer than ever before. Despite all his furious activity to safeguard his country and his people, Prime Minister Netanyahu's efforts to increase security were no more convincing than those of the Labor government that preceded his coalition.[9]

Directly after the Jerusalem bombings in July Arafat was plunged into almost as much trouble with his own people as he was with the outraged Israelis. What hurt the Palestinian leader more than Israeli charges of condoning terrorism was the accusation of the Palestinian legislature alleging corruption among members of his cabinet and demands for the replacement of all eighteen members. With two exceptions, they soon offered their resignations, but, in the turmoil after the Jerusalem bombings, he was understandably reluctant to take on a government reorganization.

Beyond that, before the outbreak of terror, Arafat already had been obliged to take disciplinary action against eight members of his police force in connection with the fatal beating of a civilian protest marcher in a local Palestinian demonstration. That, together with Israeli accusations against four other police and his police chief for allegedly plotting against the remaining Israeli settlers in Nablus, was too much for the chairman of the Palestinian Authority to handle at once.

Such were the additional trials of peace for the champion of Palestinian autonomy, a people who had been promised their own state along with the companion Jewish state in the long-neglected UN General Assembly resolution of a half-century ago. Under such compulsions, it is scarcely surprising that the usually combative Arafat vanished from his regular routine on the Gaza Strip in the aftermath of the first Jerusalem blast and returned only after a weekend of consultation in Alexandria with the president of Egypt, Hosni Mubarak.

Although Mubarak himself had nothing to say, Egypt being linked to Israel by treaty, the Egyptian radio put out a sympathetic account of Arafat's visit. The broadcast reported on "the crisis that the peace process is going through, particularly after the dangerous decisions issued by the Israeli cabinet in the wake of the explosions that took place in West Jerusalem."

Regardless of whatever counsel Mubarak may have given the Palestinian leader, or any lesser response, Mubarak was in no mood to accept blame for the terrorist assault; instead, he told Israel in effect to fight its own war in its own way against terror and refrain from "making war" on the Palestinian people. That, in turn, led to another wordy fusillade against him on Israeli radio to which he did not respond.

As for the legislative charges of corruption and the proposals for resignations from sixteen of the eighteen ministers, the Authority's chairman replied merely that there was "plenty of time" to handle that issue. He already had accepted one resignation, that of the minister of justice, who had sponsored a law authorizing the death penalty for any Arab found guilty of selling land to an Israeli. The others who offered their resignations emphasized that their move was made to "give the chairman a free hand" in responding to accusations from Israel, not to indicate any feeling of guilt in connection with the legislative inquiry.[10]

Although Arafat answered the Israeli denunciations of being soft on terrorism by seeking President Clinton's intervention, he was given no satisfaction at the White House. It was just as well. All too soon, directly after a known Hamas terrorist had been freed from an Israeli prison, Arafat embraced him and kissed him, a greeting that was celebrated with a picture on page one of the *New York Times* on August 21, 1997.

As for the Palestine Authority's financial troubles, a World Bank report had estimated early in 1997 that the gross Palestinian domestic product, never very large, had dropped more than 20 percent among the nine hundred thousand people on the Gaza Strip and the million others on the West Bank. It followed that the breakdown in the forwarding of taxes due the Authority from the Israeli government was catastrophic.

At the time, Palestinian per capita income had been estimated at only $1,300 monthly. Although the taxes were withheld, entry to work in Israel was prohibited and pay due Arafat's employees could not be obtained.

Arafat, therefore, was thrown on the defensive after the Jerusalem bombings far more than the infuriated Netanyahu. With virtually one hundred thousand Palestinians idled because they could not cross the borders into Israel for their regular jobs there, the legislative inquiry into the conduct of the affairs of the Authority was the prime subject of discussion among the discontented Arab population. Much as they mistrusted the Israelis, many also had their doubts about their own government.

The sum total of the critical report, endorsed by a large proportion of the legislature, charged widespread irregularities that affected funds other than the withheld taxes, money contributed by such major bodies as the European Union and the American Congress, together with lesser sources. There also was criticism of the high living of some Arafat colleagues and their costly automobiles. There also were negative comments against several Palestinian cabinet members who were accused of avoiding import taxes for automobiles they had received through the Gaza customs office.[11]

The report estimated that more than four thousand foreign cars had been imported duty-free, and supposedly for official use only, although their registration and licenses scarcely supported such qualifications. There was little doubt, either, about the size and beauty of some of the homes of the criticized officials and their families. Automobiles and homes, being so visible to the ordinary Palestinians who had to go jobless whenever there was trouble with Israel, were bound to arouse unfavorable comment among the people whom the officials were supposed to serve.

In the legislative report, one minister allegedly helped influence the assignment of Palestinian Authority contracts to a relative. In another instance, a minister was accused of overcharging the Authority for contractors' services and withholding the difference. Other charges in the report included embezzlement and associated evidence of misuse of Authority funds; however, the honesty and fair dealing of Arafat and a number of other ministers were not challenged.

While Israel withheld the payment of Palestinian tax funds, the Arafat regime was obliged to prohibit all but the most necessary expenditures for the duration of the emergency. The discomfort among the Palestinian people became intense and the discontent marked. But what saved Arafat and his officials during that emergency was the bitterness his people exhibited toward Israel and its government.[12]

In the search for the identities of the five suicide bombers, the two who blew up the Jerusalem market in July and the three who followed with the shopping center explosions in September, the Israelis could expect no help from the Palestinians. And as for Arafat and his ministers, they seemed to have limited their cooperation in the criminal investigation to attending meetings with the Israelis that were held on the theory that there was information to be exchanged. Except during the Albright visit and for a short time thereafter, the exchanges were noteworthy for their emptiness of substance.

Such were the trials of peace between Israel and the Palestinians in the fiftieth year of the rebirth of the Jewish state. And yet, the Jewish refugees from Russia and elsewhere still flocked to the Jewish state despite the limited security it could offer. It was more than could have been expected in the home countries of the refugees—still the reason for Israel's existence in a brutal world.

But for all concerned, there was no escaping the stinging honesty of Secretary Albright's summation at the end of her brief excursion into relations between Israel, the Palestinians, and the rest of the Arab Middle East: "The crisis of confidence there is worse than I thought. It's fairly tattered."[13]

Mrs. Albright's observation appeared to be prophetic. On January 4, 1998, Foreign Minister Levy resigned from the Netanyahu cabinet and thereby reduced the prime minister's margin to 61–59 in Knesset. It was a good question how much longer the troubled Likud regime could remain in power.

37. Israel at 50

Regardless of the ups and downs of relationships with the Palestinians and their allies, Israel is in the Middle East to stay. That is the basic conclusion to be drawn from the hard-headed record of its first half-century.

Despite all the wars, suicide bombing blasts, and propaganda offensives of its enemies, the Jewish state has developed a modern, consumer-oriented economy with a skilled workforce and a population that is bound to expand beyond 6 million. That figure, matched against the loss of life in the Holocaust, in itself represents a triumph of the human spirit over adversity.

Moreover, given Israel's expanding industrial role in the Middle East toward century's end, those nations with which it shares recognition are bound to benefit from the increased trade it develops for the region as a whole. Its enemies, however, cannot be expected to lessen their efforts to try to confuse, delay, and even halt such progress in this era of high technology.

But after Israel's first thirty years of almost constant foreign wars, together with the violence and terrorism that have punctuated the succeeding two decades, a hardy people have emerged to face the future with renewed courage and resolution. Such opposition cannot prevail against what President Clinton rightly called "a thriving democracy . . . in a hostile terrain."[1]

To rebuild an ancient state in the Middle East that had once known the glory of Solomon and the wisdom of David, the founders of modern Israel began on the shores of the eastern Mediterranean a half-century ago with little more than the stoutness of their hearts, the determination of their minds, and the mighty tabernacle of their dreams.

Despite their victories over the invading armies of six Arab powers in the War of Independence in 1948 and 1949, these widely scattered settlers of the reborn state of Israel—barely a million of them—subsisted without complaint on the meager essentials of life in their scattered towns and cities and their hard-hit communal farms. Many in rural areas had to work with guns at their side to defend themselves against interlopers.

In the cities, even in bitterly divided Jerusalem, there was no relief while enemy troops—in this case, Jordan's British-officered Arab Legion—still occupied all key positions in the Old City with all its religious treasures of the past.

Such was the desperate situation of that greatly desired Jewish homeland in its first years after the War of Independence. No one then could offer very much security or even hope to either the Zionist faithful who had restored Israel to life or to the refugees within its threatened borders who had fled the hellholes of central Europe.

In my survey of the new nation in 1950, I found no one who then could offer more than the prayers of the devout for the future, much less a forecast that this revived nation would expand immeasurably before century's end. Such remarkable growth seemed beyond belief at the time; rather, I remember the grim view of the first prime minister of Israel, David Ben-Gurion, when he uttered his own assessment: "In Israel, to be a realist, you must believe in miracles."

It took less a miracle than hard work, bravery, and military skill that brought this reborn Jewish state to maturity after fifty years. And it will require even greater effort against external aggression and internal division to preserve the nation for its first century.

The wars the Israelis already have fought in their first thirty years have been difficult enough. The War of Independence lasted more than a year during which repeated UN truce arrangements meant only that the small bands of Israeli soldiers would have to work hard to rearm for the next enemy offensives. And after that, for the remainder of those first thirty years of combat, came the Suez War of 1956, the Six-Day War of 1967, the Yom Kippur War of 1973, and in 1988, to avert the threat of nuclear disaster, the Israeli Air Force destroyed an Iraqi atomic site under construction. Even in the 1991 Gulf War to punish Iraq for its conquest of Kuwait, Israel took missile strikes from Saddam Hussein's Iraq, although the Jewish nation at the time was not a part of the American-led coalition against him.

Beyond that record of resistance to aggression from their Arab neighbors, the people of Israel—even in the relatively brief periods of peace that existed during their latter years of growth—suffered through well-nigh a score of suicide bombings of street crowds and buses in their cities as well as a continual barrage of broadcasts from neighboring radios of denunciations of the Jewish people and slurs on the Jewish faith. Nor did such peace negotiations as the White House lawn ceremonials, two Camp David sessions, the Oslo accords, and the latter-day Hebron agreement lessen the savagery of the propaganda attacks that emanated from their immediate neighbor, the Voice of Palestine.[2]

The time has long passed since the people of Israel were unable to feed themselves. In the beginning, directly after the War of Independence, the nation could provide only about 25 percent of the food needed by its people; accordingly, the burden of the economy was rural and the kibbutzim vied with the army in producing the heroes of the new nation. Ralph McGill, then the editor of the *Atlanta Constitution*, was touring the country at the time and illustrated its problems with an anecdote he picked up in a small cabaret (where you could get tea and brown bread if you were lucky):

> The master of ceremonies announces that a friend of his has started reading anti-Semitic papers. When asked why, the friend replied:
> "Well, there all is austerity. We do not have enough to eat. The taxes are high. The cost of living is great. There are many sacrifices. Life is monotonous. The papers urge one to do without and to work harder lest we starve and die. The papers warn us there may be another war. So, I read the anti-Semitic papers. And what are they saying? They are saying the Jews have all the money and are going to rule the world."[3]

McGill concluded that the story was good for a loud laugh on a dull night in town, which was characteristic of the way the earliest Israelis looked at themselves and their problems. He estimated that 20 percent of Israel's population in the early years were farmers—perhaps two hundred thousand of a million people who either worked the communal farms for group profits, if any, or individual farms at their own risk.

At one kibbutz he visited, he wrote: "Great rock walls testify to rocks picked up and pried out of the soil. Buildings, stone and concrete all are evidence of their skills." For an evening meal, which McGill shared at the kibbutz, there was "plenty of thick-sliced brown bread, bowls of plum and peach butter, margarine, raw carrots and tea. The big meal, with meat and vegetables, is at noon."

The editor commented, "It is a great and complex experiment that is being tried here. . . . It is odd, in a way, that the newest nation in the world on some of the oldest soil finds that it, too, must build on agriculture."[4]

At that time, only about seventy-five thousand acres were under cultivation by the figures that were given to me; now, I am told, the acreage devoted to agriculture has increased tenfold, with citrus, other fruits, and vegetables being widely exported to European and south Asian destinations. Although these were among the first of Israel's exports across the Mediterranean to Europe and through the Suez Canal and Red Sea to South Asia, they still are in demand along with the more important and rapidly increasing shipments of high-tech electronic equipment, clothes, medical supplies, diamonds, and processed foods.

The country, too, has changed dramatically to a largely urban society, although the farms, collectively operated or individually owned, still remain of prime importance across the land. However, because Israel now grows or produces all its food except grain imports, almost all the workforce handles industrial production for both export and domestic use. Through the development of a skilled, modern concentration of labor, Israel's ever-growing foreign trade has enlarged enormously in the past twenty years.[5]

One of the earliest problems the country faced, both for industry and home use, was a permanent water shortage. In the country's first years, water was not much of a problem. But with the increase in population and the continual growth of both industry and agriculture, government scientists were among the first to design, build, and operate large desalizination plants for the distribution and use of the waters of the Mediterranean where they were most needed inland. A network of dams and canals also was designed and created for the distribution of water wherever possible, and some, in later years, was diverted to neighboring states, Jordan in particular, where water shortages were far greater than in Israel.

As a result of such diverse and ever-increasing production, the people of Israel have earned for themselves a standard of living approximating that of western Europe and a per capita gross product valued at almost $14,000. If this is still reckoned below American living standards, an Israeli student of history could reflect that the United States, after a half-century of independence, was not in such great shape, having seen its president, James Madison, in flight before a marauding British army in the War of 1812 that had invaded the infant capital of Washington, D.C., and burned the government's buildings.

Next to the bravery, courage, and skilled development of its people, Israel's greatest asset has been the devotion and often the self-sacrifice of its leadership. Mention merely the names of the eight prime ministers these past fifty years to an audience of Israelis across the land—Ben-Gurion, Sharett, Eshkol, Meir, Begin, Rabin, Peres, Netanyahu—and there will be a pause momentarily, then a burst of triumphant yelling and applause.

Not that all have led the nation to great victories. Far from it. Mostly, the leadership has been obliged to devote itself first of all to the problems of survival. Nor have these prime ministers been able to resolve the rare Jewish problem of being a minority in every nation except in Israel where they face an Arab minority.

Yes, the Israelis are well aware that the Palestinian minority among them are mostly underemployed, underpaid, often undereducated, and abandoned to lives of wretched poverty. Yes, they realize that the Palestinians also have the urge to better their situation, to improve their lives and those of their children, to celebrate their share of the democratic freedoms that the Israelis have been able to wrest from an ancient land that has so often resounded to the march of the soulless conqueror rather than the blessings of the great apostles of peace on earth.

The problem remains, however, that the majority in this reborn land, with memories that range over five thousand years, still cannot feel itself secure from the persecution that has haunted the lives of its forebears.

The intercession of the United States eventually may make a difference but the might of America cannot guarantee the automatic creation of equality between the majority Israelis and the minority Palestinians. Even after more than two centuries of racial strife in the United States, marked by a Civil War that nearly destroyed the nation, an enormous black minority only now is beginning to force open the door of education toward equality with the still large white majority. The struggle in Israel, too, will require the healing attributes of time, patience, and continued effort.

Of all the prime ministers of Israel in its first half-century, Ben-Gurion's influence still overshadows that of his successors in shaping the policies of a Jewish state in the Middle East. For almost fourteen of the nineteen years covered by his service at the helm of the nation, his inflexible resolve and his devotion to the twin ideals of democracy and freedom inspired his people as well as those who followed his leadership in almost constant war broken by relatively few periods of undisturbed peace.

Almost on a par with him, I would rank Moshe Sharett, not so much because he was the second prime minister—his service was too brief for that; rather, he and Golda Meir as a subsequent prime minister together with the best of Israel's foreign ministers, Abba Eban, realized the importance of world opinion in shaping Israel's destiny and all tirelessly devoted their efforts to dealing with the UN. Mainly through their work, together with those of the Americans who were allied with them, did the world organization make possible the creation of Israel and initially support the infant Jewish state.

Had the Israelis who followed them devoted as much attention to the UN in its period of tremendous growth, it would not be as easy toward century's end for the nation's enemies to obtain an almost automatic anti-Israeli vote in both the Security Council (where the American veto applies) and the veto-less General Assembly. As greatly as the world organization has declined in both reputation and authority in recent years through its top-heavy small-state memberships and internal organizational growth, it remains a factor of world opinion and cannot be ignored in the way in which both the American State Department and the Israeli foreign office have operated in the century's last years. Sharett, as prime minister, never would have understood such damaging policies.

That could also be said of Golda Meir, who was tougher than most of the first ministers of the nation who followed her and yet as jealous of her femininity as any modern beauty queen. I remember once, as a reporter, telling her after a confidential talk that she reminded me greatly of my mother, upon which she muttered a sharp rebuke in Yiddish and never again spoke to me in private. When it came to raising money for Israel during emergencies, there was no one to compare with her inside and outside the government; even Ben-Gurion could not obtain the kind of dollar values she produced from America's Jewish community in every early emergency of the nation to which she gave her adult life.

For Begin, Rabin, and Peres, too, there were times when their leadership was crucial. And that, perhaps, was more important in Begin's regime than in the others, because he was the first non-Labor prime minister in the history of Israel and he had to deal with the influence of the religious minorities that were so inflexible in permitting the growth of what they feared would be a Palestinian state. In that respect, perhaps more than his Labor successors, Rabin and Peres, Begin's regime formed the basis for the equally hostile administration of Netanyahu toward the Palestinians near century's end. Say what you will about the Likud Party's opposition role in Israel's up-and-down outlook toward the Palestinians; Labor's policy of trading land for peace has its limits, too, if the Jewish state is to survive beyond Sharett's estimate of two hundred years.[6]

From Washington to Jerusalem and Camp David to Oslo, nine American presidents have tried to support Israel's efforts to attain a reasonable amount of security for its rapidly growing population within the first fifty years of its status as a rare and often quarrelsome democracy in the Middle East. The current assurance of the nation's continuous existence in a rancorous atmosphere may be ascribed in part to the efforts of at least some of the American chief executives, but this generous policy also has had benefits for the United States. As a distinguished task force of the Council on Foreign Relations put the case in 1997:

> The U.S. commitment to Israeli security is as a central component of U.S. policy. Peace and security in the [Persian] Gulf would be strengthened by a comprehensive Arab-Israeli peace. In fact, security in both sub-regions is a prerequisite for peace because Arab-Israeli peace will not be assured if established only with the front-line states of Egypt, Jordan, Syria, and Lebanon. Fear and non-conventional threats to Israel from Iran and Iraq affect those formulating U.S. policy for the region. There can be no regional disarmament or long-run economic integration until this broader security is achieved.[7]

President Truman's prompt recognition of Israel once the nation was established, President Eisenhower's continued support, President

Carter's efforts to maintain the Camp David agreements, and President Clinton's celebration of the Oslo accords with a new peace pact on the White House lawn all contributed to the creation now and then of a more agreeable atmosphere between Israel and the Palestinians. If the contributions of Presidents Kennedy, Johnson, Nixon, Reagan, and Bush were secondary to the main thrust of American policy, their views were nevertheless important because they contributed to the central American aim of eventual peace for the Middle East.

That so desirable a condition remains to be achieved was also evident in the conclusions of the Council on Foreign Relations task force saying: "Terrorism remains as a threat to the stability of states in the Persian Gulf and to U.S. personnel and interests. . . . The delays in the peace process following the 1996 elections revived serious concerns . . . reflecting both the fear of regional instability and popular concern for the plight of the Palestinian people."[8]

However, the breakdown of the Oslo peace process, like the Camp David accords that preceded them and the Hebron policy for further withdrawals of Israeli troops from Palestine areas, did not automatically bring into being the all-embracing Israeli-Palestinian agreement so many well-intentioned people had envisaged. In this interim period, even women in Israel could not pray with their husbands at the remains of the sacred Western Wall in Jerusalem without arousing the fury of Orthodox protests—a commentary in itself on what an Israeli government could and could not do to maintain peace even among its own people.[9]

It was not Israel's survival that remained in question. That had been settled by the Jewish state's self-sacrifice and success in its first thirty years of war against the encroachments of its Arab enemies. The outlook for the next century depends first of all on greater cohesion among all the conflicting elements of the Jewish state at home, a strong sense of the loyalty of its citizens to their own government, and, as always, the most vital provision of all, the support of the United States. Having achieved so much in so relatively brief a time in the history of the reborn nation, its people then could expect improved relations with its neighbors in the Middle East and the benefits of security and peace.

Notes

Bibliography

Index

Notes

Introduction: On Reality and Miracles

1. From a Ben-Gurion interview Oct. 5, 1956.
2. Harry S. Truman, *Memoirs II: Years of Trial and Hope* (Garden City, N.Y.: Doubleday, 1956); from a letter to President Wiezmann of Israel, 169.
3. Trygve Lie, *In the Cause of Peace* (New York: Macmillan, 1954), 174.
4. Truman, 168.

1. The Rebirth of a Nation

1. Lie, 158–162 passim.
2. Herma Silverstein, *David Ben-Gurion* (New York: Franklin Watts, 1988), 75.
3. Shimon Peres, *Battling for Peace* (New York: Randon House, 1995), 53; Ariel Sharon, *Warrior* (New York: Simon and Schuster, 1989). Starting on p. 158 passim, his experience with the British army is instructive.
4. Sharon, 79; Peres, 52–53.
5. Lie, 161–62, 171.
6. Silverstein, 79–87 passim.

2. A Leader for Israel

1. Peres, 60–62.
2. The background of Palestine's beginnings before the declaration of a Jewish state, as discussed in Lie, Peres, and Sharon, provided much of the factual background for this chapter.
3. The background for Zionist activities in the United States is based on my experience.
4. These other biographies of Ben-Gurion have additional factual information on his rise to power: Robert St. John, 1971; Maurice Edelmann, 1964; Ohad Zmora, ed., 1967. Ben-Gurion's autobiography, *A Personal History,* was published in 1971.

3. The War of Independence

1. Eisenhower's remark was widely published at the time China created the Formosa Strait crisis outside Taiwan.
2. Latrun detail is in Peres, 65, and Sharon, 50–60. The arms buildup in Israel is in Peres, 61–62, and Sharon, 65–66.
3. Bernadotte detail is mainly in Lie, 185–87.
4. Bernadotte assassination is in Lie, 188–92. The Sharon quote is from his book, 67.
5. The UN on Israel and thereafter is in Lie, 193–94.
6. The discussion of Truman's role is in his *Memoirs II*, 162–69 passim.

4. A Tour of Israel

1. Although I published an extensive account of my travels in the *New York Post* in 1950, what appears in this chapter is mainly reflections and analysis of what has happened to Israel over the passage of fifty years. I have consulted my notes for factual conclusions.
2. Included were the ones I knew best—Mrs. Meir and Messrs. Sharett and Eban.
3. The Israeli government provided the car, the driver, and the escort. Part of the time, I had a distinguished companion, Ralph McGill, the editor of the *Atlanta Constitution*, who published his views in his newspaper. See Harold H. Martin, *Ralph McGill—Reporter* (Boston: Atlantic, Little Brown, 1973), 142. See also McGill *Israel Revisited* (Atlanta: Tupper and Love, 1950).
4. For the beginning of the Dimona reactor, which I did not know about and could not even imagine, see Peres, 113–23 passim.
5. Peres, 113–23 passim.

5. Democracy under Fire

1. Lie, 196–97.
2. Ezer Weizman: *The Battle for Peace* (New York: Bantam, 1981), 39–40.
3. The rest of the discussion of the Israeli government and its political parties in the Knesset is based on my knowledge and observations over the years.
4. Regarding the murder of Count Bernadotte, those interested in the case should consult a footnote on p. 124 of Michael Bar-Zohar, *Facing a Cruel Mirror* (New York: Scribner, 1990), which refers to the names of those suspected of the Bernadotte murder.
5. I had a long and fortunate acquaintance with Dr. Bunche at the UN. Part of his background is from Cheever and Haviland, *Organizing for Peace* (Cambridge, Mass.: Houghton Mifflin, 1954), 493–95 passim.
6. On Churchill's Fulton speech, I consulted the text for the quotes used herein. Just before he went to Fulton, I was among the guests at a private dinner for him at Bernard M. Baruch's New York apartment and all of us then received a blunt warning of what

was to come. Appropriately, Herbert Bayard Swope, Baruch's chief associate, and another guest coined the phrase "cold war."

7. For the story of the commando force, see Sharon, 83–91 passim.

6. Crisis over Suez

1. Although a number of different authorities have made public the background of the Suez Canal crisis, I believe the most inclusive version is in Townsend Hoopes, *The Devil and John Foster Dulles* (Boston: Little, Brown, 1973), 319–28 passim.

2. Peres, 105.

3. Hoopes, 341–43.

4. Ibid., 345.

5. Ibid., 353.

6. Peres, 110–14 passim. See also a commentary by Dean Acheson in his *Power and Diplomacy* (Cambridge, Mass.: Harvard Univ. Press, 1958), 109–16.

7. War with Egypt

1. Sharon, 151–53, reflects the soldier's point of view.

2. Hoopes, 374–76, gives the American and UN response. Ike's quotes are picturesque, but I was not there to hear them so I have not used them.

3. Sharon, 146–53 passim, provides an extended view of the Israeli military action against Egypt.

4. Hoopes, 382–93, gives more of the American State Department's point of view for those who want a fuller account.

8. Treasure in the Desert

1. Coverage of the Baruch proposal for atomic control was my first major assignment at the UN. Having known the principals and their opponents and later debated the issues at Columbia after joining the university's faculty, my views were formed early on and have not changed. For factual background, see Bernard M. Baruch, *The Public Years* (New York: Holt, Rinehart and Winston, 1960), 360–79.

2. Ben-Gurion's views of an atomic future for Israel were outlined to me originally on my 1950 visit to Israel and are substantially as recorded herein. As for Eban and others in opposition, the people in Israel's government have never been bashful in stating their opinions, and I knew most of the actors in this nuclear drama.

3. For factual background, see Frank Friedel, *America in the Twentieth Century* (New York: Knopf, 1960), 565–68.

4. Ibid., 568–70. See also Elting E. Morison, *Turmoil and Tradition* (Boston: Houghton Mifflin, 1960), 635–62 passim, for a proposed U.S. approach to the Soviet Union on atomic energy as conceived by Henry L. Stimson while secretary of war.

5. For French-Israeli cooperation on atomic construction, see Peres, 120–24; for prospective atomic damage, see Arthur H. Compton, *Atomic Quest* (New York: Oxford

Univ. Press, 1956), 301–8. President Truman's views, too, are important, as witness his position in his *Memoirs II,* 294–315 passim.

9. Israel Fights for Life

1. For American policy on the Middle East and the Aswan High Dam, see Charles E. Bohlen, *Witness to History, 1929–1969* (New York: Norton, 1973); on Nasser, 426–31; on Israel, 416, 425, 509–10; on the Suez crisis, 407, 416, 440.

2. See Hoopes, for Dulles on Aswan, 330—36; Soviet-Egypt arms deal, 329–30, 338–42; on USSR aid to Egypt, 440–41.

3. On the Lavon affair, see Peres, 80–85, 87–97 passim; on political party changes, 86–87, 89–92, 149, 238.

4. On Israel and the UN, see Lie, 416–41; see also Cheever and Haviland, 367–68; 394–96.

5. For the position of the Lyndon Johnson administration in the United States, see George Christian: *The President Steps Down* (New York: Macmillan, 1970), 186–276. For Hammakjold and Thant, I used my UN notes and records.

6. On Nasser's order to oust the UN Emergency Force from the Suez Canal, see Donald Neff, *Warriors for Jerusalem: The Six Days that Changed the Middle East* (New York: Simon and Schuster, 1984), 86–88.

10. Dayan's War

1. A sympathetic portrait of Prime Minister Eshkol is in Peres, 89–93.

2. The events leading up to the Six-Day War are described in Sharon, 185–90 passim.

3. The strategic position of the Arabs and Israelis and Dayan's calculations as defense minister are given in Frank Gervasi, *The Life and Times of Menachem Begin* (New York: Putnam, 1979), 286–89.

4. Bohlen gives Khrushchev's view of the Soviet position just before the Six-Day War, 434–36.

5. The planning and actual opening of the Six-Day War, as developed by Dayan, are in Neff, 201–10 passim. See also Sharon, 186–94.

6. Peres's summary of the positions of the three Arab governments in the Six-Day War is in his book, 93–94.

11. Two Days in June

1. For the opening of the Six-Day War, there are summaries in Neff, 203–6, also 210–11; for the second day, 218–19 on the Arab side and 223–24 for the Israelis. A UN cease-fire proposal is summarized on 227. See also maps of the combat and summaries in Sharon, 193–203.

2. Damage to Syria is summarized in Neff, 203–4, to Jordan and Jerusalem, 204–5. A reflection on Egyptian turmoil was recorded in his latter years by Ezer Weizman, presi-

dent of Israel and a general at the time of the Six-Day War in his *The Battle for Peace* (New York: Bantam, 1981), 52–53.

3. Nasser's verbal attack on the United States and his severance of relations is in Neff, 219–20.

4. Damage to Jerusalem and Israel's decision to seize the Old City is in Peres, 93–94. See also Neff, 224.

5. The Kosygin-Johnson decision to stop the Six-Day War is in Neff, 212.

12. Old Jerusalem Captured

1. General Dayan's victory in old Jerusalem is reported in Neff, 231–33, Sharon, 198, and Weizman, 52–54.

2. A summation of the Six-Day War is given in Michael Bar-Zohar, *Facing a Cruel Mirror* (New York: Scribner, 1990), 7–12, and in Neff, 234–42.

3. On a UN cease-fire takes hold, Nasser quits but changes his mind, the extent of Israel's victory mounts, and a U.S.-Soviet confrontation is averted, see Neff, 261–68, Weizman, 81, and Bar-Zohar, 23–26.

4. On the war's end, the Soviet threat, Israel ceases-fire after humbling Egypt and Jordan, see Neff, 278–82. See also Ned Temko, *To Win or Die: A Personal Portrait of Menachem Begin* (New York: Morrow, 1987), 172–73.

13. Golda

1. Golda Meir, Ben-Gurion, and changing times in Israel as viewed by Bar-Zohar, 43–45, Temko, 173–76, and Weizman, 33–44, with a detailed explanation of how and why Israel must be governed by party coalitions in Sharon, 270–73.

2. Peres's views of Meir as prime minister are in Peres, 98–101; as for the Sharett incident, I was present as a reporter.

3. I had never before seen such enthusiasm in the United States for an Israeli victory. In Israel, too, the excitement was intense and the joy of victory unrestrained. See Temko, 172–73.

4. There are several versions of Prime Minister Meir's negotiations with the Soviet Union. The charge that Secretary Rogers conspired with Moscow against Israel is in *The Yom Kippur War* by a *London Sunday Times* team (Garden City, N.Y.: Doubleday, 1974), 438–56. The American position is given at length in Theodore H. White, *Breach of Faith* (New York: Atheneum-Readers Digest Press, 1975), 105–6; for Begin's role, see Temko, 172–78.

5. For a different view of Prime Minister Meir, see Bar-Zohar, 43–51. Although her coalition broke up quickly, she patched up a cabinet and remained in power until after the Yom Kippur War.

6. For Sadat's planning, see the *London Sunday Times* team, 46–62.

7. As with almost every major issue in the Middle East, there are a number of versions of "Black September." One of the most detailed is in Moshe Dayan, *Moshe Dyan: The Story of My Life* (New York: Morrow, 1976), 427–33.

8. The Allon plan and the reasons for it are in Sharon, 356–61.

14. Disaster!

1. For the start of the Yom Kippur War, a section of the *London Sunday Times* team's report makes vivid reading, "The K-Day Onslaught," 133–53. I also recommend a combatant's version, Sharon, 282–303. Since Dayan suffered most of the blame for the surprise, the account in his autobiography of the eve of war and its beginning are worth rereading. 474–78.

2. The international background is given concisely in Matti Golan, *The Secret Conversations of Henry Kissinger* (New York: Quadrangle, 1976), 62–92. Begin's experience also is worth noting; see Temko, 186–87.

3. The *London Sunday Times* team has as good a version of the surprise as any I have read. See 148–53—an unbiased report of the surprise. For a soldier's response, Sharon, 288–303, tells it plainly. Most instructive of all is Maj. Gen. George S. Patton's introduction to Frank Aker, *October: 1973: The Arab-Israeli War* (Hamden, Conn.: Archon Books, 1983), 1–3.

4. How Kissinger received the news of the Yom Kippur War in New York gives an indication of the American position in the war. See Golan, 33–43.

5. The confusion on the Israeli side is reflected in the observations of Dayan in his autobiography, 489–93.

6. The *London Sunday Times* team, 164–72, covers the Israeli holding action for the first two days of the war while the reserves were being called into action. Aker, 17–34, covers the same ground but in a more technical manner.

7. Dayan's autobiography summarizes the end of the holding action preparatory to taking the offensive, 488–93. See also Aker, 48–58, and his summary of the war at sea, 59–64.

8. The Israeli navy's role is elaborated on in the *London Sunday Times* team report, 212–17. Also, the report lists a verbatim report from Dayan on his plans at the time to wind up the war.

15. Israel Strikes Back

1. Kissinger's attempt to ration Israel's supplies and thereby control the outcome of the war his way is amply documented in the *London Sunday Times* team's report, 279–80, and in Golan, 45–57, and a concluding reference to "Henry Kissinger's perfidy."

2. The collapse of the Syrian front is summarized in Dayan's autobiography, 320–21. In the *London Sunday Times* team report, see 302, 305.

3. Sharon's crossing of the Nile with his troops is in Dayan's autobiography, 523–34, and vividly and at length in Sharon, 306–30; see also Aker, 111–22.

4. The cease-fire is in the Dayan autobiography, 543–47, Sharon, 306–28, and Golan, 74–92.

5. For a summary of the costs of the Yom Kippur War, Aker is enlightening; 126–30; on refugees, 130–35. For the beginnings of the peace process, see Golan *The Secret Conversations of Henry Kissinger*, 93–122; for the nuclear alert, *London Sunday Times* team, 399–420.

6. The most revealing account of the immediate post-Yom Kippur War era is in Dayan's autobiography, 571–608. Temko, quoting Begin, barely touches the subject,

183–88. The most detailed account is in the *London Sunday Times* team report, 469–92; Peres virtually ignores the Yom Kippur War, dealing with it briefly and harshly, 150–51.

7. Bar-Zohar, 52–56 summarizes the peace process after the Yom Kippur War and the change in the Israeli government. There are details in Dayan's autobiography, 609–24, in Golan, 211–22, and in Temko, 184–1–8. For a comment on Mrs. Meir after her death, see Peres, 101.

16. Transient Times

1. For Rabin's election as prime minister, there is a discussion in Peres, 139–41.
2. On the Rabin-Kissinger talks, the most extensive record is in Golan, 213–18; another comment is in Sharon, 341–48.
3. On Nixon's last trip to the Middle East, the record on Kissinger is in White, 306–7.
4. The end of Kissinger's negotiations in the Middle East and Ford's succession as president are in Golan, 223–27.
5. On the Rabin-Peres feud, see Peres, 144–50 passim.
6. The Egyptian-Israeli accord of Sept. 1, 1975, is in the appendix of Golan, 264–73. Sharon's comment on Kissinger as "the most dangerous man in the Middle East" is in Sharon, 346–47.
7. For the story of Entebbe in detail, see Peres, 152–69.
8. Begin's campaign for prime minister is in Temko, 193–96.

17. After Thirty Years

1. Temko, 194. Peres, 149–50, blames scandals for the defeat.
2. See Sharon's independent view of the election, 353; Begin's view is in Temko, 195; for a Labor leader's view, see Bar-Zohar, 71.
3. On Israeli political scandals, there is elaborate confirmation. See Peres, 149–51; also Temko, 193–94.
4. Temko, 193–94; Bar-Zohar, 69.
5. Begin's preparations are in Temko, 188–93, Sharon, 348–51, and Bar-Zohar, 64–65.
6. Temko, 197–98.
7. Sharon, 352; Dayan, 619–21.
8. Bar-Zohar, 71–72; Peres, 151; Temko, 197.
9. For a sensitive discussion of the role of religion in Israeli politics, see Bar-Zohar, 67–68.
10. Ibid., p. 70.
11. Sharon, 353; Bar-Zohar, 71.
12. Peres, quotation, 151. For Begin's view, see Weizman, 217–18.

18. Begin Takes Over

1. On Begin, see Temko, 196–98.
2. Ibid., 199; Weizman, 192.
3. Sharon, 353–54; Temko, 200.

4. Ibid., 199; Dayan, on the Yom Kippur War, 621–23; Bar-Zohar, 75.
5. Temko, 200; Jimmy Carter, *Keeping Faith* (New York: Bantam, 1982), 276–82 passim.
6. Carter, pp. 282–88 passim.
7. Ibid., 289–93; Temko, 201–2, 206–9.
8. Carter, 293–95.
9. Ibid., 296.

19. Sadat to Israel

1. Bar-Zohar repeats the quotation from Sadat's Nov. 9, 1977, speech, 74–75.
2. Carter, 293–94, records Fahmy's and other objections to Sadat's peace initiative.
3. The first Israeli responses to Sadat's bid are in Temko, 210–11.
4. For Carter's views, see Carter, 293–95.
5. Sadat's arrival in Israel is recorded in Weizman, 30–31, Bar-Zohar, 76–78, and Temko, 213. For Carter's encouragement to Sadat, see Carter, 297.
6. The quotations from Sadat's address to the Knesset are from Temko, 213, Weizman, 32–34, and Bar-Zohar, 8.
7. Begin's response is in Weizman, 34, Temko, 213–14, and Bar-Zohar, 78–79.
8. The Begin-Sadat news conference is in Temko, 214. Bar-Zohar's comment on Begin's policy is also worth nothing, Bar-Zohar, 79.
9. For Carter's diary comment, see Carter, 297–98.

20. Begin to Washington

1. For Carter's reflections, see Carter, 297–98.
2. For Weizman's views of Sadat, see Weizman, 56–113 passim; also Bar-Zohar, 79–80.
3. The meetings are described in Temko, 214–15, Carter, 299–300, and Weizman, 110–20.
4. See Weizman, 121–35, on the Ismailia summit; Temko 216–17.
5. On the crisis in the Egyptian-Isreli talks, see Carter, 304–7 passim. The background of the Israeli cabinet discussion between the hawks and the doves—the "Battle of the Generals" as some called it—is in Weizman, 222–28; see also Temko, 216–29.
6. Carter's resolution is in his dairy entry for Feb. 3, 1978, Carter, 306.

21. Carter as Mediator

1. Carter, 304–7, discusses the invitation to President Sadat and Prime Minister Begin as well as the PLO attack that delayed Begin. See also Temko, 218–19. Another view is in Weizman, 313–31.
2. For the PLO terrorist attack in Israel, the delay to the Begin visit to Washington, and the outcome, a detailed report is in Weizman, 264–81. A brief summation is in Temko, 210. For Carter's account, including his invitations to Sadat and Begin, see Carter, 307–08.
3. The background for Camp David is in W. Dale Nelson, *The President Is at Camp*

David, (Syracuse, N.Y.: Syracuse Univ. Press, 1995), introduction and 1–21. Carter discusses his invitation to Sadat and his wife for a weekend at Camp David and the outcome, Carter, 304–8.

4. The Begin visit to the White House is discussed in Carter, 309–13. See also Temko, 218–21, for a more sympathetic Israeli view. See also Weizman, 335–39.

5. Carter's failure during Begin's brief visit to Washington is elaborated on in Carter, 311–15; see also Weizman, 284–89 and Temko, 220–21.

6. The goal set for Camp David is in Carter, 321; details of the origin and delivery of the invitations to the participants are on 316–20. See also Weizman, 340–44, Temko, 220–23, and Nelson, 110–12.

7. See Nelson, 110–16, for the details of the background at Camp David.

8. The statement of the principals at the onset of the discussions is in Carter, 319.

22. Camp David I

1. For the opening phases of the Camp David meeting to seek peace between Egypt and Israel, Carter's account is the most thorough, Carter, 319–38; a list of the members of the three delegations is on 326. See also Weizman, 341–56, Temko, 224–28, and Nelson, 110–18.

2. For the earliest problems, see Carter, 338–64, Weizman, 356–58, and Temko, 229–31.

3. See Carter on Israeli-Egyptian disagreements, 365–72; also Nelson, 119–20, and Weizman, 359–62.

4. The problems grew intractable; see Carter, pp. 373–74, and Weizman, 363–65.

5. Carter, in despair, 375–77.

6. On the meeting near deadlock, ibid., 377–79; also Weizman, 366–67.

23. Camp David II

1. On Carter's sleepless night and his thoughts for Sadat's safety, see Carter, 389; the argument on Sadat's porch is on 383. Brzezinski's mission is in Zbigniew Brzezinski, *Power and Principle: Memoirs of a National Security Adviser* (New York: Farrar, Straus and Giroux, 1985), 264–65.

2. For a summary of the mood of the Camp David conference in the last week and of the argument over the removal of Israeli settlements from the Sinai, see Carter, 388, particularly the last paragraph. See also Weizman, 367–68, and Temko, 229–30.

3. On the seriousness of the settlement issue, both sides were inflexible, and Carter was ready to give up seeking a Camp David agreement. See Carter, 389–90. On the Israeli point of view about the settlement issue, Weizman goes into detail, 369–70; for a summary, see Nelson, 121.

4. For the way Carter averted Sadat's departure on day 11, see Carter, 391–94, Nelson, 122–23, and Weizman, 371–72.

5. For the dilemma on the settlement issue, Carter is explicit, 394–95. See also Temko, 229, last two paragraphs.

6. Carter reports the breakthrough, 396–97; See also Weizman, 372–73, and Temko, 230.

7. The successful conclusion at Camp David is covered in Carter, 399–402; Weizman, for the Israelis, 373–77; Temko, with the quotations from Begin, 231. For a summary from a variety of sources, see Nelson, 124.

24. The Price of Peace

1. For Carter's address to Congress, see Carter, 404–5. There is a detailed, and more extensive, account of both Camp David and American attitudes in Weizman, 340–97. See also Peres, 254.

2. For Sadat's advice to Carter, see Carter, 418. The first encouraging reports of the Camp David accords' reception are on 405–7. The Israeli opposition leader has an opposite estimate in Peres, 226–27, which nevertheless gives Carter great credit for Camp David.

3. For Carter's effort to sway Begin on the Camp David accords and the peace treaty, see Carter, 407. Peres has the opposition view, 178.

4. The change in spirit for the Camp David accords in the Middle East is recorded in Carter, 408–11 and in Peres, 254–56. On the position of the American Jewish community, see Weizman, 284–86.

5. On Carter's visit to Egypt, see Carter, 417–19. Begin's attitude is in Temko, 240–41.

6. On Carter's adventures in Jerusalem, see Carter, 420–24. A commentary on Sadat's position, as seen by the Israeli opposition, is in Peres, 251–52. For Weizman's view, see Weizman, 378–82.

7. The ceremonial signing of the Egyptian-Israeli peace treaty is recorded in Carter, 427–29, and in Peres, 256–57. For a different view, see Weizman, 324–31.

8. Begin's quotation is in Carter, 428.

9. For the effect of the Khomeini revolution in Iran on Carter's presidency, see Peres, 210–11. For the background of Begin's resistance to Palestinian terror on Israel's northern border, see Temko, 260–64; for Sadat's position, see 242–45.

25. War on Terrorism

1. Peres, 211–12, reports on talks with President Carter.

2. Wreckage of the U.S. plan for an air rescue of hostages is in Carter, 514–22.

3. For Peres's TV comment, see Peres, 212.

4. Carter, 524, records the dispersal of the remaining U.S. prisoners.

5. Arrangements for the release of the hostages on Jan. 20, 1980, are in Carter, 592–95.

6. For the background of the Jerusalem declaration, see Temko "To Win or to Die," pp. 246–59.

7. Ibid., 256–59.

8. Ibid., 263.

9. Ibid., 272–73.

10. Ibid., 275–76.

11. Ibid., 271.

12. Ibid., 276–80.

13. Ibid., 280.

14. Ibid., 282.

15. Ibid., 288, 290.

16. Ibid., 291.

17. Shamir's background is from *Who's Who in the World*, 10th ed., 1991–92.

18. For background of the national unity coalition, see Peres, 201–2.

19. On Peres chosen as prime minister, see Peres, 203.

26. How Much Unity?

1. Israeli troop withdrawal from Lebanon is in Peres, 203.

2. Ibid., 204.

3. Ibid., 208. The TWA jet and *Achille Laura* stories were reported by the AP on the pertinent dates.

4. Peres's background is from *Who's Who in the World*.

5. The Likud position is in Peres, 207.

6. Ibid., 208.

7. Ibid., 208.

8. Ibid., 208–9.

9. Ibid., 263–64.

10. Ibid., 209, 264.

11. Ibid., 261–70.

12. Ibid., 211–17. Generally, the Iran-contra scandal may be followed in the Associated Press file as follows. Nov. 30, 1986: First break in the scandal; Dec. 30, 1986: Reagan admits a mistake; May 15, 1986: Reagan says the contra fund was his idea; July 11, 1987: North testifies before Congress; Nov. 18, 1987: Congressional report blames Reagan.

13. The Associated Press reported the rioting at the Dome of the Rock Jan. 15, 1988; Shamir's takeover is in Peres, 269–70.

14. Bush's pardon of Defense Secretary Weinberger and five others in the Iran-contra affair was reported Dec. 24, 1992.

15. Peres, 270–71.

27. Conflict with Iraq

1. The Iraqi result in Kuwait is discussed at length in *Chronicle of the Twentieth Century* (New York: Dorling, Kindesley, 1995), 1355.

2. Peres, 183–85, 228.

3. Saddam's background is from *Who's Who in the World*.

4. *Chronicle of the Twentieth Century*, 1297.

5. For a full discussion of "the Gulf Crisis" after the Iraqi assault but before the U.S. counterattack, see *Foreign Affairs* magazine, winter 1990–91.

6. There is an elaboration of the shifting policies of King Hussein in Fouad Ajami, "The Summer of Arab Discontent," in *Foreign Affairs*. 2.

7. The quotation is from Ajami, "The Summer of Arab Discontent," 20.

8. For details of these problems, see *Foreign Affairs*, 23–27.

9. Ibid, 26–35.

10. *Chronicle of the Twentieth Century*, 1362–63.

11. Ibid.

12. For an extensive discussion of "dual containment," see an article by Zbigniew Brzezinski, Brent Scowcroft, and Richard Murphy in *Foreign Affairs* magazine, May–June 1997, 20–30.

13. Ibid.

28. A Changing World

1. The Rabin quote is from *Shalom, Friend: The Life and Legacy of Yitzhak Rabin*, by the Jerusalem Report Staff (New York: Newmarket Press, 1996), 167.

2. The Gorbachev quote is from *Chronicle of the Twentieth Century*, 1375.

3. Ibid., Oct. 5, 1995, 1269, Gorbachev meets Mitterand.

4. Ibid, Dec. 25, 1991, 1375, Gorbachev resigns. Ibid., Feb. 10, 1992, 1377, food airlifted to Russia.

5. George F. Kennan, "Communism in Russian History," *Foreign Affairs*, Winter 1990/1991.

6. The Republican-controlled Congress supported limiting immigration at the onset of President Clinton's second term; he opposed it.

7. Stanley Reed, "Jordan and the Gulf Crisis," *Foreign Affairs*.

8. "Is Jordan Doomed?" *Foreign Affairs*, Nov.–Dec. 1993.

9. "The Future of the Islamic Movement," *Foreign Affairs*, Nov.–Dec. 1993.

10. Ibid.

11. Ibid.

12. *Shalom, Friend*, 110–22.

13. Rabin 123–37; see also Peres, 271–80 for his view.

14. On Baker, see Rabin 125.

15. Ibid.; Peres, 271–80.

16. Ibid.

17. Ibid.

29. Rabin and Peres

1. Leah Rabin, *Rabin: Our Life, His Legacy* (New York: Putnam, 1997), 214.

2. Rabin's biography is from *Who's Who in the World*.

3. Leah Rabin, 214.

4. The comparison of Rabin and Peres is based on sketches by Leah Rabin, 229–31, and Peres, 274–78.

5. Peres, 279–80.

6. Ibid., 280–83.

7. Leah Rabin, 214.

8. *Shalom, Friend*, 141–43; Peres, 283–85.

9. Peres, 286–87; *Shalom, Friend*, 144–45.

10. Leah Rabin, 248–49; *Shalom, Friend*, 142.

11. *Shalom, Friend,* 143.
12. Leah Rabin, 249.
13. Ibid., 250; *Shalom, Friend,* 144.

30. The Oslo Process

1. Leah Rabin, 248.
2. Peres, 287–88.
3. *Shalom Friend,* 144.
4. *Who's Who in the World.*
5. *Shalom Friend,* 145.
6. Ibid., 146–47.
7. The examination of the agreement is based on the documents reproduced in Peres, 317–30, including "The Israeli-Palestinian Declaration of Principles on Interim Self-Government Arrangements, September 1993; the annexes and minutes, and the letters of September 9, 1993, exchanged between Yassir Arafat as chairman of Palestine Liberation Organization and Yitzhak Rabin as Prime Minister of Israel."
8. The decisions on inviting Arafat and others to the Washington signing ceremonial is in Leah Rabin, 250–52. See also Peres, 298–306, and *Shalom, Friend,* 146–48.
9. The White House ceremonial is in Leah Rabin, 253–255; Peres, 306–309 and *Shalom, Friend,* pp. 148–49.
10. *Shalom, Friend,* 148–49.

31. New Deal in the Middle East

1. The Jordan-Israel agreement on a peace pact occurred Sept. 14, 1993, the day after the Israeli-PLO ceremony on the White House lawn; see *Shalom, Friend,* 149. The agreement to "do business" is on 150.
2. The Goldstein crime and others are in *Shalom, Friend,* 257–58; see also Leah Rabin, 151.
3. For an estimate of Rabin, I would share his wife's tribute with the reader; see Leah Rabin, 306–7. He was first of all a soldier, and also a secular person, who mistrusted religious fanaticism, although in his own way, he believed in the principles of Judaism.
4. The Associated Press, file of June 6, 1997, datelined Amman, covering King Hussein's speech on the thirtieth anniversary of the Six-Day War.
5. *Shalom, Friend,* 151–57 passim.
6. Leah Rabin, 260, 262, 265–66.
7. Ibid., 263, 265.
8. *Shalom, Friend,* 206–17 passim.

32. The Sacrifice

1. On Israel's economic and diplomatic progress, international recognition, and economic agreements, see *Shalom, Friend,* 164–65. See also a later account by William Safire, *New York Times,* June 25, 1997, op-ed page.
2. On the world tour and South Korea, see Leah Rabin, 266–68.

3. On the "Larry King Live" CNN broadcast and the Kiev speech by Rabin, see Leah Rabin 268–70.

4. Ibid., 272–74.

5. On tips of potential assassins, see *Shalom, Friend,* 232–38.

6. On Rabin's own precautions, see ibid., 273–76. On his younger successors, Leah Rabin's entire book is a testimonial to their faith in each other and their trust in Peres.

7. Leah Rabin, 6.

8. Leah Rabin, 9. *Shalom, Friend,* 253–54.

9. The details of the assassination are in Leah Rabin, 2–15, and in *Shalom, Friend* at much greater length, including the background of the assailant, 218–70.

10. On Mrs. Rabin's ordeal, see Leah Rabin, 2–22.

33. Reviving Israel

1. President Clinton's remarks were issued by the White House press office.

2. The primary election of the Labor Party on Mar. 25, 1996, confirmed the emergency decision of the Rabin cabinet on Nov. 4, 1995, to request Foreign Minister Peres to serve as acting prime minister.

3. The election of the prime minister on May 29, 1996, which followed the only debate between the candidates three days earlier, was the first to be decided by popular vote of the electorate.

4. Sharon, as the champion of the far Right, was the cabinet minister whose responsibility was the defense of the Israeli settlers who tried to maintain their hold on their limited areas where Palestinians were the majority.

5. It was no secret that President Clinton and his administration, while officially maintaining neutrality in a foreign election, favored Peres and the Labor Party to retain control of the Israeli government. Although Netanyahu could scarcely make a major issue of such support for the party that then was in power, it was the main reason Peres went into election day as a slight favorite to win.

6. The record of fatal clashes between the Palestinians and the Israelis from Nov. 1995 through Apr. 18, 1996, is based on the files of the Associated Press, Reuters News Agency, and the *New York Times.*

7. The 1996 Israeli election campaign, the voting figures, and the defeat of the Labor Party are based on the coverage by the Associated Press and the *New York Times.*

8. Ibid. Much of the material about the Middle East in the American presidential election of 1996 became familiar to me during my research for my recently published work *ReElecting Bill Clinton: Why America Chose a "New" Democrat* (Syracuse, N.Y.: Syracuse Univ. Press, 1997).

34. Likud's Hard Line

1. The events described herein were reported in the Israeli press on Feb. 23 and Mar. 13, 1997. A *New York Times* article summarizing Netanyahu's troubles was published Mar. 13 and another Mar. 16. The murder of the little girls was reported by Reuters Mar. 16.

2. The Israeli press was full of Netanyahu's cabinet problems all spring and well into the summer of 1997.

3. Associated Press file, Mar. 1.

4. Ibid.

5. The Sharon secret meeting was disclosed in the Israeli press July 1.

6. The end of Peres's leadership was reported May 14 in the Associated Press file.

7. Criticism of President Weizman is in *Shalom, Friend*, 250–51.

35. Bombs in Jerusalem

1. The NBC-TV on-the-spot record of the July 30 bombing captured for millions of Americans the horrifying detail of the tragedy in Jerusalem. It was one of the most devastating—and brilliant—feats of TV journalism within my experience.

2. President Clinton's remarks also were on NBC-TV.

3. From the Associated Press file for July 31.

4. Details from the NBC-TV verbal report and the *New York Times* of July 31 and Aug. 1.

5. My wife and I listened and viewed with fascination the prime minister's barely repressed anger during his broadcast interview from Jerusalem on CNN during the "Larry King Live" program.

6. This was a purely speculative report in the *New York Times* of Aug. 1 that was not borne out elsewhere in the nationwide coverage of the event.

7. The media in the United States, TV and print, reported numerous hasty threats, few of which later were carried out. It was typical of tensions among a political leadership after a shattering tragedy such as the bombing.

8. The uncertainty of the Clinton administration in adopting stern measures to enforce peace was clearly apparent throughout the crisis. Nobody, including the president, wanted to be accused of causing a renewal of the Middle East wars.

9. Albright's comments were made on her way back to Washington after a visit to the Far East. In a previous visit to the Czech republic, she was shown while in Prague the names of her grandparents on a wall in a museum that perpetuated the memory of Jews in Czechoslovakia who had died in the Holocaust.

10. *New York Times*, June 25, 1997, A-5.

11. Reuters file, July 24, 1997, and Associated Press file, for July 25, 1997.

12. *New York Times*, Aug. 1 and 2, 1997, p. 1, and CNN broadcasts that day with the first news of the Brooklyn bomb report.

36. The Trials of Peace

1. *New York Times*, Sept. 5, 1997, and a summary telecast on CNN at 6:30 P.M., Sept. 16.

2. *New York Times*, Sept. 6, and CNN, Sept 16.

3. *New York Times*, Sept. 9, and CNN, Sept. 15; also in exhaustive daily NBC televised reports.

4. Associated Press file for Sept. 11.

5. Associated Press reports based mainly on Israeli newspaper articles, Sept. 12–15.

6. Ibid.

7. Associated Press file, Sept. 4.

8. Ibid., Sept. 5.

9. Arafat's previous activity, in which he cracked down on terrorists, was reported at the time in both the American and Israeli press.

10. The report alleging corruption among Arafat's cabinet was in the *New York Times,* July 30, 1997.

11. Arafat's actions were reported in the Israeli press July 21.

12. The response to the Arafat cabinet changes was in the *New York Times,* Aug. 3.

13. Secretary Albright's conclusion was widely broadcast and published in the United States on Sept. 16. It was at once a summation and a warning that was followed by a number of visits to the United States from the Israeli and Palestinian regimes.

This crisis was closely followed by American TV correspondents in Israel and other parts of the Middle East, who became the primary public source for a summation of the problems affecting the Israelis and the Arabs. President Clinton and Secretary Albright, too, made use of TV appearances to present their views to the American public, particularly Mrs. Albright's policy speeches beginning Aug. 6, 1997, and escalating to her warning broadcast of Sept. 16, 1997.

37. Israel at 50

1. The quotation is from President Clinton's tribute to Yitzhak Rabin at his grave.

2. The anti-Israeli broadcasts of the Voice of Palestine are on record in both the Israeli and the American press.

3. The anecdote is from McGill, 90–91.

4. Ibid., 64–65.

5. Statistics from current Israeli government figures.

6. The remarks about Israel's leadership in the past fifty years are my responsibility, and are based on reasonably frequent contact with the problems of Israel as a nation.

7. From "Differentiated Containment," a task force report of the Council on Foreign Relations, copyright by the council 1997, Zbigniew Brzezinski and Brent Scowcroft, co-chairs, 43.

8. Ibid., 42–43.

9. "Israel Melee as Women Pray with Men," *New York Times,* Aug. 12, 1997, A-6.

Bibliography

Aker, Frank. *October, 1973: The Arab-Israeli War*. Hamden, Conn.: Archon Books, 1985.

Baruch, Bernard M. *The Public Years*. New York: Holt, Rinehart and Winston, 1960.

Bar-Zohar, Michael. *Facing a Cruel Mirror*. New York: Scribner, 1990.

Begin, Menachem. *White Nights*. New York: Harper and Row, 1957, 1977.

Bohlen, Charles E. *Witness to History, 1929–1969*. New York: Norton, 1973.

Brzezinski, Zbigniew. *Power and Principle: Memoirs of a National Security Adviser*. New York: Farrar, Straus and Giroux, 1985.

Carter, Jimmy. *Keeping Faith*. New York: Bantam Books, 1982.

Chafets, Ze'ev. *Heroes and Hustlers*. New York: Morrow, 1986.

Christian, George. *The President Steps Down*. New York: Simon and Schuster, 1984.

Collins, Lapierre. *O Jerusalem!* New York: Pocket Books, 1973.

Compton, Arthur Holly. *Atomic Quest*. New York: Oxford Univ. Press, 1956.

Dayan, Moshe. *The Story of My Life*. New York: Morrow, 1976.

Friedel, Frank. *America in the Twentieth Century*. New York: Knopf, 1960.

Garcia-Granados, Jorge. *The Birth of Israel*. New York: Knopf, 1948.

Gervasi, Frank. *The Life and Times of Menachem Begin*. New York: Putnam, 1979.

Golan, Matti. *The Secret Conversations of Henry Kissinger*. New York: Quadrangle, 1976.

Haber, Eitan. *Menachem Begin: The Legend and Man*. New York: Delacorte, 1978.

Haig, Alexander Jr. *Caveat*. New York: Macmillan, 1984.

Hohenberg, John. *My Travels in Israel*. New York Post, 1950.

Hoopes, Townsend. *The Devil and John Foster Dulles*. Boston: Little, Brown, 1973.

Jerusalem Report Staff. *Shalom, Friend: The Life and Legacy of Yitzhak Rabin*. New York: Newmarket Press, 1996.

Kissinger, Henry. *White House Years*. Boston: Little, Brown, 1979.

London Sunday Times Insight Team. *The Yom Kippur War*. Garden City, N.Y.: Doubleday, 1994.

Meir, Golda. *My Life.* New York: Putnam, 1975.

Neff, Donald. *Warriors for Jerusalem.* New York: Simon and Schuster, 1984.

Nelson, W. Dale. *The President Is at Camp David.* Syracuse, N.Y.: Syracuse Univ. Press, 1996.

Peres, Shimon. *Battling for Peace.* New York: Random House, 1995.

Perlmutter, Amos. *The Life and Times of Menachem Begin.* Garden City, N.Y.: Doubleday, 1987.

Rabin, Leah. *Rabin: Our Life, His Legacy.* New York: Putnam, 1997.

Rabin, Yitzhak. *The Rabin Memoirs.* New York: Little, Brown, 1979.

Rennert, Maggie. *Shelanu: An Israeli Journal.* Englewood Cliffs, N.J.: Prentice Hall, 1979.

Sharon, Ariel, with David Chanoff. *Warrior.* New York: Simon and Schuster, 1989.

Temko, Ned. *To Win or to Die.* New York: Morrow, 1987.

Truman, Harry S. *Memoirs II: Years of Trial and Hope.* Garden City, N.Y.: Doubleday, 1956.

Vance, Cyrus. *Hard Choices.* New York: Simon and Schuster, 1983.

Weizman, Ezer. *The Battle for Peace.* New York: Bantam, 1981.

Who's Who in America. 49th ed. 3 vols. 1995.

Who's Who in the World. 10th ed. 1992.

Index